Douglas Chirnside

Douglas Chirnside was born and brought up in Scotland.
For twelve years he was an executive in several of
London's top advertising agencies, before becoming a
television producer of light entertainment and factual
programmes. He lives in London. His last novel, *Basket
Case*, is also from Sceptre.

SCEPTRE

Vanity
Case

DOUGLAS CHIRNSIDE

SCEPTRE

First published in 1997 by Hodder and Stoughton
First published in paperback in 1998 by Hodder and Stoughton
A division of Hodder Headline PLC
A Sceptre Paperback

10 9 8 7 6 5 4 3 2 1

Vanity Case is fiction, a novel set in the worlds of television
and advertising. In order to make it as authentic as possible,
several well-known people and companies make fictional cameo
appearances in these pages, but none of the other characters are
real and none of the events described here ever happened.
No reference is therefore intended to people or companies
in either industry.

A CIP catalogue record for this title is
available from the British Library

ISBN 0 340 68181 0

Typeset by Palimpsest Book Production Limited,
Polmont, Stirlingshire
Printed and bound in Great Britain by
Mackays of Chatham PLC, Chatham, Kent

Hodder and Stoughton
A division of Hodder Headline PLC
338 Euston Road
London NW1 3BH

For Kathy King

VANITY CASE ∫

Hector Quigley had been away for a while and now he was back. Portly and ebullient, he strode across the tiled floor of Heathrow Airport Terminal Four, its marble surface reflecting back the shiny undersoles of his snakeskin Chelsea boots that never walked on pavements. The welcoming committee was plonk in place this sunny Sunday morning in June.

'It's Hecka!'

Marsha Blow, personal assistant and perfectionist prop forward to the longest-living legend in London advertising, stepped forward to greet her boss. Of all Hector Quigley's 349 employees, only she had both the guts and the latent permission to abbreviate the chairman. But not the guts to kiss him on the cheek. Hector Quigley could not bear to be touched, socially, sexually or otherwise.

'My God! You're in good nick!' Marsha was stunned, but recovered well. Hector, who had always looked nice from afar but far from nice close up, appeared at least ten years younger than when she had waved him off at the British Airways VIP suite some seven weeks earlier. She brushed her own worn skin in awe.

'India agreed with me,' announced Hector plummily. While there was no trace of the Welsh accent he had once had, the resonance of that region remained. And every utterance of this self-made man was indeed announced rather than simply stated. It was as if he expected somebody to be writing it down as he spoke. Back at the agency somebody usually was.

Hector's was a powerful presence. His flawless, creaseless, timeless, three-piece pale yellow suit was a virtuoso performance of unique distinction from Gieves and Hawkes of Savile Row. His matching shirt and tie combination of broad green and lilac stripes was a bespoke Thomas Pink creation, a pastel tribute to Wimbledon where it had had its first outing a year before. The cuffs of the shirt stuck out from under his jacket like ship funnels on a steamer. They were clamped in place by gigantic cufflinks, asymmetrical golden balls, carved, one in the shape of a Roman sundial, the other a Spanish doubloon. When he wished to bring board meetings to a close, Hector would rise from his throne at the table's end and shadow-box the air, first with one cuff, then the other. 'Gentlemen,' he would say 'this is *my* business and any business is *time* and *money*.' His hands were huge – doughnut palms, pork sausage fingers, coat-button finger nails – and looked huger, adorned as they were with popish rings heavy with real jewels. From the stiff collar of his deckchair shirt sprouted Hector's perky-pink face, round and shiny and glowing and taut. His piggy-wiggy eyes sparkled amethyst blue, darting in their sockets, alert and all-seeing. To top the whole show off, his hair was worn like a crown: a concocted confection of cherubic baby curls in brassy yellow. Hector Quigley was a bottle blond.

'Where is Philip?' The piggy-wiggy eyes pierced the horizon.

'Hovering,' replied Marsha, hugging her clipboard to her bosom. 'There he is,' and she nodded to the uniformed chauffeur, an immaculate, slender black man, a few pillars away.

With a fat finger Hector signalled to his man to collect his luggage from the VIP porter. Philip shot towards the white kid bags with their thick golden zips and chunky golden padlocks. Thick and chunky because anything that was to come into contact with Hector's well-endowed hands and jewel encrusted fingers had to be large and tactile or it was an object of no great use to this so-great man.

They began the trek across the marble floor to the setting down point. As he had a thousand times before, Hector led the way with Marsha to his left, one calculated, choreographed half-step behind.

'Messages?' she asked.

In the seventeen years she had sat outside Hector Quigley's door, they had never dropped daily contact. He had even insisted on her wedding day that she walk down the aisle with a mobile phone stuffed into her bouquet. And he had rung it, too, as she approached the church on the arm of her brother: to offer his congratulations and a surprise honeymoon in Barbados for her and her husband still-to-be. But now Hector had been to India all by himself and nobody had seen or heard of him for nearly two months. 'India! What the fuck for?' the deputy chairman had harangued Marsha. He had gone out of interest, she had replied. He had gone out of touch. He had gone out of character. Hector Quigley was up to something.

'Messages,' agreed Hector.

'Nigel Gainsborough. Golf. Wentworth. Wednesday.'

'What say you?'

'It's an IPA event. You won't be stuck with him all afternoon. I'd say yes.'

'Say yes, then. Philip to caddy.'

'Yes, Philip to caddy. Dinner, Tuesday.'

'Where?'

'Château Hector.'

'Whom have I invited?' He made much of the m on 'whom'.

'It's your Chairmen's Circle idea. Get all our top clients together in one room.'

'Good God! Did I think of that or did somebody think of it for me?'

'All your own work.'

'What say you?'

'Landed it on yourself, Hecka. I can't cancel it.'

'You're not asked to. Invitations?'

'Verbal.'

'Good. Have printed ones hand-delivered tomorrow stating carriages at ten-thirty.'

'Hecka! You can't invite the chairmen of multinationals for dinner and expect them to leave at ten-thirty.'

'Eleven, then.'

'Pushing it.'

'My dear Marsha,' Hector stalled and swung his ballooning body around. 'Understand that the Great and the Good are gladdened to be organised. They appreciate being told exactly when to leave just as much as when to arrive. Write that down. I shall use that in my House of Commons lecture. Next.'

'House of Commons lecture.' It was next on her list.

'*Yes*! What say you?'

'I've got Committee Room Fourteen for you. It's historic. It's the one where they read out the result that sank Mrs Thatcher.'

'Lady Thatcher did not sink. She merely sailed on, galleon-like.'

'Shall I write that down too?'

'Don't be impertinent. Lady Thatcher is one of my friends.'

'Huh!'

'We correspond.'

'You mean I correspond with her lackey who says no to everything. You've only met her once.'

'But what a once! It was over lunch.'

'Yeah. Just her, you and 500 others. Anyway, I can't stand her.'

'And that is why you, my dear Marsha, are my personal assistant and I am master of all I survey.'

What Hector surveyed right now was the splendid sight of his gleaming buttercup-yellow Bentley gliding into place before them. Philip slipped out of the car like an After Eight from its cover and silently sprung open the rear door for Hector's embarcation. Hector turned again to Marsha. Her clipboard hung at her side.

'Is that it?'

'For now. I mean, you're interviewing a new account director tomorrow afternoon and lots of other things but those can wait until I see you in the office. I'm not giving up my whole bloody Sunday to go through your diary.'

'And why not, pray?'

'Look, Hecka, you may have had seven bloody weeks' holiday but I haven't. I've had the entire agency at my throat the whole time you've been away.'

Hector had missed their banter and enjoyed the retort. 'I'll bet you loved it, running the whole show like a proper little Madame Tussaud, first in there to measure up the severed heads, never mind the blood on your hands. *And* I have been on a speaking tour of India, *not* a holiday.' He wagged a big warning finger at her.

'What for? We haven't got any business the other side of the Channel, let alone the other side of the bleeding British Empire.'

'I am a philanthropist.'

Marsha roared with laughter and Hector did too. He was famous for the dust on his wallet.

'Oh, Hecka—' As he sailed towards the car she waved her clipboard at him. 'The Verity Tampons pitch rehearsal is at three.'

'I have not forgotten.'

'That makes a change.' She slipped it in beneath her breath. She had got hell from the pitch team for arranging work on the weekend. 'Remember this then, instead.'

'What?'

'*Thou Art Only Mortal.*' She whispered it. Hector loved a bit of theatre.

'Don't be cheeky.' He winked at her. Marsha laughed again.

'It's what the slaves said to the generals on their victory parades.'

'True. But the difference is – they *were* only mortal!' He guffawed and filled the car door frame with his huge bottom before plumping himself down and expanding into the leather back seat of the Bentley. Philip pressed the passenger door shut and slid back into the driver's seat. As the ignition started up, Hector's window slid down. Marsha looked concerned.

'Too jet-lagged to make the rehearsal?'

'I am never too tired to work,' called Hector, his voice muffled by the absorbent soft furnishings of the plush interior. 'I'll be there. No letting that lazy shower off the hook. I pays them good to slave on the Sabbath. There was something else.'

'Yes?' asked Marsha. She raised her clipboard and grabbed the pen suspended from her neck.

'What's the name of that woman I made Head of Information?'

'Joanne.'

'Yes. Terrible name. Any good?'

'I think so.'

'Send her a memo. I want somebody to go to London Zoo and calculate how much dung the average elephant excretes per hour.'

Marsha gasped. This was rich, even for Hector.

'Then find out from the Indian High Commissioner, or someone anyway, how many elephants there are in Delhi and would have been passing the Oberoi Hotel. What I am trying to say is that there was a helluva lot of shit in the street outside my room and the stench was enough to make one heave one's guts up.'

'Yuck! Did you?'

'No I did not, but that's only because a strong constitution runs in my family, which is why I have done so well.'

'So that's your secret.'

'Look, they had one bloody old untouchable coming round once a night with a utensil the size of a dustpan, God help them. No fucking use!'

'It's a third world country.'

'There is no excuse for uncleanliness. Get the head of planning to work out how often they need to sweep the streets per day based on a generous calculation of the rate of droppings at the zoo. And make sure the elephant they use is Indian and not an African one or I'll look stupid. You can tell by the size of its ears.'

Hector's window slid up and Marsha stepped back.

'Or by the size of its arsehole, no doubt. For God's sake!' She called towards the back of the Bentley. '*Bye, Hecka!*'

The car eased forward and as it did the window wound down once again. Hector's beaming face popped out, all red like a cricket ball.

'And get the correct form of address for whomever they've got as Prime Minister in India these days. Trouble is, with all the Ghandis gone, it can't be a personal letter.'

Hector nipped back in, the window snapped shut this time and the beautiful yellow Bentley glided away.

Marsha Blow waved the car out of sight and hurriedly produced a mobile phone from her summer jacket. She punched the memory button and rushed the phone to her face.

'*Eeeeeek!*' she squealed into it. 'You'll never guess what! The old fool's gone and done it. Hecka's had a *facelift!*'

'Oh, Philip, turn in here, will you?'

'This'll take us back into the airport, to Terminal Three, sir.'

'Hah!' Hector smiled smugly and sat back, comfortable with his knowing look.

Philip's death-mask expression hid his surprise. He did, as always, precisely as he was told. He was not reading Hector correctly today. In fact, he could see there was something quite different, something quite new, about Hector Quigley, and there had never been anything remotely new about Hector Quigley before. You could always read him like an open book, or more accurately, like one of his bold, brash, formulaic TV commercials. They were all always exactly the same. Yabadabadoo music and young women with great big tits. Nothing to do with the product and everything to do with Hector's hectoring.

Philip looked up and studied the chairman, centred in the chauffeur's rear-view mirror and sitting there in Tudor splendour. Something *was* different but it was going to take Philip a bit of working out to pinpoint exactly what it was. It was not the way he was dressed. Philip had driven for Hector Quigley for fourteen years and Hector had always worn the same style; *Half a Sixpence* ice-cream outfits were to Hector Quigley what floral silk coat-dresses were to the Queen Mother. His hair was unchanged. Hector's hair was one of the clauses in Philip's contract that he was under pain of dismissal to reveal. Every third Tuesday morning for fourteen years Philip had delivered Hector's hairdresser on the dot of seven to the big house in Belgravia they all called Château Hector so that Hector could have his hair cut and dyed in private. Prior to the trip to India, Philip and the Bentley had been dispatched to collect a vial of dye for Hector to administer to his own pate while on his speaking tour. Philip had not kept a strictly straight face when he had read the name of the colour on the label. Marilyn, it was called. He had been taken to task on his return to Château Hector when his millionaire master was unable to unscrew such a tiny cap on such a tiny vessel with his fumbling fat fingers, however well manicured they might be. Philip had had to decant the dye into a baby Perrier bottle when he had packed Hector's cases. It was not his hair. Nor was it his eyes. Philip leant imperceptibly closer to the rear-view mirror. Piggy-wiggy or not, Hector had eyes naturally of a colour intense enough to give Elizabeth Taylor a run for her money. It was not his eyes. But it was something around them, something to do with his face. Hey ho. Philip worked it out. It was his skin. Something to do with Hector's skin. Moisturised sagging leather had given way to stretched PVC. Something or somebody had wiped away the years with a single stroke. Philip absentmindedly turned and flicked the windscreen wiper switch and wiped away a film of London summer dust. With a single stroke.

There was less traffic than usual this summery Sunday and the Bentley soon swept up in front of the anonymous box that was the Terminal Three building.

'Pull over here, Philip, please.'

The Bentley caressed the kerb by the arrivals hall. Philip unclicked his seat belt and made to exit to open his boss's door but Hector stopped him there.

'Oh, I'm not getting out. I'll make an announcement when I wish you to drive on.'

'And will that be home, sir?' The chauffeur was puzzled.

'Home, Philip. But not just yet.'

'May I say how refreshed you look after your holiday, sir.'

'No you may not, you cheeky bugger.' Hector stretched forward, and, with an unfit grunt, hit the button to bring into place the sliding panel that sealed off the passenger section of the car from the chauffeur.

Now he sat alone in anticipation, waiting in his vehicular cocoon. He watched the chaos of arrival and departure on the terminal forecourt. Two pretty girls in shorts and T-shirts, lumbering under huge backpacks, had hysterics when they entered a narrow doorway and got jammed in side by side. A mincing El Al air steward trotted past haughtily dragging a slim black overnight case on wheels, disappearing between bronzed glass automatic doors. A middle-aged woman, stifling in a wool coat, struggled with an overstuffed plastic suitcase which had come unstuck on its own integral trolley. Flying to colder parts, thought Hector. He watched the express service porters in their bright red tunics leaning on upright trolleys, momentarily redundant. For five pounds they would unpack your car and lead you and your luggage to the correct check-in desk. Hector wondered if five pounds would seem too much to the ordinary traveller. After a few moments there was a rat-a-tat-tat at the window.

'Pssst!'

'Leave it to me, Philip,' said Hector into the intercom. He nudged open the door and a formally dressed woman dropped in beside him. She carried a small vanity case.

'It's me! Hello, Hector! How are you?' She took a second or two to adjust to the interior darkness and used the time to run her fingers over the thrillingly soft beige leather.

'I am very well.'

'You look terrific!' An air of excitement gave way to a worried look on the woman's face. 'Can he see me through that thing?'

'Philip? No. It's a one-way screen.' He addressed the intercom again. 'It's all right, Philip. Château Hector, please.'

The Bentley floated forward and the woman relaxed instantly. She went to take Hector's huge ham of a hand in her own but he pulled it away.

'I don't feel like being touched.'

She was hurt. 'You never feel like being touched.'

He pointed to her vanity case. 'What's that?' he asked.

'The documents. I'm not letting them out of my sight.'

'Do you think it's wise to carry a time bomb around with you?'

'In this case, yes. And I've brought my things for tomorrow.'

'Am I to assume that you are inviting yourself to stay the night?'

'I'm not inviting myself. I'm just pre-empting you, that's all.' She changed her tone and flashed a dazzling smile. 'Let me look at you. Hector! Six weeks!'

He corrected her. 'Seven. One in India – and *six* in Switzerland!' He let rip a throaty roar of conniving laughter and suddenly lunged and squeezed the woman's thigh tightly.

'For God's sake! I thought you didn't like to be touched.'

'I don't. But you do and I enjoy touching if not being touched.'

'Let's see,' said the woman, examining the newly trimmed version of the face that had graced a score of issues of *Campaign* in the last year alone. Even she could not detect the delicate embroidery snuggling up to his ear lobe. 'You're fortunate with your hairline. Most men can't carry it off because of their thinning. I would have thought the laser resurfacing would have left you more red but it hasn't. You look amazing. You look wonderful. You look sensational.'

'I have always looked good.'

'Of course you have. You didn't need it, really.'

'Think of it as preventative rather than curative.'

'That's *just* the way to think of it,' she flattered him.

'D'you know, when I was four years old I was so handsome I was my mother's little prince and she made me a crown out of golden cardboard and stuck Rowntrees Fruit Gums on it for jewels and I wore it up and down the parade for all the other children to see.'

'Which parade was that?'

'It was the name of the street. Albert Parade. It wasn't a parade, of course. It was a row of back-to-backs in Cardiff. I was king of nothing then.'

'The other kids must have loved you.'

'I have always sought respect, not love. If you stick your neck out you must be prepared to get your face slapped.'

The woman looked out onto the A4 and the scattering of signs pointing the way into Central London and the heart of Hector's magic kingdom.

'This is fun, being in a chauffeur-driven Bentley. It's not every day you get to live like royalty.'

'Unless your name is Hector Quigley.' He paused for effect. 'Or Mrs Hector Quigley.'

Despite the reassuring depth of the seat, the woman felt uncomfortable. She squirmed and wormed around a bit. Nervously, she patted the handle of her vanity case as if it might burst into flames. A long silence ensued. 'If I had been one of the other kids I would have pulled them off and eaten them.'

'The Fruit Gums? They didn't dare.'

She did not look convinced.

'Just as no one dares today. Little Mo and Charlie Saatchi should have taken a tip from Uncle Hector. HQ is the last wholly privately owned advertising agency in the UK top twenty. That's one helluvan achievement.'

'It is. A real accomplishment.'

'Nobody can get me.'

'Except yourself. Don't tempt fate.'

'Fate has nothing to do with it. I have not been "lucky" as that dim woman in the *Guardian* suggested. I have known good fortune, but you create your own luck. People who miss opportunities which are staring them in the face say they are unlucky. They are not unlucky. They are bad at what they do. I must put that in my House of Commons lecture.'

The woman was fretting again. 'Are you sure whatsisname can't see me through the window?'

'Absolutely. Anyway, he's hardly likely to recognise you. He has no idea who you are.'

'But he could remember me. We shouldn't be seen together.'

'Exactly why I collected you at the airport.'

'Collected me! *I* wasn't *at* the airport! *You* were. I was at home. I had to come out on the bloody Underground.'

'A taxi was a risk. You would have been logged in somebody's book somewhere.'

'I could have hailed one in the street and paid cash.'

'I apologise. I didn't think of that. I forgot you could hail one.'

'Only because you haven't walked the streets in decades. It takes an age to tube it to Heathrow. It smells of sweat.'

'Does it? How fascinating. That explains something I read many years ago in some toilet soap research about body odour. Our campaign was accused of appealing to fear. I think that was the expression.'

'What *are* you're talking about, Hector?'

'I have not used public transport since I was sixteen. I told my mother on my birthday. From now on, I said, I will always travel privately or, if I cannot, go first class. Although it has to be said that first class has declined a great deal since then. I didn't think much of the world's favourite airline. Dom Perignon! Dom Piss-in-a-bottle, more like.'

'Hector? Can we get the business out of the way first while we're in the privacy of the car? Only, you know it is a conflict of interest for me to be, well, seeing you as well as working with you.'

'How could you work with me if you could not see me? Hah! I am hardly invisible. I am high profile.'

'You know what I mean, Hector.'

'Since when have either of us cared about a conflict of interest?'

'We don't, Hector, but other people do. I haven't remotely got the resources you have. I need the money from this. I can't have "us" ruining my reputation.'

'I would never let that happen.' He took her hand this time and it was swallowed up amongst his rings. 'Fear not. We will surprise them all.' He beamed as wide as his tightened face would allow. 'This year Hector Quigley will send a shock wave through the industry that will flabbergast every last one of the lazy fuckers.'

'Hector!'

'I shall make a statement. "Just remember that all that glitters is not gold."' With his spare hand he fluffed his hair.

The woman allowed that thought to sink in.

'I am a clever man. Cleverer than credited.' He faced sideways to the window and the world beyond the hard shoulder. 'For all those of you waiting for the fall of Hector Quigley think again. Just remember that all that glitters is not gold.'

'It'll be so exciting if we pull this off.'

'*If*? Hah!'

'Oh Hector! Let me look again.' She turned her head to his and he cocked his chin at an angle to catch the midday sun. 'No one would *ever* know,' she enthused.

She was half right. No one would ever know, as long as they were the no one who had never seen Hector Quigley before. But anyone who had, would. Anyone could spot a mile off that Hector Quigley had had a facelift. They had always reckoned that he would never give up his ice-cream coloured suits and shirts nor abandon his snakeskin Chelsea boots. They had even all guessed years ago that Hector had happily helped nature along and that he was not exactly *au naturel* in the hair department. Since time immemorial Hector Quigley had been the longest-living legend in London advertising, his own cliché, a caricature of himself, an open and shut case, a nut case, a sad case, a bad case, a mad case. Now? Now they all knew what everyone knew: that Hector Quigley had been away for a while and now he was back. Now they all knew what everyone knew:

that Hector had a little secret and that everyone knew what it was. Now they all knew what everyone knew: that Hecka had had a facelift.

Of course, Hector Quigley did have a little secret. Only, that wasn't it.

She rustled in the sheets.

He stirred, opened his eyes and, turning down the alarm clock radio, nudged his sleeping partner.

She blinked, stretched out her feline limbs and rubbed her lithe body against the man, warm in the bed beside her. She purred.

He always set the radio this loud to guarantee he would actually wake up. He reached for his contact lenses and launched his naked body out of bed and towards the bathroom to pee away his erection.

'Time to get up,' he said.

She pushed her blonde hair back from her face. It cascaded across the pillow. She took one full minute to pleasure in herself. She slid her tanned legs out from under the sheet and padded nude across the floor, drinking in the June sun tumbling in through muslin-draped windows. She knew it now for sure, but she had always been a summer girl. She threw open the double doors of the wardrobe and fist-fought her way inside. She prised out her prize outfit – a sleeveless mini-dress and matching unlined jacket from Browns in South Molton Street. The colour was acid, sharp. Citrus. She held the dress out on its hanger, its two pockets large squares against her small breasts. She turned to the mirror.

'Lime is the colour of summer,' she mouthed to the golden girl reflected there and made her a promise. 'This year,' she said, and double-clicked her tongue. She stood sideways and, draping the cotton outfit about her hips, posed and pouted at her image. She remembered the time and, carelessly dropping the dress to one side, plucked a pair of La Perla panties from the drawer and ran into the tiny bathroom.

He had now showered, shampooed and shaved. His fairish hair was sparkling with L'Oréal Studio Line Design Gel, short, with just a few spiky bits on top. His slight sideburns were neatly trimmed and his finger- and toenails freshly clipped. His armpits glistened with fragrance-free roll-on, so as not to clash with the scent of the Antigua fragrance bodyspray he had applied across his upper torso. And, because he was thirty-three, the age which draws fine lines around the eyes and dries out the skin, his face was lightly moisturised and aglow.

He crossed the cream carpet to the antiqued pine chest of drawers. From the second-top drawer he selected a pair of white Calvin Klein trunks. He slipped them on in front of the mirror. Voyeuristically, he watched himself do it. His skin was bronzed by the sun of California. His shoulders were broad, his stomach flat enough and the trunks drew the eye away from his waistline down to his crotch and the top of his smooth thighs.

He opened the socks drawer and dug out a pair of beige cotton ones. From the wardrobe filing system came a Marks and Spencer duck egg blue polo shirt and a pair of Ralph Lauren bleached khaki polo chinos. He buttoned his fly with a flourish and finished off with genuine accessories. A steel and gold Santos de Cartier watch, a decent dark brown belt and matching loafers by Patrick Cox. He went in search of his Nokia Orange mobile phone, recharged overnight.

She returned, bathed, lightly made-up, giant Swatch in place. She checked her lip gloss in the mirror and hitched her panties high on her hipbones. She bent forward and shook out her damp hair. Spots of water splashed her bare breasts. From the mirror ledge she grabbed a tower of Trevor Sorbie mousse. It had lost its top. She scooshed a meringue into one hand and raked her fingers through her blonde hair, piling it high on the crown of her head. In seconds she had recaptured its designer cut. She stepped back into the little citrus dress, slid it silently up the sides of her polished body and studded it closed around her waist. As she smoothed down the skirt panel with the back of one mousse-lined hand, with the other she rummaged her way to the back of the wardrobe and the mound of shoes. She thrust her feet into a pair of lime green, block-heel, Prada thong sandals from the Pellicano sale. Their chunky silver chains uppermost in mind, she raked in the tangle of her tray drawer to produce a sparkling metal belt of interlocking circles. She slung it loose around her hips and finally pressed onto her lobes small silver Aquascutum O's to match.

'How do I look?' she asked. He didn't need to say it. She looked girly, gamine and gorgeous. Absolutely gorgeous. She ran through into the living room. 'Girls just wanna have fun,' she half sang. She punched a number into her mobile phone.

By now Duncan Cairns had located his. He held it up in front of his duck egg blue polo shirt. Caller ID told him it was Charlotte Reith calling.

'You're up.'

'And ready to go. You don't mind, do you, Duncan?'

'I haven't had a power breakfast since I left advertising.'

'Don't be silly! It's only a cappuccino with me. I don't think I could eat anything what with seeing you-know-who this afternoon.'

'Say his name.'

'Shhh,' she whispered.

'Who's there to hear?' laughed Duncan.

'No one.' She was embarrassed to lie. 'See you in five minutes.'

'Five minutes? How are you getting there?'

'On the old Ducati espresso. How else?'

'I'm walking it.'

'Better start now then. Race ya!'

Charlotte eventually found her strappy shoulder purse abandoned from last night on the back of the settee and stuffed her phone into it. She returned to the bedroom. The man in the bed turned over.

'What time is it?' he mumbled and yawned.

'Seven forty-something,' answered Charlotte.

'Where are you off to so early?'

'A meeting. Listen . . .'

'What?'

'I don't think we should do this again, Orlando.'

'Didn't you enjoy it?' Orlando propped himself up on one elbow.

'Of course . . . but I mean . . . you're my creative director.'

'So?'

'So I've got to leave right now and you'll have to let yourself out. OK?'

'Talk about it later?'

'Only to each other. Understood?'

'I won't breathe a word.'

'News travels. Seemingly effortlessly in our business – and so must I!'

She pecked him on the cheek. She quickly slipped on the little jacket, immediately removed it and stashed it back in the crush in the wardrobe. He heard the bang of the front door and went back to sleep.

Duncan pressed the red symbol and Charlotte's details vanished from the phone. He returned to the bedroom and climbed atop his slumbering partner. They began to rub cheeks and then lips. Duncan pulled back.

'You're like sandpaper. You're too stubbly, Michael.'

Michael's face matched the crumpled linen. He checked the clock radio. 'No one in TV gets up this early.'

'I'm having breakfast with Charlotte.'

'Why?'

'No time to explain. I have to rush. Feed Pushkin, will you? Where is she, anyway?'

A frantic tunnelling operation was underway beneath the duvet. The foxy face of a sorrel-coloured Somali cat popped out by Michael's chin. Her black pupils narrowed in the light. She brusquely shook out her fur.

'Pushkin!' moaned Michael.

'Miaow,' she said, jumped down and raced through to the kitchen, anticipating her crunchy breakfast. Michael buried himself back into the bedclothes. Duncan sighed and went to feed his baby.

A moment later he clipped smartly up the steps from his Maida Vale garden flat onto Sutherland Avenue. He stopped to slip on his Ray Bans then set off to deliver the lowdown on Hector Quigley.

2

At the roar of the Ducati, Duncan looked up through his shades from the pavement table outside Raoul's Café in Little Venice. Against the roast of the morning sun he could make out the silhouette of Charlotte Reith sensationally astride her motor bike, legs bared, her sleeveless citrus dress riding high at the top of her thighs. A passer-by's head turned to get the full measure of her spectacular arrival. Ignoring double yellow lines, Charlotte pulled the bike into the side of the road, yanked off her helmet, pushed her fingers through her fine blonde hair and approached Duncan's table. Like the sun above, she was beaming.

'You!' she shouted. 'How on earth did you get here first?'

'Easy peasy. I walk fast. Hi.' Duncan stood up. They exchanged kisses.

'You look so different not in a suit. I'll never get used to you looking casual.'

'I could say the same about you.'

Charlotte giggled. 'Don't wind me up. This little lot cost an absolute bomb. D'you think he'll like it?'

'Hector Quigley is known for his sartorial taste. God knows how you would define it, though. You look smart – even if you *are* flashing a lot of flesh around the place.'

She dropped into her seat and plopped her purse on the table and her helmet on a spare chair. Beneath the table her dress rode up on her thighs.

'It works well on dirty old men.'

'Didn't work on me.'

'That's because you're—'

'What?'

'Special.' She giggled again and smoothed the skirt of her dress. 'Daddy bought me this for Mummy's wedding. She wanted me to be a bridesmaid but I said no. D'you think that was dreadful of me?'

'I didn't realise she was remarrying.'

'I didn't either. She shouldn't have a bridesmaid at her age. She's married a cosmetic surgeon. Can you think of anything more ghastly? He gives me the creeps. They're still on honeymoon.'

'Look on the bright side. You can get a discount on implants. When your mum gets back she could be a whole new woman.'

'Stop it!'

'Why did your father buy you a dress for his divorced wife's wedding?'

'Don't be so Scottish. He bought it for me, not her. The thing is, Duncan, do I look like an account director?'

'You bet.' Actually she looked more like something from the centre pages of *Harpers and Queen* but she needed the assurance and Duncan let her have it. They ordered cappuccinos and fruit salads with Greek yoghurt.

'You look so brown, Duncan.'

'Michael and I went to Palm Springs for a fortnight.'

'Florida. How fab.'

'That's Palm Beach. Palm Springs is in California. It's so hot there they spray you with cooling mist by the poolside. It evaporates before it hits you.'

'Sounds fantastic. They have everything in America, don't they. Except taste. You look so relaxed.'

'It's getting out of advertising. You don't realise how much pressure you've been under until you've left.'

'I wouldn't have thought there was that much difference.'

'There is. About as much as there is between sex and masturbation.'

'Duncan!'

'Well, there is. I've been thinking about it. They're pretty much the same thing but in the end one has all the content. The other is mindless and completely self-absorbed.'

'I hope you're not suggesting we're all a bunch of wankers in advertising.'

'No. Just that television is less of a strain.'

'Well, you look good on it.'

'You look great yourself.'

Charlotte flashed her white-light smile.

'You've changed your hair,' observed Duncan.

'It's more authoritative.'

'God.' Duncan laughed, recalling the sort of lines he came out with when he was an agency man.

'Don't you like it?'

'It's lovely.'

'You know my headhunter is Audrey Goldberg?'

'Everybody's headhunter is Audrey Goldberg. She did your hair?'

Charlotte tutted with mock annoyance. 'She's got this deal going with a sort of professional makeover place that's starting up. It's called Re:Dress! – with an exclamation mark. If Audrey sends you in you get a twenty-five pound discount. I suppose they must have approached her to get a foothold on us girlies in advertising.'

'You hardly need a makeover.'

'Audrey thought I should think seriously about how I presented myself for interviews because it'll be a big promotion if I get this job.'

'She's probably getting a backhander.'

'D'you think so? Anyway, the woman who does it is very good.' Charlotte giggled. 'I'm a "summer" girl!' She made the quote marks with her fingers.

'So I see!' Duncan smiled at her warmly. He was fond of Charlotte.

'Anyway, citrus is chic for a summer girl. She felt that if I dressed older than I really am, employers would see through it. She thought I should aim to look thrusting and ahead of the game and not like every other boring old bag in her dreary navy interview suit with her pastel scarf half-strangling her. She thought I had enough panache – her word not mine – to carry off a strong image.'

'I could have told you that for free.'

'She sends you to the experts for accessories. I got thirty per cent off my hair at Charles Worthington's. You don't get him personally, of course.'

The coffees turned up, accompanied by two sundae bowls piled high with fresh fruits in shimmering wet technicolours. They dug in. Charlotte pushed her hair back from her forehead.

'David cut mine – much fuller on the crown, a staggered parting to make it bigger on top, layered throughout. He's scissored the side length to create movement.'

'Uhuh . . .' Duncan nodded but was staring into his spoon of fruit. The minutiae of personal presentation was another thing he had left behind with the agency world.

Charlotte giggled. 'Am I being too girly for you, Duncan?'

'I think you'll find I'm just as big a girly as you are.' Charlotte giggled. 'So what d'you want to know?'

'I need all the help I can get. You've been an account director. You never put a foot wrong.'

'I wish. How many interviews have you had so far?'

'Five. Two board account directors. Head of planning. Creative director. Deputy MD.'

'God. You've done really well.'

'Don't sound so amazed. Audrey's got brilliant files on the agency and really decent press clippings on its clients. She's been shit hot this time.'

'Makes a change.'

'It's a big jump for me.'

'How old are you now?'

'Nearly twenty-seven.'

'A baby. Still young to be an account director.'

'How old were you when you were made one?'

Duncan thought for a moment. 'Twenty-seven! I was lucky.'

'Well, I've had to virtually run Clancey and Bennett since you left.' Charlotte signalled to the waiter. She asked for another serviette. 'I simply can't afford to get anything on this dress. It's the real thing, not a copy.'

'It doesn't look like it's from British Home Stores.'

'Fill me in on how to handle Hector.'

'I don't think I can.'

'You must know him. Everyone does.'

'Everyone knows *of* him. There's a difference.'

'I'll just be myself. Take him at face value. That should work.'

'I don't think you should take Hector Quigley at face value.'

'Duncan, don't put me off.'

'He's had it lifted, is what I meant. For all his media appearances and his public utterances, Hector Quigley is about as well understood as the Saatchi brothers. He's very high profile but difficult to put your finger on.'

'You can't get published information on him. HQ is a private company. If he offers me the job should I take it?'

'What do you think?'

'I think yes. It's lots more money. It's a big step up. And if I stay another minute at Clancey and Bennett I'll go completely fucking bonkers.'

'Then take it. A lot of people underestimate HQ. They think because Hector does such a dated song and dance man routine he's not where it's at anymore. But all that is just a veneer. Look at their new biz track record. Nobody wins all those pitches because they're an industry joke. Mark my words. HQ is solid as a rock.'

'How old is he?'

'God. I've no idea. I've seen him speak but I've never met him. I suppose he must be Nigel Gainsborough's age.'

'Jurassic then. I think Nigel is getting pre-senile dementia.'

'Pre-?' Duncan placed his cup firmly in his saucer. 'The difference between Nigel and Hector is that Nigel *is* an old fool and Hector just looks like one. For all we know he's the shrewdest man in London advertising.'

'Stop. You're making me nervous.'

'Hector Quigley will outlast us all. He's part and parcel of the furniture in advertising.'

'Interview tips?'

'You don't need any. You look great. Talk confidently – you will anyway. He's the chairman. He won't ask you anything detailed, so answer in broad brush strokes. Think long term and strategic and not day-to-day and tactical. That's the difference between an account manager and an account director, not in being twenty-six or twenty-seven.'

'Can I quote you?'

'Yes, but only once. Now I'm in telly I get residuals. He'll be more interested in deciding whether you have board potential. You'd hardly be meeting him if the others thought you weren't up to it.'

'Oh. Duncan. It's so nice to see you again. You say all the right things to make a girl feel good.'

'Bar one. Let me know how it goes.'

Charlotte giggled. When she had worked with Duncan he had been coy about his sexuality. Now he seemed at home with it. She thought. She looked at her giant Swatch and stood up.

'I have to be in a meeting with Stella Boddington in fifteen minutes. How long does it take to get to Dean Street from here?'

'Ten seconds by Ducati. Lesser mortals take longer.'

Charlotte grabbed her purse and helmet and headed for her bike. She remembered something.

'Oh, Duncan,' she called.

'What?'

'Remember your old convertible BMW?'

'No. I erased it from my memory.'

'Clancey and Bennett sold it!'

'Did they?' Duncan felt a whiff of nostalgia.

'Well, there was no one else senior enough to deserve it rank-wise.'

'I'm flattered.'

'Anyway, guess who bought it?'

'Who?'

'My mother! I told her about it and she bought it.'

'Really?' He did not look impressed. Duncan's perception of Charlotte's family was not of one whose cars were secondhand. 'Hey,' he called after her from the terrace table. 'I thought you were paying for our power breakfast.'

'I'll pay next time.'

'Heard *that* before.'

'Let's do lunch. My treat.'
'Cliché!'
'You, me – and Hector Quigley.'
He waved her off.

3

The Paddington postman was only one half-week into his new
route, but, as he arrived in short-sleeved shirt at the bright blue
entrance of the annexe overlooking the rusty railway lines, he
already had the second post of the day correctly sorted in his
hand. He double-checked the name on the top packet. Myhill
Productions it read. He scanned the street number and address as
well because there was no company sign over the door. He rang
the entryphone bell, the door buzzed and he entered, pushing his
red trolley bag ahead of him, to the glass double doors inside.

He tried to make his way in, but through the glass he could
see that a middle-aged woman lay stretched out on the floor on
the other side of the one door that opened, denying him entry.
Propped up on one angular hip, surrounded by an array of sheets
of paper, untidy stacks of magazines, a decrepit mountain of
press cuttings and confetti scraps of discarded trimmings, she was
attempting to cut around a small photograph with a too-large
pair of orange-handled scissors.

What a bleedin' state, thought Mr Postman.

He knocked on the door and when she half got up, he assumed
it was to answer. Instead she shook the scissors off her thumb
and reached out for a large can of aerosol glue. She sprayed her
cutout till it dripped, laid it onto one of her typed sheets and
pounded it into place with her fist. She held it up in front of

her admiringly. With a knuckle sticky with adhesive and black with newsprint, she pushed a distinctive pair of thick-lensed bejewelled spectacles up her beak-like nose. She appeared to be talking either to herself or to someone the postman couldn't see. He knocked again. Behind the madwoman a tanned bloke in a duck egg blue polo shirt appeared. He stepped over the woman, waded through her tip, reached over to the double doors and undid the snib. He crossed through to the postman's side.

'Hello, Postie,' said Duncan.

'Hi there, matey.' He handed him the packet and a stack of envelopes. 'What d'you do here, then?' Postie asked.

'We're an independent television production company.'

'Is ya? Whatcha done what I've seen?'

'*The Danger Game*?'

'My better 'arf watched that. Got me down the pub, meself.' He laughed. 'No offence intended. You oughta do somethin' about that girl lying in front of the door like that, matey. That bird's a liability.'

Duncan glanced over his shoulder and saw that his colleague was generously applying more Spraymount glue to an illustration.

'That bird's not a liability. That bird's the managing director.'

'You're 'avin' me on!'

'They used to call her The Most Difficult Woman In Television.'

'Used to!' Postie looked incredulous and departed shaking his head.

Duncan clambered his way back over Karen Myhill's peroxided head. 'Karen, you and I were supposed to be having a meeting.' He jolted her.

She stopped for a second, but failed to look up. 'This is more important.'

He stood over her and checked the mail, starting with the packet.

'Oh-oh.'

Karen finally gave up. She rubbed her gungy fingers together in an attempt to clean up.

'This frank is from Channel Four. Looks like a rejection.'

'The fuckers. Are you sure?' Karen looked distraught already.

Her black hands flew to the hollows in her cheeks and left their mark when they fell away.

Duncan was carefully trying to unseal the packet without damaging the envelope. 'If they don't like something they usually send it straight back. They must be returning our proposals for the afternoon slots.'

'They can't be!' Karen shot up and grabbed the packet from Duncan's clutches. 'Stop being so namby pamby with it, for God's sake. Give it here.'

Duncan surrendered, crestfallen. Karen had been happy-go-lucky all day, spread out on the floor in the thick of things, making a mess, toiling away, creative and industrious, her genius hurdling obstacles as she turned yet another mindleap into an illustrated document with which to test the TV commissioners. It amused Duncan to watch the woman who was once one of the most powerful executives in British commercial broadcasting run her own business like a little girl playing shop. Now, in an instant her even-temperedness turned to bad, her humour to dismay, her hope to disappointment. With her gummy, grimy fingers she tore into the packet and ripped the guts out of it. Their two returned documents fell to the floor. Karen scrunched the rejection letter into a hateful ball.

'That miserable cow. What does she know! She's never produced a fucking microwave meal let alone a TV show.' She flung the letter into her tip, turned on her heel and ran for the cover of her office. She pulled the door almost off its hinges and slammed it shut. Duncan stooped to retrieve the crushed letter, attempted to follow in Karen's wake, but was restrained by a glue-drenched carpet tile stuck to the sole of his shoe.

'The afternoon is where the battle lines have been drawn, Duncan. It is to be carved up amongst the winners. The losers can leave the stage. Exeunt.'

Karen sipped the blackcurrant tea he had brought and returned to her television set and flicking through the afternoon's chat shows on satellite. The repeating images of moist eyes and big-haired women nodding concern were eventually too much for them both and Karen clicked the off button.

'What are we left with, Duncan?'

'Nothing. Nothing on Channel Four. Nothing on Channel Five. Nothing on terrestrial TV. In the afternoons, that is. Cable TV, by which I mean The Station, is our best hope now.'

'Why hasn't *Basket Case* led to a breakthrough? The ratings were great.'

'It may come back. The Station thinks highly of us.'

'They do. Martin Fox does anyway and he's the only who counts. But all we've demonstrated is that we can make expensive light entertainment. What they need to fill their afternoon schedule with is cheap factual stuff from someone who can churn it out like clockwork every day.'

'Send Martin the Channel Four rejects, then. I'll tart them up a bit, personalise them for him. They're both strong runners.'

'Yes . . .' Karen seemed to lose concentration. She sipped her tea. Duncan drank his. 'I'm depressed, Duncan. I'm too old to keep being rejected.'

'Only one in every 710 proposals ends up on TV.'

'I'll go and pick my coffin now.'

Duncan tried to be positive. 'I meant we were doing better than average.'

Karen could only be negative. 'We're not doing better than Saturn Productions.'

'Who is?'

'What have they got that we haven't got?' despaired Karen.

'Several bad series on TV.' Duncan laughed.

His boss ignored him. 'Their shows are cheap. That's their secret. Huge quantities of mass-market product at prices that commissioning editors can afford.'

'They just have great PR. It's not great television.'

'But it's great business, Duncan.'

'Shall I send our stuff to Martin? Why don't you take him out to lunch?'

'I don't need to. I know what he wants. A five o'clock show for ten K per half hour. The *Sooty Show* got more than that. If they'd had to do it for ten K they'd only have had a bare hand wriggling about.'

'Don't blame Martin. It's Channel Five that's started that ten K and under crap. Now everybody thinks you can produce on those budgets.'

'The Station is rich. Rich, rich, rich.'

'They're not coining in as much ad revenue as the initial predictions,' replied Duncan. 'I know what I was going to ask you. Didn't you make *Alive at Five*?'

'Back when TV sets were encased in wood, Duncan. Martin Fox started on that as a researcher and eventually became series producer reporting to me. God. Now I have to go grovelling to him grubbing for worms.'

The visual image did not appeal to Duncan. 'So shall I send him our proposals or not?'

'I don't think we can make those shows on his budgets, Duncan. Anyway, he doesn't want *Makeover Your Mum* items or *Blue Peter* for adults.'

'We like them.'

'I adore them. I love gluing and sticking things. You put me onto it. All my life I've been a brain, not a practical pair of hands. All this craftwork we've researched has been therapy for me. I go home, have a huge row with my son and retreat to my playroom to wrap raffia round a Piat d'Or bottle and make a Thai lamp-stand. And makeovers. I find them enthralling.'

'It's before and after, problem and solution TV. People enjoy the transformation. Proctor and Gamble have used it in advertising for years.'

'I still have more to learn about makeovers. What Martin is looking for is his answer to Oprah and Esther and Rikki.'

'Don't forget Vanessa. She's the biggest thing to hit TV in years.'

'Literally. When's the deadline?'

'In two weeks.' Karen raked around her untidy desk top for her diary. She found a business card and picked it up. 'I was looking for that earlier.' She leafed through her desk diary and confirmed the deadline. She slammed it shut and her bad temperedness returned with a vengeance. 'If that little fucker Jamie Hirst and Saturn Productions get this five o'clock show I'll spew blood.'

'Martin Fox won't give him the afternoon strip as well as the morning.'

'Why shouldn't he?'

'Because he'd have him by the balls.'

'Martin has no balls.'

'Jamie would have two and a half hours of his daily schedule.'

'Worse things have been done. Duncan, it's up to you to think of a strategy to defeat Saturn.'

'How about just thinking up a better programme?' Duncan couldn't be bothered with Karen and Jamie's pointless vendetta.

'Saturn Productions are profitable enough now to invest in their own programmes, because of the cash flow on *Megabrek*.'

'Meaning?'

'Meaning they'll use the same team, so the staffing up will cost them zilch. There'll be cost-efficiencies of scale. They'll siphon off the profits from the breakfast show into the afternoon.'

'Robbing Peter to pay Paul,' said Duncan.

'Robbing Martin to pay back Myhill,' replied Karen.

There was a knock on the door. Karen's secretary popped her head round.

'Sorry to interrupt. Karen, did you remember Paula was coming back to show us the baby. She's nearly ready to leave now. He's ever so cute!'

They went to coo over the baby boy and everybody laughed when Duncan took the screaming bundle in his arms and patiently rocked it to silence.

'Ooh. You'll make ever such a good dad,' said Paula, who Did Not Know. 'You haven't got young uns, have you?'

'No,' said Duncan quietly.

'Just you wait!' joked the girl, and everybody laughed louder.

After Duncan had performed his little miracle Karen took the sleeping baby on her lap. She whispered words of encouragement in his ear.

'My precious baby,' she said sweetly, and recalled her own new son looking up at her bejewelled spectacles with unconditional love. There was no end of conditions these days. The baby hiccuped and began to scream its head off, worse than before. 'It must be my glasses,' apologised Karen, embarrassed at being outclassed in the babycare stakes by novice Duncan. 'They've been known to frighten great men, not just little ones.' She suddenly upped and made to leave.

Duncan reminded her: 'Don't forget we're having dinner with the consultant tonight.'

'I won't,' said Karen, rushing. 'I have another appointment first.'

Duncan was left holding the baby and wondering what it was.

4

'Ring Marsha and ask her to cancel my manicurist, would you, Maria?' He pronounced it Ma-ree-ah.

'It's Mar-eye-ah.'

'"You say Mar-eye-ah, I say Ma-ree-ah,"' sang Hector Quigley happily, huge hand on hip. This glorious afternoon, this confident day of the last of the series of dress rehearsals for the Verity Tampons pitch, he was in fine form and fine fettle. And particularly in fine voice, amplified as it was in quadraphonic sound which leapt off all four walls like the voice of God – which it was to the thirty or so people assembled in the presentation theatre where HQ made all its new business pitches. The company had so expanded, it now took up two buildings in Marylebone. Quigley House, a 1950s anonymous block at the top end of Old Marylebone Road, was rendered unanonymous by the showy insertion of a post-modernist atrium and a spiral stairwell sticking into the street, not to mention a fifteen-foot-high illuminated paired H and Q hanging across one and a half storeys of the exterior. The second building, a bigger, brand new block around the corner in Seymour Place and known as the Satellite, housed Hector's favourite spot, the new business theatre.

Hector allowed himself alone the privilege of a body mike for presentations. In his eyes, there was no business like show-business except his business, the business of running an advertising agency. The megastar's fawning circle was laughing with him. All, that is, except Maria Handley.

'It's Mar-eye-ah,' she insisted, her New York twang underlining her point.

'Americans say Ma-ree-ah. Or am I wrong?'

'My mother was English.'

'An asset, I am sure, anywhere.'

'She used the English pronunciation even though we were in New York.'

'Did she really? She must have been a remarkable woman.' It was not a good idea to correct Hector, who was never wrong and who could never resist playing to a club of yes-men. His newest and youngest and only female associate director was hardly going to change the habit of a lifetime.

'"The most beautiful sound I e-e-e-ver heard,"' he sang. '"Ma-ree-ah. Say it loud and there's music playing."' He clasped his big hands. '"Say it soft and it's almost like praying. Ma-*ree*-ah-, Ma-*ree*-ah-, Ma-*ree*-ah, Ma-*ree*-ah, Ma-reeeeeeee-*haaaaaaah*!"' His hands parted and stretched wide in show-stopping climax. A ripple of applause for Hector's 150-decibel baritone did no one's Christmas bonus any harm.

'I should have been on the stage,' Hector intoned, agreeing with his own opinion. 'Broadway,' he said, acknowledging Maria. 'Your mother obviously missed out on *West Side Story*. Now run along.' He dismissed her with a camp wave of his hefty hand.

Maria's absence of humour was replaced by anger. She suppressed it. When she had been headhunted out of Chiat Day's New York office she knew the British were behind in political correctness but Hector Quigley's sexist humiliation of her was unforgivable. It made him a management criminal as well as a management monster. She ran a quick eye-search of the room. There was no telephone – an edict of Hector's so that important meetings, big clients and dress rehearsals, such as this final one for the Verity Tampons pitch, could not be interrupted. Why ask someone of her rank to leave to make a menial call? But she understood enough not to delegate it. She went in search of a phone.

'Right, that's Miss Miseryguts out of the way!' Hector's voice blasted out of secreted speakers. 'Now, the purpose of rehearsals is to polish our presentational style – and our statistics. Boys! Go back to the slide which had the research figures on our women's press proposals.'

Behind the dais on which Hector stood was a floor-to-ceiling, computer-controlled, back-projected multi-image slide screen-show on which commercials, photography, concept illustrations and verbal and numerical data appeared. A team of three were sound– and vision-linked in the control room next door. The montage of slides Hector had referred to clicked over behind him. He studied them.

'It simply isn't strong enough to say that fifty-three per cent of those interviewed placed our Verity ads over Tampax and Bodyform. That's only half the sample. Have it changed to seventy-three per cent. Keep it at fifty-three in the client's document but that's what I'll say tomorrow. Clients never read the documents and they only remember the gist. Funny word that, gist. Now does everyone agree with me? Of course you do. I am right, as usual. And the client is thick, as usual. And no telling our American cousin. She's not yet used to our little winning ways. Which is why she has come to HQ. To learn.'

Theatrically, Hector pointed to the only item which adorned the sunshine yellow walls of the room – a gold-framed printed panel, one of a collection of Hector's 'management beliefs' scattered about the agency, blown up for all to see and be impressed by. Underneath an HQ logo centred over a block of big type it read:

HQ people are more talented, more dedicated and more committed.
HQ people arrive earlier, stay longer and work harder.
HQ people don't just promise 'full service', we provide it.

The panel concluded with the flourish that was his signature and a mono photograph, credited to Snowdon no less, of Hector wearing a silken top hat bearing the HQ logo.

'OK, we'll continue as soon as Ma-reeh– . . . sorry, sorry, sorry everybody. A colossal error on my part. Forgive me, forgive me. I mean of course the one and only, all the way from the Big Apple,

Mar-eyyye-ah Ha-a-a-ndley, give her a big hand – I have!' He waved one at his colleagues, who returned the gesture with a music hall laugh. Maria re-entered the room, ears burning.

'Ah. The wanderer has returned.'

Maria scowled. She had not wandered anywhere. She had been sent out. Hector jollied her along.

'Now, Maria darling, every golden syllable, every word of wisdom, every drop of detail you utter must be delivered clearly and emphatically, so I would like you to redo your section, please.'

Maria glowered. Hector was picking on her.

'It is not a criticism, my dear. It is the purpose of rehearsals. That's why we have them. Not everybody can be as good as Uncle Hector first time round. Or any time round, you slackers.'

'It would help if I had amplification.'

'Nonsense. You're quite loud enough as it is, thank you. You're from New York and I'm sure we're all very grateful they sent you.'

'Could I stand there?' She pointed in front of the dais.

'Too close to the client,' said Hector. 'And in front of me, which is worse. You look very pretty under the spotlight there.'

'Excuse me, Hector, but that is sexist. You would not describe your other directors as "pretty".'

Hector's hired fan club braced itself for his blastback, but he was full of jovial *bonhomie* this happy day. 'How very observant of you. I would not describe them as pretty. I would describe them as a right bunch of ugly bastards.' The head of planning laughed along with the others. He felt he should. The backroom boys laughed too, for as well as amplifying Hector's every word, they recorded it for posterity and nights spent down the pub.

'Now, while you're reading out your lines, Maria, I am going to continue choreographing the end-of-presentation parade. Worry not. I shall still be listening to you in the background.'

Maria set to. Through gritted teeth she read out from the teleprompter her big piece, a partisan and derogatory review of other agencies' sanitary protection advertising. Behind her the slides montage illustrated her story in a perfect visual accompaniment. But that was in the background. In the foreground was Hector, raised on his dais, picked out by lights, pastel-suited, barking out Busby Berkeley commands to a troop of slim secretaries selected for their looks. Hector's young ladies had each been obliged to slip into her HQ outfit: white stilettos, yellow leggings, tight yellow T-shirt imprinted with a big H and a big Q, one on each breast. During the course of the rehearsal Hector had been handed a series of overlarge mock-ups of designs for ads, new packs, vending machines, logos, promotional gifts and suchlike. Each was reverentially brought to him by a different girl – wearing white gloves so as not to smudge the precious artwork – who then retrieved it and withdrew when Hector had explained its purpose to the client's empty chair. Now at the end of the floorshow, as they had done for so many previous pitches, the girls returned with their wares in a climactic line-up of all the agency's ideas. Strategically placed speakers pumped out the campaign jingle and the back-projected screen flicked through illustrations of the TV commercials and press ads. The gloved handmaidens attempted to culminate in a semicircle behind Hector.

'You're in the wrong order!' spotted their ringmaster and they shuffled around. 'Don't worry. That's the purpose of rehearsals, ladies. Yes! Good! Better! Excellent! A veritable parade of Verity tampons! I shall call it my "tamponade"!' he announced to more canned laughter. 'Come on, you sad shower. Look happy! I hope you all have your tampons in today, inside your nice yellow leggings. Hah!' Maria Handley, who had given up, ignored in the background, looked daggers. She had never expected this.

The last of the young ladies stepped forward. In her white-gloved hands she bore a yellow velvet cushion with a voluptuous golden tassel suspended at each corner. On top of the cushion was a parchment contract, tied with gold thread. Hector took the contract and stepped forward off his dais. The girl ran ahead of him and placed the cushion on the carpet in front of the chair intended for tomorrow's senior client. With some difficulty, Hector lowered one knee onto the cushion and delivered his last excruciating line.

'I may be a self-made multimillionaire but I am not too proud to implore – to *beg* you – for your business.'

He gently placed the contract on the client's chair and rose to take a bow. His colleagues cheered, Maria half-clapping too.

'There,' said Hector. 'That must be worth five million big fuckers.' He asked the cushion-holder, a new girl, to ring his personal assistant and arrange for a cup of tea to be sent down. Maria wondered where the secretaries had been when the manicurist had had to be dealt with.

'I make a terrific cuppa,' offered the cushion girl to the man whose initials were branded on her breasts.

'I do not care for ordinary tea. Marsha will send down my lacquer tray with my Wedgwood cup and my Queen Anne caddy. She knows what to do.'

The cushion girl ran off to do her duty. In the background Hector's colleagues had clubbed in excitable, noisy chatter.

'A-a-a-a-ll right!' boomed Hector from every corner of the theatre. He re-ascended his dais and danced a soft shoe shuffle centre-stage. 'Quiet please! In your places everybody. Don't worry about mistakes. That's the purpose of rehearsals. Now. Everybody look at me! Check boys in the backroom? Check planning? Check media? Check creatives? Check young ladies? Check Ma-*ree*-ah, Ma-*ree*-ah, Ma-*reeeeee-hah*!? Good girl. OK, everybody! Let it roll, One More Time!'

5

Charlotte's Ducati zipped around a black cab jettisoning a passenger and pulled up in front of it. She dismounted and thumped her bike onto the pavement. She locked it and whipped off her black helmet. It was hot and humid inside. Her fine blonde hair tumbled out like a Timotei girl's and she mussed it back into its cut. She smoothed down the skirt panel of her lime green mini-dress and checked the hang of her silver belt. She breathed deeply and stretched back her shoulders, pulling up her breasts and, with them, her already high hemline. In her pre-interview stress she failed to notice the cabbie behind her enjoying an eyeful or hear the honk of his appreciative horn. Charlotte composed herself and swung her strappy shoulder purse onto her bare brown arm.

She was well aware that trumpeting her arrival on the Ducati could create the wrong first impression. First impressions are the only ones that count in advertising. So today she had stopped in York Street, five minutes short of HQ, intending to walk the last few hundred yards to the agency and the interview with Hector Quigley. But before she could take a step forward she received a jolt. A hand appeared in front of her face. It held a business card.

Daniel Mainwaring. UK Casting Director. Hollywood Pictures.

It took a minute to sink in. She turned to the young man at her side. He was exceptionally tall, six foot five she guessed. He was exceptionally slim, exceptionally freckly-faced and, despite shoulder-length strawberry blond hair not usually to her taste, Charlotte found him exceptionally sexually charged. He wore a dark green suit.

'I'm on the lookout for talent. And you look like a talented girl to me.' His accent, Estuary English in full flood, was in contrast to her cut crystal.

Charlotte giggled. 'I think you've got the wrong girl.'

He clasped his forehead in comic horror. 'Whoah! Don't go breaking my heart.'

She snatched the card from his hand. 'What is this anyway?'

'We're casting for a major motion picture being filmed in London. They're making it a lot easier to get street filming permission in the capital these days and it's opening up new opportunities. I'm looking for a young English girl who can ride a motor bike.'

'Would a Ducati do?' She motioned with her eyes.

He clasped his forehead again. 'Whoah!' He heaved with infectious laughter and checked out the bike. 'I never saw that.'

Charlotte was incredulous. 'Liar,' she said.

'I never did, I swear it.'

'You must be blind.'

'Nope,' he said, edging closer. 'Just dazzled.'

Charlotte giggled and licked her dry lips. He gently took her fingers and sweetly prised the business card from her hand. 'I can't afford to give too many of these away,' he said and slipped it inside his jacket. It was lined with dayglo pink silk.

'Wow!' said Charlotte.

'Had it made in Hong Kong.' He seemed terribly proud of that fact. 'What's your name?'

'Charlotte Reith.'

'*Ex*-cellent!' He clenched his fist and laughed again. So did Charlotte, though she had no idea why. 'The American market likes English stars with classic names. Emma. Sir Anthony. Kate. Winslett, I mean. Do you mind if I ask how old you are?'

'Twenty-two. Nearly.' Charlotte shocked herself at her automatic lie, but she'd done enough model and actress castings for commercials to know that you had to slice five years from the truth to stand even half a chance. 'I'm awfully sorry, but I'm on my way to an appointment.'

'Are you a model?'

'At five feet five?'

'Naomi's not that tall. Tara is, mind you.'

'Do you really know all those people?'

He was bashful. 'I'm a bit of a namedropper, actually. I'm telling you the truth because I like you. You engage me. If you can do that for the lens – wow!' He laughed again and so did she. They dangled by each other, unsure of what to do next. While not releasing her from his green-eyed gaze he lightly fingered his jacket button, twirling it between fingertips. He was saved by the bell. He produced his mobile phone.

'Yup . . . yup . . . nope . . . OK . . . Brad, yup . . . who else? . . . no, I know Gwynneth . . . yup, but if he does that he'll have the fucking funeral without the four fucking weddings, won't he? Bunch of arse mate. Fucking dickhead . . . well you pace the streets trying to pick up the next fucking Julia Roberts. It ain't easy. I'm gonna end up doing time for this, matey . . .' He suddenly laughed. '. . . yup . . . yup . . . love you too. Big kiss.' He replaced the phone in his jacket. Suddenly he looked embarrassed. He was all little boy lost. Charlotte wanted him to be big boy found again.

'Trouble?' she asked.

'Everything under control,' he said. 'I'll let you get on your way. Call me.' With a flash of dayglo pink he returned the business card to her possession.

'Might do!' Charlotte shot him her white-light smile.

'I know this great little club . . .'

'Go on. Surprise me.'

'Yeah. I admit it. Too quick. Damn. Ruined my chances.'

'Oh, go one. Which one?'

'Well, look . . .' He seemed unsure now Charlotte had encouraged him. 'How about the Ministry of Sound?'

'It doesn't get going until rather late. It's a bit noisy.' For a smoochy evening, she meant.

'Try something different. The Atlantic?'

'Know it well. It's quite chi-chi. Older crowd.'

'I'm a grown-up. And on expenses.'

'In that case count me in!'

'See you in the foyer, seven-thirty?'

Charlotte giggled. It would be something to do after her interview.

He turned and almost ran off then turned back.

'Charlotte Reith!' he called.

'Yes?'

'Imagine that in plastic letters!'

Charlotte giggled. Plastic letters! She suddenly remembered the huge plastic letters on the building she was supposed to be heading for. She panicked and picked up pace. She couldn't be late for Hector Quigley. Crash helmet under arm, she sprang forward, started to swing her shoulder purse ahead of her and then to skip. She was smitten.

6

'Hiya, handsome.'

'Hello.' Duncan pulled the blue door to, and turned the mortice lock. As he crossed the pavement the passenger door of the grey Mercedes 300E swung open and Duncan dropped in beside his lover. Michael Farnham had all the windows wide open to allow a balmy blast through the interior. The car crept into the evening rush hour traffic and, as Duncan belted up, he looked back at the annexe where he worked.

'She really ought to have something done about that building.'

'Did I catch you locking up? This early?'

'Yes. Why?'

'A bit cruel, isn't it?'

'What is?'

'Locking Karen Myhill in. I know she's The Most Difficult Woman In Television but she's not a danger to the public.'

'She left even earlier than me.'

'That must be a first. That *is* unusual, isn't it?'

'It is.'

'I wonder why.'

'I wondered why too. She's not been concentrating recently.'

'Losing her touch?'

'Losing her mind.'

'Losing her grip. On her son.'

'He's hard on her. He's growing up. He's going through the argumentative stage.'

'That lasts twenty years.'

'I don't think so.'

'It has in your case.' Michael laughed. Duncan did too.

'If you're going to be unkind, Michael, I'm not going to help you.'

'*You've got to,*' wailed Michael. He rattled the steering wheel like prison bars.

'You agreed to be her godfather.'

'Only because they're old friends. She's been alive for ever and she's still a toddler.'

'She's sweet.'

'Why can't children grow up and grow more interesting more quickly? I mean, what do you buy a four-year-old girl for her birthday?'

'Try going into a toyshop and asking.'

'I hate going into shops. It's an ordeal. There are only cretins behind counters.'

'Turn left here.' Duncan directed Michael to the Early Learning Centre in the King's Road in Chelsea.

'You may love shopping, Duncan, but I detest it.'

'Think of the child.'

'You may love children, Duncan, but I detest them.'

'Well, you shouldn't have agreed to be godfather then. Imagine her little face when she opens your present. She'll remember it for the rest of her life.'

'Listen to you! I haven't adopted the little brat, you know. Show me the contract where it says I have to contribute!'

'The lawyer speaks.'

'She costs a fortune. When I was a child, kids got pennies. Now everything they need starts in three figures.'

'We'll find her something small and special that won't break the bank. Start looking for parking.'

'When I was a kid, adults dressed like adults and children wore what they were bloody well told, no matter how humiliating. Now adults dress like children used to and kids pose and pout like prostitutes.'

Duncan laughed. 'You were raised in South Africa. It was probably a bit more old-fashioned there.'

'It was the same here. If you misbehaved your parents gave you a good thrashing. Now they have to negotiate. Talks about talks about bedtime.'

'Children have rights now. You of all people should understand that.'

'Why me of all people?'

'Because you're a South African. The black mammy who bottle-fed you in the fifties was barely better than a slave.'

'I don't think "black mammy" is the accepted expression.'

'I wouldn't know. I'm from Scotland.'

'Brigadoon.'

Duncan snorted.

'You're always going on about Scotland but you only go there once every hundred years.'

'Huh! Parking!'

'How much is this going to cost?' asked Michael, reversing into a slip of a space. 'I'm deducting the price of the parking meter from the present.'

'It's past six-thirty.'

'It's an eight-thirty limit here.'

'We can afford it. We're a two-car, three-home, five-holiday family.'

They got out and Michael zapped the central locking with his key fob. He left the roadside and joined Duncan on the pavement in front of a row of miniature pastel Chelsea terraced houses.

'Is that how you see us? As a family?'

'Yes. The three of us.'

Michael was lost.

'You, me and Pushkin! We might find something for her in the Early Learning Centre. A little ball or something.'

Michael laughed. 'Would you like a child, Dunky?'

'Not a possibility. I'll think you'll find I'm fucking the wrong person.'

'I know. But would you like to be a father? You'd be a good one.'

Duncan sighed and stalled. 'It's not something I can ever have. I don't think about it. I've never thought about it.' The look on his face suggested otherwise.

'You, me and Pushkin!' Dadda, mumma and baba,' said Michael in a baby voice.

'I can't stand you being queenie like that,' Duncan snapped. 'And I'm not fucking mummy, either!'

'No, but I am!' goaded Michael. He pushed up to Duncan and nuzzled in his ear. 'And I'll tell you, she's one helluva girl!'

Karen Myhill was depressed. She dragged her feet reluctantly over the paving slabs of Chiltern Street, an elegant row of shops hiding behind Baker Street and a hotel named after Sherlock Holmes. Right now, Karen could do with his powers of deduction. She needed to know why her programme proposals were getting rejected at the rate they were. She and Duncan were a good team. Everybody said so. But recently they had not sold a single show. Was it just a lack of demand in the market place? Was it just an oversupply of independent producers? Was it just all budget cutbacks and referral of investment out of programming and into new technology? Karen never had been one to look on the bright side, nor one to lighten her own load, nor one to spot a silver lining. A shy Sherlock with manic moods, she searched dark corners in her own and other people's minds.

Tonight, Karen was on an investigative mission with a three-fold aim. One: to cheer herself up. Two: to research Duncan's *Move-Over! Make-Over!* programme idea. Three: to impress the new man in her life. But she was not cheering up, she had no need to research programme content herself, and the new man in her life seemed not to want her to be in his. Or at least not very often. She trailed past the boutiques. These were terribly London shops. Small, low-key, discreet, drawing discerning people of taste not catered for elsewhere. There was a shop for wide, shapely shoes for wide, unshapely feet. There was a shop for uncommonly huge hats for rare grand occasions. There was a shop for tall female executives, women above the height of *prêt-à-porter*. Karen should have tripped gaily along Chiltern Street because she was one of its classic customers and the line of traditional, wood-edged windows was welcoming. But instead of feeling tailored for, she felt hemmed in. She hated W1. She hated being at the heart of things. She preferred to position herself on the periphery, which is why she had placed her production company in Paddington. There, there were no huge hat-makers and no outsize outfitters. Karen was not catered for but she was in control.

She stopped. She stooped in her loose waistcoat and long brown hobble skirt. A vanity case hung from her hand, empty but for crucial contracts, private papers and draft documents which never left her side. Karen slumped inside her clothes, feeling unattractive and rejected, her wine-bottle shoulders falling away from her thin neck even more than usual. Marvellous makeover material, in fact, for Julie Anne Bolton.

'Julie Anne Bolton.' She sang it through lips luscious in hyacinth.

'Hello. I'm Karen Myhill.' Karen faltered. She had barely crossed the threshold and she wanted to leave. Julie Anne, a picture in pink, floated forward. She had obviously been at the happy tablets and was on gush factor twelve. There was still time to make a run for it, only Karen could only hobble in her hobble skirt. And Julie Anne's rose-taloned tentacles had trapped her. They were already wrapped around her arm and were pulling her into her parlour.

'I know exactly who you are. Welcome to Re:Dress!, Karen. Can I just check? Karen with a K?'

Disarmed by this unprecedented line, Karen nodded. Julie Anne beamed like she had come first in a regional spelling bee.

'M.Y.H.I. Double L? Get it right, right from the start, that's one of my Five Fantastic Philosophies.'

'I have a six-thirty appointment.'

'That's just what it says in my little pink book. And you're in television, Karen? How fascinating for you! How exciting for me! Come in here and tell Julie Anne *all* about it.'

Karen immediately resolved to clam up, but, like a sparkling synthetic strawberry milkshake, Julie Anne continued to froth. She bubbled over and out of the reception room, leading the way. Karen wanted to vomit. There was no way Julie Anne Bolton was going to get a guest spot on her hoped-for afternoon show. She was all wrong. Karen was already able to rule out the first two aims of tonight's mission. She was not going to get cheered up and she was not going to learn anything about makeovers. She would struggle on simply to impress her man. Annoyed but resolute, she followed the vapour trail of Julie Anne's fragrantly feminine perfume. Karen had forgotten all about her secret appointment when she had dressed in the dark this morning and now felt diminished in the presence of this pink pavlova. It was only as she was leaving home that she had remembered and had run back to get the vanity case Julie Anne had suggested she bring to fill with freebies.

They entered a small room, a cross between a theatre dressing room and a Romanov boudoir in mauve. From beneath the low floodlit dressing table Julie Anne rolled out a plush purple stool and beckoned Karen to sit down. Karen did, and looked into the mirror. She could have wept. She could have cried. She could have cried off but she didn't dare. The penalty was too great. She might be tied up in tutu netting or powder-puffed to death. There, under the glare, the reflection in the mirror who returned her look of panic was hardly The Most Powerful Woman In Television. Nor was she possibly A Quite Powerful Woman In Television. She was not even The Most Difficult Woman In Television, Karen's very own epithet. Instead, she was The Original One-Hundred-Year-Old Withered Woman. She Who Must Be Obeyed after re-entering the flame. Nefertiti dug up and displayed unwrapped in the British Museum.

'Well!'

Karen did not know if this was a bad 'well' or a very bad 'well'. It certainly wasn't a well 'well', whichever 'well' it was. Julie Anne stood behind her in the mirror and Karen could thankfully no longer see her pork chop face, only the gold weave buttons on the breast pockets of her suit.

'Well! What have we here.'

'This is me at my worst,' said Karen defensively.

'Well!' Julie Anne ignored her. 'Haven't we lovely hair.' She plunged her fingers into Karen's loosely cut coiffure and began to make pastry.

'I spend my money on my hair,' said Karen, comforted. Her peroxided hair, a model of controlled cutting and colouring, was her one small triumph over the unkindness of a Nature which had given her a great mind and then taken a break. Julie Anne stopped her kneading and ran her fingers up and down Karen's hollow cheeks.

'And haven't we fine bone structure.'

'My nose is too prominent.'

'And haven't we hands to write home about.'

Karen snatched her hand back and placed it in the dark of her lap. Other women only noticed your hands when you were ugly.

'I see we're not wearing make-up, this evening.'

Karen wanted to spit back that 'we' were wearing just the right amount of make-up this evening, only one of the two of us seemed to be wearing all of it all by herself. She desisted.

'Do we wear make-up? All my products are hypo-allergenic so there's absolutely no reason not to.'

'I do in the evenings or if I'm going to a function.'

'Functions! A glamour puss! I knew it. And do we always wear our spectacles?'

Karen instinctively clutched onto both legs of her trademark multicoloured bejewelled glasses, protecting their position with her fingertips.

'Yes,' she threatened.

'I wear contact lenses, myself.'

Karen couldn't have cared less if the woman had the Hubble telescope strapped to her forehead. 'I'm not into sticking things in my eyes.'

Julie Anne tried without subtlety to nudge Karen's hands from her head.

'Let's just take a peek at what we look like without them.'

Karen brushed the woman away.

'I look better with them on. I never take them off in public.'

'Deary me. We're not *hiding* behind them, are we?'

Julie Anne smelt a rat and rats had to be caught and eliminated. She took firm hold of the spectacles by the corners and gave them a little tug but Karen gripped them to her head.

'I'd rather they stayed on, actually.'

However, Julie Anne was deadly determined. 'I'd rather they came off.' She took firm charge of each spectacle leg with three fingers and thumb, her little fingers extended downwards like claws of prey in flight. Karen cowered into her collar and clung on for dear life. Her face reddened and she screwed up her eyes. She pulled her beloved bejewelled spectacles back towards her face.

'Leave me alone.'

Pull. Push. Pull.

'There's no need to be shy.'

Push. Pull. Push.

'Stop it!' Karen was close to tears. 'You'll break my glasses.'

Pull. Push. Pull.

'They won't break if you'll just let go!'

Push. Pull. Push.

'For fuck's sake!'

'Language, language!'

Pull. Push. Ker-r-r-runch.

'*Ow-aagh*!' Julie Anne sprang off her violent victim as 2,000 volts of agony shot through the little finger of her left hand. She shook her wrist out vigorously to quell the pain. Her finger had turned pure white while her face was now as unpleasantly pink as her suit. She had dangled her finger in front of her client's mouth and Karen had bitten into it. She was in a state of shock and took a moment to calm down. Karen was ashamed of herself but had no intention of sinking to an apology. She braced herself for Julie Anne to dish out one of her Five Fantastic Philosophies or a Horrendously Happy Homily but none was forthcoming. Instead, Julie Anne regained her composure and stood a good four inches further back from the untamed beast before her. She decided to compromise with The Most Difficult Woman In Television.

'Shall we agree that your spectacles are part and parcel of your personality and that we'll keep them as is?'

'OK by me,' replied Karen. Her posture improved and she sat up straight on her stool.

'Would you like a glass of white wine?' asked Julie Anne.

'You couldn't run to a bloody mary, by any chance?'

'You're mistaking me for a barmaid, dear. I do do white wine though.'

'Thank you.' Karen tried to smile and sound sweet but she had failed miserably to manage that in her first five decades and she did not accomplish it now. Julie Anne nipped behind and returned with two freezing glasses of semi-sec and a stack of coloured cards. Karen sipped while Julie Anne, stiff and detached, galloped through her script.

'Your hair is . . .' Flick. Flick. Flick. '. . . the colour of a sandy shore.' She matched a coloured card to it. 'Your skin . . .' Flick. Flick. Flick . . . has the pink sheen of rose petals.' She matched another card. 'Your eyes are . . .' Flick. '. . . the blue of the July sky. Your lips are apple red.'

'Apples are green.'

'Apples are red. Grapes, grass and greengages are green. Yes! You say summertime. That's what my charts are telling me. See?'

Karen felt flattered for the first time in a long time. She liked being summery already. It was better than being winter's woman, which is how she usually felt.

'In a minute or two I'll do your make-up based on what I've just discovered and I'll let you have a list of all the products I've used so you'll be able to repeat it at home. I'll give you your discount coupons too. But first – stand up!'

Karen stood up and looked in the mirror. Julie Anne pulled the plush purple stool away from behind her calves.

'Your dress sense is, there's no other word for it, dreary, Karen.'

Karen of the sandy shore under July skies was too pleased to disagree.

'Your skirt is too long for your long legs and those layers shroud your figure. You're not just wearing autumn and winter clothes, you're wearing autumn and winter colours. But *your* chart says summer! Think bold and bright! Think shimmer and shine! Think short and sleek. Think . . . small suits in citrus!'

'Citrus?' Karen didn't follow.

'It's *the* colour.'

'What colour is it exactly?'

'I'll show you.'

'Why aren't you wearing it?'

'I don't go past May. I daren't.'

'Eh?'

'I'm a Spring Slumberer. A bit of blossom does me best. The chart says it. But you're Summer Sunshine. For you, zest is best. You're to wear citrus. Grapefruit! Orange! Lemon! Lime!'

Julie Anne appeared to be roll-calling a pack of Opal Fruits. A right load of pith, thought Karen. But she felt happier. She wanted to impress the new man in her life and this was a lot better than nothing.

'Come behind this screen, Karen with a K. We'll slip you into some samples. We need to smarten your silhouette. Bring drama to your legs. Heap harmony upon your hips. Add detail by design. Make a shape statement. I'll show you what to do and you can pop along the street after and check out the boutiques. Look on spending soundly on the foundations as an investment and not an expenditure. I pass on my discount with the neighbouring stores, too. Generous Julie Anne, that's me! More wine, or are we tipsy on our tiptoes?'

Two hours later a new figure emerged onto Chiltern Street. It was undeniably Karen Myhill, but she stood straight, shoulders back, slimline in citrus, chic in summer shades. Julie Anne Bolton had pulled off the most magical makeover since Colonel Pickering had whipped Eliza Doolittle off to Whiteley's. As she legged it long-leggedly to her car, only the peroxided hair and trademark bejewelled spectacles revealed to the world that this was the same dead-beat, defeatist, reptilian Karen Myhill who had miserably crawled up out of the ether earlier in the afternoon.

She flung open the driver's door, swinging her vanity case of files and redundant garments onto the back seat. She heard the high-pitched tone of her mobile phone. She grabbed it from the glove compartment. She checked the caller ID facility. No number showed.

'Karen Myhill.'

'Hello, Ms Myhill. This is Tim Lutyens speaking.'

The phone slipped within Karen's grip. Tim Lutyens had been her son's deceased father's solicitor.

'Why are you calling me?'

'I wondered, Ms Myhill, how shall I put it, if I had been in your thoughts of late?'

'Why the fuck should I be thinking of you?'

'You remember who I am?'

'I remember exactly who you are.'

'You recall our meeting about one year ago?'

'I do. Do I win a prize?'

'Ms Myhill, I must ask you a question. Did you discuss that conversation with anybody?'

'If you must know I dined out on it for six months! I told it on a cable chat show! I turned it into a twenty-six-part international TV series! No, of course I didn't discuss it with anyone! It affected my son's life and that is one thing I do not play with.'

'Did you perhaps mention it to your son?'

'He knows he will inherit a million-pound trust fund in less than ten years. I did not tell him the details. I don't know them anyway. Why?'

'Did you give your son my name and address by any chance?'

'No, I did not.'

'Hmm.'

'Hmm, yourself. What's that supposed to mean?'

'It means nothing, Ms Myhill. As you know, these matters are always confidential. I'm so sorry to have troubled you. Goodbye.'

He hung up.

'Hang on a minute. You can't just—'

But the solicitor had gone.

In frustration Karen closed the call and switched the phone right off. Her new nylon-coated nails touched her new sorbet de cassis lips. Her shoulders slumped, her spine stooped, her newly revealed legs went limp. It wasn't her apparel that needed a going over, it was her life. As she lamely pulled the car door shut and caught her sleeve on it, her head pounded with thoughts of the solicitor, his deceased client and their son. She retrieved her new jacket from the door's grip and examined the cuff. It bore the mark of black rubber. It was only five minutes old and it was ruined already. Citrus had seemed a sweet colour but it was a sour one too. Oh, dear. What would the new man in her life think of what she had done?

8

'Mr Quigley, would you care to inspect the table?'

Hector nodded over the back of the overstuffed, overbuttoned leather armchair by the library fireplace. On winter evenings it would flicker purple and blue with a flame-effect gas fire. At the height of summer it played home to an equally fiery display of white and crimson tiger lilies, orange gladioli and white and yellow chrysanthemums. The head of the hired catering company held open one of the mahogany double doors and Hector passed through into the dining room.

When he had purchased the lease on the six-storey stucco-fronted corner mansion in Belgrave Place, Hector had briefed his interior designer to come up with something reminscent of the Hall of Mirrors at Versailles for his dining room. Hector adored Versailles. Hector adored mirrors. Hector adored dining by reflected candlelight and if he ever got bored he could always enjoy watching himself in charge out of the corner of one eye. The dining room was literally palatial. Eighteen feet high and iced with confectionary cornicing and mouldings, the room was long, lit naturally by a magnificent bay window at one end. From the ceiling hung three reproduction Louis XVI gilt chandeliers. Each chandelier was reflected to infinity by one of three pairs of ornate gilt mirrors hanging opposite one another on the long walls. The outer pairs were full-length floor-to-ceiling jobs, the inner pair amputated to accommodate an Adam fireplace and mahogany doors leading, eventually, to the kitchen. Running the length of the room, and given a guard of honour by a procession of gilt-backed Louis XVI chairs, a linen-draped table was laid for eighteen. Tonight was the turn of Hector's new club, the Chairman's Circle and their first dinner. Each man would have four solid silver knife and fork sets to tuck in with, five gold-edged crystal goblets to sip from, six translucent gold-leafed china plates to sup off. Gilt candelabras, to match the chandeliers, and gold cherubs holding high horns of plenty and showering sprays of yellow flowers, occupied the no-man's-land in the middle of the table. At the centre, a lone cherub had swapped his horn of plenty for a golden pitcher from which flowed dyed turquoise water, invisibly pumped through a hidden plastic tube. The cherub revolved on a raised turntable to enable all Hector's guests to appreciate it to its full effect.

He inspected the arrangements and gave his seal of approval to his hired head of catering, but for one piece of self-admonishment.

'I really should buy a canteen of gold cutlery. The silver doesn't match. The trouble is that gold scratches, don't you find?' And he showed the hired head of catering his Roman sundial and Spanish doubloon cufflinks.

The double doors to the kitchen suite parted.

'I'm off now, Hecka.' It was Marsha Blow. 'I've checked everything downstairs and it's all tickety-boo. You're having ever such a nice claret with the venison and the dessert is just to die for. It's a huge great big pile of profiteroles stuffed with white chocolate ice-cream and glued together with bitter brown chocolate.'

'Don't spoil my surprise!' Hector's huge hands covered his ears. 'My pudding is my surprise!'

'Don't be such a big baby, Hecka. Anyway, you'll be glad to know that I've played food taster and no one's trying to poison you. Unless of course it's me – in which case I'm lying and see you at the funeral.'

'Hah!' laughed Hector. He intoned to the head of the catering company. 'She was dropped on the head as a child. Her mother was driven to it.'

'I've checked with all seventeen secretaries and the nobs are all *en route*. So they should be here between seven-thirty and eight.'

'Better make yourself scarce then, hadn't you?'

'I've called a cab. You'll be in at eight tomorrow morning for the set-up?'

'I will indeed. Then it's time to show Verity Tampons what we can do.'

'How was that girl you saw? Caroline Reith.'

'Charlotte Reith. I liked her. I'm sleeping on her, if you know what I mean.'

'Poor girl, she'll get squashed flat as a cold crêpe.'

'Don't be cheeky.'

A peal of bells chimed.

'That's the cab! Good luck, Hecka. Have lovely din-dins. Bring me a doggy bag.'

'Thank you for your help, my dear Marsha.'

Hector turned and studied the table, turning the seating plan over in his mind. The bells chimed again.

'What's she forgotten this time?' When Hector had hired staff in, which was most of the evenings he spent at home, he did not usually answer his own front door, but he could deal with Marsha on the doorstep. However it was not Marsha under the portico. It was his lady friend.

'Goodness me!'

'Charming!'

'And I was just saying I liked surprises. I have very important guests coming.'

'What? Not just averagely important ones? Don't worry, I'm not staying. I was on my way to a business meeting and a cab pulled out right in front of your house and there was a parking place so I thought I'd stop and see if you were in. And to show you my new look.' She flicked her eyes up and down herself and he followed.

'It's not a new look. It's a transformation.'

'Dr Frankenstein, I presume! Show a little more enthusiasm. I was very sweet about your – you know – *thing*.'

'Leave my thing out of it.'

'It was only a facelift . . . Not a penis enlargement.'

'Shhh. That is one thing I have no need of. That colour is so sharp.'

'That colour is citrus. It's *the* colour. I've been for a professional makeover. She said my skin tones are the colour of summer.'

'She didn't mean summer pudding, did she?'

'Don't be nasty. And I should dress younger than my age so I've been squeezed into small suits.'

'Squeezed is the word.'

She tutted. 'Can I come in?'

'I thought you didn't want to be seen with me. I have company chairmen on their way here now.'

'Just for five minutes. Standing here I can be seen by the whole of Belgravia. There's a camera over there on the Portuguese Embassy.'

'So you'll be famous for five minutes in Portugal.'

She moved forward. 'I've had a phone call. I think you should know it affects our little . . . arrangement.'

As she crossed the threshold, Hector searched left and right across the square for spies Portuguese and others and, assuming none, shut the door behind her.

9

Charlotte's haircut was performing well. It had been pushed in and pulled out of her crash helmet all day and still fell back effortlessly into style every time. Charlotte's little citrus mini-dress was performing well too. It had ridden up her thighs and been tugged back down again more times than she cared to think about, but she looked the part in it, she looked the wannabe account director, the wannabe starlet, the girl about town. And Charlotte Reith was performing very well herself, thank you very much. She had had breakfast with Duncan Cairns, run a good client meeting in one ad agency, headed off to another and sailed through the interview of her life with the legendary Hector Quigley. She would have to wait and see, but she thought she had pulled it off. He had steamed through her c.v. like an ocean liner, she had tacked about his like a yacht. They were not chips off the same block but they had impressed each other. This summer evening Charlotte Reith was positively brimming with confidence.

Now, just off Piccadilly Circus, as she passed the bouncers on the door of the Atlantic Bar and Grill in Glasshouse Street, she intended equally to impress Daniel Mainwaring of Hollywood Pictures. He had turned up opportunely, if out of the blue. She had needed a last-minute distraction before meeting Hector and Daniel had been that. She had needed a fun wind-down session after her interview, and he had arranged that too. And she had need of a new man in her life and well—

'Charlotte Reith!'

It took a moment for Charlotte to focus in the dim interior. As she ventured down the staircase into the ox-blood art deco foyer she could just make out his chiselled silhouette flanked against the dark brown marble. At six foot five, he was the tallest man in the room. And though not conventionally so, with his long strawberry blond hair, Daniel Mainwaring was the most handsome.

'Watcha!'

'Hello, Daniel.'

Charlotte wondered if he might peck her on the cheek but he did not.

'Dick's Bar? The other one's crowded.'

'Dick's Bar,' agreed Charlotte. 'We can lounge on the settees.'

'It's me who's meant to drag you onto the casting couch.'

'Yes, well, these are modern times, Mr Zanuck.'

'Who?'

Charlotte was surprised that Daniel did not know the name of the man who had organised the biggest search for an actress in cinema history, but then he had probably grown up playing football at weekends and not sitting indoors with his mother glued to *The Making of Gone With the Wind*.

While Charlotte was acclimatising to the dark burgundy spaces, Daniel sorted out drinks at the bar. She flopped into one of the highly accommodating sofas and lay back, flinging her shoulder purse to one side and spreading out her brown arms. Her mini-dress rode to the very top of her bare thighs and, hanging on to her hemline, she swung one prominently over the other. She wiggled her Prada sandal from side to side. Perhaps they should have sat out somewhere in Soho. But this was peaceful and air-conditioned and very grown up. Daniel returned with glasses, a champagne bucket and a bottle of Moët.

He placed them on the low table between them. He removed his jacket and, folding it neatly into a square, turned the dayglo pink lining out to show. He placed it on his settee and sat opposite her, sliding his tall frame down to her level and spreading wide his long legs. He poured.

'Champagne,' said Charlotte.

'Had it before, have you?'

'I've had a lot to celebrate.' She took a sip.

'Such as?'

'Oh, I've been successful in my career. I'm not badly off for money. I've been lucky in life.'

'Whoah!' He clutched his forehead. 'For a moment there I thought you were going to say "lucky in love".'

'I *am* lucky in love,' she giggled. Daniel looked perturbed. 'Lucky enough to be free to choose.'

Daniel raised and lowered his eyebrows suggestively.

'So, Mr Producer, tell me what this film is you're making.'

'Oh, I only handle casting. I just put the girls forward to the director. New talent, I am. There's another department does established talent.'

'D'you cast the boys as well? I get the impression men don't figure much in your line of work'

'Just girls, on this occasion.'

'I can't believe they have a guy just to lure women off the street into auditions.'

'It's a hard job.'

'Punishing. How old are you?'

'How old am I?'

'You look young to wield such life-changing power.'

'I'm twenty-eight.'

'I *thought* you were about my age.'

'You're twenty-two.'

Charlotte realised she'd forgotten she'd lied earlier. She made amends. 'I *thought* you were about the same age as me but you're obviously a bit older. Tell me what the plot is then.'

He leant forward across the low table. 'We down the champagne, I take you through into the restaurant – I've booked a table for nine p.m. – and then back to my place for wild kinky sex.'

Charlotte laughed at his audacity. 'Well, at least you haven't mistaken me for a cheap tart. That's reassuring.'

'If you were, we'd be at Stringfellows, this would be Asti Spumante and no dinner. Never shag a bird who's just had curry.'

'The posh girls get the Atlantic, do they, and the scrubbers get Stringfellows? Charming!'

'It's not a classless society.'

'Actually I wanted to know the plot of the film.'

'I know. The script isn't finalised yet exactly.'

'I've seen *The Player*. Pitch it to me.'

'Whoah! An expert! It's, er, sort of *Pretty Woman* meets *Clueless* crossed with *Seven*. Set in London.'

'It sounds appalling.'

'It is. But it's commercial.'

'Who's in it?'

'Charlotte Reith.'

Charlotte laughed again. 'You want to watch her. Stardom has gone to her head. Apparently she's a real bitch.'

'But you have to admit she's one helluva good-looking bitch.'

She giggled. 'The guy who gave her a leg up was such a schmoozer.'

'Leg up, was it? And that bastard claimed it was a legover.'

'Did he?' She tugged on her hemline, which was riding high. So was she. 'I heard it was her who took him back to her place. Apparently she has a voracious sexual appetite.'

Daniel Mainwaring gulped. 'Really?'

'Really,' promised Charlotte.

10

Duncan smiled to cover the pause in the conversation and subtly revolved his arm to catch sight of his watch. It was almost ten o'clock. Still no sign of Karen. He wondered whether he should call it a day and say goodnight to the afternoon television woman they had chosen to take consultancy from.

Donna Silverstein was a forty-something New Yorker who had married an Englishman and now earned a few bucks in Britain by drawing on her experience as a producer of American syndicated talk-shows. She sank the dregs of her Greek coffee and dared to ask the charming and polite Duncan Cairns a question.

'Do you think she's coming? It's been nearly two hours.'

'She's usually very reliable.'

'That's not what I've heard. I've heard she's—'

'—The Most Difficult Woman In Television?'

'Yeah. True?'

'Not really.'

'She's not married?'

'No.'

'Relationship?'

'Not that I know of.'

'Peculiar.'

'I don't think so.'

'No. That she should want to do this sort of TV. Afternoon talk is all about the housewife and her love life. Women's problems.'

'Karen has had her share of those.'

'But you need to be so domestic to identify with the target audience. I mean, Duncan, these are women who slave over hot stoves and worry about dye running in their laundry. The best TV engages with the trivia of their lives yet disengages with it, delivering their dreams. And their nightmares.'

'Their nightmares?'

'You know the sort of thing. Daughters who sleep with their stepfathers. Teenage boys who want to be teenage girls. I sniffed my husband's secretary's perfume on his underpants.'

Duncan laughed. Donna laughed too.

'It's idiotic, but that's what makes it so entertaining. Home-makers feel guilty about watching TV while they should be doing their housework. The material has to be light but compelling, never unfamiliar, always something unexpected. And move the show on every five minutes. English shows are so slow, they get bogged down on one-topic issues that just don't hold the audience. It's a shame Karen isn't here. I would like to meet her.'

'Actually, this is her now. At least I think it is.' Duncan was gobsmacked. He had never seen Karen looking so well turned out, so head-turningly glamorous, so every inch the professional woman. She thumped into the seat beside Duncan without eye contact.

'I'm sorry I'm late, I had to drop in on somebody on the way here. Hello, Donna. If you can bear another Greek coffee you can run through a summary of what you've told Duncan and then I'll let you get away.'

They did just that. After she had left them Karen and Duncan talked.

'You've made notes, Duncan. I wish I could be so efficient. I try to absorb it all and let it soak in. You make a point of detailing what you're told and referring back to it. I forget things, you file them.'

'It's different styles, that's all. We make a good team because we both bring something different to the picnic.'

'I wish it was a picnic, Duncan. We've got to get this afternoon show off Martin Fox.'

'We can do it. He's commissioned us before and he will commission us again. Maybe not this time, of course.'

'I want it this time, not some cast-off crap that Jamie Hirst can't be bothered with. He can outgun us on anything we do.'

'He can outgun everybody. He's going international. In adver-tising, though, it's often the smaller agencies that are more creative and can outmanouevre the giants. Remember David and Goliath.'

'Right now I half think I do. I feel so old I've probably just forgotten I met them once.'

'You don't look your age tonight, Karen. You look stunning.'

'It was meant to be part of my research for *Move-over! Make-over!* Anyway, tell me what Donna had to say for herself.'

Duncan turned a page on his black leather clipboard.

'It's all American daytime stuff. I don't know if we can use it, but it's interesting. She had charts of the US ratings to prove these things actually work.'

'We could use those in our proposal.'

'She wouldn't let me have copies. She filched them from her last employer.'

'God. I can't stand people with morals. Run through what she said.'

'The host should be a woman. Women viewers prefer it. She should be between twenty-eight and thirty-five when the show starts its run so she can last. She should have a catchy name: Oprah, Ricki, Sally Jessye. She should have public setbacks in her personal life and be seen to overcome them. Women don't empathise with thin women. She'll get the highest ratings if she's been fat and *then* sustained dramatic weight loss, the second highest if she puts it all back on again, the third if she was always big. If she was always a stick insect she's a no-no.'

'That explains Vanessa Feltz, then.'

'She should be touchy-feely-tactile, prone to crying, gagging to giggle at naughty things, quasi-religious, totally liberal and totally uncritical.'

'Jesus. There is only one woman in the whole of fucking Europe who fits that bill.'

Duncan looked up. 'Who? Gaby Roslin?'

'Princess Diana. She fits everything so far. We'd have to call her Di, though.'

Duncan had absolutely no idea if Karen was serious. 'If we do a talk-show we should have a small audience.'

'Is it a talk-show or a chat-show?'

'Apparently a chat-show is where celebrities do a one-to-one interview revealing the minimum possible in front of their fans, and a talk-show is where unheard of ordinary people debate the intimate details of their lives with an audience of complete strangers who don't really give a fuck as long as it's raunchy.'

'That sounds pretty accurate. Would we really need an audience? That's expensive. We've got ten K per show remember.'

'Donna thought we did. The audience should be as rigorously cast as the programme participants. They should be recruited in the workplace or local community groups. Audience members of opposite viewpoints should be sat next to each other to create friction. They should be free to shout out and to participate in a loose debate.'

'Housewives are boring. What have they to say?'

'Donna said the same format and topics minus an audience rated twenty per cent lower than with. The cutaways are crucial.'

'What cutaways?'

'Well, say the main protagonist admits to being unfaithful. You see his wife by his side then immediately cut away to an audience member with her hand over her mouth shaking her head. It encourages viewers at home to take sides.'

'It encourages them to believe something is happening when it's not. But we're British. People here just won't spew all that American diarrhoea out of their mouths.'

'I think you need to watch *Confessions*. Or *Blind Date*. Or *Richard and Judy*.'

'Hmm. He's thin and she's fat. No wonder they get such good ratings. Anything else?'

'Triangles and two generations. That's it.' He snapped his clipboard shut.

Karen imagined a studio set hanging with triangle shapes. 'I don't get it. Triangles?'

'There are three sides to every high-rating story. The husband, the wife and the lover. Have all three in the studio. Oh, yes, and surprises. Don't tell the first two that the third is there and coming on in a minute. That helps to increase the tension and leads to fights, which always get higher ratings. That's how that man got murdered in America.'

'Jesus. Have they no shame?'

'Oh, yes. Have no shame. Donna didn't say that, but I added it to the list.'

'And the two generations thing?'

• Douglas Chirnside

'Two-generation stories double the audience. Don't do *I Turned To Prostitution To Finance My Drug Habit*. Do *My Mother Whored For My Hard Drugs* but she's still the best mom in the world to me, sort of thing.'

'Oh, my God.' Duncan had triggered something in Karen's mind.

'What is it?'

'I have to get home or my son will kill me.'

'Yeah. That works. First-person confessional. Two generations. Conflict. That's the formula.'

'Duncan, we may know the formula for relationship television but I wish to God I knew the formula for the relationship I have at home. I must go.' She asked Duncan to get the bill and departed. He was suddenly left with only himself to speak to.

'Two generations. Not a problem I'll ever have.' He sighed. 'Well, thanks, Duncan. You've done a great job.'

11

Karen was frantic with frustration but at last she located a parking space. She bashed the bumpers of the car in front and the bull bars of the one behind as she reversed in. She nearly fell from the car in her haste to get into the house, almost slamming her vanity case in the door and hitting her infra-red key fob over her shoulder. Flask Walk, a street of higgledy-piggledy doll's houses, was shrouded from the light of the summer night sky by rows of dense plane trees and Karen stumbled in the pitch black. She pushed through the gate and raced up the path to the heavy Victorian door of her home. She thrust the key into the lock and barged in.

• 60

'Max!' she called through the unlit hallway. 'Max! I'm home,' she called up the echoing staircase.

Her new short skirt let her leap the stairs in bounds. She pushed open her bedroom door and threw her case onto her bed. She tiptoed to her son's door.

'Max,' she whispered. She pushed it ajar. There was no light inside. 'Max', she said more firmly.

She switched on the light. The teenager's room was as neat and tidy as the cleaner had left it. It had been unoccupied since morning. Karen sighed. Her shoulder slump returned. Her face took on the cares of the day, then the lines of a lifetime. In her dressing room she took off her little citrus suit and left it where it fell. In her bedroom she slipped on her bathrobe and tied it comfortingly about her. In her bathroom she removed the new make-up and brushed out her hair. In her living room she sat up and waited up and dreamt up nightmares.

Max was not at home and Karen had no idea where he might be or what he might be up to. Except that whatever it was he was doing with his life, it did not include her.

With a palm on each of Daniel's cheeks, Charlotte pushed his devouring face up from hers.

'Enough.'

'Sure?' he asked. He unpicked their entwined hair.

'No,' she giggled and pulled his mouth back onto hers like a plunger on a plughole. He was a tonguey, chewy, wet kisser, rough, maybe not an artist in love but certainly a beast in bed.

He had dragged her mini-dress below her shoulders and rucked the other end above her waist. He abandoned it on her midriff, exposing on one side her small breasts and on the other her tiny panties. He mushed his face into one and then the other. Charlotte squirmed. His right hand ran up the inside of her left thigh. It found its way to the junction with her G-string. He began to rub her and arouse her there and to finger his way inside.

For a while she floated with pleasure. Then he swung himself up her body and they lay cheek to cheek. His flesh raged and she felt her bosom seal to his. She slipped her hands down the front of his stomach to undo his belt. She giggled as she fumbled with it.

He rose in a press-up and she undid the buckle. She unbuttoned his waistband and half-unzipped his fly while he breathed deeply and irregularly. She tugged his trousers down his thighs. He was wearing thinly striped boxer shorts wide apart at the opening. His long slim cock was sticking straight out and straight up.

'Hello,' said Charlotte.

'Hollywood salutes you,' joked Daniel. He was proud of his erection. She slid down the bed on her back to go to work with her mouth and tongue. He sat back on his knees, arched his back and fondled her hair.

'Yup, yup, yup,' he said, gently pushing in and out of her face. 'Enough,' he said later and drew her away. 'I'll come too soon.'

'Not over my dress.'

He repositioned himself over Charlotte and pushed his penis between her breasts. They were small but large enough for his requirements.

'Give me a tit wank.'

'Charming. What do I get in return?'

'How about a pearl necklace?!'

'In your excited state I'd expect at least a tiara!' She giggled and rolled out from underneath him, the lime green band around her middle. 'Look. I'm still wearing my sandals. Prada, you know.'

'I checked the brand on the soles when your legs were in the air.' Daniel laughed. 'This is my best suit.' His trousers and boxer shorts were bunched up around his ankles over his shoes and socks. The lovers parted for a moment and, on either side of Charlotte's futon, stripped themselves of their dishabille. Charlotte bent over in her displaced knickers to fold her dress on the chair.

'Nice bum,' noticed Daniel. He, too, bent over to chuck off his socks.

'Nice arse,' said Charlotte, returning the compliment. She tiptoed over and drummed her fingers on his backside. They fell back onto the futon naked, their bodies hard and hot against each other. They snogged for a bit. Then, as Daniel lay dreamily on his back, Charlotte stretched one arm to the bedside table. She felt around for something. She found his business card there where she had put it, picked it up, read it and grinned. Then she replaced it and collected a second small object.

'Are we going to get down to some top-level shagging or what?'

'Patience.' She held out her left arm and he saw her hand was clutched close. He knew what it contained.

'Nah,' he said.

She opened it to reveal what looked like a golden coin, a foil wrapped condom.

'No way. No fucking condom.'

'No fucking condom, no fucking me,' she said.

'Bunch of arse.'

'We should practise safe sex. I know exactly how to slip it on. You won't even notice.'

'I won't be able to feel anything.'

'The boy wants feelings!' she mugged. 'How sweet.'

'Come on. Forget the johnny. Try a spot of bareback riding. Sit astride me. See if we can come together.'

'What about our deal. Do I get a large part?'

'Yeah. This.' He nodded to his flashing friend.

'I knew you just wanted a quick shag, you bastard.'

'I do,' he said and lifted her up by her breasts and dropped her back down onto his throbbing member to give her one.

Hours later, in the blackness, he rolled over. He quietly collected up his clothes. He silently retrieved his card from by the bed. He carefully crawled from Charlotte's bedroom and soundlessly stole into the night.

The clock on the library fireplace chimed twelve times. Hector looked at it from his leather chair. The night was bare. He heard each single strike of the bell and counted it out.

'Twelve o'clock and all's clear,' he said quietly. 'Too bloody clear.' He drained the Scotch from his crystal beaker and ran an enormous finger round its lip to make it sing. It didn't. He sighed. He didn't feel like going to bed. His guests had left *en masse* an hour earlier, their 'carriages' at the door, their schedules set for six a.m. rises. Hector had no trouble rising. He rose easily in the morning as he rose easily to every occasion. He was becoming an insomniac. He hated his nights alone.

He rose now and passed through the mahogany doors to the hallway, his full-length navy blue velvet dressing robe skimming the polished floor. He crossed the passage and opened a pair of sister doors. Entering, he reached for the light switch but stopped at the last moment. Instead, he moved into the darkness and felt around for a tall table lamp set by a silk *chaise-longue*. He switched it on and its yolky light sent a warm glow around the creamy walls. Hector trailed his glass to the rococo piece of furniture he used as a drinks cabinet and filled it with Cragganmore. He moved around the room again, this time to the Bernstein grand piano. He stood in its nook and, downing the whisky in gulps, picked up in turn three ornately framed portrait photographs of his family. First the wife who took his money. Next the wife who took her life. Last the wife who took his child. The women smiled back stonily at him in the shadows, still not prepared to say in the dark to his face what they had said about him in broad daylight behind his back. My three witches he called them, for the tragedy they had wreaked on his kingdom. He kept their photographs prominently positioned on the piano, a portent from the past for any future female he might find for himself. He had found one now, of course . . .

He wandered round to the keyboard and tinkled in the upper register. He had a thought. He put down his glass, crossed to the lamp and switched the room back to night. He retraced his steps and sat down on the fat stool. By and by, he began to play pianissimo and to sing softly in the dark.

'Michael?'
    'What time is it?'
    'Are you awake?'
    'I am now.'
    'Sorry.'
    'What?'
    'Do you think we'll always be together?'
    'Yes. Go to sleep.'
    'I love you.'
    'I love you too. Now go to sleep.'
Snuggled up on top of them, Pushkin flicked open one almond eye, closed it again, pulled her head into her body, placed a padded paw across her face and purred her way into her dreams.

'Sorry we're late.' It was Duncan apologising.

The man clung limply to the chipped door frame like a wet rag of seaweed waiting to be washed from his rock. He looked distraught and wailed at his visitors.

'I thought you were going to be Anton.'

'Well tough, we're not,' said Michael, foot in the door. 'I'm starving.'

'Don't look so pleased to see us,' said Duncan. 'Isn't he here yet?'

'No-o-o!' whimpered their wan-faced host. 'I hope he hasn't been in an accident.'

'Perhaps he's stuck in manacles or suffocated inside his flagellation chamber. Is that the correct expression?' Michael nudged Duncan and they suppressed chuckles.

'Don't be nasty to me, you two. You've got to be on your best behaviour for Anton.'

'Shut up. We can do without the histrionics. We brought you this,' said Michael, thrusting a bottle of chilled white wine into his hands. 'It's South African.'

'Well, there's a surprise,' said the host, miffed. 'Come in and meet the lipsticks.'

'The who?' asked Michael.

'The lipstick lesbians. It's my midsummer Friday night couples' dinner. Michael and Duncan. Lesley and Sarah. Anton and Paul.'

'Will he be wearing his executioner's mask?' asked Duncan, laughing.

'If he's boring we can always zip his mouth up.'

'Fuck off,' snapped Paul. 'It's a dinner. We leave the S&M gear for the privacy of our own dungeon. Look, this is the first time Anton and I have ever done anything social and I don't want it spoiled.'

Paul McCarthy led Michael and Duncan into the sparsely fur-
nished front room of his rented north London flat. Surprisingly
smartly framed posters of Expressionist paintings advertising art
exhibitions for the cognoscenti hung over the settee . On it were
seated two young women in similar dark trouser suits over white
T-shirts. Paul introduced everyone and, making a fuss, left to
open the bottle of wine which was a godsend. He had not been
able to afford to buy enough for the whole evening.

'So you're getting to meet the famous Anton too,' joked the
girl with the boy's haircut. Paul had introduced her as Sarah.

'Notorious,' said Michael.

'We feel privileged,' said the other girl, Lesley. She smiled.
Duncan thought she was rather pretty in a natural sort of way.

'You should feel privileged that Paul has asked you to dinner,'
he said. He returned her smile. 'He entertains so rarely.'

'I don't think he's had much work lately,' said Lesley. 'I think
he must be quite hard up.'

Paul traipsed back into the room in a fluster.

'Where can he be, d'you think? I invited him half an hour
earlier than you lot and you—' he gestured at Michael and
Duncan, '—were half an hour late.'

'Duncan was faffing with his hair.'

'At least I have hair with which to faff.'

'Have you rung him?' asked Sarah.

'Only about twenty times. There's no reply. Not even the
answerphone. Should I call the police?'

Duncan laughed. 'D'you think that's wise? They may put out
a radio alert for a perv in chain mail and a harness!'

The women laughed. Paul shot Duncan a furious look.

'I wouldn't have invited you if I thought you were all going
to make fun of me. Tonight is a very important night for me.'

'Oh, shut up,' said Michael. 'Where's the bloody wine?'

'I couldn't get the cork out of the wine. I'm in such a tizzy
I couldn't raise the stamina.' He held up the bottle with the
broken half-cork still stuck in the top. He caught Sarah's look
of disapproval. 'Here. You're the butchest one here. You do it.'

'Don't be politically incorrect. We're supposed to be sisters
under the skin.'

'I'm not your sister even under my moisturiser,' retorted Paul.

'Oh, give it here,' said Sarah and she set about sorting out drinks and refills.

'*O-o-oh*!' Paul's screech died only when his hand hit his mouth in panic.

'*Jesus*!' gasped Michael. 'What is it?'

'The pasta! It'll be boiled to mush. I completely forgot about it. I've been such a bag of nerves I had to go and take an E and it's quite flown my mind.'

'What mind?' Sarah enquired of the others beneath her breath.

'We'll help you, Paul,' offered Lesley. She stood up and smiled at Duncan. 'Let's go and sort things out.'

Half an hour later, Michael and Duncan and Sarah and Lesley were seated around the kitchen table. Duncan and Lesley had de-steamed the room, rustled up fresh penne and rescued Paul's Rocquefort sauce. Duncan had dressed a big bowl of salad and they had found candles for the table. Duncan had also discovered that Lesley worked in market research and was swapping stories from his days in advertising. Meanwhile Michael had learnt that Sarah was a solicitor, and he was regaling her with tales of the media and his job as as head of the legal team for Britain's largest interactive cable TV channel. The couples were getting along famously. The couples were relaxed with each other. The couples were a success. The two couples that is. The third couple had not materialised. Anton had not shown. Paul had sunk into gloom, if not actual drug dependancy, lost stewardship of the evening, burst into tears, abandoned his carefully chosen guests and fled to his bedroom to sob into his shirt and his substances.

There were two conversations going around the table but a remark from Sarah to Michael brought Lesley and Duncan into theirs.

'Have you ever wanted children?'

'If I did I've been sleeping with the wrong sort of girl,' joked Michael and grabbed Duncan's hand across the table. It was snatched away.

'No, seriously. Have you?'

'I can't stand children,' said Michael. 'Until they get to about fourteen or fifteen and they're a boy. Then I take an interest.'

Duncan tutted.

'I have a goddaughter. We had to buy her a birthday present. I hadn't a clue. But Duncan is wonderful with children. He took me to the Early Learning Centre and picked out a plastic house thing. She loved it and so did her parents. It was fun *and* educational.' The way he said the last phrase he was obviously poking fun at his lover.

Lesley smiled at Duncan. Her eyes were flirtatious. 'I think that's lovely,' she said softly. 'Would you like to have children, Duncan?'

Duncan thought. He took this more seriously than his partner. 'When I was young I had an image of myself as a grown-up and I would be married with children . . .'

'You just didn't see yourself as the mummy with a cat for a baby,' jested Michael.

Duncan tutted again.

'D'you miss children then?' asked Lesley.

'I don't think about it. We're very lucky. We have three homes – we each own a flat in London and we share a cottage in the country. We have two cars and several holidays a year. If you're gay you can be quite selfish. You can have your career. You can have white carpets. You can go out where and when you like. I feel sorry for straight people sometimes. If you have kids you can do none of those things and when your little angels grow up they thank you for nothing and do the opposite of everything you've ever told them.'

'That's a bit severe.'

'I'm only joking . . . you put it out of your mind, don't you?'

'We haven't,' said Sarah. But she got no further. Paul, or it could have been Blanche Dubois, entered the room. He was wrapped in a sheet. His glass was empty.

'Are you lot still here?' His eyes were red.

'Don't worry, Paul,' said Duncan sweetly. 'He'll call you later or he'll turn up in the morning.'

'I never want to see him again.' Paul sniffed.

'You haven't seen him this time,' observed Michael. He tried to be kinder. 'He'll probably send you flowers. A big bouquet.'

'He's not the type. He didn't want to meet my friends. He doesn't like me.'

'Paul, you shouldn't drink and do stuff at the same time,' said Sarah. 'You're getting yourself down. I'll make us all some coffee.'

'Don't bother,' said Paul and he staggered back out of the room. Sarah ignored him and found the kettle on its side in the debris of the preparations for dinner.

As they were letting themselves out and saying goodnight, Lesley spoke to Duncan.

'Do you have a card? On you?'

'Actually, I don't. I'm in the phone book. My surname is Cairns. As in Australia.'

'We *have* thought about it,' said Lesley and she lowered her voice so that Michael could not hear them.

'What about? Australia?'

'No. Having a baby. Together. We have everything we need bar the obvious.'

Duncan yawned. He was sleepy. 'What's the obvious? A cot?'

'No, stupid.' She looked him in the eye. 'A father.'

13

Karen Myhill was taking the dishes out of the dishwasher when she dropped a stemmed glass and it smashed on the floor. Her round-shoulderedness slumped about her. She didn't usually bother to empty the dishwasher. She usually used it as a sort of cupboard. But on this Sunday afternoon she had time to kill, minutes to murder, hours to bury slowly and forget about. She was angry with the glass for breaking. She was angry with herself for having nothing better to do with her time. She was angry with Max. She was angry with Max for letting her sleep the other night in her armchair and not waking her up on coming in. She was angry with Max for not telling her where he was today. She was angry wth Max for never telling her where he was, for no longer making her a part of his life.

She delved inside the cupboard under the sink and pulled out a plastic dustpan and inset brush. She began to brush up the glass fragments. The glass had shattered and scattered across the terracotta tiles that Karen had paid so much for. It was not a good idea to invest so much in something initially that was going to cause accidents in the future that would cost you even more. She made note of the point particularly, because she had recently arranged for the other ground floor rooms in the house to be redecorated. She liked the warmth of the terracotta and wondered whether that should be continued into the dining room.

Karen collected up the shards and made a final, half-hearted sweep of the corners under the hand-painted cupboards. She sloped off to the dustbin through the back door and tipped the fragments into it. The doorbell at the front of the house rang. Karen made a face. In London the only people who called unsolicited at the door were people who wanted money or people who had come to the wrong address or people with bad news. Karen did not rush and allowed the caller to ring twice more before she reached the heavy Victorian door. She opened it. It was the Collins girl, a neighbour's daughter, younger than Max but looking older and never around unless there was trouble. Karen had an intrinsic distrust of this girl whose first name she had never bothered to learn. Before the girl had time to open her mouth, a horn honked beyond the gate. She turned and ran down the path. Karen did not know whether she was expected to stay or to shut the door. A rusty old banger reversed slowly into her view and she saw the passenger window jerkily wind down. The girl leant in and spoke to the driver, a young man with long reddish hair. He seemed to be pleading with the girl but she dismissed him and ran back up the path to Karen. Karen, who did not like to be kept waiting, was abrupt.

'What do you want?'

'Is Max in?'

'Why?'

'Is he in?'

'No, he's not actually. What did you want him for?'

'Where is he?'

'What do you want to see him about?'

'Just to see him. I've got some problems with . . . my home-work and Max is very good at that sort of thing.'

'I thought teachers had given up on homework? Well, he's not here.'

The young man in the beaten-up car honked his horn again. The girl turned round, embarrassed, and mouthed to him to eff off, which he did in a trace of black exhaust smoke and a hacked off wave of his green-sleeved arm.

Karen felt she was being mean and tried to be more amenable. 'Sorry.'

'What time will he be back?'

'Am I my son's keeper?'

The girl frowned.

'It means,' explained Karen, 'that I don't know where he is or when he'll be back. You should've phoned instead of coming round. You would've saved yourself a trip.'

The girl smiled nonchalantly. 'It's only a few yards.' She made to leave.

Karen closed the door. 'Don't bother to say goodbye, then.' She immediately reopened the door. 'Shall I tell Max you called or what?'

'No. No!' There was an urgency in the girl's voice.

'It was meant well. What's the big secret?'

The girl's face took on the contorted look of someone's whose secret has been unearthed, though Karen had no earthly idea that there was a secret and hadn't meant to suggest that there might be.

'Is anything wrong?' she called.

'No. Nothing.' The girl got as far as the garden gate and then turned and caught Karen's concerned eye. She spoke too softly and Karen couldn't be sure she heard her correctly. 'It was too important to phone about. That's why I came round.'

'Pardon?' called Karen.

The girl shrugged her shoulders. Suddenly her face burst into a smile. Young Mr Myhill had appeared on the pavement on the other side of the Venetian wrought-iron gate. Karen smiled too. Her baby was home. But to her abject displeasure and to her total despair the girl sidling up to him blocked her view of her lanky son. What was she doing? What was she saying? Karen did not like the Collins girl. She thought Max did not care for her either. Max did not care much for any girls. Max did not care much for any people at all actually, something he had inherited from his unsociable mother. But now Max was smiling and now looking sympathetic and now looking worried. Come on, come on, Max, she thought. We can talk indoors. We can catch up. We can go out. We can be together. We can be a pair again.

But Max turned his back on his mother. The girl wrapped a skinny arm around him and proceeded to lead him away.

Is he coming back in a minute, Karen wondered. Is he coming back in a while? Is he ever coming back, my baby, she asked herself. What was going on between Max and that girl? As far as Karen was concerned, there was only room for one woman in Max's life and that was his mother. She was jealous of the girl, she was protective of her boy, and she mistrusted them both. She shut the door and re-entered her Sunday solitude.

14

Of all the buildings in old Marylebone, HQ's was the one that stood out most. Of all the girls in Old Marylebone Road, Charlotte Reith was the one that stood out most. And of all the days in young Charlotte's life, this first Monday in July and her first as an account director was the one that was going to stand out most. Only she didn't know it yet. She thrust her Ducati into a slip of a space in the underground car park. She braced herself in front of the brick and glass building. She plunged through the double doors into reception.

Good morning. Welcome to HQ. Monday.

It was not Hector Quigley who personally greeted Charlotte at the revolving door. Nor was it one of the board. It was not even one of the twin receptionists. No. It was the doormat. Hector Quigley had hand-designed his own company buildings in his own image and no opportunity to impress upon his client list the agency's unmatched commitment to commerce and the agency's unmatched attention to detail and the agency's unmatched creative flair had been missed. When it came to pounding home any point, Hector Quigley believed in saturation bombing. The two receptionists' first task each morning was to lay out the mat bearing the name of the correct weekday at exactly 8.00 a.m. Later they would turn it over to its afternoon side precisely as, across the West End, Big Ben was striking twelve. Hector had not shared the concern of his colleagues that naming the day on the doormat was possibly overstepping the mark. 'Most of the stupid bugger clients have no idea which day of the week it is,' he had said when he had had the idea. Or rather copied it off a company he had visited on a trip to Dallas.

Charlotte skipped over the mat and tripped into the swanky reception area. It was yellow. All yellow. For Hector had a thing about yellow. Powerful people do have their team colours. Margaret Thatcher the former prime minister had a thing about blue. Bruce Gyngell, once a breakfast TV chieftan, had a thing about pink. Hector Quigley had a paler palette. He had a thing about yellow and if Charlotte had not spotted it previously, she would realise it by the time she had made it to the first floor. Hector wallowed in yellow. Sunshine, buttercup, canary, any variety would do. Hector believed that yellow was happy, humourous and heavenly. Yellow was upbeat. Yellow was energising. Yellow was a selling colour. Yellow was young. Yellow said yes. At least Hector thought it did when applied to every item in his business environment. Yellow chairs, yellow table tops, yellow folders, yellow name badges, yellow desk lamps, yellow desk tidies, yellow staplers, yellow pens, yellow notebooks. And in reception, where Charlotte was now, yellow walls, yellow soft furnishings, yellow counter tops, yellow-framed ads, a yellow-edged video wall. And two twin yellow-suited receptionists. It suited neither of them.

It was the first time Charlotte had seen middle-aged receptionists in an agency. Normally anything over twenty-two was put out to pasture but these two were pushing fifty. In their air hostess suits and with their beautician-lady hair and – probably, thought Charlotte – false eyelashes, they were a pair of spare beauty queens who had found a role in mid-life instead of a crisis. To meet and greet at the portal to Hector's magic kingdom.

Charlotte announced herself and the women beamed. They were co-ordinated like synchronised swimmers. Instinctively they knew who would chat and who would call upstairs. Charlotte sat and waited on the sunflower settee under a blown up print of one of Hector's management homilies.

> Too many advertising solutions fail, not because they are the wrong solutions but because they address the wrong problems. At HQ we never fail to identify the real problems and always provide the right solutions.

Charlotte was convinced by its certainty. It felt supremely satisfying to be joining an organisation which had an opinion and knew its mind. She made her mind up there and then that from now on she would lead from the front.

'Oh, Charlotte.' It was one of the receptionists. She was holding up an enormous white envelope. 'I almost forgot. This was hand-delivered for you.'

Eyebrows raised, Charlotte collected it and returned to the settee. She tore it open to reveal a collossus of a congratulations card. By the size of it she had known it would be naff but it was even naffer than she had feared, a pastel drawn puppy, turquoise-eyed in a basket and holding a slipper in its mouth. How ghastly. She checked herself for her sheer lack of gratitude but she hardly wanted to be caught holding this huge, unmissable bad taste souvenir on her first day in her new job. Who on earth could have sent it, biked round? The answer was neatly inscribed inside.

'Congratulations. Grow my little acorn. Love Audrey.'

So Audrey Goldberg was on intimate enough terms these days to patronise and sign off with love. Charlotte was half-touched and half-resentful. She supposed it was sweet really, and handed it back to the receptionist to hide it away for now. She'd collect it later. She scanned the yellow table in front of her. With the sun streaming in, it hurt her eyes. She was attracted to the new copy of *Tatler* but, earning her promotion, instead pretended to flick through the *Financial Times*. She was caught with it by Marsha Blow. Charlotte followed her into a stunning atrium area. For five floors overhead Charlotte could catch glimpses of glossy offices and agency goings on. Across the ground floor to the left there was a chromium deco bar area.

'That's for cappuccinos,' Marsha pointed out. 'They're free.'

They came to the glass bubble lift and made the ascent to Hector's inner chamber. Charlotte could feel all eyes on her as she was whisked upwards in what felt like a display cabinet.

'So your Hecka's new girl, then?'

Charlotte did not wish to be referred to as a girl, particularly Hector Quigley's. On her first day as an account director she wanted to step up into being a grown-up. She had hoped that that would come with the title.

'I'm the new account director.'

'I know. Audrey Goldberg's girl. Did you see what she sent in about you? Very impressive. Do you think she's had a facelift, Audrey Goldberg? Hecka has.'

Charlotte smiled. She was yet to cross the path of a discreet PA.

'What accounts has he dumped on you then?'

'I'm finding out now. It depended on new business wins.'

'Didn't you discuss them before signing the contract?' Marsha was surprised.

'We discussed the agency and my role in it. The accounts are secondary.'

'Sure. But we've got some real bummers here. Hecka's completely out of touch with the day-to-day business. If you don't like what you get, insist on them changing it. Otherwise it'll take you two years to swing it.'

Charlotte nodded, another message of the day sinking in. They left the lift at the top floor and sank into the deep pile carpet which covered the management corridor only. This was where chairmen walked on their way to the boardroom and no expense had been spared in a business that spares none anyway.

'Charlotte Reith for you, Hecka.' Marsha pushed open one of the flat oak double doors and Charlotte was left alone in Hector's cocoon or pond or web or whatever was appropriate to whatever sort of insect he would turn out to be. Hector was plump behind his Napoleonic desk, framed within a set of frames on the wide window behind him. There were three, each showing a black-and-white studio portrait of a woman, each accompanied by a young girl. Charlotte assumed these were Hector's three wives and three daughters and that they were not recent studies and that the wives were not as good-looking as the portraits suggested and that the daughters had long since flown the nest. That Hector believed in family – albeit serial families – suggested he was a decent man. The decent man got down to business.

'Welcome aboard my little ship, Charlotte. I am delighted that you have elected to join London's most prestigious private advertising agency and to further your career with us. Our critics say we are the last of the big private agencies, but I believe we are the first of the new generation. The plc is an overrated structure. I hope I can assure you that this will be the wisest move you will make in fulfilling your destiny.'

'I'm—'

'Now about the accounts, my dear. You will be reporting to an associate director rather than a board director to begin with, but think nothing of this. It is not a reflection on your youth. I would like you to join Maria Handley's team. She is going to head up the Verity Tampons business, a new business win I will be announcing shortly. She needs someone solid and you look like a solid girl to me. She is an American and still needs a bit of cross-cultural fertilising.'

Charlotte nodded. 'I—'

'To support you in your role I will be giving you our very best account manager. He is young and very bright and very able. His personal style will complement yours very well. He's more of a fixer, a streetwise personality, an Artful Dodger, and I think with you in a strategic planning role I hope and believe you will be a very sound team. Bottom heavy. No disparaging Maria Handley, of course, but you know what I mean. She is only an associate director.'

Charlotte absorbed the implication while Hector picked up the telephone.

'Marsha. I would like to introduce Charlotte Reith to her new account manager. Ask him to nip over from the Satellite.'

'The Satellite?' Charlotte got the least necessary of her questions in.

'We are an expanding company, my dear Charlotte. Too big for this building these days but I own this building myself and now is not the time to sell it. Profit at your peril or some such expression. So we have leased a building in Seymour Place. That is where you will be. Tell me. Some American companies put employees' salaries on their desks so others can judge whether the recipients are worth it. What think you?'

Charlotte flinched. The question had come sideways at her. 'I think that would be a disaster. The clients might see. Who in advertising is worth their income?'

'A shrewd observation, Charlotte. None of the buggers I employ, that's for sure. I see we will get on very well. Now, what I know and what you do not is that although HQ has won the Verity Tampons account against very stiff competition, the client has rejected our creative work. They have bought our strategic thinking and business planning but not our ads, the buggers. So the very first thing that you will have to take command of is rebriefing the creatives and developing and researching new ads and then presenting them in a very big presentation indeed with me and Maria. Possibly without her. It may be that an American presence may be inappropriate. This is, after all, a woman raised in a country where pile preparations are rubbed in on television. We may need to be more subtle than she is capable of.'

Charlotte was concerned how this Maria Handley could handle the business if she was not a group account director, not a UK native and not favoured by Hector. Charlotte hoped she was not being set up. The telephone rang. Hector answered.

'Ah, good. Send him in.'

Hector smiled. Charlotte's eyes flicked round his hairline

seeking out signs of surgery. She wondered once more how old he might be but she had absolutely no idea and, at the sound of the oak door opening, she spun round smiling to welcome her new account manager, the bastion of whom Hector had spoken so highly. The first person ever to report to her. The first man she would be responsible for. The rock on which she would rely. The team-mate who would be crucial to her career.

'Here he is,' said Hector. 'The man himself.'

To Charlotte's abject horror it was the man himself. He took the word right out of her mouth.

'*Shit.*'

Six foot five. Long strawberry blond hair. Dark green suit, pink silk-lined. It was Daniel Mainwaring. Who was not with Hollywood Pictures after all.

15

Duncan turned through the revolving door and was surprised to find Karen already there. She was wearing her citrus suit and it was crumpled. He wondered what had made her so punctual. He half-waved to her but she seemed deep in gloomy thought so he checked in at reception and picked up a magic key fob which would allow him access through the turnstiles of The Station's corridor security system. The Richard Rogers building, just behind King's Cross, was an inspirational crashing together of silver steel and liquid glass, a breathtaking, idiosyncratic gesture that encapsulated everything you'd ever need to know about Europe's most technologically advanced cable TV channel. The architect had hung the world's largest single suspended sheet of glass at a diagonal on the front of the building as if all six storeys of it were about to crash down and shatter into fifty million fragments. Karen sat at its base beneath a multilayered criss-cross net of cobweb-thin steel wires which held up the huge pane. The tension of the supporting cables was less than the tension on her face and, were the glass to fall, the crash would be less dramatic than the collapse of her expression when she saw Duncan.

'What's up,' he asked. 'Isn't Martin here?'

'He's very much here, Duncan, but we're under-prepared for this meeting.'

'It's for Martin to brief us, isn't it?'

'It's up to us to stimulate him with our ideas.'

'It's up to us to stimulate him with our enthusiasm and our generic ability. There's no point in flinging ideas at him because we don't know what he's going to say.'

'We've got to get this commission and we're going about it all wrong.'

Duncan sat down beside her on the Mies Van Der Rohe-inspired settee. He hated Karen when she got like this. The role of management, Duncan had learned in advertising, was to bring light to darkness. No one could hold a candle to Karen for talent but when you held one up to her for management technique she just blew it out.

'Hello, people.'

Duncan and Karen were startled. Martin Fox, the Head of Programmes for The Station had crept up behind them. Martin was an old friend of Karen's and had worked with her in the seventies at Trafalgar TV. As a one-time protégé of Karen's and now the man who would or would not commission her, he had moved from her support to her saviour, from her lackey to her lord. Though he knew Karen better than any other man, that was still to have only a vague idea of what might go through her mind. Karen and Duncan followed him down the curving ramp into the canteen, the cool slice of modernism where The Station's executives ate. They put together their own Italian coffees in big white cup and saucer sets and sat with a view in the sun.

'How's business?' Martin asked Karen.

'*Terrible.*'

'Rubbish. You must have made a fortune from *Basket Case*.'

'It was expensive, Martin. The set-up costs have to be retrieved on the second series. '

'The second series?' Martin smiled mischievously.

'You'll recommission it.'

'Don't anticipate me. I'm not letting you have a monopoly on being unpredictable. They call me The Sly One.'

'My arse,' said Karen. 'That's because your name is Fox and no one in TV creates much else other than clichés. Except Duncan of course.'

'Look you two. I can't hand you another huge series. Not for the afternoon. We want something cheap and cheerful.'

Karen tutted.

'That's all I can afford.'

'I've checked your income and expenditure figures,' said Duncan.

'Cheeky!'

'Well, I used to work in advertising and I believe in doing my homework. Your ad revenue is bang on target. Your capital expenditure on the building and studios is on budget. Why do you need to save money? The afternoon schedule is where everyone is slugging it out. You need to invest in it.'

Karen grinned fiercely. Nice one, Duncan.

'I need to invest in it with creative quality, not necessarily money. You're basically right, Duncan. I'd forgotten you'd been a businessman before you became a producer. So you'll understand it when I say that the board has decided to capitalise on our success by consolidating. If things dip later we'll have reserves. But at the moment we just don't need to throw money at everything like we've been doing since we launched. We're a success.'

'Is that the rebrief. Cheap?'

'Well, I don't want a magazine show. I want something that is a breakthrough. Something small and clever that the critics will talk about. That will be a cult. That will grow a dedicated, quality audience.'

'What's all that meant to mean?' Karen was snippy-snappy.

'I don't want pap from women in pink suits. I want something uniquely interactive but which is an idiosyncracy.'

Karen was annoyed. 'Martin, if you'd been so inexact when you worked for me I'd have beaten you up. When is it to go on air? September?'

'Earlier if you can. As soon as possible. A late summer filler. I have a hole in the schedule. This is a last-minute commission. If it does well I'll keep it through the autumn.'

'It's halfway through summer now. How on earth can we get on air before September?'

'Try.'

'It's all so mishy-mushy what you're saying. All that's coming across is that you want something cheap. All—' Karen caught sight of someone from the corner of her eye. Vinegar fumes evaporated off her expression. 'What's *he* doing here?'

The two men looked up. Peering through the glass vista into the canteen from reception was Jamie Hirst, maker of *Megabrek* for The Station and Karen's arch rival.

'Oh, it's Jamie,' said Martin. He checked his watch. 'He's early.'

Karen exploded. 'What are you seeing that arselicker for?'

'He has twenty-two million pounds of my business. Is that a good enough reason?'

'No! Is he pitching for this?'

'Karen.' Martin was warning her.

'Well?'

'He may be and he may not be. People bring me ideas all the time.'

'Piss. Fuck. Shit. I hate him. He has so much business already. Look at him.'

Martin made what he hoped was a foxy wrinkling of his nose. 'Would it be an incentive for you to work a bit harder if I did put him up against you?'

Karen was vitriolic. 'It would be an incentive for me to kill someone. It could be you. It could be him. It could be myself.'

Duncan stood up. 'Martin, that's a good brief. I understand it. And I understand about the level of investment. Don't worry about Jamie Hirst. We can see him off. And don't worry about The Most Difficult Woman In Television. I can handle her too.'

'Don't be unkind, Duncan. You're supposed to be on my side.'

'I am. Which includes saving you from yourself.'

From behind the glass screen Jamie Hirst was clocking the lot and shaking his head imperceptibly from side to side.

16

'I don't know what Charlotte thought she was doing going to that place.' Serena Sark screwed up her dry-skinned face and pulled her Tiffany pen from her teeth. 'We could just as easily have promoted her here if she'd had any patience. If we win the other half of the Verity account she could even have worked with the same client. Silly, silly, silly.'

Right now Charlotte Reith might have agreed with her ex-employer but she was no longer the up and coming young account manager at Clancey and Bennett, the MCN International subsidiary. Clancey and Bennett's joint managing directors had just learnt that they had been picked to pitch for the launch of Verity home pregnancy and ovulation predictor kits, the sister business to the tampons Charlotte was going to be working on. Serena stared at the press release she had prepared for her partner's approval.

'What d'you think, Nigel?'

'I think she should have confided in us, old girl. I could have told her a thing or two about old Hector.'

'I didn't mean about her. I meant about the press release. I'm trying to make it look as if we've had a run of new business wins capped by this pitch, rather than a shock enquiry out of the blue.'

Nigel glanced at the sheet of paper with one eye. With the other he tried to focus on a black hair sprouting at the end of his left nostril which he had caught between his fingertips. He gave it a tug but all that happened was that his nose stretched for a second and fell snap back into place. He winced. The pain was excrutiating. He gave up. As it was, he was going cock-eyed over Serena's sad attempt at sensationalist publicity. He had a go at making his contribution.

'I think . . .'

'What?'

'Don't know, old girl, to be honest. Perhaps we could pop downstairs to MCN and see if we could copy one of theirs.'

Serena huffed with indignant frustration. Nigel was deliberately being no use. These days he was leaving everything to her. With Charlotte Reith just gone, Serena had been left running ten pieces of business virtually entirely by herself. Now she had a complicated pitch for complex business to pull off. She had had enough. But Nigel had a question for her.

'If we could find out which other agencies we were pitching against we could mention those, couldn't we? Show us in good company, up there with the big boys, success by association. Make us look better than them, sort of thing.'

'Oh, Nigel, that's brilliant.'

'C&B to pluck preggers tester from snatch of JWT. Imagine that on the cover of *Campaign*. Well, possibly not those exact words.'

'I wonder who the other agencies are? Will the client tell us?'

'Probably not.'

'It's worth asking. They always used to tell you. It's unprofessional not to. I suppose everyone wants it confidential these days. They'll be livid we press released it.'

'Just deny it. How will they find out?'

'We need the story in *Campaign* more than we need their business is the truth. Anyway you ask them who we're up against. Clients never tell me anything sensitive. They think I'll use it against them later.'

'They're not wrong there, are they old girl?'

Serena's face slashed with her serial killer smile. A plan quietly crept across her expert brain. 'I know who I'll ask. Drop out of lunch today.'

Nigel look appalled. 'What?'

'Drop out of our lunch with Hector. I'll go on my own. Say you had too much to handle. Hector and I are old friends.'

'Hector and I are old friends. Golf means something, you know. You wouldn't understand, being a woman.'

Serena ignored his taunt. 'Hector and I go back a long way.'

'We go back all the way round the bloody golf course to the nineteenth hole.'

'Nigel!' Serena's sharpness became shrillness. 'I thought of pumping Hector and you didn't, so I'm going for lunch with him, leaving in five minutes. You're disinvited.'

'Why?' Nigel was hurt.

'To make it casual. Put him off his guard. I'll practise my feminine wiles on him.'

'Blimey. I hope he's not allergic to snake venom.'

'Don't be rude. And don't use words like blimey. There's enough vulgarity around without you joining in. You know you'll never get the info out of him.'

Nigel scowled and deflated and descended until he was down in the dumps. He liked his lunches. The appalling strain on his shirt buttons was testament to that fact.

'What's Hector up to anyway?' he asked. 'Why has he asked us – oh, excuse me, you – to lunch?'

'No doubt he wants to co-ordinate our Verity business with his.'

'We haven't won it yet, the old bugger.'

'We'll have to fall into line with him because he's so much bigger. You can't have the tail wagging the dog. At least HQ is old-fashioned about prices. We can charge full whack on the pregnancy and ovulation kit accounts and know he won't be undercutting us and making us look expensive. With a bit of luck we can run up a profit to please the MCN board.' Serena smiled. If she just managed to win the last stage of the pitch process, it was in the bag. Then she would need someone to work on it. Desperately. Nigel had not even been sure what ovulating was when they had first been approached. He had asked the client if it was that thing Negro women in African huts did. Thank God only she had realised he was thinking of ululating. She winced with embarrassment.

'Nigel?'

'What? I thought you were leaving.'

'Why don't I take charge of Hector and you take charge of recruitment? I can't believe I'm saying this, but on the basis that we haven't seen anyone we liked, why don't you ring up that Audrey Goldberg woman and see if she's free for lunch?'

'Audrey Goldberg? You can't stand her.'

'I can't but I'm not having lunch with her. Take her somewhere cheap. We don't want to waste money on her.'

'I don't want a cheap lunch.'

'Don't be ridiculous. You're supposed to be on a low-calorie diet. Look. Audrey Goldberg is the doyenne of headhunters. She has all the best candidates. Girls like Charlotte.'

'I wish we could get her back.'

Serena sighed. She wished so too. Her mind burred and computed for a second.

'Nigel?'

'What? Perhaps I could have sirloin with no sauce. That wouldn't be fattening.'

'Nigel! I've had a thought.'

'I thought you were meant to be leaving. Go on then, spit it out.'

'We could do just that.'

Nigel was lost. 'Just what?'

'Get Charlotte back. We could get Charlotte back and much, much more.' Serena's eyes twinkled. A blueprint emerged inside her head. 'I'm going to use my lunch with Hector to good effect. Getting Charlotte back will be just part of the plan.'

'Good. Can I cancel Audrey Gold-thingy, then?'

'No. You can't cancel her anyway because you haven't rung her yet. Do it now and remember to be charming. And don't tell her all about our business because she leaks like a sieve. She's a frightful old gossip.'

'She's a frightful old gargoyle.'

Serena stood up and slipped on the jacket of her little suit.

'Good God!' Though Nigel had partnered the prismatically attired Serena Sark for many years, even he had never before seen her in such a sharp colour.

'It's for lunch with Hector. He likes bright colours.'

'He has a thing about yellow.'

'This isn't yellow. It's citrus.'

'Is it? Acrid yolk, I'd call it.'

'It's the in colour this year. I have the colourings of a summer day or something. I can't remember what that woman said now. But I have another makeover planned.'

'Bugger off. I'm not having my nose hairs plucked out by some demented lesbian.'

'Not you! Us! Clancey and Bennett. The biggest small agency in the world. I'm off to lunch with Hector and off to seal our fate. And Charlotte Reith's.'

17

Charlotte Reith did not need her fate sealing. It was already staring her in the face in the more than familiar form of Daniel Mainwaring. She steeled herself and, at the same moment as Serena Sark was thinking of her, tried to remember how Serena might take charge in the face of adversity. It was hardly a management style of which she approved, but right now she needed to be more Rosa Klebb than Florence Nightingale.

'In here. Now!' Her arm made the firm gesture of a traffic gendarme and Daniel marched into the meeting room ahead of her. She did not slam the door but shut it hard for effect. She backed onto it for support.

'Just what, exactly, is going on?'

Daniel opened his mouth but nothing came out. He looked sheepish.

'I want a full explanation.'

Daniel made a lugubrious face.

'Correction. I demand one.'

Daniel looked at the floor.

'You've got five seconds to come up with a bloody good one or . . .'

'Or what?' He said it out of curiosity. It was not a counter-threat.

Charlotte knew that as a non-board account director she was in no position to fire Daniel at all, ever, let alone on the spot, within five minutes of turning up on her first day. It was a bad tactic to introduce ors and threats into the conversation. If you could call it a conversation. She abandoned the shrill Serena Sark style and tried Duncan Cairns as a role model for her next line. Firm and formal if not without sympathy.

'Do me the courtesy, Daniel, if you can, of explaining how the person I thought was the casting agent for Hollywood Pictures turns out to be the poxy little account manager reporting to me on my new tampon account?'

'Well how was I supposed to know you worked in advertising? I don't try it on with birds in advertising. Not that trick. It never works. I mean they're not that stupid.'

Charlotte bristled. 'And I am?'

'No. Of course not. Obviously not. It's just a great way of picking up birds. It's – oh, I dunno. It's a laugh. I mean, you have to laugh, don't you?'

'My ribs are cracking.'

'Jesus. I think this is the worst day of my life. I wouldn't have done it if I'd known. Shagging the boss lady is something I do not get a kick out of.'

'Charming.' Charlotte gave up. Daniel seemed as embarrassed as she was. She could cry. She could break down and weep. Instead she sighed and walked past him and slumped into a swivel chair. It was too high. She found the release lever on the side and pressed it. Slowly she descended, brought down closer to earth. Daniel loomed even larger over her. She looked up and spoke in a more empathetic tone.

'I mean, what sort of pathetic individual, what sort of sad fuck goes round approaching vulnerable women in the street offering them parts in non-existent films in order to get them into bed?'

'Me.' He looked pleased with himself. 'Me and Bonzo. Although it doesn't work for him on account of his acne. He hasn't had a shag since Christmas. He'll need thicker glasses the way he spends his nights in alone with his right hand.'

Charlotte's ears pricked up. 'Who's Bonzo?'

'My mate, that's who Bonzo is. He's my flatmate. And we share one account.'

Charlotte spun right round and sat bolt upright. This was too ghastly for words.

'He works *here*?'

'He's the account man on all the retail stuff. He gets the crap. He's dead bright but you can't have blackheads in advertising and expect to get put on blue chip business. I mean, can you?'

'Do I look like I would know? What have you told him about us? What have you told him about me? He sounds vile.'

'Nah. He's a real sweetie. I haven't told him anything.'

'You work with him and live with him. I can't believe this is happening to me. If you as much as breathe a word to him I'll kill you. Or anyone else for that matter. I'll probably kill you anyway.'

'D'you honestly think I'd bomb in here and say I had this great shag last night?'

'Yes!'

'Whoah.'

'Of course I do. I know what boys are like. I've worked at Saatchi's. I wasn't born yesterday.'

'Or twenty-two years ago.'

'What?'

'You told me you were twenty-two.'

'You told me you were twenty-eight.'

Daniel grinned. 'Works a treat. Still, you denied me the extra *frisson* of knowing I was getting some top-level shagging with an older bird.'

Charlotte should have bristled again but actually she rather liked the idea of bedding a younger boy. The thought flashed across her mind that she would never grow up, that she would never be adult enough to hold down the job of account director. Perhaps she should have waited for promotion to come to her rather than to chase it. But it was too late now.

'Listen Daniel. I might as well as be honest with you. This is horrific for me. I should be furious with you and I am but because of what's happened . . . you know the truth and I won't pretend – I do like you and I know you like me and we're going to have to get on together and work with each other and we've both got good jobs at HQ because we're very professional and very ambitious and despite the fact that you have the sexual maturity of a twelve-year-old I know we can be very grown up about this.' She was losing track of her pep-talk-lecture-cum-dressing-down-cum-bury-the-hatchet statement. 'Look. This job is of paramount importance to me and I'm not having you or anyone else fuck it up. What happened between us meant nothing and is completely forgotten. Nobody, absolutely nobody, is to hear of it. Understand?'

Daniel nodded.

'You are never to make any sort of . . . you know . . . unsuitable approach to me, ever. You shouldn't to any woman in any office because that is sexual misconduct and an automatically firable offence. And if you as much as mention it to me ever I'll . . . you'll . . . regret it . . .'

'Yup.'

'Understand?'

'Yup. ' Daniel smiled sweetly at her. 'I enjoyed it too. You're a great girl, you know.'

Charlotte was furious. 'That's exactly the sort of thing I have in mind. Never, *ever* speak to me like that. Understand?'

'OK. I get the message. Look—'

'What? Make it quick. I want you out of here and out of sight as soon as possible.'

'Hold on. Hecka's put me reporting to you. We have to work together. I can do it. It's not a problem for me.'

'How very reassuring, you obviously being the sensitive type.'

'Look, I'm an honest guy.'

'Pull the other one. It's got bells on.'

'I am. I did tell Bonzo—' He was stopped by the aghast look on Charlotte's face. 'Hang on, matey, let me finish the sentence. I did tell Bonzo but, like, in the abstract. I didn't tell him your name or anything or that you worked here because I didn't fucking know that, did I? But I did tell him I'd had this great bird and a prolonged night of top-level shagging. I mean blokes do that.

They brag about it. Most of it's a bunch of arse but there's only so much you can say about football.'

'Jesus.'

'He doesn't have the personal details, just the sexual ones. He has to have those otherwise we can't score the performance.'

Charlotte choked. '*Score the performance*?'

'Yeah. Bonzo does know there's a nine out of ten out there somewhere. He just doesn't know it's you. And he won't ever do. I promise. Your secret is safe with me.'

'Nine out of ten?'

'Well I never give ten. But you're the highest so far this month. Year.'

'I'll put it on my c.v. for my next move.'

'We do it with cards. We hold them up and then average them. It's like ice dancing. We got the idea watching Torville and Dean at college.'

'Remind me never to sleep with Bonzo then. I'd hate to slip down the charts.'

'You wouldn't fancy him. He's got skin like braille.'

'And I don't fancy you either, is that clear?'

'Yes, meine Führerin.'

The door swung open. An older woman in lurid smock dress and caked in make-up strode in to what little standing room remained.

'What are you two up to?' she barked. Her accent was New York. She ignored Daniel and spoke stiffly to Charlotte. 'Hi. You're Charlotte, right? I'm Maria Handley. You're going to be reporting to me. Hector's filled you in, right?'

'Yes, he has.' Charlotte stood up. 'Hello, Maria. I'm pleased to meet you.' She offered her hand and they shook. Daniel sniggered.

'What's up with you?' snapped Maria.

'Women look funny shaking hands. It's like standing up to take a piss. It ain't right.'

'You have an attitude problem, young man,' warned Maria.

Preconditioned by Hector, Charlotte took an instant dislike to Maria. The woman was a cold fish, a robot, a humour-free zone. Though Daniel Mainwaring ought to be her deadliest enemy Charlotte sided with him. She could not stop herself liking him and admired his braggadocio if nothing else. Charlotte was up for a good time in the office too and Maria had no-nonsense written all over her plain face in plain English.

'Is Daniel briefing you on the accounts? That's my job.'

'I was only filling her in on how the office works. Hot-desking etcetera.'

'He was.' Charlotte reassured her colleague with a smile. 'My own desking is still a bit lukewarm.' She had no idea what she was saying. She was bonded to Daniel further by the lie.

'I was explaining how we have no secretarial staff and do all our own admin on our own monitors.'

Charlotte's face fell. 'We don't have a secretary?'

'Nope.'

'What none at all?' She realised she would have to rely on Daniel even more than she had first thought.

'It's more efficient,' said Maria. 'Hector is pretty unreconstructed in many ways but he's white hot on technological innovation. It's quicker to do all your own memos and client correspondence yourself and e-mail it than have to brief some half-literate girl to half-do it for you half-badly. Modems and monitors cost less than Moiras and Monicas.'

Charlotte gagged at the mediocre motto. This was meant to be a senior woman in advertising. Her taste in copylines was clearly as crap as her taste in clothes.

'And what do Marias cost?' asked Daniel. He was pushing it.

'You have an attitude problem, Dan.'

'You have a stuck needle.'

Charlotte changed the subject before World War Three broke out. 'I'm reporting to you, Maria? I'll get my diary and we can fix up lunch to discuss how I'll be running the business.'

'Excuse me. I don't do lunches. And I will be running the business.'

Behind her Daniel was shaking his head in disbelief. Charlotte was ready for home already. She had had enough. She did not wish to be put in her place. She knew exactly where Maria Handley stood in the rankings but professed ignorance.

'You're on the board aren't you, Maria?'

Maria, scalded, was hopping mad. She guessed Charlotte knew she was not.

'I'm an associate director.'

'So you're just an account director like me then, really?'

'I am the most senior account director in the agency. You are the most junior.'

'I am the most new. I don't intend to confuse the two.'

'Well, don't confuse this: you report to me. You have a lot to learn.' Maria rotated round and exited. She banged the door behind her.

'You can go and fuck yourself,' said Charlotte to the quivering door.

'Yeah. Well no one else is going to.' Daniel realised he had an ally.

'Is she always such a complete cow?'

'No. That was her with her human face on. No one likes her. She's Dagenham.'

'What?'

'Two stops past Barking.'

'She had no right to speak to me like that in front of an account manager. How dare she try to put me in my place.'

'You're a big success with the team so far, aren't you?' He gave her a grin.

'Listen Daniel, I'm going to make this work. And you're going to help me. I help you and you help me. OK?'

'Sounds fair to me.'

'What was all that about warm desks and no secretaries? God. That's all I need.'

''Strue. Look.' He led her out of the meeting room into the open-plan office area. 'When you come in each day you collect a laptop there and sit anywhere you like. No one has their own office or their own desk. You pull the team around you as and when you need them. That's hot-desking.'

'It sounds appalling.'

'You get used to it. Admin will issue you with your own radio phone. Works anywhere in the two buildings and anyone can always get hold of you.' He took her to a desk where a laptop computer sat abandoned. He pulled the mouse over. 'Are you familiar with Windows?'

'The sort with curtains on. You jump out of them when things get desperate.'

'Don't worry. If this company's done one thing right it's to get an easy 'puter system. Everything you see on the screen is exactly how it prints out on paper or will read out on electronic faxes etcetera.'

'Is that a big deal?'

'Yeah. We have wysiwyg.'

'Wizzy what?'

'Wysiwyg. What you see is what you get.'

Charlotte didn't know whether to laugh or cry. She opted for a fit of giggles. She couldn't help herself. She looked up, red, desperate, but amused. She put her hand on Daniel's sleeve.

'In your case, obviously not!' she said.

18

Paul McCarthy was in a state. He was a bag of nerves. The sweat was pouring off his forehead and making his tinted moisturiser run in orangey bronze lines into his eyebrows. He could not bear driving in London – in fact, he could not bear driving at all anywhere, ever – and wondered now why he had brought himself out into the lunchtime traffic in the rusting hulk that was his car. So uninterested in driving was he that he could not actually remember what model of car he drove, its name badge having being torn off or fallen off long ago. He should have gone on the tube, only when he had looked at the A–Z to plan his journey to have lunch with Duncan, he realised that despite the clarity of the primary-coloured snakes and ladders plan of the London Underground there did not seem to be an efficient way of going from A to B today by public transport.

The traffic lights changed. He swallowed. He refocused. He depressed the clutch and braced himself for the lurch into first gear. He waited for the car in front to move off so that on his lurch he would not smack straight into the back of it. Paul was, in fact, one of the few people who knew by heart the roll number of his car insurance policy, so many times had he given it out to strangers he had pranged. Still, there was a chance that at nearly forty he was maturing. He was getting better. He was developing more self-confidence. But . . . oh no. He dropped dramatically into despair. He had been approaching a T-junction with the intention of turning right but the no right turn sign indicated he was obliged to turn left. There was only one way in which one was allowed to drive. He would be heading in exactly the wrong direction, heading into Marylebone instead of towards Knightsbridge.

Fuck. Fuck. Fuck it, he thought. He just simply could not head off in the wrong direction. He was already hideously late and Duncan would be sitting in the restaurant already. Duncan would be getting in a strop. Duncan would kill him. Duncan was the ayatollah of timekeepers who turned on latecomers and meted out dismemberment on his more lenient days. Duncan took no prisoners. Oh help. It was all extra pressure on Paul. He had to turn left. He had to. He had to? He looked right, just a peek. He really was not sure whether the street to the right was one-way or not. There were no signs and no clues. There was nothing in it. Not a car nor a pedestrian in sight. Well . . . nobody would see, would they, if he quickly sped along it and, if it *was* one-way, that he was driving in the wrong direction. He made the decision, then he rethought, then he changed his mind back and then he went for it. No. He wobbled. He started to turn right, quickly thought better of it and swung back to the left then, at the last minute, spun round to the right and turned blatantly in the face of the no right turn sign. The car behind him hooted twice but Paul was off on his own and heading towards the next cross junction and the escape to Knightsbridge. In one quick manouevre he had solved all his problems. He might even make up some time and not get it in the neck from Duncan.

But he had been over-confident. Already he was becoming jittery. He could hear a siren on the horizon. Nana-nana.

He had no idea where it was. It might be behind him. It might be behind the buildings on the right. It might be behind the buildings on the left. Wherever it was, it was already nearer than when he had first noticed it. Nana-nana.

He could see the cross junction ahead and his escape route. The siren grew louder. Nana-nana.

A car a long way directly ahead in the street opposite the junction flashed its lights. It could not be at him, could it? Was it? Why? Paul had a quick convulsion and then calmed. God, it was hot. The other driver was trying to be helpful, a kind and considerate knight of the road. He checked his own lights. That was the sort of thing that straight men did in these circumstances. He switched them on and off quickly. They were working. They were off. They should be switched off. Nothing amiss there. The siren was surging nearer. Nana-nana.

The lights flashed their warning again. What was he doing wrong? Oh. He was driving the wrong way down a one-way street. That's what he was doing. Well, at least he knew now. The other driver was not being friendly. He was being hostile. He was giving him a V-sign and beating his fist in a wanking gesture. Paul did not like the other driver. Paul did not like driving at all. It was too heterosexist for him. The siren was very loud now. Nana-nana.

Still, Paul had almost reached the cross junction. He would just need to confidently head out into the moving traffic on Marylebone Road. Only there would be no space to drive into and no one would make one, mainly because he would be heading out of a non-exiting road on a blind corner. He shut his eyes and willed himself forward. The noise of the siren was deafening. Nana-nana-nana-nana.

He opened his eyes. It was deafening because the source of it was directly in front of him. A speeding ambulance previously unseen in the throng of traffic on Marylebone Road was now heading straight for the front of his old wreck of a car. The shock of what was about to happen dissolved his watery panic. Paul confidently decided to indicate he was turning left out of the street and the ambulance might back off for a moment to give him time to do so. Unfortunately, instead of flicking the indicator switch Paul hit the one for the windscreen wipers. They came on at full, alarming speed and on the dry windscreen left a trace of burning rubber. The scrape could not be heard over the sound of the siren. Nana-nana.

Paul flicked off the wipers and flailed around the dashboard for the indicator switch. But it was too late. There was no way the ambulance was going to reverse back onto the main road. He could see the whites of the eyes of the black driver of the white amubulance. He literally was a rabbit caught in headlights. The ambulanceman indicated with one hand that Paul was to reverse back down the road and get out of the way and do it now. Nana-nana.

Paul gulped. Orange sweat was dripping from his brows down onto his lips. Paul McCarthy had never been able to reverse his car. Left became right and right became left and you got all confused and all dizzy. You didn't know your back from your front passage, he had always joked. What was he going to do? He was going to break down and suffer an involuntary attack of weepiness and a heart attack victim would die just off Edgware Road because of his selfishness. He was going to abandon his vehicle and make a run for it and be traced in two days and get sent down for two years by a rugby-playing jury who choked on the word homosexual. He was going to get out calmly, walk over to the ambulance, smile pleasantly at the driver and explain that he could not reverse his car and could the paramedic do it for him. He was – going to humiliate himself in the eyes of the pedestrians who had gathered on the street corner to see what was causing the commotion? No. He was going to do none of these things. He was going to hit the gear lever into reverse and run the car backwards and beyond the junction behind him where he had made his illegal turn earlier. That would give the ambulance an exit point. Paul knew he could do it. He believed he could do it. He willed it so. It was straight all the way. Now, he had never done anything straight or backwards before, but there had to be a first time.

He thrust the stubborn gear stick down and into reverse and, without as much as a look behind him, he pumped the accelerator. He could not hold the steering wheel straight while turning over his shoulder so he used the rear-view mirror. He shot back, beyond the junction where he had made his illegal turn.

He was lucky, lucky, lucky. When it got there, the ambulance turned to its left up the other street and he was suddenly free. Yes! He had not had to back around a corner or do anything difficult at all. And he had learnt to reverse. He wiped tinted moisturiser onto his cuff. He was drained. Enough was enough. He decided to park and get out and take the tube the rest of the way to lunch with Duncan Cairns. Bloody Duncan Cairns. Why did these things never happen to him?

Paul looked to his left. This had all happened very quickly and because London drivers are trained to compete in nineteenth-century narrow streets, to seek out endangered parking bays and to reroute regularly for emergency vehicles, so they have become the hurdlers and obstaclers and egg and spoon runners of city drivers and these ones today had understood why he was sitting on the wrong side of the road pointing in the wrong direction. But his good deed was over. The ambulance was over. The peace treaty was over and the law of the internal combustion jungle returned. Paul knew exactly what beastly nastiness that would mean if he did not get a move on. His tiger-striped sweaty brow furrowed in angst, but not for long.

Over his shoulder Paul spotted that rarest of London occurrences, that minor miracle of modern times, a streetside parking space. All he had to do was reverse drive into it. Simple. Unless you were Paul. He had only just learnt to reverse at the behest of the ambulance driver and what he had actually done was back off on pain of death, either his own or the ambulance's passenger. But there was no choice. And there was nothing to lose and everything to gain. He could park and get out and head for Marylebone Underground and let the train take the strain.

He put the car into gear, depressed the clutch and jolted back. He looked in the rear view mirror. Two fat ladies were standing, almost leaning, on the back of his hatchback, yacking, blissfully ignorant that Death was out for a lunchtime joyride, victim-spotting, sitting just a yard away next to Paul McCarthy, scythe dripping with orangey brown tinted moisturiser. But the ladies were frightened off by the roar of Paul's mistuned engine and black exhaust. Paul had once filled his tank with diesel by mistake and it had had lung cancer ever since. He took a hard grip of the steering wheel on its lower right-hand side and pulled down and down and *down*. He stopped, exhausted, confused.

He let the wheel return. He should be pulling the other way, shouldn't he? To turn the car to the right in reverse, turn the steering wheel to the left. Or to the right. Paul didn't know. A horn tooted at him. Peep.

He ignored the aggressor. How to reverse park? There wasn't time to look in the book that came with the car and it probably didn't tell you anyway. He'd better just do it one way and see what the car did. If it did it right do more of it, if it did it wrong stop it and do the other thing. That made sense. Peep. Fuck off. He thought he was doing it right. So there.

Bang, bang, bang. A pedal cyclist in bumble bee cycling T-shirt and black lycra shorts was thumping on Paul's window. 'You nearly fucking killed me, you stupid twat!' he yelled, riding off.

Don't distract me, thought Paul, wondering where the hunk had sprung from. It was unlike him to miss a good-looking man to his rear. How was he supposed to realise that the front of the car would swing right out into the traffic as he buffed his way into the space.

Uhhg. Nearly in. There. Success. Paul sighed and withdrew the key from the ignition. He had made it. He leant into the rear-view mirror and touched up his hair. It was wet with perspiration. His golden-stained skin did not look too bad in the dim car interior, so he was not to notice the tiger stripes. He got out of the car and reached over the driver's seat to get his large rucksack in which he carried all his man-about-town possessions and a generous helping of a tapestry he was working on.

He backed out into the street and locked the car door. It was only now he noticed that his ancient vehicle seemed to dip down at the front right hand corner. Damn. He had reversed the car half onto the pavement. Would he get a ticket for half-sitting on the kerb? He didn't know. He didn't care. It was all too much of an ordeal. The street was busy, busy with spectating pedestrians particularly just at this stretch. There was a gathering crowd. He wondered what might be going on. Perhaps the Landmark Hotel was expecting a celebrity. Perhaps they were having a charity lunch with a Princess Di type coming. Paul thought he might just check to see who it was. It was only then that he became aware of a small commotion at the far corner of his car. Of all things, a nun appeared to be preaching to the group collecting in the street. Bloody cheek, thought Paul. After all the Roman Catholic church had done for homosexuality he was not well disposed to nuns. She stood rigid on the other side of his car and, as he stared, she slowly and stiffly turned to meet him with her gaze holding his. He walked around the car. It was only once he was on the other side that he realised this strange woman of religion was standing plank stiff at a peculiar, gravity-defying forty-five-degree angle to the pavement. Her lilac habit rustled on the side of his rusting wreck.

'You!' said the nun. She appeared to be accusing him of something.

Paul stood open-mouthed. He was damned if he was going to be dragged into her sideshow. She could preach for all she liked at the others but not him.

'You!'

'Me?'

'Yes. You!' Her accent was broad Belfast brogue, her face was throttling red, her habit light purple, short and nurse-like. Paul decided that all the sensuality and glamour had just gone right out of Roman Catholicism.

'What are you on about?' He made to look as if he was in a hurry.

'I was trying to cross the road.'

'So?'

'I was trying to cross the road and you stopped me.'

'I'm not stopping you.'

'Believe me, you are, m'dear.'

'I do *not* believe. Period.' He puffed up with the put-down.

'Ugh!'

'So?'

'So, before I pass out, m'dear, you couldn't manage me the small courtesy of driving off me fuckin' foot!'

Her eyeballs rolled to heaven, her sockets turned porcelain white and inconveniently and all of a sudden Paul McCarthy had an unconscious nun on his hands.

Charlotte and Daniel were leafing through a folder of press advertisements for sanitary protection. It was an historic file that had been put together with ads from over the years.

'Some of these are so naff,' he said.

'They're just amazing, aren't they?' Charlotte found the exercise culturally interesting. 'They're so patronising. Even in the 1980s they were still showing women decorating in white overalls, sitting astride ladders with one leg out here like Darcy Bussell and the other stretched up behind their ear.'

'You gotta see that crotch in a tampax ad.'

Charlotte giggled. 'Look everybody. I'm having my period. So I'll just jump around in a public place in skintight white dungarees with my legs spread like a cellist so you can all see there's no blood gushing down between my legs.'

'Vomit. These ads for tampaxes must have been thought up by some sicko.'

'Tampax is not a generic. It's a brand. The word is tampon.'

'The word is muff blanket. Look at that.' He pointed to an ageing ad for a sanitary towel in which a side-by-side test used blue ink to make a comparison.

'A blue period. Very Picasso.'

'That fucking thing looks like a nappy. It makes my stomach churn. Imagine getting inside some bird's knickers and finding she's got a cotton wool Weetabix stuffed in there.'

'The terrible thing is towels *are* like nappies. They sit there outside the body with a damp patch.'

'Whoah!'

'It beats me how any modern women can wear them. According to this research the market is still split half and half between towels and tampons.' Charlotte abandoned the portfolio to flick through the stack of research documents. 'It's all fascinating stuff.

It really illustrates what's happening to women and how fast. The developments in the market place are huge.'

'These towels are huge. Who wears them?'

'Pregnant women. Women who don't go out to work or the sort who take a day off when they're having their period and sit at home clutching a hot water bottle.'

'Oh-oh.'

Daniel was shaking his head from side to side.

'What?'

'Is this bleeding daft or what? This bird's in a stadium, right?'

'Try young woman. That would go down better with me.'

'Yeah. This young bird's in a stadium watching football – as you do if you're a bird. I mean that's realistic for a kick off.'

'Some women do.'

'Ever been to a football match?'

'Not me personally. I'm more the polo type.'

'Nuff said. Right – and Alan Shearer, our man of the match, fifteen million transfer fee and a bottle of Newcastle Brown Ale into the bargain right, scores from a nail-biting penalty shoot-out climax or whatever, right?'

'Right.'

'So what do you do, bearing in mind you're a luscious yummy young girlie smack in the middle of a double-page-spread sanpro ad?'

'Something appalling obviously. Eh . . . you jump up and down vigorously in tight white hotpants doing leg-splitting high kicks while pointing at your fly with a candy floss?'

Daniel chuckled.

'Creative, but may I say twenty years out of date, madam art director.' He pulled the huge portfolio and held it up on the table top so that Charlotte could see what he had been looking at. '*This* is what you do. You whip your knickers off and throw your panty liner four hundred metres in the air so eighty thousand blokes can get a whiff of it. That's what you do. And you hope to God it blows back in your direction and doesn't end up on some poor bastard's head as a snow-white toupée. Jesus fucking Christ. Sad. Sad. Sad.' Sure enough, that is what the advertisement appeared to show.

'Silly old me. I'd never have guessed. But then I'm an old-fashioned sort of girl. Speaking of panty liners, I haven't seen any Verity ones or read anything about them in all this literature. I don't see how they can get away not competing in that sector.' Charlotte looked up. Daniel had locked his head in his hands and was killing himself laughing. 'What's so funny?' she asked. 'It's a logical point.'

'Superglue.'

'Superglue?'

'Yeah. Verity being Britain's most backward company—'

'Oh don't say that. I've had enough bad news already today.'

'I'm good news. Not bad news. You just met me in unfortunate circumstances.'

'Which we will never refer to again.'

'Yeah. OK. Verity decide to expand into panty liners and into Europe at the same time. So they buy into a small factory in Denmark and decide to do a local test.'

'When was this?'

'Last year. Still going on. I think so anyway. But they have production problems. The first batch goes out and women are ringing in like crazy – and you know how laid back the Danes are, so it must have been bad – saying that they're running to catch a bus, getting on a plane, teaching a bunch of students and, whoah, what happens is their panty liner slips out of their knickers and drops on the floor in front of all and sundry because the glue is no fucking use.'

'Oh my God, I'd die if that happened to me.'

'Well, I mean, what is the etiquette? Does a gentleman step forward and say excuse me miss your used panty liner appears to have become disengaged, shall I pick it up for you and stuff it back in.'

Charlotte giggled.

'So what the general manager of the factory does is over-compensate with a new batch of bunch-of-shite cheap glue from China. Next thing, the women of Denmark are ringing in saying they were in the toilet at work or at the theatre or wherever and, when releasing their liner from their knickers, the adhesive strip was so fucking powerful that they've had a fight half-bent over inside their own underpants and ended up ripping the crotch completely out of their knickers.'

'Oh, no!'

'Yeah. So there they are. Stuck in a public place with split-crotch knickers and a whole day left in which to walk round with unsolicited air-conditioning in the fanny department.'

Charlotte laughed. 'Is this true?'

'Might be.' He grinned.

'D'you talk to Maria Handley like this?'

'I don't talk to her. Period. No pun intended.'

'She's your boss.'

'I think you'll find she's your boss. I report to you now.'

'Where is she anyway?'

'Who cares.'

The door of the meeting room opened. Charlotte half-assumed it would be, speak of the devil, Maria Handley. Instead it was Hector.

'Charlotte and Daniel. You make a first-class team. I am very good at putting young people together and keeping ahead of the competition. Only the best work for HQ.'

'Only the best—' interjected Daniel, '—and Maria Handley.'

Hector's taut face gave nothing away but Charlotte judged that if Hector had not enjoyed that remark Daniel would have had a huge penalty to pay.

'I have been thinking about the creative re-pitch for Verity Tampons.'

'We've been working on that too,' said Charlotte.

'And what say you?'

'Well, basically sanpro communication seems to be all about trust.'

'Trust! Exactly.'

'Daniel and I have reviewed the history of the market. Sanpro boils down to having to reassure even today's pro-active, worldly-wise executive women that they will never face embarrassment. They want to have the greatest freedom and the most discretion during their period. The regulations say we can't appeal to fear or talk about leakage or odour, but – I can't believe I'm saying this – that's actually what you have to do to trigger women into reconsidering their choice of sanpro. Appeal to fear. Subliminally of course, not overtly.'

'Very interesting, Charlotte. I too have had a thought.'

'Yes?'

'An idea actually, born of my innate genius. I have had Marsha bring in pack samples to my office and go through them with me and I have noticed something.'

'Verity packaging is completely out of date.'

'It is, but not just that. On the back of Tampax packs there is a woman you can write to called Barbara Lee.'

'It's not really a woman. It's a fiction. It's their consumer affairs department.'

'Exactly. And Barbara Lee, who is she?'

Daniel answered. 'She's supposed to be like a big sister or a kindly aunt, the one in your family you'd run to with your period questions, so help me Bob!'

'And,' continued Hector, 'Dr Whites have Sister Marion, a nurse to whom you can make enquiries. It's all about trust. It's all about having a woman with whom you can identify. Well I have a project for you two.'

'Ye-e-e-s?' Charlotte didn't know why but she cringed.

'Verity Tampons have nobody to represent *them*. With Verity you just ring an anonymous telephone number and get some feeble girl. They need more than that. They need more than Tampax's Barbara Lee or Dr Whites Sister Marion. Your task is to find the woman to represent the Verity brand.'

'When you say "find", Hector, you mean think one up?'

'Oh no. I don't mean that at all. When I say find, I mean find. Verity will have a real flesh and blood woman to personalise the brand.'

'Less of the blood, please,' chipped in Daniel.

'Not just someone you write to whom you never see. No. Someone who appears in public. Who appears on television. Who attends sales conferences and goes into schools on educational exercises. Someone who is an authority.'

'D'you mean like a celebrity?' asked Daniel. 'Like Joanna Lumley? Is she still likely to be menstruating or is she knocking on a bit?'

'She's to be a spokesperson not an endorser,' said Charlotte, annoyed. She could guess that once Hector got a bee in his bonnet it would overtake and undermine everything else they were doing.

'No. Not a celebrity. An unknown. It must be someone whom you can trust absolutely. Who do you trust absolutely, Charlotte?'

Charlotte shuffled in her seat. In her present frame of mind she trusted neither Hector Quigley nor Daniel Mainwaring for that matter, after the way he had tricked her.

'What sort of woman?'

'I . . . I . . .' Charlotte did not know.

'My dear Charlotte,' beamed Hector, egged on by his own self-belief. 'I will tell you exactly who you can trust absolutely.'

20

'Cooeee!'

Duncan looked pained but it was no use. Before he could protest Paul was all over him with orange moisturised kisses.

'You're late, Paul. What time do you call this?'

'Relax, darling. No one'll notice if you're late back.'

'Karen Myhill will notice.'

'Ugh. Don't mention that woman's name.' Paul finished stuffing his rucksack under the table and wormed his way into his seat. He shuffled about a bit, more so than usual. 'Anyway, you and your boyfriend were half an hour late for my dinner party the other night.'

Duncan did not like Paul bandying terms like 'your boyfriend' in front of the waiter. While they ordered their drinks, a diet coke refill for Duncan and a Campari and lemonade for Paul,

Paul detected Duncan's smarting at the reference.

'Relax, for God's sake. He's a right bender if ever I saw one. And I've seen a few, I can tell you.'

'A few hundred, more like. What kept you? Being fashionably late for dinner at home is a little bit different to virtually standing someone up for lunch in a restaurant .'

'Hark at madam,' said Paul. He regaled Duncan at great length with the triumph of his reverse parking and the confrontation with the nun.

'I hope to God you didn't just leave her doing a Long John Silver in the street?'

'Oh, she was just playing up. She was a nun, for God's sake. I expect she'd been begging for someone to crush her foot for years. Have you never seen Jennifer Jones in the *Song of Bernadette*? It was my grandmother's favourite film. Nuns enjoy nothing better than staggering round supurating with ulcers, lashed in bandages, hearing muffled voices, earning a martyr medal or two. It's the highlight of their frigid little lives.' He unwrapped a bread stick and took a crunch. 'It's all sexual, of course. Sexual, sexual, sexual. RC is very S&M. I mean, all that black and white constricting material, self-denial, single-sex bed arrangements, spartan ritual. How else do nuns get their kicks? They're just as horny as the rest of us, even you, Duncan.'

'I think you'll find women have a different sexuality to what you have in mind.'

Paul dabbed at the breadstick crumbs on the corner of his lips. 'Personally I've always thought that Linda Darnell in false eyelashes was a bit miscast as the Virgin Mary. Funny how all those cripples go to Lourdes.' He shuffled some more in his seat.

'Perhaps you should make a trip yourself. You were in a real state the other night.'

'A bunch of terminal cases in wheelchairs is not my idea of a hot group session.'

'Look. You have to take better care of yourself. You're turning into a drug addict. Not to mention an alcoholic. And you abandoned us.'

'Oh stop being an old pair of iron knickers. I'm fine. I was upset, that's all. Anton rang me at two a.m. with profuse apologies and everything is fine now.'

'What happened?'

'He had to go away for a fortnight at short notice and hadn't been able to get through before from the third world.'

'Where was he? What does he do?'

'I haven't an inkling, darling. He's very big in something international and glamorous that he chooses to keep mum about. So he says, anyway.' He swung back and forth in his chair.

'Well, there you are. You see. There is always a simple explanation for everything and you were knocking back the booze and pills. You must be careful.'

'Don't lecture me. I'm not as tight-arsed as you are.' On 'arse' Paul's hand tweaked at the seat of his pants. Duncan was fazed by Paul's constant twitching.

'Can't you sit still?'

'No, I can't.'

'You're over-excited because you parked your car and disabled only one pedestrian in the process.'

'That's not it.' Paul winked.

'What then?'

'Well . . . I shaved my arse the other night and now it's growing back and itching like hell. You know what it's like. Stubble bum.'

'I have no idea what it's like.'

'Oh, go on, you must.'

'I can assure you I do not. Do I look like someone who shaves his backside?'

'Don't say you use Immac?'

'I have no idea what you're talking about.'

'It's a female depilator. I tried it once but I squirted it too far up my bum like toothpaste. Jesus. It felt like oven cleaner. I'm not doing that again in a hurry.'

'Serves you right.'

'You must have shaved your nou-nou?'

'I beg your pardon!'

'Your nou-nou!'

'I don't have a nou-nou.'

'Oh, don't be so square. It's so incredibly sexy. It's a turn-on if two of you do it together. Before you know it, there's jiminy gism erupting all over the place.' Paul's waving his baton of breadstick rivalled Georg Solti bringing in Beethoven's Eroica to its last beat.

'Keep your voice down,' chided Duncan. 'People are eating their lunch.'

'So? Shaving your nou-nou makes your dick look that much bigger. You get about one added inch. If you're a grower rather than a show-er it's ever such a good idea. All the porn stars do it. Are you a grower or a show-er, Duncan? I'm a show-er. Nine inches at the last count.'

'Shut up.'

'Why should I? Everyone does it. All those suited young chaps in the City, get them home, whip their bowler hats and pinstripe knickers off and what do you find? They've spent just as many hours as me squatting over a mirror checking their five o'clock shadow. Testicles as smooth as two scoops of sorbet, a bottom you could eat your breakfast off of.' Paul was squirming in his chair again, almost as much as Duncan was at his flamboyant hand-gesturing.

'Leave it out, for God's sake.'

'The thing I notice is—'

'What?' snapped Duncan, not at all desperate to know.

'—that when you've shaved your arse it does feel funny when you fart. You know, like when you burr with your lips.' Paul did it and smiled.

That was it as far as Duncan was concerned. As the waiter arrived Duncan was ready with his order. It had been an age since he had sat down. But the waiter stood at the adjacent table, and fingering the back of a chair he addressed Paul, who was now lifting first one buttock and then the other.

'Having trouble with your seat, sir?'

Paul sniggered. Duncan made a face.

'Am I ?!'

'Would you like me to exchange it for this one?'

'Oh, that sort of seat! I thought you meant my—'

'Don't say it!' Duncan was not amused.

'Aren't you ever so butch, Duncan.'

Paul and the waiter snorted together and lunch collapsed into mayhem.

21

'He's off his head.' Charlotte shook hers as she leapt down another half-flight of the Satellite stairs.

'Who is?'

'Hector Quigley.'

'You mean you've just found out? There was me thinking you were a bright girl.'

'Daniel. I've warned you about being over-familiar.'

'It's a laugh. You've got to laugh.'

'It's not a laugh. It's totally unfunny. It's a crisis. It's completely wrong for the brand. And apart from that it's a total impossibility to achieve ever, let alone in the next couple of hours. I can't believe this is happening to me.'

'It isn't. It's happening to us.'

'It's such a stupid idea. I should have argued back more effectively.'

'Everyone says that about all Hecka's ideas. But by the time he's got the client outspending their competitors ten to one he's usually proved right.'

'Look, Daniel.' Charlotte had one hand on each hip. She had to bring someone to their senses. 'I have every intention of making a success of this. Since I arrived here I've spent all my time genning up on the sanitary protection market. Hector is right strategically. Tampons are all about trust. But he's wrong executionally. He'll make the agency a laughing stock. He'll make himself a laughing stock. He'll make me a laughing stock.'

'Which is what you're really worried about.'

'No it's not. Unlike everyone else in advertising, I am not completely self-obsessed.'

'Whoah, boss lady. Let me go first. I can take these steps two at a time.'

Charlotte turned on the landing to face her junior partner. In a spate of energetic angst, she had decided to leg it down the stairs rather than take the lift. She had somehow hoped that this way she and inspiration would meet by the time she reached the bottom flight. Only one more storey to go.

'You're not going first. You'll only lead me into trouble.'

'Look, if you don't mind me making a suggestion, why don't you go back upstairs and try to do this on the telephone? I'll make the house calls.'

'You have no car.'

'Neither do you.'

'I have my Ducati. You can ride postillion.'

'Now who's being over-familiar.'

'Look. Concentrate on the matter in hand. What are we going to do?'

'You're the boss.'

'I am well aware of that fact.'

'So you think of something.'

'I have no idea what to do.'

'I don't know either. I'm just following you.' His wide grin was equally irritating and amusing.

'Oh, Daniel, where are we going to find a *nun* before two-thirty?'

But then, as Charlotte turned into the agency reception, her prayers were answered. There on the settee, lying prone as if dead of some mediaeval lurgy, her lilac habit rucked up, her veiny hands clasped across her bosom, her flat black shoes sticking into a decorative tub of fronds, lay the very thing they were looking for. A nun. She was a miracle dispatched from heaven. And she was snoring loudly.

Charlotte took three steps backward rapidly, bang into her tall accomplice.

'Whoah. Put your reverse lights on, boss lady. What's up?'

'There's a nun lying in reception.'

'Lying as in telling porky pies or lying as in having a kip?'

'Is this some trick of Hector's? What's a nun doing in our reception?'

'Waiting to see someone. Perhaps we've won a convent account.'

Charlotte puckered her lips. She crept into reception and found herself standing in front of one of the receptionists with big hair. It being lunchtime, only one was on duty.

'A pinch of nutmeg . . . and half a teaspoon of cumin. Hang on. I'm getting a filthy look from the new girl.'

Charlotte was annoyed at that remark but she needed the woman's help, so she feigned sweetness. She nodded towards the nun.

'Do you know who that is?'

'She's a nun.'

'Is she sleeping?'

'She's having a lie down. She came in here in such a state I said she could. Hecka won't mind. Hang on . . .' She returned to her telephone friend. 'Oh you *must* be able to get chutney in New York.'

'Are you calling America just to read recipes down the telephone?'

'I have to do it during my lunch hour because of the time difference. To catch my friend before she leaves for the salon she's got. They start early over there.'

Charlotte decided to have one last try. 'What was she in such a state about?'

'She thinks you can't get chutney in Manhattan but I'm sure you can. They must have Indians there. There's millions of them everywhere. I mean they've got the Irish haven't they, so they must have Indians.'

Charlotte failed to see the logic, but it wasn't New York she had had in mind anyway. 'Not your friend. The nun. What was she in a state about?'

'Hit and run. Some bastard ran over her shoe with his car and buggered off. I told her to take the weight off her feet. I haven't done a bad thing have I?'

'No of course not. Haven't you called an ambulance?'

'I suggested that but she went mental. Took my breath away.

I've never heard a nun swear before. I suppose they must do. To relieve the pain anyway. So I suggested she waits till Judy gets back from lunch.'

'Who's Judy?'

'The nurse. Or rather the girl that runs the sick bay. She's really in personnel but we call her the nurse. I think I did the right thing. Hang on . . . Crush the spices with a pestle and mortar and shallow fry dry in the frying pan, very hot, until they begin to jump.'

Charlotte signalled to Daniel to join her over the nun. When he did, she nudged her. The nun stopped snoring and turned over, away from Charlotte. She nudged her again harder and then again very hard. The nun awoke with a start. She immediately put her hand to her left foot and grimaced.

'Are you all right?' asked Charlotte.

'I'm fine, m'dear. Which is why I'm laid out here like a mouldering corpse. What d'you think, sweetheart? I'm in sheer bloody agony.'

Charlotte noticed the language. The poor woman was in shock. Perhaps she would not mind sitting out the afternoon at HQ.

'Can I do anything to help? Would you like a Nurofen or something?'

'Nope,' said the nun.

'An aspirin?'

'Never touch 'em,' replied the nun.

'How about a brandy?' asked Daniel.

'Now you're talking!'

Charlotte was taken aback, but before they all knew it they were upstairs in the meeting room and the strange woman in their midst was chatting away nineteen to the dozen in her Irish brogue and agreeing to meet the clients for one meeting only for the grand sum of two hundred and fifty pounds cash in hand. Charlotte had originally offered fifty but the nun had quickly negotiated the rate upwards – and won herself a room at the Metropole Hotel for the night into the bargain.

'What's your name?' asked Charlotte.

'We're all the same in God's eyes,' explained the nun. It was not an explanation at all of course, but Charlotte and Daniel were hard pressed to notice.

'It's just that we would like you to agree to one more thing.'

'Uh-huh.'

'Just for this afternoon.'

'What, m'dear?'

'Would you mind if we gave you a new name? You know, to suit the brand.'

'For two hundred and fifty big smackers you can call me any name you care to, sweetheart.' The nun grinned.

'So you wouldn't mind if we called you, say, Sister Verity?'

'Sister Verity? I have no objections at all. For this afternoon, like.'

'Brilliant. It is only for this afternoon. I think I can reliably say that this exercise will lead to nothing, so you can rest assured that this whole thing will go no further.' Were Charlotte to remember those words in a month's time she would have felt her prognosis to be remarkably bad, but they were forgotten as soon as said. 'Oh, it's so kind of you. I can't tell you how lucky I feel. I appreciate it enormously.'

'And I can't tell you how lucky I feel, m'dear. And I'd appreciate it enormously if your young boyfriend here could find me another of those wee miniatures of brandy.'

'Whoah.' Daniel had watched her sink three already.

'For the medicinal effect, you understand.'

'Of course,' said Charlotte. 'To ease the pain.' She grabbed Daniel's cuff before he could leave. 'Make it three, Daniel. One for each of us.'

22

'Hello, Duncan?'

'Speaking.'

'I didn't think you'd be in at this time of day. I thought I would see if you had an answering machine and leave a message on it. I'm not disturbing you am I?'

'No, not at all.' Duncan still did not recognise the voice. 'Sorry. Who is this?'

'You don't recognise me. I'm crushed.'

''Fraid not.'

'It's Lesley Turnbull. You met me at Paul's for dinner the other night. Remember?'

'I do! It's Paul McCarthy I can't quite place, we saw so little of him. How are you?'

'Fine. Are you having the day off?'

'Oh no. I'm trying to get to grips with afternoon television. I've been viewing cable and satellite stations for inspiration.'

'Inspiration? Good God. I thought you might like to act as my guinea pig.'

'Your guinea pig?'

'Remember I told you I was a market researcher?'

'Yes.'

'Well I have a questionnaire that I've been asked to write and I normally try it out on a few folk in the office or friends at home to see how it pans out. Trouble is, to be absolutely honest, most of my friends have worn out. I spotted you had lots of opinions so I thought you might like to try.'

'Sure, I love giving my opinion. So does Michael.'

'I don't need him. Just you.'

'He'd be happy to help.'

'No. Just you.'

'OK. Are you going to do it down the phone?'

'Only if this is a convenient time. It'll only take a few minutes.'

'Yeah, it's fine. I need a break.'

'Fabulous. It's just that men are so reluctant to state their true feelings.'

'Straight men are. Gay men yack.'

'There are questions about sex in this.'

'Is it a gay questionnaire?'

'No.'

'Then won't my answers be misleading? I'm not straight.'

'Never!'

'I thought you should know.'

'I'm flabbergasted,' she jested back. 'No matter.'

'Also, I did tell you that I had worked in advertising so I have commissioned a lot of research in the past. I may be preconditioned.'

'Let me be the judge of that. OK. Here goes. How old are you?'

'Thirty-three.'

'How long have you lived in London?'

'Twelve years.'

'Do you think you'll stay in London in the short term, medium term, or long term or do you not know?'

'I can't imagine living anywhere else. We have a weekend home in the Cotswolds.'

'You have to choose from the options I give you otherwise it doesn't work.'

'Right. Well, we'll stay in the long term. What's this for?'

'I can't tell you. It would prejudice the outcome of the research.'

'Clue then.'

'No clues.'

'Blast. A professional.'

'Is there any known genetic illness in your family? Heart conditions, epilepsy, a tendency to alcoholism, allergies, anything like that?'

'None that I'm aware of. Homosexuality.'

'That's not an illness. We don't know that it's genetic.'

'Hah. Not so professional. You're not meant to give your opinions to the respondent according to the market research society rules.'

'You're a friend. Now. Are your parents alive or dead and if alive what age are they and if dead at what age did they die? That's not what's written down here but I'm paraphrasing because I know you. Saves time.'

'I appreciate your concern. Both living. Aged sixty-one and sixty-five.'

'Good. That's nice. Next question. Do you think that it is preferable for a child to be raised by one parent or two or no preference?'

Hell, thought Duncan. She'll think I'm a reactionary if I tell the truth. 'No preference,' he lied. Duncan was rather old-fashioned about these things. Karen Myhill and her relationship with Max came to mind. Mind you, it proved the point either way, since she was equally a brilliant and a useless mother both at the same time.

'And do you believe that the sexuality of the parent or parents affects the child's upbringing for better or worse or makes no difference or don't know.'

'God.'

'Not a box on my form.'

'I suppose I don't know.' Duncan was sure he could hear Lesley flinch at the other end of the line.

'How do you feel about a child raised by a lesbian couple in a stable and loving relationship? It is better for the child than being raised by a traditional straight couple, it is about the same, it is worse, don't know.'

'About the same.'

'And would it make a difference if I phrased the question how would you feel about your own child being raised by a lesbian couple.'

Duncan laughed. 'Too hypothetical to answer.'

'No it's not.'

'I'm not likely to have a child, am I?'

'You might. Just answer the question.'

'I suppose I should say that it would make no difference.'

'You don't sound very convinced.'

'I don't know, is the honest answer. It's an extremely complex issue and I have never thought about it because I never have had and never will have children.'

'You might. You told me at dinner that you liked children.'

'Liking one and fathering one are not the same thing.'

'You can do it by artificial insemination.'

'I know. But liking children and liking shopping for presents is not the same as having a child of your own and bringing it up. Particularly if you are homosexual.'

'You wouldn't be bringing it up. It would be being brought up by a female gay couple. I mean, in the hypothetical situation we're discussing.'

'I understand. What is this research for anyway? It sounds like a political questionnaire or something.'

'I'm not at liberty to say. We're near the end.'

'Good.'

'Do you know your HIV status?'

'No, I don't actually.'

'Do you have any objections to taking an AIDS test?'

'Not if it's anonymous and doesn't go on my medical records.'

'Hang on. Give me time to write that down . . . medical records. OK. And what do you think the result would be if you were to take an AIDS test?'

'I would hope that it would be negative.'

'Hope and think are not the same thing.'

'I think it would be negative. But I don't know. Put down don't know. Hey. This is confidential, isn't it? I'm just a guinea pig. This is not going to appear anywhere.'

'It's going to be headline news in the *Guardian* tomorrow. Of course it's not going to appear anywhere.'

'Next question.'

'That's it.'

'That's it? That was a strange survey.'

'Well, I paraphrased it. I'm just asking the questions I need to check out the wording on or the sort of rogue answers I might get. I skipped three-quarters of them because they're all standard.'

'When it's done will you let me know what it is for?'

'I think I can guarantee I will let you know what it is for.'

'That interesting is it?'

'I think you'll find that it will be. Goodbye Duncan.'

'Oh.' Duncan thought she was being rather abrupt, but then she must have lots of other people to ask. 'Goodbye.'

He replaced the receiver and returned to 'I married an axe murderer', or whatever today's TV chat topic was. But his mind couldn't focus on the banality of the show. Instead, he had Lesley's questions repeating in his mind. What would he really think about fathering a child, by natural or the progressive methods mentioned by his caller? Why was she so keen to know what he felt about his own child being raised by a lesbian couple? Was she really tripping through an office survey for a commercial client? It didn't much sound like it and she hadn't gone much out of her way to dress it up as one. Duncan was beginning to feel that Lesley was sending him a secret message, one that would not stay a secret for much longer.

23

'Who is Marsha Blow again?' Charlotte turned to Daniel, who was sitting at a circular table behind her in the Satellite's hot-desking area. They were alone.

'Hecka's PA.'

'God. Imagine forgetting that. I've only met her three times.'

'Yeah. Better known in the biz as Marsha Blow-job.'

'Does everybody have to have a nickname?'

'"Fraid so.'

'What's yours?'

'Dan the Man.'

'That's original. What's mine? No doubt something revoltingly sexual.'

'You haven't been here long enough.'

'It's supposed to be a creative hot-shop. How long do they take?'

'Depends on the character of the victim. I'll get Bonzo on to it.'

'What's *his* real name?'

'D'you know, it's so long since I last heard it I've forgotten. Even his clients call him Bonzo. Come to think of it, even his mother calls him Bonzo.'

'It's a dog's name.'

'It's a dog's life, his.'

'What about Maria Handley.' She said it Ma-ree-ah.

'It's Mar-eye-a.'

'I'm so sorry. Ever so.'

'We've got a corker for her. Mainly because she has no idea of the reference. She has no idea, period. No pun intended.'

'Don't tell me. Maria Hand-job.'

'Nah. Myra Hindley.'

'The most evil woman in Britain.'

'She's never heard of her. We're waiting till the real Myra turns up on the front page of the *Sun* again. Then we'll score a direct hit. She has a complete humour bypass.'

'I thought Americans were supposed to be relaxed.'

'They expelled her from New York. She didn't fit into the Big Apple because she wasn't enough of a Big Cheese.'

'She's a Big Disappointment as far as I'm concerned.' Charlotte smiled. She was feeling more relaxed with Daniel these days, not least because she had been forced to bond with him in order to gang up on Maria and because she needed someone to explain HQ's peculiarities to her. 'Why does Marsha Blow want me to go across to Hector's office?'

'No idea. At least it's not five o'clock.'

'What happens at five o'clock?'

'You haven't heard of the five o'clock car?'

What now? 'No. I have not heard of the five o'clock car.'

'Well, that's what happened to Gareth Thomas.'

'Who?'

'An account manager. Known as the account damager.'

'What happened?'

'Got the five o'clock car. Never seen again.'

'You mean he was fired.'

'You have to hand it to Hecka. He has style.' Daniel threw back his long strawberry blond hair, leant forward, and adopted the deep, quiet voice of the naturalist documentary narrator. He had a story to tell. 'It's your last day at work, of your career maybe, only you don't know. You're sitting in your office and the clock on the Landmark Hotel begins to peal. There are five chimes. Ask not for whom the bell tolls, it tolls for thee. In harmony – a little counterpoint here – your phone rings. One long steady ring, an internal call. Hector's House to the Satellite. You pick it up. Marsha Blow-job, for it is she, requests the pleasure of your company in Hector's office. Beads of sweat form on your forehead. There's a tremble at your wrist, a shake in your hand. But there will be no handshake for you. You make your way downstairs and into the street to cross over to Quigley House. And there she is on the steps of reception. Marsha Blow for Freedom. Not upstairs at all. Not upstairs festering in her attic but live and livid on the steps of the house that bears the name of the great man himself. And there on the forecourt is the five o'clock car.'

'God, Daniel, it's so gothic. You're frightening me.'

'It's a gleaming Mercedes if you're an account director, a mere BMW for the damagers. It awaits you. Your name alone is inscribed on the driver's chitty. At her beckoning, you get in one side and the high priestess gets in the other. A short conversation of regret ensues and she hands you your P45 and other papers of termination. She exits. The car rolls off and you're a footnote in advertising history.'

'How ghastly.'

'I enjoy telling that story.'

'I can tell.'

'One of the birds down the corridor had a good line on it. She said you become like Rebecca, talked about in whispers, a memory haunting the corridors, never officially referred to again. Meanwhile, Marsha Blow-job morphs into Mrs Danvers. She waits until the setting of the sun and she can venture out into the night without shrivelling to dust. The Satellite empties. The innocent go home for their tea. Marsha Danvers crosses over in the dark. Silently in the night she slips to your locker and removes your personal effects until no trace of you is left. She caresses your company credit cards to her bosom, runs her fingers through your files, strokes the apple you were going to have for a snack. She boxes everything up and leaves without a trace. Last thing she does is to pop your nameplate into her parcel and pack it up for dispatch to deliver to your door in the morning. With her best wishes. And a kiss from the spider woman.'

'You've seen too many movies.'

'Nah. Done too many drugs, mind you.'

'I'm having palpitations. I can't bear to go over there.'

'You're safe. Has the bell tolled for thee?'

'Oh stop it. I suppose he just wants to go through the rehearsal with Sister Verity. She's great, isn't she?'

'I thought you thought she was a mistake?'

'The strategy is a blunder in my opinion, for what it counts, which is nothing. But the execution is perfect. And I'm only responsible for the execution.'

Charlotte tapped the door and waited. She could hear faint piano music on the other side. At Marsha's beckoning, she slipped inside. She could sense Hector's presence but could not see him over the raised lid of the baby grand piano which sat to one side of the office. She had not seen it with the lid up at her interview. He was tinkling something trite and trivial. Anywhere else, for the chairman to have a piano in his office would be regarded as an indulgence, an eccentricity. Here it was par for the course, routine, expected. Charlotte was already getting used to being unfazed. And after all, this was the lair of the legendary Hector Quigley, Lord of the Jingle. There were fewer jingles around these years, almost none, but when called for – and when not called for too – Hector would compose something suitably foot-tappy and hummable to repeat in the brains of the Great British public and drive them demented.

Hector stopped with a ripple in the upper register and turned his bright, shiny, taut face onto hers. His piggy eyes were all atwinkle. She noticed that he wore stretch gold armbands around his shirt sleeves to raise his cuffs from the keys.

'When I was a youngster,' he intoned, 'I had an ambition to play piano American-style in one of the great hotel cocktail bars, the Grand in Cardiff or the Majestic in Bristol. But for that one must have a background personality. I had presence.'

Charlotte could only think to say yes.

'I had a voice too. What Welshman hasn't?'

Charlotte stuck with yes again.

'Sister Verity is a triumph, Charlotte. I congratulate you on the idea.' He underscored her achievement with a cadenza on the keyboard.

'Your idea, Hector. My execution. We must put the concept into research. I mean, I know she won't be in the commercials or press adds but we should still test the back-of-pack references and the leaflets and things.' i.e. Kill her off.

'I have been thinking about that. Sister Verity must be a spokesman for the brand. We should push that home with the client today. Where is she, anyway?'

'We put her up at the Metropole. It's cheaper than the Landmark. She's being collected at two and brought round to the Satellite. She has an injured foot.'

'Has she? Well, tell her to hop in a cab! Hah! What do you think of this?'

Hector played the familiar four-bar phrase with which he had been tinkering when Charlotte entered.

'It's . . . nice. What's it for?'

'Sing it back to me. Let's give it the Old Grey Whistle Test.'

Charlotte cringed. Jesus. She was being asked to sing to one of the most powerful and richest men in British advertising. Red-faced, she lah-lahed the tune back.

'Yes, well don't call us Mrs Worthington! It passes. It passes. You have heard it once and can repeat it perfectly.'

Charlotte felt relieved. She had in fact heard it twice but she wasn't letting on.

'We could use it as our campaign theme.'

'We need something modern. More Spice Girls, perhaps.'

'Never heard of 'em.'

'We'll have to research it.'

'Very keen on research, aren't you? Well, we just have and it works.'

'I'm not the target audience.'

'You're a young woman, are you not?'

'I'm not twelve. Most girls move onto tampons at school. I mean it's not scientific.'

'You're beginning to sound like our American cousin.' Accompanying himself on the keyboard, Hector bawled out a bit of *West Side Story*. 'Mareeah, Mareeah, Mareeeee-haaah! No bloody sense of humour that broad from Broadway. Not scientific, eh? You young uns consider advertising too much of a science and too little of an art. That is why I am here. To stop you. Creativity is the cure. Progress is made in imaginative leaps and bounds, caution in calculated small steps. Give that man a banana! Write what I just said down and have it made into a wall plaque.'

Charlotte had nothing with which to write it down nor felt that it deserved to be. Her fingers flustered in the air for a second and then she realised that Hector seemed not to notice. Write that down was something that tripped off his tongue as lightly as the platitudes that were encapsulated in Hector's Homilies.

So that was it. Hector had wanted her to hear his music. He was going to land that on the campaign as well as the nun. Heck. Charlotte was going to have to work full time just to keep the nun out of the TV commercials. She knew that already. At least Maria Handley would be on her side for that, as would Daniel, and surely the client. She hadn't even met the client yet. She needed Dan to fill her in.

On her way out, in the anteroom that was Marsha's domain, she thought that Daniel had the high priestess Danvers completely wrong. She was cheery and chatty.

'Don't worry. I listened in. I got the phrase. I'll have a plaque made up and tell him you did it.'

'Oh, thank you.'

'It'll go in the bin. They all do. He doesn't know what he's talking about most of the time only most folks are too gutless to stand up to him.'

'How old is Hector, Marsha?'

'Too old but not old enough.'

'Meaning?'

'Meaning that he's got at least another ten years in him. He's had a facelift, you know.'

'So I've heard. Not really, though.'

'Oh yes, really. He's been going for clandestine meetings. There's some woman involved. He's been making his own appointments. Well, that's unheard of. I thought to myself, "What's he up to?" So I did last number recall on his phone. You'll never guess.'

'No I won't.'

'He's going for electrolysis.'

Charlotte had visions of Hector having a permanent wax on his bikini line. 'Surely not?'

'Behind the ears. That's where they do it.'

'Behind the ears? Electrolysis?'

'Yes. When men get a facelift they have to have some hair-bearing facial skin pulled up behind the ears. So unless they have electroysis they have to shave there.'

'Uggh. Are you sure?'

'Sure enough to tell absolutely everybody I can think of.'

'Where do you get your information from?'

'Anywhere I can. Philip the chauffeur is a good source. He has a mother who is deaf and he learnt a few tricks from her. He reads Hecka's lips through the screen in the Bentley. It's supposed to be one-way only, but when it's sunny you can see straight through it. Apparently.'

The telephone rang. Marsha took the call and put it through to Hector.

She pointed excitedly at the telephone.

'Who is it?'

'Her. His fancy woman.'

'Never?'

'Always. Can't keep her away.'

'Who is she? Anyone we know?'

'Imelda Marcos for all I can tell. He keeps his private life very private indeed. You used to work at Clancey and Bennett, didn't you? With that Nigel and Serena? Hecka's great chums with them.' Charlotte grimaced. 'He had lunch with Serena the other day. She's married, isn't she?'

'Yes. She's having an affair with Hector? She's supposed to be having one with Nigel.'

'It could be her. She puts on a pretend voice. She'll be his fourth wife.'

'He's not going to marry her?'

'I reckon. I was right the last time. You'll have to be strong on this nun thing.'

'I intend to be.'

'Once Hecka gets into his stride there's no controlling him. It's up to you or there'll be nuns in lightbulbs and on posters and balloons and bus tickets all over England.'

Charlotte grimaced again. 'The only nun I intend to see is none of the above.'

'It's her mother.'

'One moment please, Mrs Reith.'

Morella St Charles smiled at the sound of her former name, somehow so familiar, somehow assigned to the dustbin of history, if her conventional Southeast English life could be termed anything as grand as history. Like the majority of middle-class women of her age, she had done little of lasting note after an undistinguished adolescence at cheapish minor girls' public schools near places like Eastbourne and one term at a copycat finishing school in Montreux. Lac Leman. Lausanne. How to press a pleated summer skirt. How to make a floral arrangement last a few days more. How to sign a cheque. *Never* with a ballpoint pen. They knew their market. They were the offspring of families in decline in an empire in decline learning manners in decline. Manners did not matter. Within a half-decade it was all as dead as the dodo. There was only just time to be flown back to London, to be thrown a coming out, to be picked on by the nearest bachelor, to be led down the aisle on the arm of your father and back up it on the arm of your shiny new husband. Then all that sort of thing was swept away on the surf of the sixties. By the time Charlotte and Robin had been born and farmed out to nannies and prep school teachers, the froth in which Morella had expected to flit had given way to fondue parties for people in marketing who did their own washing-up. Dresses were drip dry. They did not have pleats. Flowers were fake. Cheques were superseded by credit cards.

She had not seen much of it coming. She had not seen much of Frank either until she caught him out. Then she saw nothing at all. He had not been on an overnight stay at a conference, but to an overnight session in a seaside hotel. The fact that it was his secretary made it all so shabby and predictable. The fact that it was Eastbourne where she had grown up after the War made it worse and Morella had filed for divorce. So nobody cared anymore that you got divorced. Morella felt that it mattered. She was just a little old-fashioned. She was just a little proper. She was just a little redundant. All she had been raised to do, she had failed at. Despite the fact that it was Charlotte and Robin's father who had done the beastly deed, it was she who was the failure. She had not reverted to her maiden name, Penn. She stuck with Mrs Reith for more than twenty years until at a preview for a young Pole's art exhibition she had bumped into Anthony. Anthony St Charles. One of Harley Street's top cosmetic surgeons. Anthony St Charles. Single. Rich. Well-preserved if not conventionally handsome. A naturalised Briton, no hint of an accent, no trace of a past. Anthony St Charles. The man who could provide the life she had been waiting all her own to live.

So here they were. Back from South America via New York, The QE2 and Concorde. This was the first engagement at their white stucco to-die-for home in The Boltons. This was what she had been trained for. At last, at past fifty, Morella St Charles was in her forte, in her element, at her best, in her prime. Morella and Anthony St Charles At Home. Home from the honeymoon. There had been no reception for friends after the wedding, just family. Now it was friends, no family. Except for Charlotte.

'Wednesday 20th July. This is the voice mail of Charlotte Reith. I'm sorry I can't take your call at the moment. I'm in a presentation this afternoon but will try to reach you later.'

'Darling. It's mummy. I know you're doing your tampon meeting today and you're under lots of pressure but just to remind you that it's six-thirty now and the party will be going on to nine or so and Anthony and I will be having a little supper round the corner so do try to come. And, darling, I really don't know a soul and I need the support. Seeing the whites of their eyes takes on a whole new meaning when none of one's guests can quite close their eyelids after radical blepharoplasty. Bye darling. And good luck even though I know it's over by now.'

'Where would you like these, madam?'

Morella turned to the Philippina girl who had come with the caterers. She held a vase of flowers in yellows and golds.

'There's an occasional table in the hallway by the cupboard under the stairs. Put them there in front of the mirror. The guests will see them when they come in.'

Charlotte was not here. Anthony was not here. Most of the guests were his choice and most of his choice were his patients. Morella had made him promise that, though she was not against the idea in principle, she did not wish to be forced into an early facelift as some sort of proof-of-purchase advertisement for her husband's skills. She knew exactly who had had what. Anthony had shown her the album of before and after photographs. Patients loved having them taken. Despite the fact that they insisted on complete discretion when they booked in, they always ended up bragging about the benefits after they had gone back out stretched and nipped and tucked and into the world. She had news for Charlotte. Anthony had flown to his Swiss practice immediately prior to the wedding to perform an endoscopic brow lift, a classic deep plane lift plus a bletharoplasty on one of Britian's leading, not so anonymous, businessmen. There were no before and after photographs of *him*, but it fitted with what Charlotte had told her. So much for the Hippocratic oath and the swearing to secrecy.

She was on edge. There seemed so little to do. The staff opened the black front door. They greeted the guests and put their summer jackets on hangers and onto the rail in the cupboard under the stairs. They served their drinks and cantered round with the canapés. Morella was left to be scintillating, sparkling and glittering at light conversation. She was good at it. It was the one thing she could do. Putting on a good show. Without Anthony St Charles, who was up to his wrists in some woman's breasts at this very moment, augmenting them. How much would any of this lot know of how she really felt about her second marriage? How much would any of this lot care?

The eldest there, a gentleman of the old school, was patting his flannels pockets and reaching inside his jacket. Only he had forgotten he had taken it off as he had come in, at the suggestion of the Philippina girl. Morella crossed to him.

'Lionel! What have you lost?'

'Left me damn lighter in me jacket, Morella.'

'Let me get it for you.'

'Are you sure?'

She cupped his ear. 'Give me the chance to slip out of the room and this conversation I'm having. Which is your jacket?'

'Burberry check. It's in the top inside pocket.' He winked. Old-school old gentlemen were frequently fond of old-fashioned Morella.

She slipped into the grand entrance hallway. Anthony had had it done up in black and white by a Royal Opera designer whose pectorals he had padded out in a barter deal. Morella stopped by the yellow and gold flowers on the occasional table. She lifted them up and let them fall back more gracefully than before. She checked the line of her little suit in the mirror. Its acidic brilliance clashed with the creaminess of the flowers. She had been encouraged into citrus by Charlotte's own choice of it for her wedding. Her wedding. She sighed at the thought. She stepped sideways to the panelled door of the cupboard under the stairs. She touched the little gold handle and pulled upon it. The stairs flew up to the next floor at a height of twenty feet: this was a large understairs cupboard. She flicked the light switch. The bulb blew. She repeated her sigh and slid into the darkness.

Forgetful old Lionel soon forgot that he had sent Morella St Charles off in search of his jacket. Instead, he accepted a light from a rather charming middle-aged woman with a dramatic jawline. Conversations were continued. Canapés were consumed. Drinks were downed. No one noticed that Morella made no reappearance. No one missed Anthony's low-key new wife. Not even he when he hurried home at last and was caught with the overflow by the flowers in the hall. Morella had been forgotten. She had slipped from sight. She had entered into a black world and become consumed by her own curiosity. She had been trapped by her own trepidation. For she had indeed discovered something in her search of the dark and dreadful cupboard under the stairs and it was not old Lionel's lighter at all.

'Michael?'

'What?'

'Are you going to be moody all night?'

'I'm not being moody. I have these contracts to read through.'
He muttered aloud. '". . . whether now existing or developed in
the future to include without limitation by analogue or digital
terrestrial cable and or satellite broadcast and or delivery near
video on demand and or radio transmission broadcast and or
delivery." It's all small print stuff.'

'How about the small print in our lives? That's worth checking
out too.'

'God, Duncan, the way you manipulate words.'

Michael pushed the papers of the day across the low table and
downed the last of his mug of coffee. He smiled wearily.

'Would you like a refill?' asked Duncan.

'No. I have an early start. I need the sleep. Pressure, pressure,
pressure. That's all The Station's been since it started. We're
already into another season and another batch of programmes.
No rest for the wicked I suppose.'

'You enjoy it.'

'I've been through the honeymoon period. I've had the seven
month itch. What comes next?'

'The divorce?'

'I'm not leaving.'

'We need the income.'

'I'm not leaving.'

'I don't earn enough.'

'Read my lips. I'm not leaving.'

'People who say "read my lips" do that so you don't look them
in the eye when they're lying to you.'

'Look me in the eye then.'

'I was. I was warned about men like you.'

'And couldn't wait to seek them out as soon as you got the
chance.'

Duncan laughed and jettisoned himself from the settee. He padded barefoot into the tiny kitchen of his flat and helped himself to more black coffee from the cafetière. It was cold. He stuck it in the microwave to warm it up.

'We should get one of those little hotplate things for cafetières.'

'God. You're so LMC.'

'Come again?'

'Lower middle class.'

'Don't be such a snob.'

'A cafetière hotplate is the sort of ghastly thing they advertise in those naff magazines that come with the Sunday papers. Who reads them?'

'Me.'

'You read everything. That's why you know everything.'

'I'm glad somebody notices. I probably know people who've written the copy for them. Agency copywriters do it moonlighting. Like academics writing porn under pseudonyms. "We all have trouble with navel fluff. Well, no longer. This tiny miniature vacuum has been specially designed to reach the crevices of your belly button. Available in taupe, cerise and . . ." what's another terrible colour?'

'Chocolate? No. Shit.'

'That'll do. "Taupe, cerise and shit."' Duncan laughed and returned with his mug. He swung his bare legs up, sank into the settee and sighed.

'Do you think Lesley and Sarah are seriously considering me?'

'As a father? That's risible.'

'You're just jealous they haven't asked you.'

'I am not. Anyway, they haven't asked you either.'

'They're obviously considering me as a candidate. The conversation we had was dead obvious. She was just being diplomatic in case they change their minds. They want me to take an AIDS test. I deduced that much from the questions.'

'You're not taking an AIDS test.'

'I would if they wanted me to.'

'Look Duncan, I lost two of my closest friends to AIDS and I'm not going through all that again.'

'One of your closest friends. The other was an acquaintance.

Anyway, what difference does the test make? If you have it, you have it.'

'Knowing and not knowing are the distinguishers, not having and not having.'

'Well, I know I haven't got HIV. I mean, I don't know, but I'm pretty sure.'

'Just keep it that way.' Michael returned to mutter over his papers. '". . . but not limited to all other television rights theatric rights non-theatric rights videogram rights video on demand rights and multimedia rights to include without limitation CD-Rom CDI videodisc video CD laserdisc and all other software platforms and Library Extract Rights." What have they forgotten?'

'If they insisted I had the test I'd have to have it.'

Michael stopped work again. 'Duncan, you are not having an HIV test and you are not fathering anyone's child. I forbid it.'

'Forbid it?'

'I'm asking you as your partner not to do it.'

'Telling me not to do it more like. You're just jealous they haven't asked you and you're feeling left out of the party. Well, tough titties.'

'Duncan. You can't have a child. You are a gay man. A child would just be a sop to your own personal vanity. You are a gay man in a long-term relationship with me. You're not in a relationship with those two lesbians whom, I might point out, you have met just once at a disastrous dinner party. There is no room in our lives for a child. We're not suitable parents whatever political correctness says.'

'Speak for yourself. I could be. I am.'

'Duncan, you couldn't abide having your child raised by two dykes. You know that. You're not sufficiently relaxed about your own or their sexuality. You'd be embarrassed by the whole thing and wish you'd never done it. Think of sitting at the school nativity play with two shaven-headed mothers who've turned up on bikes in leather with rings through their noses waving rainbow flags from the back row. That's just not you.'

'It's not exactly them either.'

'It's a lifelong responsibility. You need to think of the consequences very seriously.'

'I'm doing just that. And don't hector me. You're not my father.'

'And you're not anybody's father either and you're not going to be. Think it through.'

'Most straight people don't think it through. They get drunk, get laid and get a baby.'

'Don't exaggerate.'

'Gay people are more responsible. I'm taking my responsibilities very seriously.'

'Gay men are more self indulgent. They're more selfish. A baby is not a fashion accessory, nor is it a two fingers gesture to the rest of society. Just think about it. You couldn't bear to have your kid brought up in a liberal household run by two left-wing lesbians.'

'They're not left-wing.'

'They are compared to you. And who's going to pay for it?'

'Me. Us. Us and them.'

'That means me. I'm not paying for some nasty little experiment with two ugly women we don't even know. They're friends of Paul McCarthy's, for God's sake.'

'So are we.'

'They could be drug addicts. It's them who should be having the AIDS test, not us.'

'You're just jealous, listen to you. You're all hurt because they didn't tug at your wrist going "daddy, daddy". Well, it's nothing to do with you.'

'How can it be nothing to do with me? I'm your lover. I live with you.'

'Oh, is that who you are? I was wondering. I knew you came in somewhere.'

'Dunky, don't get quarrelsome.'

'It's not me who's being quarrelsome.'

'It is. They haven't asked you and they probably won't so let's not discuss it. You're not to do it and that's final.'

'If I want to have a child I will. So there.'

'You'd have one just to spite me.'

'Probably. If Lesley rings back—'

'—If she rings back you know what to say. Just say no.'

'I don't want to say no. That's your answer, not mine.'

'You're impossible. Look. Why are we arguing? She hasn't even asked you.'

'Yet,' said Duncan under his breath, his mind set.

26

Charlotte was by nature a biker. She hated being driven and right now she was being driven to her new client by Maria Handley. She was annoyed that Maria had insisted Daniel be left back at the agency, putting Charlotte in the position of the junior member of the agency team. She would have to minute the meeting in the contact report, something Maria had no doubt planned in order to make her look secretarial.

'I can't believe they haven't got your car for you yet,' said Maria. She was coping well with driving on the 'wrong' side of the road. However, her level of concentration was so great that it rendered her already stilted conversation even more terse. 'This country is so inefficient.'

'I haven't chosen one yet.'

'You didn't choose one yet? You'd better get a move on.'

'I thought about getting an MX5. A red one.'

'Black is better. What is that anyway?'

'You call it a Miata in the States. It's a Mazda. Skimpy and sexy.'

'Well, they say people are like their cars.'

So why you're not driving a hearse I shall never know, thought Charlotte.

'Is that what you think I am? Skimpy and sexy?'

'I don't like to say it, but you have bare legs for a client meeting.'

'It's very hot.'

'Bare legs are not formal enough for management.'

'I think I'm very smartly dressed.'

'You are from the waist up.'

'I can't believe an American is lecturing me, an English woman, on formal dress.'

'I'm half-English.'

'You don't sound it.'

'Well I am. I'm not lecturing you. Just pointing it out.'

'Then you won't mind me pointing out that younger women consider bare legs formal. As long as they are smooth and tanned and your shoes are expensive, which mine are.'

'They are noticeable. You know how to draw attention to yourself, don't you?'

'We do work for an advertising agency, you know. We're supposed to be state of the art about our presentation. That includes our clothes as much as our creative work. And bare legs are *de rigueur* these days. *Tatler* says so. Even at society does. Look at the Princess of Wales.'

'Exactly. Look where she got herself. Kicked out of the royal family.'

'Hardly for having sensational legs.'

'She flaunts herself.'

'And Camilla Park-and-Ride does not, I suppose.'

'She's not exactly a role model either.'

There was a pause as Maria's attention was taken up by the traffic.

'Anyway, to continue where we left off, I don't need a car. I have my bike.'

'You can't show up at Verity on that thing. You need to communicate the maximum status, being such a junior account director.' Charlotte's body blinds slamming down were detected by Maria. 'I'm sorry. I know you don't like to hear that, but it's true. People make judgements about you by what you turn up in in the parking lot.'

'I don't think HQ could come up with anything much to rival a Ducati. They *are* the finest bikes in the world.'

'It's not the brand, it's the mode of transportation that's wrong. Charlotte, can you and I talk?'

That's what they were doing wasn't it?

'I don't see why not.'

'Why can't British people just say yes. What I said required only an affirmative response not a complicated double negative.'

Charlotte was damned if she was going to let that pass.

'We tend to make – what? – quite a subtle and sophisticated use of words over here. You should look out for that in advertising, both in the meetings and in the creative work. It's very important.'

'I'll try to ignore the inbred stuck-uppedness in that remark. Look, Charlotte, I don't want to fall out with you but we need to discuss the way we work together.'

Charlotte flushed. She stared straight ahead into the back of a Ford van they were following into West Sussex. The round green trees, the buttercups by the roadside, the redbrick walls and red-slated roofs of the domestic-style architecture reminded her of growing up in Hampshire. It was very beautiful. Why did Maria Handley have to spoil it all?

'I think you should know,' continued Maria, 'that I am about to go on the board. I can see that, as usual, Hector Quigley and his guys did not bother to tell you the exact reporting structure on this business before you arrived and that it has somehow put your nose out of joint that you have to report to an associate director.'

'I don't even know what an associate director is.'

'Someone who is on the associate board.'

'Who else is one?'

'I'm the only one.'

'Some board.'

'Don't be so hostile. You'll soon realise that I am a very senior account director with years of quality experience behind me.'

'How old *are* you?'

Maria flushed beneath her pancake make-up. Now she stared straight ahead.

'Look at this guy! Where does he think he's going. Come on. Gimme a break, dumbhead!'

Charlotte sat firmly, not letting Maria off the hook.

'I'm in my early – mid-thirties.'

Huh. Pushing forty more like, thought Charlotte.

'Anyway, the point is that these guys are pitching you and me against each other. It's a male strategy. I studied this at business school. Men of Hector Quigley's age see women as unclubbable. They place men in positions where they can work in teams and women in positions where they work in isolation and against each other.'

'I hadn't noticed.'

'Well I have. Look around you, girl. If they think I can't work that out they're badly mistaken. I intend to get on that board if it kills me. I intend to smash through that glass ceiling.'

Charlotte willed Maria to smash through the glass windscreen instead, but to no effect.

'I don't believe that glass ceiling theory. Some women don't get to the top because they just don't want to. They give up and have babies or whatever. If they want to, they do. Look at Serena Sark.'

'I know that name.'

'I suppose that's another disadvantage of your being new to London. She was my last boss.'

'You reported directly to her?'

It occurred to Charlotte that if Hector Quigley really rated Maria Handley surely she would at least have had to have had a courtesy interview with her to get the job. No interview, no power. That was a useful little thought to keep up her sleeve.

'Serena is the managing director of Clancey and Bennett. It's a small part . . . it's a very important part of the MCN International group in the UK. In Europe actually.'

'I know where I read her name. Have you seen today's *Campaign*?'

'No.'

'You'll have to do better than that, girl, if you want to be in my team. It's on the back seat. Check it out.'

Charlotte leant over onto the back seat. The copy of *Campaign* lay there beside a small vanity case. Charlotte took the paper and wondered what could be in it. A reference to Clancey and Bennett? Surely not. A story about Nigel and Serena? In *Campaign*, the sly, witty, exposé trade tabloid of Britain's hottest creative business? Never.

But there they were. Third-page news. The photograph took her back. Somebody had actually bothered to go to Nigel and Serena's offices and shoot them. Serena was grinning from ear to ear like a gypsy.

'She's got flick-ups.'

'What?'

'Her hair. It's not her strongest point.'

'That's the sort of comment men use to diminish women's stature. I'm surprised at you.'

'Sorry. I didn't realise I had to be politically correct.'

'What you need to be is ahead of the game not behind. See the story?'

'Yes. They're pitching for the launch of the ovulation and pregnancy side of the Verity account.'

'Did you know they were pitching for it?'

'No.'

'But you worked there. It's not a large agency.'

'Well, actually it is. It's part of MCN. They were not pitching for it when I left. Not to my knowledge anyway. I wonder who they're pitching against? It doesn't say. It doesn't matter. They won't get it.'

'Us.'

'Us?'

'We didn't push for it. The client has asked us so we couldn't say no. They'll split that smaller business off when they realise we're too big to do it cost-efficiently.'

'Nigel and Serena are hardly cheap. Just them and us?'

'No. There is one other. We don't know who. So you see?'

'What?' Maria was being smug so Charlotte knew that some criticism was on its way.

'You should have known about that. You could have walked into a new client meeting and not known the most important thing they're doing this week.'

'You could have told me. Pre-meeting meetings are very important. I do need to be briefed.'

'I just did that. What do you think of Daniel?'

A wave of self-consciousness swept across Charlotte. She did not agree with Maria's criticisms of her, but she knew her fling with Daniel was a weak spot waiting to be exposed.

'I think he's good if unconventional.'

'Insolent is the word you're looking for. And lazy. He wouldn't last five minutes in a New York agency.'

'He's not working in one so that doesn't matter.'

'Do you get on with lower-class men?'

Charlotte laughed. 'He's not lower class.'

'He talks like a cockney.'

'No he doesn't. It's an affectation. I've seen his c.v. He's public school. I think it's good having a man on the team. Tampons should not be girlie business.'

'I disagree. How can a man know what it's like to have a period?'

'We can tell him. Most of our advertising is aimed at pre-pubescent girls. They don't know either. Anyway, Daniel's role at his stage is to get the work out of the agency and do the accounts and admin and stuff. I will do the creative briefing.'

'That's my role. You assist me.'

'I intend to be an asset to the account and to the agency. The creative work needs special attention. I think I have developed the skills to do that.'

'We'll see.'

'Don't worry. I won't step on your toes.' I'll stamp on them, thought Charlotte.

'What about Sister Verity? You've already gone behind my back on that one.'

'That was nothing to do with me.'

'You went out and found a nun.'

'I didn't go out actually. She came to us. Anyway, it was Hector's idea and it won't get anywhere.'

'The client adores her.'

'She won't be in the advertising. She'll be back of pack copy, that's all. Anyway, they haven't put the concept into research yet. The first group will kill her off. I wouldn't get your knickers in a twist over nothing.'

'It is not nothing. It's unstrategic. It's unprofessional. It's unintelligent.'

'Tell that to Hector Quigley not me. Then see if you smash through your glass ceiling.'

'I will. And I will enjoy it.' Maria's mood changed. She seemed to grip the steering wheel tighter. 'Hector and I are a lot closer than you think.'

She turned and smiled coldly at Charlotte, her bleached American teeth as dazzling as her little citrus suit.

27

Michael scanned the horizon of the smart staff restaurant. The Station canteen was a massive projecting balcony at the rear of the building where Michael worked amidst four hundred others of the highest paid people in TV. The conservatory room provided views of a much-commented-upon Japanese sand garden. Unfortunately that had basically blown away over The Station's first winter and, now wiser and wearier and without wealth, The Station's house management committee had opted for York stone paving and tubs. The workmen could be seen putting the finishing touches to the uninspiring replacement design, setting traditional park benches into a grey concrete mix. No one knew what the celebrated architect of the building thought about this. No one had sought his opinion this time.

Next to the steel and glass outlook point a slight woman in her mid-thirties stood with her back to Michael, her nylony white-blonde hair whipped up like spun sugar and hanging about her shoulders. Her right hand twitched nervously by her side.

'Hello, Briony,' said Michael.

'Ooh! You made me jump.' She turned and smiled. To Michael, Briony Linden, The Station's Head of Marketing, was fascinating-looking rather than conventionally attractive. Her colouring, or rather the lack of it, was exceptional, her near-white eyebrows almost invisible against white limpid skin. On her eyelashes she wore electric green mascara. She always wore something about her person to distinguish herself from the crowd of identikit executive females at The Station. Today it was the turn of a citrus scarf, which she had knotted and clasped at the neck with a brutal-looking Celtic brooch, something Boudicca might have worn into battle. Wrapped around her right wrist, where her hand still fidgeted, was a matching bangle, bold enough to be a piece of protective armour handed down from the Queen of the Iceni.

'I'm desperate for a cigarette.' Briony beamed broadly. 'You wouldn't like to take a pre-lunch stroll around our new garden would you?'

'You're absolutely right. I wouldn't like to take a stroll outside. It looks like a British Rail station. What on earth do they think they're doing?'

'Cutting back like the rest of us. Now they've got the whole show off the ground the board are looking to maximise profitability. I'm surprised they've gone as far as tubs. My marketing budget isn't enough to launch a regional freesheet let alone a new season on national TV.'

'I miss out on all that budget stuff in my department.'

'Lucky you. If you ever want to swap jobs you can have mine.'

'Shall we go in? Is Martin here?'

'Oh, I forgot. Old Foxy rang and said he was running late. He'll join us for the main course.'

'I only want a main course. I don't want a starter. If I have a starter I can't have a pudding.'

'I've never been a pudding person. I used to get to smoke at the end of the main course before nicotine fascism took over the world. So I never got into puddings.'

Briony led the way. She was the colleague whom Michael liked most of all. A top brain herself, she appreciated his experience and observations and acted upon them. She did not treat him as the boring company lawyer in the way the programme-makers did. They probably dismissed her as that publicity girl herself, now she came to think of it. They walked down the great curving slope, round the arched back wall, and made their way through their colleagues to a table by the glass wall with more views of the pedestrian garden layout.

A waitress was upon them in seconds and they chose from the menus. Then Briony opened up the conversation.

'I've been here for more than a year. I realised the other day I had missed my anniversary.'

'I suppose I must have been too.'

'It's funny how you don't notice that sort of thing despite the fact that work dominates your life so much.'

'It *is* your life.'

'Mmm. I have my two children I suppose. They're my life really.'

'And your husband.'

'Him too. But you never take your children for granted the way you do your husband.' She winked.

'How old are they now?'

'Six and seven.'

'So you're at sixes and sevens, then?'

'I'm not. I have a house-husband. He looks after the girls usually.'

'You don't have a nanny?'

'I have never resorted to one. If my husband couldn't ever look after the girls I'd bring them into the office for the day or something. They're at school mostly.'

'You seem to have it sorted.'

'We thought it through. I don't believe in farming my children out to a stranger. I'm old-fashioned that way.'

'You're the least old-fashioned person I can think of.'

'Actually you're right. They did a piece on me in *Options* the other month. Briony Linden, modern ms about town sort of thing. She has it all – top job, top home, top clothes, top kids, top husband.'

'It's true.'

'I know. That's what was strange. Every word was true, but it didn't seem to be about me. I still see myself as the progeny of Lancashire mill folk.'

'Trouble at t'mill type, are you?'

'Trouble in t'marketing department type. Clancey and Bennett have rather fallen apart since Charlotte Reith left.'

'Oh do tell. Has it? Pass on the gossip. I'll tell Duncan.'

'She was that girl who worked for him, remember? Imagine. She abandoned this modern ms about town in t'top telly company for a stand-up war with Tampax tampons.'

'That'll be a bloody battle.'

'Yuk. That's nauseating. I'm surprised at you, Michael!'

'What are you two arguing about?' It was Martin Fox, Head of Programmes. He pulled out a seat next to Briony, its metal legs making a tinny, scraping noise on the industrial floor surface.

'Michael was being disgustingly masculine, that's all.'

'A camp old thing like him?'

'Less of the camp, please. Less of the old too, for that matter.'

Martin sat down opposite Michael.

'These bloody metal chairs. They're so uncomfortable. You'd think whoever designed them had never seen a man's bottom.'

'Ah,' said Michael, 'that must be why gay interior designers are so popular. They see so many.'

Briony laughed. 'It's all part of the plot, so we get back to our desks quickly. Being an American company they realise that the British have to have their lunch but being puritans they try to make it as undesirable an activity as possible. Like banning smoking in the entire compound.'

'Compound? I've not heard it referred to as that before,' joked Martin. 'You make it sound like a prison.'

'Subliminal reference, I assure you. Freudian slip.'

'So what's on the menu today?'

'You're briefing us on the afternoon strands. The big battle is in the afternoon, you said. Hopefully the big budget will be there too.'

'Actually I meant quite literally what was on the menu?'

'We're having the chorizo sausage pappardelle,' said Michael. 'Are we going to be naughty and have a glass of vino?'

'A glass?' responded Briony. 'A bottle each, please. Or will Colonel Bogeyman have a problem?'

Martin ordered. They ate. They reached coffee time and still no afternoon briefing.

'Martin, The agency will be here shortly,' said Briony. 'Tell us about the afternoon schedule.'

'It's quite simple really, I suppose. Think cheap. Think two women sitting on a sofa discussing the soft issues of the day – tampon ads, since that seems to be in everybody's minds for some reason. That's the level we've sunk to.'

'Surely not?' asked Michael.

'It took Channel Four ten years to get that bad,' said Briony gloomily. 'How come The Station is collapsing after only three seasons? It's not even summer ratings you're talking about.'

'The board's policy is to maximise profit. The shareholders want a dividend.'

'The shareholders want a good thrashing,' said Briony. 'They've hacked into my budgets so bad I've had to recycle the paper clips.'

'The truth is we have to reserve our funds for where we need to compete with high-investment programming. Daytime programming is naturally light and frothy and needn't be expensive. Look at what the other channels are doing. It's all simple stuff stripped daily.'

'Aimed at simpletons,' said Michael. 'From what I hear. I don't watch it myself. What have you commissioned?'

'Not a lot. Yet. Karen Myhill and Jamie Hirst are vying for the three o'clock slot.'

'Oh my God,' said Briony. 'Take cover, everybody.'

'Nonsense,' said Martin.

'No it's not, Martin,' said Michael. 'And it's you who puts them up to it every time. You enjoy playing them off against one another.'

'They enjoy it. Ask your boyriend, what's his name, Donald?'

'Duncan.'

'The truth is that both Karen and Jamie pull out all the stops if they think the other is up to something. I don't see why I shouldn't encourage a competitive spirit. What they don't sell to me the BBC usually picks up later. Or Granada Sky or whatever those guys are calling themselves.'

'Bigger than us,' said Briony. 'That's what they're calling themselves.'

'That's not true,' said Martin.

'If you fiddle the stats enough you can say anything. It was in a press ad in the cuttings the other day.'

'Sue them,' said Martin.

'Let's not sue anybody,' said Michael wearily. 'Send it to the ITC.'

'I've sent it to the Advertising Standards Authority. They regulate press ads. The ITC regulates TV.'

'Ruins TV is the expression you're looking for,' said Martin. 'Well. I was going to tell you about afternoon scheduling, but since we fixed this meeting everything has fallen behind. I've had to start again since the cutbacks were announced. So treat this as a jolly and we'll have a proper meeting about it all in a few weeks' time.'

'When Myhill Productions have come up with the goods,' said Briony.

'What makes you think they'll win?' asked Martin.

'Oh,' said Briony. 'I was just supporting my old friend Duncan Cairns.'

'Michael's on his side too.'

'I'm a disinterested third party.'

Briony checked her watch. 'Shit! The agency will be here. I'll catch up with you soon, guys.'

Michael rose in acknowledgement of her departure. She dashed through the dining room like an unwinding rubber band. Michael sat down, at home with his old colleague.

'She runs off like that all the time,' said Martin. 'She's desperate for a cigarette, I expect.'

'I'm desperate for some more vino,' said Michael.

'You've had a whole bottle.'

'You and Briony helped yourselves all through lunch. Let's have another glass.'

'Well . . . we might as well make merry now. When the afternoon starts, it's going to be hell.'

'Duncan. I'm glad you could make it.'

'I wouldn't stand you up, Alan. How are you? I haven't seen you for ages.'

Alan Josling made a half attempt at a smile which did not conceal weariness. 'I'm fine. Basically.'

'Have you heard from Cindy?'

Alan appeared not to know how to respond.

'Oh. You haven't.'

'No. I haven't. Have you?'

'A few postcards. Just chat. Nothing much.'

'I think it may be the end.'

'You do?'

'I do this time. She threw me out of the flat before she left for Oz.'

'She told me it was a mutual decision.'

'She confuses mutual and unilateral.'

'Michael and I keep separate flats in London. We don't live together but we have a relationship.'

'But you never moved in with each other. Moving back out is different.' Alan took a sip of the whisky sour he had been palming in his hand. His thoughts seemed to be elsewhere. 'She's looking for a job in Sydney. Cindy is.'

'She's in Sydney *pretending* to look for a job, Alan. She always says that. She does bugger all about it. She goes home to see her mother.'

'She said she was fed up with London.'

'Aren't we all? Do any of us ever leave? As soon as we go somewhere else – anywhere else – we realise what makes London so incredibly exciting.'

'What she really meant was that she was fed up with me.'

'Oh.'

'We've had an on-off relationship for so many years now I don't know what to think.'

'Cindy says that herself. To me anyway.'

'You know her better than I do. She says that too.'

'I don't think so. We're very good friends. But you're partners. Lovers if I'm allowed to use that word. Perhaps you just need to sit down and talk.'

'We're not partners. We co-exist. We fit each other in, in between appointments. Half the time we meet up it's at the opera or the theatre or in a group for dinner. We have no time alone together.'

'Quality time. The Americans call it that.'

'They would have a stupid name for it, wouldn't they? But they're not wrong I suppose.'

'Why didn't you go to Australia with Cindy?'

'Work wouldn't allow it.'

'Six weeks apart every year is a long time. Why don't you go out for the middle two weeks or something like that. You'd have a great holiday.'

'It's been suggested, I can assure you.'

'You've suggested it?'

'Some years. Some years she has. There's always been a reason it hasn't happened. We have had weekends away together. But Cindy and I are both running small businesses – in her case she is the business entirely by herself – we just can't take the risk of jumping on a plane and flying off together and buggering the consequences. She closes down each year for a six-week period and that's it. She works every weekend the rest of the year to make up for it.'

'Well . . . I don't think that's completely true. She spends a lot of free time with me. We go out all the time together.'

'That often?'

'She feels . . .'

'Go on . . . tell me.'

'She says it's because you're never around, always late, just want to lay around doing nothing – I'm not taking her side. I consider you both friends.'

'I've lost her.'

'Have you called her?'

'No. I could, I suppose. It's not expensive to phone Australia these days.'

'Oh come on, Alan. I saw your brand new TVR parked outside. You spend more on one night at Covent Garden Opera House than a year's worth of phone calls to Australia. The cost has nothing to do with it.'

'She's only once gone home in the summer before. Their winter. She hates the cold. She wants to end it.'

'She would tell you if she did.'

'She would tell you.'

'She hasn't. In fact, she gave me the impression it was the exact opposite. After you had your car crash last year she said you were growing closer.'

'Yeah. Then I had to devote double the time to Thurrock and Josling. Which, actually, is what I wanted to see you about. Cindy and I had a really bad row about nothing and a big bust-up again. Still . . . I have to sort her and me out myself. I'm sorry.'

'Don't be. You're my friends. But don't expect me to have any solutions. I don't know which is more difficult, men and women, who don't know how the other sex works, trying to live together, or two men, who know exactly what's going on with each other all the time. Both seem a recipe for disaster, actually.'

'You and your, eh, friend – Michael isn't it? – are not getting on either?'

Duncan shook his head. 'Oh, no we are.'

Alan looked marginally disappointed.

'But I was just thinking of something that we had been discussing and we could read each other like a book. A bit of mystery and a bit of cloudiness can help a relationship. You don't want all your motivations under a spotlight. You need room to manouevre.'

'I agree with that sentiment entirely.'

'Anyway . . . You mentioned Thurrock and Josling. I don't know anything about the company.'

'You know what we do. We dabble in advertising, a bit of local retail and trade press, not TV. But we're mainly into graphic design and doing company brochures and that sort of stuff. It's very profitable if you get the right contracts.'

'Interesting business.' Duncan faked it. Actually he thought it was rather the bum end of things and that Alan's real kick was in controlling his own little empire and making a fast buck. He could sell second-hand cars and be quite as content.

'Good. I'm glad you say that. It's just that Cindy did say that when you went into TV if things didn't work out that well you could always get an offer to tempt you back into an agency. Well, I may be looking for someone like you so I wanted to sound you out.'

Duncan was caught off his guard. This he had not expected. He did not feel Alan was in robust enough mood to be told straight to his face to forget even asking.

'I'm . . . eh . . . I'm . . . I suppose I'm quite happy in TV, really. I haven't thought about going back at all, since I've left.'

'You can't be making the same sort of money.'

'True.'

'I can afford to be very generous.'

'I like the lifestyle in TV. I like the writing and the creative side. I like the fact it's not so commercially orientated. I don't miss being in a service business.'

'You don't know what I'm suggesting.'

'No.'

'I thought that without any commitment either way you might like to consider a bit of consultancy.'

'Consultancy?'

'Yes. For me. I'd pay you cash in hand. There would be no requirement to write anything down. Just report back.'

Duncan put himself on alert. Alan Josling was an old hand at under the counter espionage and dodgy dealing. He wondered what dirty deed he had in mind.

'Report back? On what?'

'You may or may not know that Verity Tampons have appointed Hector Quigley as their new agency. God only knows why, but they have.'

'I do. The account director on it worked for me at C&B on The Station account. She's a friend.'

'I know. I thought you might like to take her out to dinner and pummel her for a bit of information. I'd pay for the dinner and for you to do it.'

Duncan was shocked. If there was ever going to be an Advertising-gate, Alan Josling would be there holding the tapes.

'Alan . . .'

'Come on Duncan. It's only what she would tell you anyway. And it's not about *her* business. I don't want to know about the tampons. Verity have other products. Self-testing pregnancy and ovulation predictor kits. I'm pitching for the launch of those against Clancey and Bennett.'

'Oh my God. Them.'

'It's money for old rope, Duncan. The pregnancy testing market is so small that HQ couldn't handle it commercially. It has to go to a little shop like mine or C&B. You know as well as I do that Nigel and Serena are the kiss of death for any brand. You don't want them to get it.'

'Well if you do your job thoroughly, they won't will they?'

'It doesn't work like that as well you know. Serena Sark is dead crafty. I know for a fact that she's hanging out a lot with Hector these days.'

'Serena is? Really? What has Nigel got to say about that?'

'What has he got to say about anything? He may not even know.'

'HQ aren't being asked to pitch then?'

'I don't know. I'm being honest.'

That makes a change, thought Duncan.

'I only found out that C&B were pitching when they press-released it to *Campaign* themselves. They must be desperate to have done that.'

'Alan, I can't pummel Charlotte for information if HQ is pitching too. That's disingenuous or dishonest or dis- something.'

'I don't *think* HQ is. The fact that's it's me against Nigel and Serena must mean they want a certain kind of agency to handle the kits.'

A small, slithery, slimy, corrupt one, obviously, thought Duncan. He liked Alan Josling as a friend but was less inclined to trust him in business.

'So will you do it, Duncan? If I get the businees there's a big job in it for you. I need a deputy managing director. Colin Thurrock wants to retire.'

Duncan sighed. 'I don't really want to get dragged back into marketing. I'm in telly now.'

'Well we'll see. There's a sizeable consultancy fee in it at least.

You know Charlotte. And you're the last person who'd want to help Nigel and Serena. Wouldn't you rather be on my side? And Cindy's? And Charlotte's. Charlotte'd die if she had to link up again with Godzilla and Dracula.'

'How do you know? You've never met her.'

'I know Serena Sark well enough to know how Charlotte would feel.'

'That's true. You're absolutely right, of course.'

'And any documents she could pass on to you would be most helpful.'

'Alan!'

'I need to get my hands on the HQ pitch stuff. Hector is barmy and his circus act is a hoot but actually his planning people pile all the facts into the presentation documents. The ones I have seen they do at any rate.'

Duncan sighed again.

'And, Duncan, if you could use your connections within MCN to get any fresh dirt on Nigel and Serena I'd be grateful. You know all the MCNers hate them. Any one of them would spill the beans to you because they'll just assume you're just out for a gossip, you not being in the business anymore. I'll pay your expenses. It has to be cash in hand though. Don't bother with receipts.'

Duncan tutted. Alan Josling was as subtle as Lucretia Borgia caught picking poison toadstools.

'Alan. I'm not passing confidential documents for anyone. That's illegal.'

'Balls.'

'It is. And it's not my style.'

'Think of the money. Do it for me and Cindy.'

'I am not a go-between.'

'In our relationship you are, Duncan. And I'm very grateful. If I could just pick up this business I can afford a deputy managing director. Then my workload will halve. Cindy and I will be able to spend more time together. You could be the person to bring all that about Duncan. You'd be making Cindy so happy. I love her.'

Duncan's expression soured.

'Think about it, anyway. We still have a few weeks.'

Duncan said nothing.

'Will you think about it? Please, Duncan. For me and Cindy.'

'I'll think about it,' said Duncan dryly.

29

'You're absolutely sure you know what you're to do?'

'I am.'

Charlotte now meted out her instructions.

'Just follow Hector's lead. You don't have to say anything other than the three lines on the script. If anything goes wrong I'll be in the front row with Daniel. Catch my eye and I'll give you the appropriate sign. Thumb up for yes, thumb down for no. But they won't ask you any questions anyway. And ignore the clients.'

Charlotte smiled reassuringly and dabbed a little excess powder from the nun's nose with a tissue. It was time to open the doors and let in the dozen journos of the retail and marketing trade press. But before she could get to the back of the HQ theatre, Hector was amongst them booming in quadraphonic sound on his radio mike.

'Maria. Charlotte. Daniel. I have wonderful news.'

As he approached, Charlotte began to wonder who was slapped with the most pancake – Maria Handley with her normal theatrical overdose, Sister Verity with her pit-plugging skin cover or Hector. Hector had not managed to stop at a matt base but had felt obliged to define his eyebrows and eyelashes with brown mascara. The result was Marlene Dietrich at her most artificial. His skin tones, blond hair and facial features each seemed to have originated on a different colour palette. Or planet. Charlotte was not inspired by the prospect of wonderful news.

'We're going to start just a few minutes late. Joining the ladies and gentlemen of the trade press will be a camera crew from L!VE TV.'

Charlotte gasped.

'Who are they?' asked Maria. She was already in her front-row seat awaiting her client's arrival, miffed that Hector Quigley would do all of today's talking. She herself was mentioned nowhere in any of the handout literature.

'Well might you ask. They are a cable television company which covers parties and press launches of events of considerable interest in central London.'

'They'll never show it,' said Charlotte. 'It's not big enough.'

Maria seemed to agree. 'We're only telling the trade press about the Verity Tampons campaign. And that the Sister Verity character is going to do a regional tour of schools.'

'Oh, but they will show it. They're going live. We've struck lucky. Naomi Campbell failed to show at the Fashion Café and something got cancelled at Planet Hollywood. Marsha tells me there is nothing happening at Wembley either and they have to fill a live half-hour right now. So it's better than nothing for them and absolutely fabulous for us. I expect my own reputation as a strong media performer has not escaped them. Make sure we get a copy of the tape and circulate it to all exisiting and potential clients. It will make us look big. More importantly, it will make me look big which, in fact, I am. Brilliant. Another masterstroke from the foundry of invention. Write that down somebody. So. Let the press in. Let the games commence.'

Maria and Charlotte went to the door and greeted the journalists who had been stuffing themselves in the buffet, the only reason they had been fagged to come. They would get this done in five minutes surely, cribbing off the handouts Maria and Charlotte had spent two nights rewriting.

The L!VE TV team of three people arrived and ran in quickly, a camera man, an interviewer doing her own sound and a teenager in checked shirt left untucked over torn jeans. They were by a very long way the three least smart people in the glamorous HQ theatre. The boy ran to the yellow curtains drawn over the window and signalled to the outside broadcast satellite van in the street below. With everyone assembled, Charlotte was aware that she had not seen Daniel come upstairs with the rest from lunch. But now he rushed into the room. He made straight for the nun. On the table in front of her on the dais he placed a plastic cup and two small miniatures of brandy. Sister Verity unscrewed the cap off the first one and, ignoring the cup, plunged the bottle onto her upturned lips. Daniel dropped down beside Charlotte.

'What the hell d'you think you're playing at?' she whispered angrily.

'Her request. To steady her nerves.'

'She doesn't suffer from nerves. Haven't you noticed?'

'Steady her hands then.'

'She's already knocked back six glasses of wine up here while we were at the lunch.'

Daniel clutched his forehead pretending shock. 'Now you bleedin' tell me.'

'*Shh*!' Maria glared, her finger at her fuchsia lips. Daniel mouthed an unseen fuck off at the back of her big hair.

'Stand by everybody,' shouted the boy. He was sweating profusely. He seemed nervous. 'Quiet, please. There's a studio programme going out and they'll be cutting in and out of here with links and things, but you lot won't hear nothing. OK. And counting. Four, three, two, one, action.'

Like the puffed-up professional he was, Hector lost no time in beginning his slide show with a prolonged account of his own career highs and the history of HQ. Charlotte was fascinated. She learnt more in the next quarter of an hour about the company than she had since she had turned up a few weeks back. She could hardly believe it was being broadcast even if it was only on L!VE TV. In fact, little of it was, but they were not to know. It was time for the question and answer session.

'Are you a real nun or an actress?' asked the L!VE TV interviewer, a beautiful black girl in micro-skirt and legs that lasted for ever.

At the beginning of a big career, that one, thought Charlotte. She smiled. She had anticipated the first question correctly and had rehearsed the answer with Sister Verity. Discreetly she made the thumbs up gesture to the nun. Irritatingly, Sister Verity gave her a great big thumbs up gesture back, which sent Daniel into shoulder-heaving sniggers. And the retail and marketing trade press people, who were no fools either.

'I am a real nun. Sister Verity is not my real name but I am a real sister of charity from Belfast, happy to do practical work of information and education in the wider community.'

'And why is a nun representing a tampon brand? Isn't it just a gimmick?' The interviewer ran forward and held her microphone up to Hector, unnecessarily for a man who boomed in quadraphonic sound.

'It is not a gimmick,' assured Hector from his voice of God speakers. 'We thought that people, particularly young people, girls anyway, would like to write to a nun with their problems and perceptions about periods. And indeed all our research shows this is the right thing to do and we hope and believe it will be very successful. Our track record is as Britain's fastest-growing agency. Our work stands eyeball to eyeball with the people.'

'But isn't it all rather commercial for the Catholic Church?'

'Sister Verity is not representing the brand. There is a distinction. She will not be in the advertising. You can see from the commercials that I have shown you today that she is not.'

'So what will she be doing exactly?' The interviewer moved the microphone across to the nun's side of the table. From the front row of the gathered press Charlotte made a stop signal with the flat palm of her hand, but Hector had already grabbed the microphone and pulled it back. He would decide when he had nothing left to say, not some bloody woman from L!VE TV.

'Sister Verity is a spokeswoman for some of our related marketing activities which are of an educational nature for the youngest section of our target audience. She is a morally responsible figure who can be sympathetic to the young teenage girl starting her periods while being at the same time a figure of reassurance to concerned mothers. One of the characteristics of the usage of tampons is that young girls are keen to start as soon as possible while their mothers are reluctant to allow it. They have a thing about it, naturally, and wish to delay the inevitable switch from sanitary towels to tampons. We know this from our research.'

While Hector had been speaking Sister Verity had been nodding vigorously so much that the camera man from L!VE TV had been unable to decide who made the better picture, the showman or the nun, such a visual treat were they both.

Sister Verity stopped nodding and, to Charlotte's concern, left the script.

'It's a little bit like sex, isn't it?' she said.

Charlotte's heart leapt. Her concern ran to panic. While Hector arched an eyebrow – with difficulty since his forehead lift had left him immobilised below his hairline – the nun took a swipe from the second miniature bottle of brandy. At the same time, the first bottle, lying empty on its side, noisily rolled across the tabletop, noticeably underscoring her reliance on drink. The camera followed its drop onto the carpet and cut back.

'I don't understand,' said the interviewer. She placed her microphone to Sister Verity's chin.

'What? And you a black woman, too? Of course you understand. Just look at the legs you're showing off there. Young girls are keen to learn as much about sex as soon as they can and their mothers are keen to keep it from them. That's the big challenge of parenthood. You hide from your children the facts of life for as long as you can. They hide from you the fact that they already know.'

'And do you think that getting into tampons as a teenager is related to early sexual activity? I mean that's a big problem in this country, teenage pregnancy.'

Charlotte glared at Sister Verity and made as prominent a thumbs down gesture as possible. The nun was to answer no. The clients were fidgety enough already. But Sister Verity's confidence was growing by the second. She loved the attention and had forgotten all about Charlotte and, in her Northern Irish brogue, rose tremendously to the interviewer's challenge.

'Look. The Roman Catholic church was always of the disposition that once a virgin stuffed a tampon inside her young, untrammelled body what was going up there next? A penis, no doubt. That was what was on the Pope's mind. A penis.'

Now Hector was as alarmed as Charlotte. He moved swiftly, chortling to cover the crisis.

'Well, ladies and gentleman, I think that brings our question and answer session to an end.'

'I'm sorry,' said the interviewer. 'I didn't understand Sister Verity's point about the Pope having a penis on his mind? Could you flesh that out for me—'

'—as the actress said to the cardinal.' Sister Verity, who had shown no talent for it previously, was suddenly exhibiting a strong line in spontaneous repartee. 'Well, where would you expect the Pope to have a penis? Hah! That's a cracker. Now I'm not talking about the present day Pontiff, mind you. I'm not being disrespectful. I'm talking about history. The 1930s. You see that's when tampons were invented and they were thought by the more old-fashioned Catholics to be the spawn of the devil himself. And you wouldn't want the virgins of Ireland inserting into their vaginas the spawn of the devil, cardboard applicator or no, would you? That's the way I was brought up and terrible it was too. But times have changed. We are all modern now. We have to be progressive. Even nuns. Our habits are shorter and we show our legs these days, though not as much as you are showing, m'dear. If you don't mind me pointing it out, I can virtually hear the snap of elastic on your black thighs. We show our practical side more too. If the young girls want internal protection, then so be it. And my job is to tell their mothers that nothing dreadful or dirty or otherwise will come of it.'

As Hector wound down and Maria and Daniel saw the press out, Charlotte sighed with relief. Sister Verity had drifted off the script but had had enough command of the English language and her senses to come round before things got too out of hand. Charlotte put it down to nerves, the drink and the Irish in her. They were all a bit like that in Ireland were they not, although she had thought the Northern Irish were meant to have less of the blarney about them. Sister Verity was a Roman Catholic and that had its problems in Northern Ireland and perhaps there was a publicity angle in that that could be explored to the benefit of the brand. She would mention this to the client at their next meeting.

'Well. I thought that all went rather splendidly,' said Hector, no longer miked and only slightly less intimidating.

'Bleeding marvellous, if you ask me,' said Daniel. 'Well done, Hector. Well done Sister Verity. Well done Charlotte.'

Charlotte was not so sure. She was turning into a worrier.

In her Paddington office, Karen Myhill flicked the remote control to off. L!VE TV. What level would they stoop to next? But in her search for afternoon tips and tricks Karen had spotted something. A nun who could chat on social issues and whose moral and social advice tripped easily off the tongue. It had never been done before. It had a regional accent. It had a gimmick. It had audience appeal. It had publicity value. The nun was not camera shy. She was a TV natural. She was a TV treasure. It was timeless. It was cheap. It was bang on brief. She jumped up from her seat and, scrunching up her latest proposal in her hand, threw it at the wastepaper basket. It missed. She leapt to the door and called.

'Duncan! Duncan come in here will you. I have an idea and I think Martin Fox will love it.'

30

Briony Linden had sat and listened patiently for what seemed an eternity. Now she saw her chance to interrupt Jamie Hirst's flow. His uncharacteristic pause also provided an opportunity to plead her own case in front of Martin Fox.

'Jamie, it may surprise you to hear that I'm on your side.'

'It doesn't surprise me.'

'Well it surprises me because I don't usually feel I am. I agree with everything you've said. Or most of what you've said. Yes, *Megabrek* is our only daily programme outside of news. Yes, it is crucial for our advertising revenue. Yes it does provide twenty per cent, or something like that, of our total income. Yes it is operating in one of the healthiest and most creative sectors and the most dangerous. Yes, the non-core audience does have to be sustained by constant marketing as well as on-air promotion. That's the gist of what you're saying and I agree with all of that. But I'm only the head of marketing. I'm not the financial director.'

'Only!'

'Yes, only, I'm afraid. My budget is to be cut right back in the next year and the bulk of the spend is to go on the afternoon launch. The board hasn't bought my argument that I need additional monies or that at least I should have executive control of where those monies are spent. I'm out on a limb as much as you are. God, I wish I could have a cigarette just once in this fucking building.'

'I thought you liked our architecture,' said Martin, chuckling.

'It wasn't the architecture I had in mind. It was the old men who run this place. It's supposed to be a TV station, for God's sake. The only other place I can think of like this is my daughters' school. Next thing they'll hire the headmistress to stomp in and check we've all got clean fingernails and done last night's homework.'

'Not everyone here does their homework like you, Briony,' said Martin. 'Well, you two. Why do I feel you're ganging up on me? All I can say, Jamie, is that you know that we know how big *Megabrek* is to us. There is no way The Station will allow a ratings slippage. But you know as well as I do that we have given you the biggest budget of any show of this sort in the history of non-terrestrial television and that you are easily talented enough to make it work without Briony's box of tricks. Your producers will just have to keep on their toes and continue to be more inventive than the ones at GMTV or *The Big Breakfast*. They will be, don't look so sad. What I am prepared to do is to talk to the financial director and to Michael Farnham. We will look at the renewal contract – which like everything else in this business no one has signed yet despite the first one having expired – and see if there is a way in which we can allow you to redeploy production monies into programme-related activities.'

'Huh. Martin, I've heard that one before. What you mean is that we can get the ad spend out of the programme budget. I want additional money, extra money.'

'It's only a suggestion. I will arrange for Michael to give you clearance to do it. If you don't want to do it then you don't have to. But at least this way you have a reserve on which to draw. There. That's as far as we can go today. The thing about *Megabrek* is that it is holding up.'

'I'm glad you think so.'

'I do. Don't be so self-critical.'

'I didn't think it was myself I was criticising.'

'Ouch. Look. Unlike the competitors, your show does not have an over-reliance on name presenters or set pieces. It's a constant daily invention. And you are still the only company to use interactivity well, let alone stretch it to its limits. So you didn't get the UK TV Awards nomination this year. That's only because you don't fit into any award category.'

Briony checked her watch.

'Are we through, boys?'

Jamie turned to her but was actually addressing Martin.

'I have some thoughts on the afternoon for you.'

'Ooh,' said Briony. 'I suppose that means you'll want me out of the room.'

'No, stay Briony. There's no reason why you shouldn't hear this. Jamie'll only tell you in some wine bar later.'

'I think you'll find wine bars are a bit 1980s, Martin,' laughed Jamie.

'Good God. Are they really? So where do you slope off to? Not some ghastly gym and tonic establishment.'

'That's me just behind Princess Di at the Harbour Club in the photographs,' joked Briony. 'We don't go anywhere. I've no idea why you think Jamie confides in me. He's never taken me for a drink.'

'I will after this meeting.'

'You're on.'

'Good. Well, look. How shall I start? Saturn Productions has mushroomed since you gave us *Megabrek* and we've never sat down and told you what's been happening to the company.'

'I read *Broadcast*,' said Martin.

'So you'll know five per cent of what's happening three weeks after it happened.'

'Ouch. Again.'

'Saturn is the fastest-growing and now the largest of the real independent companies. Companies like Grundy and Action Time are owned by big financial organisations – we're not in that league but they're not in ours for invention. In our class we're the largest. But we're still young and lean. The average

age of our employees is twenty-four. We have a very successful radio arm and are pitching for franchises in our own right.'

'Really. Are you intending to get your own cable station one of these days?'

'One of these days.'

'Need a marketing director by any chance? I have experience!'

Jamie smiled. 'As well as a marketing department, we have a rights and formats sales team. Where we can't sell our own shows into other territories we've been selling our formats but with a controlling interest. We also sell some of the vignette items from *Megabrek* into other markets. The English speaking ones.'

'Do you?' asked Briony.'I thought the Americans took nothing from us.'

'Not necessarily. In our VT items we use no presenters in vision. We just lift off the English language voiceover and sell the film on with a written text. The buyer simply rerecords it into their own accent or has it translated, redubbed and dropped into their own show.'

'You little bugger,' said Martin. 'You're coining it in from material we own.'

'I own it,' said Jamie. 'Check with Michael Farnham.'

'I will. I'll ring his neck.'

'It's standard business terms.'

'I know. So where is all this leading to?'

'I'm just updating you on how sophisticated our operation has become. Compared to, say, other leading companies. So-called. Like, for example, Myhill Productions.'

'Funny how her name aways springs up, isn't it Jamie?'

'I'm her keenest rival.'

'You've left her well behind. In size and turnover anyway.'

'We have.'

'But you can't drop the rivalry, can you?'

'I wouldn't want to spoil your fun. Or hers.'

'You enjoy the jousting as much as any of us. Well, the afternoon is where you have to slug it out this round.'

Jamie reached into his soft leather bag and slipped out a multicoloured document. Briony spotted the word *Snakatak* emblazoned across the cover as it flew onto Martin's desk.

It landed with a soft pat. Martin picked it up and laughed appreciatively at the title. Jamie made a low-key pitch.

'I'll leave that with you as a taster of the sort of thing you could expect from us. We've done a lot of research. No one knows your audience better than us because no other company has broadcast so many hours for The Station. No one else has our scale of production in interactive television. Only we can provide quality programming at a truly effective cost per hour. We have provisional sponsorhip deals in place already.'

'You do?'

'Really?' asked Briony.

'Yup.'

'Who with? Not Proctor and Gamble, I hope.'

'I can't tell you at this stage.'

'There's a surprise.'

'I hope that's not a conflict of interest,' said Martin.

'Why should it be?'

'Well, like everyone else we like to keep our sources of financing and editorial completely separate. I don't want to find out that my afternoon show has turned into some secret subliminal campaign for acne lotion or something.'

'Check it out with Michael Farnham. He understands the rules better than anyone. Sponsorship deals are perfectly acceptable. Saturn Productions never puts a foot wrong.'

'That's what I'm afraid of,' said Martin to Briony after Jamie had left.

'Martin, I know it's not my area but you can't give Saturn Productions the daily afternoon show as well as the morning one. They'll have complete control of hours and hours of our daily schedule and a third of our advertising revenue. They'll have such a grip on us. The tail will be wagging the dog.'

'I know. But I also have to think about the editorial issues. He produces the best material. I can rely on Saturn Productions to come up with the goods. Karen Myhill is clever but she has a streak of unreliability. He's way ahead of the rest of the pack. I can't just dish out all the work "fairly". Programme makers seeem to think they have a God-given right to get a commission when it's their "turn". Don't they understand its dog eat dog out there?'

'Why is Jamie so obsessed with Karen Myhill?'

'Because he's vain. Because she's good. She's not in his league in terms of turnover of money, but she's easily in his league in terms of turnover of ideas.'

'And people, I hear. When I last saw Duncan Cairns he was telling me how fast the staff move on.'

'They do at Saturn too. I can tell you. It's the nature of the business.'

'She's awfully difficult to work with, apparently.'

'I worked for Karen for years at Trafalgar Television and it did me no harm. So did Jamie, for that matter.'

'Well, it's up to your judgement but I think if we give the afternoon show to Saturn they'll have us stitched up.'

'Maybe. Maybe not. But Jamie Hirst is a keen operator. No one is going to run rings round Saturn.'

'Ouch,' said Briony.

31

'I never know whether you're meant to kiss a lesbian hello or not.'

Duncan sat down and smiled at Lesley. Her hair and her face looked flatter under the high level of lighting. She was somewhat annoyed by his remark but she took it with good humour. She liked Duncan. After all that was why she had asked him to rendezvous with her at Yo! Sushi in Poland Street.

'We're not green-headed monsters from Mars, you know.'

'I didn't mean it that way. This place is amazing.'

'Fun, isn't it?'

The tables of the modernist-minimalist sushi bar were

arranged around a thin, winding conveyor belt which ran at chin height the length and breadth of the restaurant. On it, a never-ending supply of tiny saucers of raw fish and rice dishes topped with plastic domes wobbled past, their trundling constancy reminiscent of glass bottles in a processing factory. It was all very concrete meets plastic, fluorescence meets neon, Tokyo meets Soho. It was not very Duncan Cairns. Still, it was fun. Lesley reached out and plucked a couple of bite-sized plates off the supply line. Duncan followed suit.

'It's just that nowadays,' he said, 'there are so many right and wrong ways of doing things. If you're gay yourself you're not allowed the excuse of not knowing the etiquette. But I don't know. I don't read *Gay Times* or the *Pink Paper* and I don't go to gay clubs. Well hardly ever.'

'I know what you mean. Society is changing at such breakneck speed it's difficult even for us metropolitan queers to keep abreast of modern manners.'

Duncan smarted at the phrase. He used his chopsticks to dip a piece of raw salmon into its dark brown sauce. A mouthful later and he was halfway through his meal.

'I can't think,' continued Lesley, 'of a married white straight couple I know with two children where the father goes to work in an office and the mother bakes at home. Yet that's what everyone still thinks is normal.'

'I'd say they were an extinct species. Although it's how I was brought up.'

'In Scotland? Don't they have a very good education system up there? Where are you from?'

'Edinburgh.'

'My absolute favourite city. Whereabouts?'

'D'you know it?'

'A bit. I've done market research forays around the whole country at some time or another. Edinburgh is so beautiful. They have the highest standard of living in the UK in Edinburgh. They spend more hours than any other group of people in art galleries and more money on lined curtains than anyone outside London. And they eat soup every day. Even when it's hot.'

'I can't say I do.'

'I bet you did once.'

'Hmm . . .' Duncan smiled. 'Maybe.'

From the corner of his eye he saw a stainless steel robot trolley slowly self-propelling across the floor past the side of their table. On it were bottles of Japanese beer and saki, thermos flasks and small porcelain teacups. He snatched a bottle of beer and a large glass. Before the trolley was gone for good Lesley reached out and grabbed herself a bottle too. She dispensed with the glass.

'I've spent many a happy year at the festival,' she said.

'Have you? The Edinburgh Festival?'

'That's the one. I've appeared on the fringe.'

'That wasn't you I saw in *Lesbian Leather Bikers Butch it up in Hell*?'

'No. I'm completely ashamed to say I was the third nun in the disco version of *The Sound of Music*. It was the end of the seventies. Maria von Trapp was a black girl with an electric guitar. The children were a rainbow family of adopted Vietnamesy refugees. We got very good reviews actually.'

'Whomever from?'

'Most Edinburgh people are meant to hate the festival.'

'That's because they turn up for that nice *Sound of Music* and get black lesbians and rainbow politics.'

'Where in Edinburgh are you from?'

'The New Town.'

'Ah. Georgian homes to die for. Which street?'

'I was born in Moray Place. We moved to Great King Street later.'

'Isn't that where Walter Scott and Robert Louis Stevenson lived?'

'Sort of. Ish. Not together, of course, and not in my time.'

'Do you go home much?'

'Not as much as I should.'

'Your parents are still living?'

'You can't stop interviewing me, can you? You asked me that question the last time.'

'Sorry. I do it for a living. And do you prefer full fat or low calorie Hellmann's mayonnaise, bearing in mind that a boy from Moray Place wouldn't know what Salad Cream was. See. I can't help myself. '

'That's a remarkably good joke. For a lesbian. Relax. You're not at work now.' He picked a piece of moist ginger from a small bowl on the table and bit into it. 'Where is Sarah? Is she coming?'

'No. I'm allowed out on my own.'

'I just thought . . .'

'What?'

'Well. Look. You're not being incredibly subtle, are you?'

'Damn. And me a lesbian too.'

'You want to check me out about you two having a baby, don't you?'

'I came on that strong?'

''Fraid so.'

'Well. Are you up for it?'

'Unfortunate use of words.'

Lesley laughed. 'What do you think?'

'I don't know what to think. Persuade me.'

'Well, Sarah and I have discussed it. We would like to have two children.'

Duncan looked surprised.'Two?'

'Yes. One each.'

Duncan looked alarmed. 'I don't know if I could manage two.'

Lesley laughed. 'Sarah is going to have hers first. It suits us job-wise to do that. Then in a couple of years I'll have mine. By a different father.'

'A different father?'

'Yes. Of course.'

'Why "of course"?'

'Well it may not seem obvious to you but we have . . . well . . . like a shopping list of requirements for each of the fathers.' She went on while Duncan stood up and grabbed a few more saucers from the miniature railway line. 'One of them is that the father of each of our babies should look as much like our partner as possible. So Sarah and I are considering you because she thinks you look like me. I do too.'

He sat back down with a thud. 'I look like you?'

'Well, similarish. Same colouring, same shape of face, same sort of interests.'

'Same broad shoulders and manly voice.'

'Be serious!'

'I am. I'm not following you.'

'Well, this way, our first baby will be Sarah's genetically but there is a chance that it will look quite like me too and perhaps inherit from you some personality traits or interests that could have come from me. We want our two children to reflect both of us as much as possible. D'you understand?'

'Sort of.'

'You don't like being told you look like me, is that it?'

'Like any woman.'

'Like a lesbian.'

'Particularly a lesbian.'

'Anyway, we both liked your looks and your intelligence and I've checked out your medical and educational and personal history and as long as you haven't got, you know, the big A, then you move up to the top of our shortlist. As long as you want to do it.'

'And what is it that I have to do, exactly?'

'I'm getting there. Have you discussed this with Michael?'

'He's quite keen on the idea.' Duncan rarely lied but when he did he did it properly, huge big ones, laced with spades of genuine sincerity. If he'd learnt one thing in his years in advertising it was how to do that.

'Good. He's not offended we haven't asked him?'

'You could ask him next time round.'

'He doesn't look like Sarah.'

'I forgot about that bit.'

'Well the truth is, no offence, but if I have a boy I don't want a baby that's going to grow up bald with hairy arms. And he's a South African by birth and I certainly don't want their genes in my family thank you very much.'

'But apart from that you think he's completely gorgeous.'

'Sorry. I didn't mean to be rude.'

'The baldness gene, as I understand it, is passed onto you from your mother's side. If you don't want a bald baby, check out your mother.'

'Mine's not bald.'

'Then you're completely safe.'

'I'm sorry. I didn't mean to be rude about your boyfriend, but we need to be really honest with each other. Bringing a child into the world is an incredibly important thing and these children will have to face a hostile society.'

'Maybe. Maybe not. By the time they grow up it'll have changed out of all recognition again. It's getting more and more liberal. Too liberal for me actually. I'm not sure *I* approve.'

'Well, whatever happens, we want to have two kids who are intelligent, attractive, equipped for life with the best genes possible.'

'Didn't Adolf Hitler have a similar programme?'

'That's unfair. His wasn't run by lesbians.'

'That we know of. They'd have looked great in those boots, mind you.'

'Don't tell Paul McCarthy. It'll get him going.'

They laughed. Duncan was shocked by the genetic engineering but flattered to be selected and to receive the attention. He liked the professionalism of the whole thing. He didn't have too much time for disorganisation.

'So, well that's it, really. You need to come and meet Sarah. We have one final stage in mind.'

'I was intending to deliver the goods bottled. Not on draught.'

Lesley laughed. 'You could send it round on one of these automatic robot trolleys. No. I mean before that. A final interview.'

'You mean I haven't got the job?'

'Well, we thought it was better that I did the negotiating because although it's very personal for me it's obviously even more personal for her and I thought she should not get involved in case things don't work out between us or someone changes their mind later and there's a tussle over the child. I mean I know with you there won't be but . . . well, it just makes it easier in the future if there's an intermediary. We felt.'

'What do you want me to do?'

'Oh, yes. Well. Look.' She dug in her bag. She produced something Duncan had never seen before. It was a lilac box.

'What's that?'

'It's a Verity Ovulation Self-Predictor Home Test Kit. It's barely on the market yet. They haven't launched it. I read about it in *Chemist and Druggist* at work and ordered it as a trade sample.'

Duncan checked out their fellow diners. He was surprised she had taken it out in a restaurant. He recalled his meeting with Alan Joling who had mentioned the launch. 'I recognise the name Verity. They make tampons.'

'They make these too. It's like a pregnancy test thing. You use it to work out when you are ovulating and therefore at your most likely to conceive. Sarah will use this and then we'll invite you round to do your bit. I could use this on myself and it would give just as accurate a reading.' She stood up and helped herself to the conveyor belt once more. She did repeats for Duncan too. 'Sarah's and my periods have been bang in rhythm for years. That happens to women who live together. And work together. It was like that at Greenham Common. Of course in the modern workplace half the woman are on the pill, which buggers things up. But we don't need to be for obvious reasons.'

'And what will you expect me to do? I mean are you . . . you know . . . intending to be in the room at the same time?'

Lesley laughed.

'Eeeugh. No! You can bring Michael round if you so wish. You do it into a vessel, syringe it up, give us a call.'

'A vessel.'

'We've got a sherry glass. Will that do?'

'I'd rather it was champagne. We might as well do it in style.'

'We'll buy one for you then. I'll rush it through and whack it up Sarah. It'll be at exactly the right moment for conception. Just in case, we'll do it three days on the trot. We have friends who did it this way. It works. It's ironic but gay people are strangely better at conceiving than breeders.'

'I think it would mollify Michael if he were there.'

'Mollify?'

'He won't have a problem with it but it might make him feel more a part of things if he were there.'

'Well, if you need him. Can't say we mind either way. It's nothing to do with him.'

Duncan felt awkward that Lesley had said that. He and Michael would bring up the baby together on their side, just as the girls were planning to do on theirs. But he left it. He needed to bring Michael on-side before he went any further.

'So? Anything else?'

'Not just now. Well, just one thing.'

'What?'

'You need to have the AIDS test and bring the result written down so we have proof.'

'That's all right.'

'You don't mind having one done?'

'You can have them done anonymously.'

'It can't be anonymous.'

'I mean under a false name. So it doesn't affect your medical records.'

'It can't be under a false name.'

'It can. You can get it done. I know people who have.'

'How will Sarah and I know that it's your result if it hasn't got your name on it?'

'Do you think I would lie about such a thing?'

'No. But we don't know you very well and we don't know your past and . . . well, we can sort something out. Sarah will want proof. I would too.'

'I understand,' said Duncan. He eyed up the conveyor belt of food again. Sushi was a change, but it was unsatisfying. Suddenly, the stream of plastic domes jammed abruptly. It lurched forward again, but this time irregularly, and saucer began to pile upon saucer upon saucer, a film of falling dominoes played in reverse.

'*Stop! Stop! Stop!*' The staff behind the central bar area yelled into the kitchen to turn the conveyor belt off. The amused diners called out too and tried to encourage the chaos. Duncan and Lesley joined in. The conveyor belt halted. Somebody had switched it off. With the food line at rest the restaurant seemed more prosaic and more peaceful.

Duncan gave Lesley a reassuring nod. 'We can work something out.'

32

'Michael, have you got five minutes?'

'Is this Briony?'

'You mean you don't recognise my voice? Meet me in reception in two.'

'Why?'

'Surprise. Just do.'

When Michael arrived in the reception that looked out over King's Cross he saw Briony standing on the shallow front door steps chatting to Martin Fox. She was smoking. What are they up to? he thought.

'Your guess is as good as mine,' said Martin when Michael came out and the Head of Programmes caught his expression. 'Perhaps Briony has discovered a great tobacconist's she wants us to endorse.'

'Hah, hah. I think it's just interesting that you two don't know, considering.'

'Don't know what?' asked Michael.

'You'll find out soon enough.'

Briony led them around the corner and onto Euston Road. The massed traffic of lorries, vans, buses and motor bikes lined up in dirty, noisy lanes like light industry. The shops were tatty. On the sides of bare brick walls the grime was covered only by advertising hoardings whose contents had been scraped away layer upon layer leaving the sad goodbye of a thousand commercial quips on faded paper. Briony marched with the depressed crowd of commuters making their way into the rail terminus. The plain brick of the old handsome station was spoiled by 1970s thoughtless additions of porch roofs and a blistering rash of directional and commercial signage. She led the two bemused men to the head of the Underground station. She took one last deep puff of her Camel Light cigarette and dropped it to the ground, where she flattened it underfoot. She stepped onto the down escalator.

'I'm not going down there,' Michael protested. 'I haven't been on public transport for donkey's years.'

'Don't be so namby-pamby,' said Martin, following Briony. 'It'll do you a power of good.'

'You use the tube, do you?' asked Briony over her shoulder, through her near-white curls.

'Occasionally I do.'

She looked up from a few steps beneath him and smirked.

'I do,' protested Martin.

Michael reluctantly took the escalator down with Martin. The two men caught up with Briony at the automatic ticket machines. She snapped her fingers at them over her shoulder while she typed in the cheapest destination she could find.

'What?' asked Martin.

'It isn't free, you know. The plebs have to pay,' said Briony again over her shoulder. Martin handed her the coins.

'Where do you think you're taking us? I have to be back in the office in two minutes. I'm not coming.'

'We're not going anywhere.'

'Then why are you buying tickets?'

'Just to get us onto the platform. There.' She collected the last of the three pink tickets from the mouth of the machine, turned inside the huddle the two men were making and, with a wink, pushed them aside.

The queen bee led her two drones to the ticket barrier, where she inserted the tickets and pushed first Martin and then Michael ahead of her through the turnstile. She caught them up as they climbed onto the escalator taking them down to the Northern Line.

'I hate the Northern Line,' confessed Martin. 'It's the black one.'

'Where does it go? Brixton?' asked Michael.

'Spot the South African. I didn't mean it was the one for black people. I meant it was the one which is black on the map. I always liked the yellow one as a child because it went round in a circle.'

'Nothing changes then,' joked Michael. And he was about to

laugh but his mouth opened in surprise instead. 'How did that get there?'

Ahead of them, as the escalators fell steeply, where the ceiling lowered was a huge 96-sheet poster. It was orange and yellow and red and blue and every other colour. In a Roy Lichtenstein cartoon design in 'Kerpow' and 'Wham' type writing was printed the word Snakatak. Smaller and more conservatively, the words 'See it every afternoon next season only on The Station', appeared at the foot.

'What sort of a joke is this, Briony?' asked Martin, annoyed. The poster was getting larger as they were getting nearer.

'I thought I might ask you that. Only on the way here I realised you knew nothing about it.'

'You've jumped the gun. I don't know what you think you're playing at. I haven't commissioned this show.'

The poster was even huger now. They were almost right underneath it.

'I didn't do this. You know I wouldn't dare have a poster put up for something that hasn't been commissioned.'

'You did last year.' Martin strained his neck as they passed the critical point and entered the tubey bit of the tunnel, leaving the poster behind them.

'That was a one-off research poster for *Basket Case*. And that *had* been commissioned. I ran it as a test to prove the advertising worked. But this has nothing to do with me. This is Jamie Hirst's doing.'

Martin fumed. 'Bugger him.'

'He should be so lucky,' said Michael.

'Honestly. If this is meant to impress me it hasn't worked,' Martin blasted. 'I've never seen such wallowing in one own's personal vanity. Excuse me.' He ran to the bottom of the moving escalator down the side of the column of bored commuters. If they had seen it they didn't look as if they were hurrying home to catch *Snakatak* on TV. Not that they could, of course.

Briony and Michael stood into the side to let people past and took the ride on the moving stairs. Meanwhile Martin was hoofing it up the sister escalator riding in the reverse direction. Michael waved from his side. Martin tutted unheard. He could see Michael and Briony laughing. It probably had not occurred to either of them that their programme strategy for the next season, at least, if not the actual execution, was plastered forty feet across the whole of the London bloody Underground.

By the time Michael and Briony had reached the top of the up escalator Martin had calmed down. He was already into the middle of his opening sentence by the time they were within earshot.

'What's it meant to mean? Who's it meant to appeal to? It looks like a cartoon.'

'I'd like to know how Saturn Productions got someone to print a one-off poster for them,' said Briony. 'I assume it didn't cost them a fortune.'

'I wouldn't assume that for a moment.'

'You have to hand it to Jamie,' said Michael. 'It's an incredibly clever thing to do.'

'It's an incredibly stupid thing to do,' said Martin. 'I suppose we're meant to see it and go "Wow, they're so clever those Saturn boys." But I don't use the tube, so how would I see it?'

'But you are seeing it,' said Michael. 'So it's worked.'

'It wouldn't have if Briony hadn't spotted it.'

'I didn't. A secretary rang my secretary to say that a friend of hers had seen it earlier in the day. Half the office is talking about it and saying isn't it brilliant that Saturn have got the afternoon show.'

'God,' said Martin.

'Apparently there were photographers down here earlier on.'

'Jesus, that's all we need.' Martin turned to Michael. 'Sue anybody who prints anything.'

'They'll have been from Jamie's PR company,' said Briony. 'That's how he'll spread the word.'

'I don't understand the strategy,' said Martin. He was baffled.

Briony explained. 'He's trying to build up a head of steam for *Snakatak*. He's trying to get it talked about in the business so positively that you come under pressure to commission it. He's trying to make it inevitable.'

'Is he now?'

'It's called a whispering campaign.'

'Whispering campaign? Jesus. I can't wait to hear him shout it from the bloody rooftops!'

'Well, I admire his spunk,' said Briony. 'Don't you, Michael?'

'I think I'd rather not answer that question on the grounds I might incriminate myself.'

'Well, I've a good mind not to commission it now just to be spiteful,' said Martin as the TV triumvirate walked back to the turnstiles. 'Why can't we go back to the good old days when people just mailed in their ideas. Now you get a whole song and dance and publicity shuffle built around no idea in the first place. Do programme makers honestly think that sort of thing convinces me?'

'I think it shows application and enthusiasm and willing,' said Briony. '*Snakatak* is a good idea. You said so yourself.'

'I did? Now that's a good idea!' Martin was looking at a poster for Hennes and Mauritz. In it, a gorgeous black girl with hugely unwholesome hemispherical breasts modelled a skimpy bikini in an animal print. She was pouting suggestively. 'Look at the size of her tits.'

'I don't need to,' said Briony. 'I already noticed.'

'I didn't,' said Michael, catching up with them.

Briony stopped in front of the poster and lit up another Camel Light. She examined the model. 'I wish I had shares in silicon,' she joked, but the men had moved on. They made their way back to the office side by side by side in silence.

33

'Switched on your voice mail?' Daniel was mocking her in the way her mother ran through her checklist before Charlotte was ever allowed to do anything.

'God. Why do I have to do it all myself?' she retorted, turning back from the door of her office. 'When I came into the business an account director had a fleet of staff and a PA to put everything into their hands. Now I'm one myself all I seem to have ended up with is an answerphone, a personal fax, a crap coffee machine and a simplistic word processor that's got wizzy something or other.'

'Wysiwyg.'

'Wizz off, would you?'

'Don't bother to include me on your list then.'

'You're not a robot.'

'No mechanical parts.' He grinned.

'Watch it, you,' warned Charlotte. She was under so much pressure she could do with an office hug but Daniel was out of bounds. They did not seem capable of putting what had happened between them behind them. 'Where is old hag features?'

'Maria's not coming.'

'She's not coming?'

Charlotte looked pleased but Daniel cautioned her. 'She's not coming because she said this was a meeting between you and your friend. She's put on her citrus suit and taken the press ads down to Verity.'

Charlotte was furious. 'I haven't even seen them!'

'She has.'

'I'm supposed to be the fucking account director. What the hell does she think she's doing?'

'Playing politics.'

'Have you seen them?'

'Nope. She left a message on my desk. I'm surprised she knew where it was. She told Bonzo to tidy it up too.'

'I've had enough of her. This is war.'

'Fab. Can I sell tickets?'

'Daniel, you are to support me.'

'Whoah!'

'I demand it.'

'Well, you were the better shag.'

'*Shhh*!' Charlotte was startled by his indiscretion. 'You'd just better because I have every intention of winning.' She flicked the switch on her telephone to activate the voice mail. The telephone rang immediately. They watched and waited.

'Hello. It's Tuesday and you've reached the voice mail of

Charlotte Reith. I'm in the agency today and will be in meetings periodically. Please leave a message and I'll return your call as soon as I can. Alternatively call Daniel Mainwaring on extension two four three four or press one after the beep to reach the switchboard.'

'Never use the term periodically on a tampon account,' laughed Daniel.

'Shhh.'

'Charlotte. It's Maria.' She was on her carphone. Charlotte made a V sign at the telephone. 'Daniel's not answering his phone either. If you're not in your meeting yet could you fax me something at Verity? They asked me to pop down urgently with the new press ads which I didn't have time to show you. But I've left the creative briefs and the strategy papers and planning things on my desk. Can you fax them so they are there when I arrive. I'll fill you in, of course, when I get back at the end of the day.' The machine clicked off.

'What a shame for her,' said Charlotte, 'that I was in my meeting when she rang. "I didn't have time to tell you. I'll fill you in, of course." Cow.'

Daniel laughed.

'Daniel. Do something for me, please?'

'What?'

'Go into Maria's office and find all the documents she referred to and hide them in your own filing cabinet. Go on. Hurry.'

'Why?'

''Cause she'll ring someone else and get them to fax them. This way no one will be able to find them. We'll put them back before she shows up later.'

'Aye aye, captain!' Daniel grinned and sped off.

Charlotte called after him. 'I'll see you downstairs in the meeting!' She stayed put for one more second to check her lip gloss in her purse mirror and then, hitching up the bust of her lycra top, she headed for the lift. She was pushing her fine blonde hair into its cut when the doors opened onto reception.

'Hello, Duncan,' she said and he rose from his seat and came over and they embraced.

'I hope you don't keep your clients waiting this long.'

'I'm sorry. I'm under so much pressure at the moment.'

'I can't believe *you're* hiring me,' he said.

'Haven't done it yet,' she replied. 'We need a bit of consultancy. We've got great meeting rooms here. Come on in. Would you like coffee or a cold drink?'

Charlotte poured two black coffees from the pot on the sideboard.

'Did I tell you my mother had bought your old company car?'

'You did.'

'She loves having a BMW. She loves putting the roof up and down. I'm really pleased she got it. I negotiated the deal for her with MCN.'

'I would have thought they would have given it to another director rather than sell it off.'

'Everyone in that place has got some humungous car already.'

'What does that tell you about advertising?' Duncan looked round the windowless meeting room.'Hector Quigley does like yellow,' he said referring to the walls.

'It's the agency colour.'

'Don't think much of that.' Duncan pointed at the management statement panel on the wall.

> HQ people interrogate the product.
> We strip away the layers of veneer until we discover the essential truth which lies within.
> That is the secret of great advertising : the revelation of truth.

Duncan grinned back at Hector's studio portrait.

'I know,' said Charlotte. 'Embarrassing isn't it? It works for a certain type of client, though. So, how is life in the fabulous world of television?'

'Fine. Actually, it was a coincidence you calling me for some consultancy. I was about to call you. I think we may have a crossover between projects.'

'Really? What?'

'Tell me first what you want to know.'

'OK. I've had my first meetings with Verity Tampons. Oh, have you seen who's pitching for the pregnancy and ovulation predictor kits launch? Nigel and Serena. If they win it I'll die.

We'll have to have co-ordination meetings. It's too ghastly for words.'

'I wouldn't worry. It'll never happen. Are you pitching for it here?'

'Yep. I just hope we win it. Nothing would give me greater pleasure than beating Nigel and Serena in a straight fight.'

'Who else is pitching?' Duncan already knew the answer. He wondered if Charlotte did too.

'The client is keeping it a secret.' She didn't.

Duncan decided he was not going to use this meeting to pump Charlotte on Alan Josling's behalf. He could tell Alan that HQ and C&B were not onto him. That was enough for now. The door opened and Daniel came in.

'Mission accomplished, boss lady,' he said to Charlotte. She introduced him to Duncan.

'Hi there, matey. ' There were a few pleasantries before Charlotte got down to the meeting for real.

'Verity Tampons have a small budget for the size of brand and the market and its sensitivity to ad spend. One of the things that they are interested in doing is, well, not overt TV advertising. Quite a lot of women reject tampon advertising on TV. One lot see it as coy and clichéd, the other as embarrassing in front of their fourteen-year-old sons. The problem is that there are so many disparate parts of the target audience and so many disparate messages that it's difficult to put out one national TV campaign without just being bland. So, in a nutshell, they are considering putting a little money behind a TV sponsorship test.'

'Do they have a series in mind?'

'Our media department has approached the commercial terrestrial channels and looked at existing series, but what between the broadcasters and the programme makers it's proved difficult to find a high enough profile series that will agree to have a strapline about periods splattered all over the beginning and end of every programme. The series ought to have a strong female theme.'

'What about a holiday show? Lots of shots of women in bikinis on the beach. You can't go swimming with a sanitary towel.'

'We've already discussed it. Holiday series are big-budget shows which require big-budget sponsorship. We haven't got enough money. Also, bikinis and swimming are old hat in the world of internal sanitary protection.'

'And,' said Daniel, 'you get your *double-entendres*. Judith Chalmers saying, "Here I am with my towel on the beach." And she holds up a six-foot white square. You can't cut from that into "She should have used a tampon."'

'How about a movie series?'

'We looked at that on Channel Four. We went off it as soon as we saw *Return of the Mummy's Curse*. Then you get things like arts programmes about Picasso's blue period. It's such a tightrope.'

'Hey,' volunteered Daniel. 'There's a great press ad we could do. A female acrobat walking a tightrope in a snatch-hugging leotard. You can climb to new heights with Verity Tampons.'

'I don't think circus performers are the aspirational role models they used to be,' said Charlotte, but she smiled appreciatively. 'You don't realise how many creative teams are men, Duncan, until you work on a tampon account. I can't believe Maria Handley showed the shark ad to the client.'

'Which one was that?' asked Duncan.

'It was a spoof of the famous poster for the movie *Jaws*. Seventies retro is back in in advertising. It's the woman swimming the crawl with a fin closing in behind her. The line says, "If only she'd used Verity."'

'Sick-o, ' said Daniel.

'It was a stitch-up.'

'The creatives hate Maria,' said Daniel. 'They do things like mount three ads for presentation on an L-shaped board so she has trouble getting through door frames. She puts it down to British inefficiency.'

'She must be daft,' observed Duncan.

'She's American,' said Daniel.

'Half-American,' corrected Charlotte.

'Half-witted, more like.'

'That's enough about her,' said Charlotte. 'The reason we were thinking about hiring you, Duncan, is that Verity want a show they can sponsor. It should be targeted at women and be cheap and cheerful enough for them to be able to afford a three-month trial. When we said we couldn't find a slot for them—'

Daniel sniggered.

'—Daniel there is nothing funny about the word slot – they told us that they'd heard that Proctor and Gamble and Pepsi created their own shows and they wanted us to look into that. So I instantly thought of you to give us consultancy on the rules and regulations and come up with a few formats that we could present to the client. I could pay you fifteen hundred pounds to do, say, a two-page summary of how the system would work and give us, say, three programme ideas. What d'you think?'

Duncan smiled.

'I think . . . I think we need to talk about your nun. What's she called?'

'Sister Verity? How d'you know about her? We're trying to kill her off.'

'Karen Myhill saw your press conference on L!VE TV.'

'God. I'd forgotten about that. I thought no one watched L!VE TV. They told us that themselves.'

'Well it's not quite true. She loved Sister Verity.'

'She's very sweet. But it's my intention to let her wither on the vine. Literally in her case – she drinks. She's all wrong for our brand repositioning.'

'Well, possibly not. Let me fill you in on what I have in mind because I think we could be in business together.'

'Daniel?'

'What?'

'Where's your notebook?'

'Upstairs where I left it. I thought this was just a chat with your old mate here.'

'Well it isn't. Go and get it and take notes.'

'Bunch of arse.'

'It is not a bunch of – that expression. It's an opportunity.'

'It's an opportunity to impress your client,' said Duncan.

'It's an opportunity to run Maria Handley ragged,' said Charlotte.

'We should be very pleased with ourselves.' Serena's hand left the steering wheel and patted the string of pearls and diamonds at her throat.

'We are, old girl. Pleased as punch. What do I do now?'

'Turn left. Are you at the high hawthorn hedge?' Her paint-scraper voice was tinny on the squawk box.

'There are hedgerows everywhere. I thought they were meant to have cut them all down. There was this woman on the radio the other day, bleating on about voles and foxes and those sorts of things. Saying all the hedgerows were being removed and they had nowhere left to live. Obviously she hadn't been to Sussex, the old lesbo. Turning left.'

Nigel and Serena were driving in convoy to Glyndebourne. Exclusive, upmarket, small-scale, jewel-like opera in country house surroundings. Champagne in the formal Italianate gardens before Act One, silver service picnic on the English lawn in the interval. As always, they communicated between their matching maroon Jaguars via their matching hands-off car telephones.

'Have you turned?'

'In my grave, old girl.'

'I can't see you in my rear-view mirror. I don't think you were where I thought you were.'

'Bloody hell.'

'I'm down to thirty-five. Put your foot down and if you haven't caught me in five minutes you'll have to stop and check the map. Isn't the English countryside gorgeous?'

'Too many bloody voles. Shoot the damn things.'

'They couldn't have been voles. Voles are water rats. They don't live in hedgerows. That's what Ratty was in *Wind in the Willows*. He wasn't a rat, at all. He was a vole.'

'Really.' Nigel couldn't have cared less if he was pigeon pie.

'I expect he couldn't call him Voley because he had Moley

and you couldn't have Moley *and* Voley so he called him Ratty,
I suppose.'

'I'll tell you who's bloody ratty right now.'

'Well you weren't looking at those lights. I knew where I was
going. You should have followed me.'

'I was picking up my wallet off the floor. When I slammed on
the brakes it shot out of my jacket pocket.'

'Pay more attention, Nigel.'

'Bugger off,' said Nigel but he forgot that he had the speaker
phone on.

'I heard that. Ah. There you are. I can see you down the hill
and off to the left. You'll catch me on the next bend. Stick closely
with me and I'll lead the way.'

'That'll make a change.'

'I heard that too. There.' She waved in the mirror and Nigel
gave two hoots on the horn behind her. She waved back again.
Now she could see Nigel's mouth in her mirror moving in
lip-synch.

'I hope this is not one of those bloody avant garde things.'

'It's *Arabella* by Richard Strauss. It's supposed to be very
beautiful.'

'Supposed to be. Some fat old bag warbling away about being
a virgin in a foreign language. It strains credibility.'

'No it does not. They are always pretty productions at Glyndebourne. I've been priveliged to come here for many years. Of
course, it's not the same now. The new opera house is very
architectural and all that but it doesn't have the charm of the
old building. But I suppose it means we can bring our clients
and they'll feel it's special but not beyond people of their class.
There's no point taking them out of their depth because they
only resent it.'

'What's in the picnic?'

'No idea. You have the cool boxes?'

'Boxes and boxes of booze, don't worry.'

'Well I do worry because you know what you're like and
don't call it booze. Call it Dom Perignon because clients can
only discern by labels. I know what I asked Margaret to get
for the hamper but she can't be relied on. She doesn't know
Harrod's Food Halls like I do. She can't even tell farmed from

wild salmon. One must be so trapped having to rely on public transport.'

'I'm starving.'

'Well we can't eat until the interval. I asked her to pack lobster for six and—'

'Lobster! I need filling up, woman!'

'I'm switching you off if you're going to complain. There'll be plenty of stuff.'

'There'll be plenty of that pretentious plonky German music. When was Richard Strauss, anyway?'

'Not completely sure. 1940s, I think.'

'Nazi.'

'He wrote *Der Rosenkavalier*. That was mummy's favourite. Poor mummy. Read the programme.'

'I can't do that and drive at the same time.'

'Funny. I thought that's what you *were* doing!'

'Hah bloody hah.'

'You know Nigel, I'm not one to crow but—'

'—but you'll make a rare exception on this occasion.'

'Well, we have fought off very strong competition to bring this into the agency.'

'Such as?'

'Such as Hector Quigley and A.N. Other. Tonight will be an impromptu celebration.'

'Hardly impromptu. It's been in the diary for three months. Sitting there like a skull and crossbones.'

'Well it's a coincidence but it's nice we have something to tell the others about. Brag a little. They need to hear we're doing well so they don't get restless.'

'I wonder who A.N. Other was?'

'Verity will tell us now we've won. Hector didn't know either. I did ask him.'

'You think he'd tell you, old girl?'

'He'd tell me.'

'He would, would he?'

'Don't get jealous.'

'I'm not. You can flirt with him as much as you like. See if I care.'

'JWT I expect.'

'Don't change the subject.'

'Or McCann's or St Luke's or somebody like that. Now we've got Verity Kits, Charlotte will be kicking herself she left. She could have stayed and worked on the very same client. Silly girl. She could be with us tonight celebrating.'

'What? An account manager?' Nigel was appalled at Serena's social lapse.

'She's an account director now. Hector spoke very highly of her.'

'Not mentioning the fact she never wears knickers, no doubt.'

'Nigel, don't be crude. I said it was because I'd trained her myself, which in a sort of way I have. She probably tries to model herself on me. She could have come down for the picnic. She could have come down on her motor bike, changed into something not too showy and been waiting for us when we came out. It's such a bore having to lay out one's own picnic. Let's bring a butler next year.'

'A butler?'

'People do. Get someone from the agency to dress up. I mean, what do we pay them so much for?'

'Personally, I'd be miffed if I missed the opera. That's what it's all about.'

'That's the last thing that it's about. She's only young, is Charlotte. She won't be into opera. Pop music would be more her thing, wouldn't it? Take That.'

'Take what?'

'It's a pop group, silly. Take That. It's the only one I've heard of. It came up in some research on the ovulation predictor test. I think they might be defunct now, based on the comment that was made. It's funny the things some women will do just to get pregnant when they get desperate. I've never wanted children myself so I can't really identify with all that peeing into a test tube.'

'Difficult enough to hit the bloody target with your old fellow in your fist. How you girls manage it I can't imagine.'

'I should think they do quite a lot of decanting.'

'We could do with Charlotte on that account.'

'I have plans to get her. Ah, here's the turn-off. Follow me, this time.'

'I'm right behind you. Any slower and I'll bump your car.'

'Nigel, if you bump my car I shall never forgive you.'

'Don't tempt me,' he muttered.

'I heard that.'

He made a grumpy face.

'And I saw that in my mirror, too.'

Nigel stuck out his fat tongue and pulled in to park.

35

'There's a story here about a woman having eight babies.'

'Where?'

'In *The Times*.'

'Jesus. It's as bad as the *Daily Sport*. Next they'll have "I had Elvis Presley's love child ten tears after he died."'

Duncan and Michael were halfway through Saturday at their cottage in the miniature Cotswold village of Wychwood Lea, one of a row of tumbledown stone houses blanketed in clematis. On the village green the pink horse chestnut had already flowered and was now lush green. Their weekend home, a three-storey house, was opposite the ancient Swan pub and adjacent to a tiny Norman church.

On their arrival the evening before, Pushkin had growled and sniffed her way round all three floors. The cottage was much smaller than it appeared from the outside, principally because it was only one room deep and had two foot thick stone walls.

Now on Saturday, Duncan and Michael had shopped in Oxford and finished their lunch of frankfurters, mashed potatoes and sauerkraut. After the food they had made coffee in the cafetière and were reading the papers. Pushkin had alternated between laps and, bored of being pushed away as articles were finished and pages turned, had padded upstairs. She lay on her back on the sunny carpet and dreamt of escaping out through the window onto the branches of the old yew tree to swipe at the doves from the churchyard.

'It is possible,' said Duncan.

'What is?' Michael was deep in a law report.

'Fathering a child from beyond the grave. They do it with frozen sperm and IVF and that sort of thing. If Elvis had had it done when he was alive it could be true. It's possible to have babies long after you're dead. If you're the father.'

'Perhaps you could put your little escapade off until that point then.'

'Or the mother. You can have your eggs frozen and then some other women bear the child. There was an infertile woman whose age-old mother gave birth to her own grandchild.'

'Society is becoming weird. It's breaking down.'

'I had the very same conversation with someone the other day. We're turning into a normal couple by default.'

'We're turning into a boring, middle-aged couple.'

'I'm in my early thirties. That's hardly middle-aged.'

'Real middle-age is in your thirties. I mean you're not middle-aged when you're sixty. How many 120-year-old men do you know?'

'Let's see. You.'

'Hah hah.'

'I can't be halfway through my life. I haven't done anything.'

'Yes you have.'

'Like what?'

'Like your relationship with me. A career in advertising. A new career in television. Your name on the credits. Three homes. Holidays abroad.'

'It sounds more the way you say it than it feels.'

'It's better than squatting in a hut in Africa.'

'You sound like Nigel Gainsborough. There. You *are* an old man.'

'I sound like him?'

'The words you use. He was always going on about the darkies in Africa squatting in their huts or running round.

White Europeans never seem to squat at home or run round outside.' Duncan hid himself behind his broadsheet.

'It's just an expression. Everyone has their prejudices. Look at you and that woman with her octuplets.'

Duncan came out from behind the paper again. 'It's like puppies. It's like she's an animal or something. Here's another story of two lesbians who are being refused treatment to have a baby.'

'Well, they should be.'

'Refused treatment?'

'Absolutely. That comes off our taxes. There's people dying of AIDS and cancer and things and the resources should not be spent on social engineering.'

'It's not social engineering. Everyone is entitled to have a child.'

'No they are not. There is no such entitlement. Particularly if you're a lesbian.' Michael meticulously folded over the page of his paper and spent a second or two refining the crease before reading on.

'Why are you so against lesbians having children?'

'Because I believe quite honestly that single mothers and latch-key children are leading to an undisciplined society.'

'I thought I was supposed to be the right-wing one around here.'

'You're right-wing about money. You've always been like marshmallow on social issues.'

'You mean soft?'

'Yes. You're a big softie.'

'Listen. While we're on the subject?'

Michael sighed and threw down the *Independent*. 'Don't tell me. Lesley the Lipstick Lesbian has been begging for a bottle of sperm fresh from the tap again.'

'Not quite.'

'She's a can of worms. Stay away, Duncan.'

'Why are you so against it?'

'Because she and her partner will come between us and split us up, that's why. Because they think we're wealthy and can pay for their little baby after they've fucked up its education and God knows what else. They can see you coming, Duncan.'

'They won't be seeing that bit. That's behind closed doors.'

'I hope you haven't been talking to her about it again.'

'No,' lied Duncan. 'I haven't. I would have to have an AIDS test.'

'Which we've agreed you're not doing.'

'We have?'

'It's a bad idea. Why should the fall guy they pick on have to have it done anyway? It's an insult.'

'It's a sensible precaution. For at least three reasons I can think of. So that the baby is born healthy. So that the mother does not become infected. And to make sure that the father doesn't have a potentially limited lifespan. He should be there for his child.'

'You had that all worked out. You're to have nothing to do with them.'

Duncan could only have been more infuriated if Michael had wagged his finger at him. 'I lived with Hitler.'

'If you're not fathering a child you don't need an AIDS test.'

'I ought to have one anyway. I don't know my status.'

'How could you be positive?'

'I could be. Anyone could be.'

'And how would you feel if you were found out to be positive? That wouldn't just put an end to your little let's-make-a-baby party game. It would put an end to your life.'

'It ends your life whether you know or not.'

'That's not true. Look at Piers. Look at Rik. They were both fine and then they had tests and when the results came back they were devastated and they went straight downhill and died.'

'Don't exaggerate.'

'I'm sure if Piers hadn't known he might be around today. There is a thing called the will to live.'

'There is a thing called a complete load of old bollocks.'

'Dunky. I love you and I want to to spend the rest of my life with you. I don't want you to start sharing it with a pair of lesbian harridan hags and I don't want you shrivelling up with depression because you get bad news from a don't-care doctor. Just leave things be. We're happy as we are. Everything is going well for us in life at the moment. Don't spoil it.'

'Hell hath no fury like a bitter old queen scorned. You're just jealous.'

'Bollocks.'

'You're jealous they asked me and they didn't ask you and now you're coming up with every feeble excuse you can think of to stop me. It's my life and you don't control it. If I want to do something with it, something that's very big and very important to me I will. You can't stop me. Why do you always have to be top dog?'

'I've given up loads of things for you. I've chosen to live with you and share my life with you. I don't want anyone else in it, genetically related to you or otherwise.'

'That's the most selfish thing I've ever heard.'

'Selfish? You want to make some little baby with a woman who you can't even fuck and then trip round every second Saturday to play daddy when it suits you. It's called vanity, Duncan. You are selfishness personified.'

'Don't adopt that tone.'

'I'm not adopting a tone. And you're not adopting a baby.'

'I don't want to *adopt* a baby.'

'You're not having one. It's not a fucking fashion accessory.' Michael returned to hide behind his paper. 'Get back to your *Daily Fascist*.'

'Excuse me, but you're the fascist round here. God. You can take the boy out of South Africa but you can't take South Africa out of the boy.'

'But you can take the piss out of the Scotsman. Go and get me more coffee.'

'I'm not your black servant you know. I'm not your boy.'

'You are my boy, Duncan. And I'm yours. And we're not having another one, your son or mine or anybody else's getting in the way. And that's final. Coffee. No milk.'

Duncan sighed and got up to do his bidding. 'Coming up, massa.'

36

Martin Fox blew a jet of air from his bottom lip. It breezed up the front of his face.

'It sounds dubious to say the least.'

'It'll be a sensation, Martin.' Karen punched her point and her programme home.

'It could be the wrong sort of sensation, that's what I'm afraid of. I just don't know. Nuns are such a joke. Apart from anything else, there are hardly any in the country anyway. I mean, when did you last see a nun who wasn't Julie Andrews or Whoopi Goldberg or that other singing one. Who played her? Debbie Reynolds? Or was she the Flying Nun? Oh, my God. A flying nun. Who in hell's name thought that up?'

Karen ignored him. 'Look. We only need one and we've found her. Anyway, the point is, it isn't a show hosted by just any old nun. It's a show hosted by Sister Verity. She's brilliant. Even her name is brilliant.'

'She may be brilliant in person but people who are good in reality are often poor on TV as well you know, Karen. She may freeze on film or not look right or not sustain. You have nothing on tape. You have to have something pretty unique to last half an hour every day for years on end.'

'She's been on TV. Just once. That's where I saw her. I know my instincts are right.'

'What was she on?'

'L!VE TV. She was amazing.'

'L!VE TV had something on and it was amazing? I find that concept staggering. I thought they had rested their laurels on a woman with a cleavage giving the weather in Norwegian and a man dressed up as a giant bunny reading the news. God forbid that The Station should ever become like that.'

'Look, Martin. Look at my proposal.' Karen waved her own

copy of her document across the Head of Programmes' desk. 'Duncan Cairns and I did it together and, while I admit I'm not, he's very strong on sticking to the brief and we've fulfilled yours exactly. Each show can be made for less than ten thousand pounds per half-hour, it's completely interactive, it has strong female appeal, and it's lurid-ish without being as bad as Jerry Springer or one of those other shows from the States.'

'I know. On paper you have done exactly what I've been looking for. But a nun?'

'BBC2 has Sister Wendy.'

'She's an art critic, for Christ's sake.'

'Yes she is. Literally.'

'And she has buck teeth. I hope Sister Verity is better-looking. She has to have credibility.'

'She's not Pamela Anderson in a sequinned habit split to the crotch if that's what you mean. But that's not what women want to see on TV. They want to see romance and compassion and understanding and someone with integrity. Someone who's been through the mill of life and learnt about things on the way. That's the Sister Verity story.'

'Well. It would seem that the most appropriate action to take is to commission a pilot. I mean it's only ten thousand pounds a show.'

'How much for the pilot?'

'The full whack.'

'Ten thousand pounds?'

'I don't see why not. But I want titles and on-screen graphics and real callers to the show. I don't want it rigged. I don't want researchers with pre-rehearsed questions and answers. That's an old Saturn trick and I'm not falling for it twice.'

'You'll have to broadcast it. Brilliant!'

'Not quite. We'll put it into Milton Keynes only. They can still take a regional opt-out there since we started them off as a test area prior to launch. I want to trail it within the fortnight.'

'Jesus!'

'Look, it's July now. I want it out while it's still summer. If it doesn't work I want to have time to bring on something else in October.'

'It'll work.'

'Good.'

'Fantastic.' Karen stood up and looked as if she was going to jump up and down with excitement. Instead she removed her trademark bejewelled glasses and rubbed them on the front panel of her blouse.

'There's something else,' said Martin quietly.

'What?' Karen replaced her glasses slightly askew on her nose, making her look only slightly less like a vulture.

'Don't look so worried, Karen. It's more good news. I *would* like another series of *Basket Case* for next winter. Same budget, same number of episodes.'

Karen whooped for joy, surprising herself and Martin, let alone the bank of secretaries sitting outside in the open-plan area. She composed herself but the grin remained unwiped from her face.

'We'll need to review the budget,' she said. 'Production costs have risen.'

'We will not need to review the budget. Series inevitably get cheaper as you do more of them. You've learnt how to make the show now. Just repeat your magic formula.'

'But we're not shooting in bulk. It's a live show. The people are expensive.'

'Karen!' Martin was cross. 'Don't push it. It's all verbal at the moment. Why don't you hold off until we've sent you a letter of intent. That's the right time to talk about the money. Get Duncan to make a case for an increase and if it stacks up, we'll look at it. Possibly. Maybe. Big if.'

Karen laughed. 'You have such a charming way of saying, "No bloody way will you get another bean out of me." That's why I respect you, Martin. You say it the right way but you can be read like an open book.'

'And it's the end of another chapter. I have to go and see the chief executive now. He's over from the States. Come back to me with a running order for the pilot, a schedule and a budget breakdown.'

'When?'

'As soon as.'

'When's that?'

'Tomorrow. Before Jamie Hirst gets his bovver boot in the door.' Martin laughed but it was no joke to Karen.

'Don't even contemplate giving that little bugger the business, Martin. What idea has he got that's better than mine?'

'I wouldn't like to say. I don't pass your ideas on to him and you would not expect me to pass his to you. It's a jungle out there, Karen. I have to take the best show the monkeys make for me. Make sure that it's yours.'

Karen hurtled up the garden path. Her hands were shaking with suppressed excitement. She could not get the key in the door without first dropping it and having another try. She faffed and fumbled. She realised she was trying to open the front door with her car key. It was difficult what with a briefcase in one hand and a polythene bag of cakes and pastries in the other, the same one as both bunches of keys. The bag of cakes was spinning, winding around itself. Max would be home from his sixth form college in five minutes or less and Karen wanted to have a sweet surprise for him. She needed his opinions on what teenagers would want to see in the show. Teenagers love new technology and were always the first to find the new shows on cable and satellite TV. Max would know exactly how to hook them into Sister Verity.

Inside Karen dropped everything on the hall floor as she threw her light summer jacket onto the hook. It hung on for a second and then gave up the fight with gravity and slipped to the floor. Karen did not bother to notice. She picked up her shopping and swept into the kitchen, spotless because it was so rarely used these days since Max had abandoned breakfast. She barely saw her son in the mornings anymore. With the polythene bag still in her hand she hit the switch for the kettle and, hearing it come alive, Karen bent into the dishwasher to find two mugs. She placed them on the counter beneath the cupboard where she kept the tea. The Earl Grey teabags were in a sealed clear plastic tub. She pulled out a pair joined like Siamese twins. Why do they join them up in twos, she thought, tearing them apart and dropping a detached bag into each mug. The manufacture of teabags had never concerned her before. Because you make a pot with a pair, of course. Karen never made tea in a pot, she just dunked a bag in a cup. But today was special and it would be lovely to give Max and herself a treat. They had done nothing together for ages and with his exams upon them and her battling for success with the afternoon schedules, they had barely seen each other for weeks. Not properly. Not to converse. Well, today they would, even if it was only for an hour over a cup of tea.

Karen knelt down in front of the carousel corner cupboard which held the blue and white china teapot. She spun the door and the tea pot revolved into view. Beside it sat a matching little milk jug and a sugar bowl, all presents from her mother in the last year of her life. So that made it all the more special because despite the circumstances of his birth, Granny had adored baby Max. As she removed the teapot Karen spotted an item she had not seen for at least five years. In fact, she had forgotten that she owned it. An oval-shaped electro–nickel plated silver meringue basket with a high handle like on a flower trug. It had been a wartime wedding gift to her mother from the girls in her office. Her mother had often told her the story of it. And before she had died she had asked Karen to have it. 'But, mummy it's your wedding gift and it belongs to you and daddy.' 'Your father will never miss it,' her mother had replied. 'And, I'm afraid darling that you're obviously never going to get any wedding presents of your own, so take it.' She had kept it out for a year and then eventually it had receded further and further from a position of prominence until now it lived lurking at the back of the under-counter carousel cupboard. Karen tepidly lifted it from its hiding place and blew the dust from it. She was more excited now she had the tea set out to do it all properly. Why had she and Max never done this before?

She found a tray and used a new linen dishtowel as a tray cloth. She laid out the cakes and pâtisserie in the meringue basket and arranged them. It was a shame she had no doilies. Did anyone, anymore? Her mother would have known where to buy some. With a brainwave, she remembered they had some paper napkins left over in the drawer and soon the cakes and pâtisserie nestled on a bed of white. A golden cream horn with raspberry. A madeleine with coconut and a cherry. A slice of tarte tatin. She would have that. A slice of pistachio pie. A marzipan frog. A chocolate choux bun with caramel filling.

The plastic jug kettle boiled and clicked itself off. Karen did as she had seen her mother do all those years ago. She swirled boiling water around the interior of the pot and when it was warmed dropped the Earl Grey teabags in and topped up with water. She placed all the items on the tray and a pretty picture it made. For once the house in Flask Walk felt like a home. For a moment Karen wondered that if she had not had to work – if she had been married and Max had had a father – would this have been the life they would have lived? It did not bear thinking about. She switched her attention back to the present and checked her watch. She knew Max would walk up the garden path any moment now. She would greet him at the door. She stepped into the hall. Through the windows of the solid Victorian door she could see his shadow approaching. He was walking slower than usual. His gait was different. She wondered why. She strode to the door and pulled it wide open.

'Max, I've got great news and I've had—'

But it was not Max. It was the Collins girl from along the road. What did she want this time?

'Is Max in?' she asked.

'No. He's not home yet.'

'Can I wait for him?'

Karen was cross. She didn't want the girl spoiling their treat together. 'He's got something on as soon as gets in. I'll get him to call you.'

'Please,' said the girl.

'Please what?'

'Please can I wait here until he gets home.'

Karen sighed aggressively. 'It's really not convenient. Come back in another hour. And a half. Or two would be better.'

The girl watched Karen's expression turn from irritation to a smile. She turned and saw Max at the gate. He was slightly bent over under a backpack. When he saw the girl talking to his mother he faltered and then carried on towards them.

The girl got in first.

'Max. I really need to see you. It's really important.'

He did not look at his mother. 'Sure he said. Come in.'

Karen's heart sank. The girl would spoil their tea by being there.

'I can't come in. It's a private thing I want to tell you about.'

'Oh,' said Max.

'Walk me up the street and I'll fill you in.'

'OK.'

'Max,' said Karen. 'Don't go off just yet, darling. I have to talk to you too.'

'I'll be back in a while.'

'No. Now, Max. Mummy needs to talk to you now.'

'Don't call yourself mummy in front of my friends. It's humiliating. I'll be back in another hour or something. It can wait.'

'She can wait, can't she?' called Karen. But Max had already taken the girl by the arm and was leading her off towards the street.

'Max, I've made tea and everything.'

'Tea?!' Max did not call it back to her. It was merely an expression of incredulity to the girl whose arm was linked to his. Karen had never seen a girl on his arm before. She had always been the one by Max's side until now.

She closed the door quietly and sloped back to the kitchen. She poured the tea into one mug. She checked herself. She should have put the milk in first. Her mother had taught her to do that. You got a different chemical reaction or something and no scummy layer on the top of the tea. She poured the mug out into the sink and started again with the milk. She stirred her tea and stared at the cakes. She was trying as hard as she could not to feel rejected. Max had not meant to hurt her feelings. She knew that. But here she was, alone again, trying to cheer herself up, trying to struggle on. She was supposed to be the Most Something or Other Woman in Television, wasn't she? The most powerful or the most difficult or the most creative. But not the loneliest, the saddest, the most unsure of what would happen next, of what would happen to her. As the sadness welled she selected her cake from her mother's meringue basket and settled herself in her living-room settee, munching her madeleine, mired in her misery. It was moments only before she broke and began to cry.

'When I said "Make it cheap" I hadn't expected to be taken quite so literally.'

From the polished plate-glass viewing window of the studio gallery Martin Fox peered down. In the heat of the first week of August he was perspiring under his cotton jacket. It was barely a fortnight since he had given Karen the go-ahead but he had expected more. He looked onto the set. There was very little of it. A collapsible desk made of medium density fibreboard which looked suspiciously like a decorator's wallpapering table. An office swivel chair in grey weave with the rusty stain of somebody's cappuccino down the back of it. Lighting cables and other wires roped around and over and under the set. A transformer for the radio mikes. Three arc lights which flattened everything out and exposed it for all it was worth, which was very little indeed. That was it.

'If you don't mind the expression, Karen, "Where's the beef?"'

Karen Myhill looked up over the computer console in front of her. Its tiny lights twinkled beneath her and were reflected on her face. Drawn and aged of late, it had become animated and youthful with the thrill and the risk of a live broadcast pilot. Her hair was flattened by a set of headphones. A tiny microphone jutted out onto her hollow cheek. She sat twitching beside her do-as-you're-told director and his PA, the three of them underneath a bank of monitors positioned over the window showing the full spectrum of angles available from the five-option multi-cam system.

'Sister Verity is the beef.'

'It's only going out in Milton Keynes. Do we really need five cameras?'

'We do for the pilot. If we don't have a use for them all we'll drop one or two for the series.'

'How about dropping four? She only needs one.'

'Wait and see. Anyway, we have no camera men so we're

saving there. We've locked off each camera on a fixed view and I'll direct which ones to cut to from here.' The director glared at her. Wasn't that his job?

'Too many cameras are confusing,' said Martin. 'And that—' he stabbed his finger at the window—' looks appalling.'

'Look, Martin, I changed my mind at the last minute, which is my prerogative.'

'Perhaps the prerogative of a lady. Not that of a producer.'

'The Station is a glamorous channel. This is a very small studio. Our set was made of very small, very cheap bits of cardboard and looked like exactly that on camera. So I had it taken out and burnt.'

'Burnt?'

'Burnt.'

'She's supposed to be Sister Verity, not Joan of flaming Arc.'

'We're supposed to be progressive and ultra-technological. One of Duncan's contacts has found a brilliant alternative for us. So last night at rehearsal I decided to introduce blue screen. It's fabulous. No show like this has ever done it this way before. It's a genuine breakthrough. And it's the perfect setting for Sister Verity. Can someone get me a coffee, please? Where are the runners, for Christ's sake?'

'Locating more blue fabric, I think,' said Karen's director.

'You think or you know?'

At that moment the soundproof doors of the gallery opened and Duncan stepped in, followed by Briony Linden. She looked excited. She took a moment to adjust her eyes to the darkness and, unexpectedly catching her own reflection glowing clearly in the plate-glass window, she fluffed up her barley sugar hair. She stepped forward and, taking her place beside Martin, looked down.

'Oh. I thought this was the studio we were broadcasting from.'

'It is,' said Martin dryly.

'Where's the set? That looks awful.'

'Ditto my words.'

'We're blue-screening it,' said Duncan before the crispy Martin Fox could get any drier. 'Sister Verity will sit on the chair at that table. We'll drape it all in blue and we'll chromakey in the background around her. It looks stunning.'

'You've lost me,' said Briony.

Karen sighed rudely and made a face at Briony's back. She could do without amateurs in the gallery thirty minutes before they went on air. Briony ignored the face, which Karen had not realised was clearly reflected in the gallery glass. Duncan cheerily continued.

'Look down there. See the studio walls have been painted royal blue? We had that done last night. They've painted the floor blue too. Now, over there, there are two guys unfolding a huge blue curtain?'

'Is that what they're doing?' said Briony. 'Can we smoke in here, Duncan?'

'Nope. 'Fraid not.'

Karen let slip a 'Hah.' Perhaps the wretched woman would go away.

Martin Fox turned to her.

'Karen, do you know Briony Linden?'

'No,' said Karen giving no indication she wished to. Her eyes did not leave the screening notes she and the director were going through quietly in front of the screens. As they read out numbers, the PA repeated them into her talkback microphone and headphone system. Differently angled shots of the studio flicked over on the central monitor.

'Camera four,' ordered Karen.

'Camera four,' repeated the director.

'Four,' said the PA. 'Did you mean four?'

'No I meant seven hundred and twenty eight,' snapped Karen. 'What do you think I meant. It comes after three and before five.'

'Well, that's the wideshot. I thought you'd want ECU.'

'Try not thinking, then,' said Karen. 'You're paid to do as I say not to analyse every fucking word.' The pressure was getting to her and via her to everyone else.

'ECU stands for extreme close up,' whispered Duncan to Briony, pulling her to one side.

'I know,' she said. 'They use it on agency scripts for commercials. "ECU beans being scooped out of can to reveal viscous sauce." That sort of thing.'

'So they do. But they rarely use blue screen. Watch the guys draping the table and the chair with the blue fabric. When Sister Verity sits down they'll switch on the chromakey and you'll see what happens on the monitor.'

'What *will* happen?'

'She'll appear to be in this amazing background we've found. It's computer-generated animation. It comes on a CD. We just insert it into the machine and up it comes around her. It's in 3D. It's a fantasy pseudo-cathedral interior. It moves. It's got shimmering stained glass lighting effects like a kaleidoscope which change colour continuously. And beams of light which glow on and off according to random cloud patterns you can glimpse through the hole in the dome.'

'Blimey. I can't wait to see it.'

'Neither can I,' said Karen in a stage whisper. 'Where the fuck is it? And where the fuck is Sister Verity?'

'What are we going to do about Maria?' sang the director. He clipped it short as Karen's glare made it clear that that joke had worn thin the night before.

'If the runners have let her trip back to that fucking bar . . . We could get this series sponsored by Gordon's Gin let alone Verity Tampons.'

'What's this?' asked Martin.

'Karen's little joke,' said Duncan. He didn't want the Head of Programmes to think their presenter had a drink problem. 'She's in wardrobe,' said Duncan.

'Any good?' asked Karen.

'Completely brilliant.'

Duncan addressed Martin and Briony. 'We've given her the full makeover. Sister Verity's own lilacy habit was breaking up on screen. It's made of nylon. It flared when we chromakeyed in the picture. So we've been out to Bernhams and got an absolutely fabulous black-and-white habit for her. It's much more nunny. More old-fashioned and showy. And wardrobe have found these gorgeous, gem-studded crucifixes, costume jewellery style. She's agreed to wear the lot. Altogether and all at the same time.'

'Christ,' said Martin through gritted teeth. 'She sounds like Boniface VIII.'

'More like Madonna, actually,' replied Duncan.

'Same difference.'

Karen swung round in her chair. 'In what she normally wears she could be mistaken for a nurse. It has to be clear that she's a nun-type Sister Verity and not a ward-type Sister Verity. This is showbusiness, Martin, not reality.'

'It's virtual reality, actually,' said Duncan. 'The computer animation is modelled in 3D. They've linked the cameras up to the computer so that whatever angle we shoot her from the background moves round automatically. It's awfully clever.'

'It sounds awfully expensive,' said Martin.

'Jesus! A minute ago you said it was too cheap,' moaned Karen.

'I said it *looked* cheap. As I know to my cost, *looking* cheap and *coming in* cheap are two entirely different things in TV production. Look at *Noel's House Party*.'

'I rather make a point of not looking at *Noel's House Party*,' said Karen. 'I get so easily depressed. OK. I'm going downstairs to the dressing room to give Sister Verity her final briefing. Anything I should be saying on your behalf, Martin?'

'No. Just "break a leg . . ."'

'If she's anything less than completely heavenly, Martin, I shall be breaking both her legs in two personally myself. But that won't happen. I suggest you come down with me and grab a drink from the green room before Sister Verity hoovers up the whole of hospitality by herself and then I'll meet you in the call monitoring room and show you how that works. We've already got thirty people on the responders with some great problems. Stunners.'

'Genuine calls, I hope.'

'Yes, yes, yes. We got the point. The researchers are briefing Sister Verity on them now. Bring Brenda with you too.'

Martin turned over his shoulder and smiled at Briony.

'Come on then, Brenda.'

Briony looked to Duncan to save her.

'I'll run the titles for you if you like,' he offered. 'It's a great sequence.'

'I'll be down in moment,' she said taking up Duncan's excuse to stay wide of Karen. Martin and Karen left the gallery, closing the black felt soundproofed door behind them.

'How are you using the responders on this show?' asked Briony.

'Viewers use them to call in.'

'How is that different from phoning?'

'Well, it's free for a start. Small production companies like ours can't bear the cost of all the incoming calls and on this sort of show we felt some people would not pay premium rates to stay on the line. So we get the responders to classify the calls for us.'

'You've lost me already.'

'No I haven't. The viewers have to enter a category number into their hand unit and we can then tell what subject area they are calling about. If we want to take a call on that subject we call them back on the phone. We have all Station viewers' phone numbers on our database. If not, we don't. That way we have editorial control without having to employ a huge team of telephone counsellors to pre-test every call before it gets through.'

'So the responders are a benefit to you and to us. Clever.'

'And to the callers. When you enter a category number and send it we automatically download text advice on that subject to your screen. We pretend it's a letter from Sister Verity, or at least that's the idea. It runs along the bottom of the screen as she's talking.'

'How do you know how to reply? Where do you get your answers from?'

'Easy. Victim organisations. Charities. Helplines. That sort of thing. It's all done by desk research. So every person who sends us a message gets a benefit, not just the ones who get through.'

'Clever.'

'It was Karen's idea.'

'She's awfully unpleasant, isn't she?' remarked Briony.

The director and PA nodded in unison.

'I mean, threatening to snap the legs of a nun in two. That's a tasteless thing to say. Even joking.'

'She wasn't joking,' said the director. 'She omitted to say she'd start with the neck and work her way down, vertebra by vertebra, limb by limb. That's after I've been hanged, drawn and quartered and had my personal bits thrown to the worms.'

'Well, I like her,' said Duncan. 'And she adores Sister Verity. It's because of that we're all here. Now watch these titles and you'll see why Karen is a genius. Then maybe time for a quick drink – eh Brenda?'

38

Duncan yawned. He caught sight of himself, bleary-eyed in a mirrored pillar. He checked his Santos de Cartier watch, its steel strap discreetly studded with forty-four eighteen-carat gold screws. Wearing it was the last remnant of his days in advertising to which he still adhered. Its glittering formality was a contrast with his blue-white T-shirt and stone-washed chinos. He could barely believe the time. Six-fifteen a.m. Smart Roman numerals and a rock crystal face eased none of the pain of the early rise. It felt earlier, much earlier. Notwithstanding Duncan's smart watch or his personal bodyclock, Heathrow Airport Terminal Three was on its own twenty-four-hour timetable, alive and abuzz and milling as always. Suited London businessmen and women who knew their Euro-routes by heart and now chased planes as their predecessors had once chased trains shot past, their schedules slashed to the reality that everything flies out of Heathrow at least a quarter-hour late. Their urgency was that of people with decisions to make rather than people who have planes to board.

A fleet of exotic Eastern beauties sailed past, short women in sharply cut red suits, immaculate in matching make-up and a cute beret and silk scarf combination. They were stewardesses for Japanair. In contrast, a wave of arriving zombies dribbled out of the customs exit, quickly disappearing into the diaspora of visitors to London and comers home. Duncan looked out for his friend. He was still too early.

He continued to pan the interior of the terminal. This was Duncan's favourite at Heathrow, if people were allowed to have such a thing, because of its smartness and sexiness and because of its shops. But to those who are neither arriving nor departing, merely meeting, the thrill of the airport shops remains a frustratingly close one, kept out of reach. Duncan was stuck on the wrong side. Not the shop till you drop side, but the stand till you die of boredom side. He wondered whether to go for a coffee or whether to go for *The Times* or whether to go on standing staring at the TV monitor showing that flight Q231 had landed. It was yet to show that the passengers had reached the baggage hall. Duncan yawned again and moved the weight on his feet from side to side within his pale suede Timberland boots. Another wave of arrivals was superseded by more and more until Duncan gave up trying to spot different plane-loads of people. It didn't work like that anyway, as well he knew.

Then, hidden in the crowd, he spotted her. Despite the hour and the twenty-four hours of flying, despite the large Vuitton-style suitcase, wheeled, and its matching vanity case, carried, despite the carrier bags and the coat over one arm, here she was – a perfectly poised and genuinely beautiful woman. Tired she may have been, she did not seem as tired as her co-passengers. Her olive skin, covering impeccable bone structure, was neither lined nor worn. Only the little extra weight beneath the chin hinted at her age, perhaps three years older than Duncan. Her well-cut light brown hair, highlighted in hazel to hide the onset of grey, was in no intentional style. Her natural-colour, natural-fibre clothes were creased like everyone else's but the crushes in her linen looked a deliberate gesture of style. So here she was, looking good, looking like she knew how to travel, looking like she knew London, looking like she knew the world. Which she did. A bit. She spotted Duncan and, breaking into a smile, threw her eyes heavenward to indicate the fuss and nonsense that had been going on behind the scenes for ever since they had landed.

'What's that?' asked Duncan nodding to her folded coat. He lifted the vanity case from her hand.

'Every other time I land in London it's raining.'

'It's the middle of August.'

'Like that means it doesn't rain in England? Some welcome, Dunky. Don't I get a kiss?'

Duncan gave her two, one on each cheek and then they put the luggage on the floor and hugged hard. To passers-by, with their good looks and fit bodies, in their expensive, low-key clothes and stylish accessories, with their smart haircuts and good grooming, with their confident poise and clever conversation, they seemed the perfect thirty-something couple. But that was not their story.

'Thanks for collecting me.'

'Straight to the car or coffee? We could have a catch-up. I don't have to be at work till eleven-thirty.'

'What time is it now?'

'Six-thirty.'

Cindy Barratt placed her trolley case on the floor again and adjusted her watch. 'Eleven-thirty?! What sort of time is that to roll up? You've got five hours.'

'Actually I was at work until midnight last night, which is why I'm so knackered this morning.'

'What were you up to? You know, you hear nothing about England in Australia other than whether Di's been at the Harbour Club or the hairdresser's.'

'You hear nothing else here either. We've been commissioned to make a thirteen-week-long test series for The Station.'

'Congratulations.'

'It's all being done in a terrible rush. This is our first week on air nationally. We just made the pilot a few weeks ago. We only did a test in Milton Keynes, but it did so well in the ratings there they've brought the airdate forward. If this thirteen weeks goes well, we'll go on air in the spring on a fifty-two-week contract.'

'Champagne all round.'

'There's been no time for any of that. No congrats. No sleep. No thanks. It's a sort of agony show.'

'I love it already. Who's doing it? Anyone I know?'

'A nun.'

'A nun! Not that ghastly Sister Wendy with the buck teeth. I can't stand her.'

'She's an art critic.'

'Not much she isn't. She's always standing in front of some modern art of some fat woman with her tits out and her legs splayed bleating, "I think this is so touching, don't you?" Nuns know nothing of sex, yet they can't shut up about it.'

'Sister Verity has the same problem.'

'Any good?'

'She's a star.'

'She's a Catholic, isn't she?'

'She's not very catholic in the advice she gives. Or rather she is. She's catholic with a small c.'

They finally reached the car park. Duncan queued at the automatic ticket machine and prepaid. They loaded Cindy's luggage into the hatchback and began their descent from the multistorey, the route onto the A4 and the drive back into Central London.

'Look at this traffic!' exclaimed Cindy.

'Welcome back to the big city. How was your mother?'

'Glad to see me when I arrived. Glad to see the back of me when I left. That's not true. Actually we get on well and every time I leave she breaks down and weeps and says she'll be dead and buried before I go back again.'

'You see more of your mother in Sydney than I do of mine in Scotland.'

'She wants me to get married.' She mimicked her mother's Ozzy accent. '"You're nearly forty, Lucinda."'

'And what do you say?'

'"Don't call me Lucinda. And I'm not nearly forty." I'm almost thirty-seven and I'm a free agent again. I'm dropping back to saying I'm thirty-ish. I can pass for thirty-two, can't I?'

'Dunno. Think I'm with mum, Lucinda.'

'Piss off!' Cindy playfully punched Duncan on the arm.

'Careful. I'm so tired if I don't actually fall asleep at the wheel I'll crash because you pushed me.'

They drove on into a succession of roundabouts, strung like pearls on the dual carriageway.

'Is that it, then?' asked Duncan.

'Is what what?'

'Are you really a free agent. Have you and Alan split up?'

'Look in the mirror, Duncan. Is that Alan Josling you see driving me home from the airport?'

Duncan had not told Cindy he had had lunch with Alan while she was away.

'You told me he was out of town.'

'As far as I'm concerned he is. Out of town. Out of sight. Out of my life.'

'What happened?'

'Oh, I don't know. Nothing really. I'd rather not talk about it. I'm too tired. I might slip up and say something I actually mean.'

'Meaning?'

'Meaning I don't know what to think. My mother doesn't exactly help. In her book you're born, you get married, you give birth, you show up in a big hat at your daughter's wedding and drop dead shortly afterwards, overcome by an overwhelming sense of achievement. She just can't fathom my life in England. Just as well really. I can't decide whether I've invested all these years in Alan or wasted them. We never had one serious conversation. He was always at work. He never had time to talk. He never had time for me. Not when I wanted it. Only when it suited him.'

'That's not unusual.'

'I know. Men are only interested in themselves. They're so vain. But women don't tolerate that sort of behaviour anymore, Dunky. We're supposed to have a full-time career and still run the home and raise the children and turn out for dinner looking like Sophia Loren *circa* 1956. Men go to work, where they spend half the day out at lunch or golf or shagging the temp, come home late, look in the mirror and flatter themselves they're gorgeous when they're not, burp, fart, flop out in front of the TV and then moan like hell if they're not waited on hand and foot.'

'I don't do that.'

'I didn't mean you. I meant straight men.'

'Oh.'

'Then they wimp out in bed.'

'Ah,' said Duncan.

'Well, anyway. I'm sorry I buggered off to Australia without telling you.'

'I'm not your keeper. I understand. But you could look for a cheaper bolt hole. Every time you have a tiff with Alan you fly to the other side of the world.'

'It wasn't a tiff. We've parted.'

'Are you sure?'

'Yes. It was to do with, you know, the big question.'

'Marriage.'

'No. I've never thought of getting married. More the patter of tiny feet question.'

Duncan took his eyes off the road for a second. He made light of it.

'Are you getting a kitten?'

Cindy smiled. 'You know what I mean.'

'No. What? You wanted children and he didn't?'

'He already has a daughter by Terri. He said he didn't want another child. I mean, how fucking selfish can you get? What about me?'

'You could talk him round.'

'Alan doesn't talk. Or listen.'

'Couldn't you just – get pregnant?'

'Huh! It'd have to be the world's first immaculate conception in two thousand years.'

'Oh. Dear.'

'We went off sex.'

'You and him or you or him?'

'Both. I don't know. I think when things begin to go wrong everything just disintegrates. He associated sex with me trying for a child. I caught him counting my pills one day. The bastard. He didn't even trust me.'

'I can't see you as the maternal type.'

'Gee, thanks.'

'No. I mean you'd be a terrific mother but I thought you liked your time to yourself.'

'I have too much time to myself. I want to share my life with someone. Perhaps I'll just have a child on my own. Everyone's doing it these days. It was in *People* magazine or *Hello!* or something I read on the plane. All these Hollywood women are bringing up babies by themselves and even their best friends don't even know who the father is.'

'So what will you do? Hang around Soho bars sizing up the gene pool?'

'Maybe. Or find a nice friend to help me make a baby. You must have heard of DIY AI.'

'Didn't they pick up the British Airways account from Saatchi and Saatchi?'

'Be serious. I just need to find the right fella.'

'Criteria?'

'How about you, Dunky?'

'What?!' Duncan stared at the car in front.

'Why not?'

'Don't be ridiculous.'

'I'm not being ridiculous.'

'I'm embarrassed.' He was. 'End of conversation.'

'We would make perfect parents. We would have such a beautiful intelligent child. We'd be doing the world a favour.'

'Forget the world and just do me a favour. Shut up. Or I'm driving you straight back to the airport and putting you on the first flight home.'

'This is my home. Anyway, it's winter in Australia. It's too depressing. I shouldn't have gone at this time of year. I thought you'd like to be a father, Dunky.'

'I would. In theory.'

'Put it into practice.'

'I might well do. But, no offence, not with you.'

'You won't get a better offer. You won't get another offer.'

'Well . . . actually . . .'

'You're joking.'

'I'm not. Someone has, as they say, placed an order.'

'Who?'

'No one you know.'

'Piss off. Don't be so mysterious. Who? Not that awful woman you work for.'

'That rather nice woman I work with is over fifty and has a child all of her own already. Almost grown-up.'

'Who then?'

'I have to respect their confidentiality.'

'Bollocks!'

'Immediately I've dropped you at your flat I'm going to see them.'

'I don't believe it. Oh, Dunky it's not fair. You're not even straight and you're going to be a parent and I'm not.'

'Only possibly.'

'Definitely. I know you, Dunky. When you set your mind on something it happens. It always works out for you. Every time.'

39

Nigel was bored and stirred his beverage half-heartedly. 'I'd rather have had tea.'

'I asked Margaret for tea. I don't know what's got into that girl. She half does everything I ask her to do and the half that she does do is usually wrong. Have you *any* idea at all how this thing works?'

Serena aimed the remote control at the television monitor and, holding it at arm's length like a duelling pistol, repeatedly squeezed the button. Nothing happened. The TV set remained switched off.

'Are you pressing the right tit, old girl?'

'Of course. And don't use that expression. It's unfortunate to say the least.'

'Why? No one squeezing yours these days?'

'Nigel!' Serena was horrified.

Her partner chuckled and continued to stir away. He licked his lips in anticipation of a biscuit, but there was none in sight.

'I shall ignore that remark – and any more like that and I shall ignore you. Altogether.' She studied the remote control and then launched into another session of pointing and pressing. 'The trouble with this whole set-up is that that silly interior designer woman has had the TV set and all its cable and satellite bits built into the wall. One appreciates the fact that it might look all very smart for clients and everything, but how are we to know if it's even plugged in? And the technology is far too complicated. I mean, look at this.' She waved her weapon at Nigel. 'There are at least thirty buttons and each one is dual function. I mean, are the people who design these things aware of the level of intelligence of the average person? I went to Cambridge and I can't even switch on the set.'

'Shouldn't worry, old girl. There's nothing on for people who've been to Cambridge. It's all rubbish.'

'I couldn't agree more. Channel Five. Granada Sky. Carlton Select. Wall-to-wall drivel. It was better when we didn't have any of them. And The Station is worse than the lot of them. I don't care if they are our biggest client. One has to be objective. I was asking Briony the other day to fix me a meeting with their Head of Programmes – what's his name . . . ?'

'That Malcolm Fox chappie. Not a golfer.'

'It's Martin. *Martin* Fox, Nigel. Try to get it right.'

'Why are you in such a snap? You didn't know his name at all. At least I was half right.'

'And you were half wrong, which isn't good enough. Well anyway, I think Briony could at least fix a meeting with Martin Fox. She's incapable of getting the advertising strategy right all by herself. But she seemed to think it was all rather a rum idea. She's so political. Protecting herself, I suppose. Doesn't want to get found out. Well, we found her out long ago.'

'Did we? I thought we thought she was quite good.'

'If I ever said that, I was damning her with faint praise. She's quite good for a woman who's background is frozen fish fingers. Oh, this is ridiculous.'

Serena trotted to the side of the room. She picked up the telephone receiver.

'I'm just about ready to scream. They've installed that new-fangled phone system in this room too. Innovation is supposed to make things easier. How on earth do you dial out?'

'Haven't had my telephone training yet.'

'Telephone training. How ridiculous. Why does one need to learn how to use a telephone? We've had them for over a hundred years. One never needed to go on a course before . . . oh, hang on . . . I see . . . I've got to follow the prompts. . . Oh, how awful. It's playing the most ghastly music imaginable. Ravel's thingummybob, Torville and Dean style. It's ringing now. Where is Margaret? She's never at her desk when you want her. What's the name of the technician downstairs in MCN? That fat chap with the perspiration problem?'

'Oh him. Bob, I think. Or Bill. Who's Ben?'

'Ben is the rude one in production. It's not him. I'll try reception. They'll know. They'll send someone up.'

Five minutes later, the MCN technician, whose name was Brian, had been in, switched on the meeting room TV monitor, tuned in The Station and left. On the screen, seated in her computer-animated set, was Sister Verity, looking to camera, nodding attentively and pondering a caller's problem.

'Dammit,' said Serena. 'We've missed the beginning. We'll have to wait till the break to see the Verity branding. It looks awful already. Cheap. I don't know what Verity thought they were doing getting involved. I shall have to watch them like a hawk in future. Allowing their nun on it is one thing, but sponsoring it is another thing entirely. How much money is going on that? At least it's out of the tampon budget and not our bit.'

'Ours wouldn't run to it. We've got the beggar's budget. Duncan has the bugger's! Hah!'

'Don't be mindless. It's him I blame. Duncan should have known better than to concoct this whole scheme. I thought he was an intelligent boy, but I was wrong on that one.'

'Wrong?' Nigel couldn't believe Serena had said it.

'And as for Charlotte Reith, she's given some very bad advice to our clients.'

'She's a bit junior to take the rap? Must have been someone higher up.'

'Well, whoever it was she should have tried to stop it. No doubt Duncan led her on. They were all rather chummy in his little club. I assumed that was all in the past but look at things now. I mean, who is this woman?'

'She's a nun. Irish by the sounds of it. Esther Rantzen in a habit. Not Jewish though. At least doesn't look it. Do you get Irish Jews? Must do, I suppose. They get everywhere. But you don't get Jewish nuns. Or do you?'

'She must be a Roman Catholic. That's a retrograde step for a start. No wonder they're a dying brand. She's *far* too old for their positioning.'

'She's not going to be in the campaign, the nun. Hector told me. Said she's back-of-pack stuff. You know, in the leaflets the little uns read when they have to finger their fanny first time round.'

'*Nigel*! I've warned you already.'

'It's a fact of life. If you want to get in there you have to use your fingers.'

'Verity Tampons are like Tampax. They have an applicator. They're not digital.'

'Digital?' Nigel was thinking of digital watches back in the seventies.

'Digital tampons are ones you insert with your digits. Verity are applicator tampons. You haven't to touch yourself down there at all. It's very civilised and if I had a teenage daughter that's what I would allow her to use. Listen to this!' Sister Verity had strayed into teenage drug abuse. 'This woman's advice is next to useless. Platitudinous clichés. Is that the best the Church can do? No wonder it's in such a state. No wonder there are no Christians left.'

'Not the Catholics. Breed like billy goats. An aversion to rubber. That's what causes it.'

'She needs to be more robust. If I had my own series on televison I'd be much harder hitting. If people ring up for advice, they can jolly well expect to have it dished out right and proper.'

'I don't think they screen book-burnings, do they?'

'Nigel, think of this, what those stupid Verity clients haven't realised is that this reflects on our ovulation and pregnancy kits. They haven't just put the tampon symbol on TV. They've sponsored the programme with generic branding and that reflects on what we're going to be doing. We're being dragged down by this whole sad affair. And—'

'Hold on, old girl, here's the commercial break.'

Nigel and Serena peered into the pastel pink light as the break bumper into the commercials came up. Sister Verity's name appeared in the scroll-like script of the tampon pack and then the word Sister faded from the screen and was replaced by a voiced-over line. 'The truth is it's Verity.'

'Was that Judi Dench's voice? I would have thought she wouldn't demean herself by doing tampon voiceovers for cable television. Once they get made a dame they just can't resist cashing in on it.'

'Think of the repeat fees, old girl. It's a daily show and they must use that line four times a show.'

'She may need the money, of course. She probably hasn't done as well as me. I expect the National Theatre pays buttons. No doubt they still run that as a communist co-operative. The stars'll get the same as the tea boy.'

'Really? How appalling. Never could stand the luvvies meself. Too pink around the gills for my taste.'

'It may not have been her, of course.'

'Who?'

'Dench.'

'Ah yes. Difficult to tell. Which one is she anyway?'

Serena tutted. 'Whoever she was, she was far too old. Make a note that they need a younger voice. If nothing else, we should get her sacked.'

'Second half!' Nigel sat up alert, his shirt buttons straining as his belly shifted forward. But Serena flicked her remote control at the screen and switched off.

'I can't bear it. And we have proper work to do. I need to call Verity right now. They simply haven't understood the difference between supporting the product and crucifying the whole brand. Really, Duncan should have known better. We bent over backwards to accommodate him and his – you know what I mean.'

'No bloody idea what you mean, old girl. About the last thing I'd do is bend over in any direction near the likes of him.'

'Well, anyway. Someone has to put a stop to this and it obviously is going to have to be me, because no one else has a modicum of sense. If it's the least I do for Verity Ovulation and Pregacy Kits, it's going to be to get that woman off TV. I know I can do it. If I'm right and I usually am—'

'What? Not always?'

'If I'm right, we must be the only people who know all of the players in the game. So we have the best chance of controlling it. I enjoy being in control and in this case I intend to make a very thorough job of it.'

40

Back to England. Back to Haringey. Back to home. Back to boredom. Cindy Barratt could not bring herself to get back to business, to make the first phone call to her clients from her basement bedroom office. Instead, she had put off client contact for a few hours more and taken a wander around her flat, searching for the TV remote control. Her mother had once thrown hers out with the rubbish and Cindy was begining to think she should check in the dustbin. However, she became side-tracked, reacquainting herself with interior flaws and reinventing improvements she needed to make. But she had no funds to afford any. She had blown her savings on the trip home. It seemed a waste now. She had returned to Australia to her mother's farm in the Blue Mountains in the middle of winter. There was not much doing there at the best of times and winter was hardly the best of times. She should have kept the money to improve her home and to fend off the taxman yet one more time. Instead, she was down to three figures in her building society savings account. Before, she had always had Alan to fall back on. He had been there to help her make the transition from advertising agency to self-employed consultant. She had never actually needed his money but he had made the offer and that had given her the courage to take the plunge. And when she was having one of her cash flow crises it would be his credit cards which carried them through dinners or trips to the opera or binge shopping in Harrods. Now she had turned her back on him, she had turned her back on all that too. Who did she have now to share her woes with? Duncan. But he only went so far and was committed elsewhere and there was no question ever of his financing her. When he had been in advertising that might have been a possibility, in theory at least. Now he had leapt into telly that thought could take a dive.

Cindy sighed. Telly. Where was the remote? She hummed to herself and sorted through her Deutsche Grammophon CDs and slipped a silvery disc of Maria Callas hits into her Sony player. She sought out a vacuum-sealed bag of Aribica ground coffee from Sainsbury's and boiled up the kettle. She made her coffee in a giant cup with painted piggies on it and settled into her settee with a copy of Australian *Vogue*. She had packed it in her hold luggage and had not been able to leaf through it on the plane. There was something odd about Australian *Vogue*. It was below Britain in the hierarchy of Vogueishness. You got Italy then France then Britain then Australia. American *Vogue* didn't seem like anyone else's *Vogue* at all and therefore didn't count, even if it was the original. Funny how the cultures crossed over but failed to meet. Maybe that was her problem. She had crossed the great seas to Europe but had never quite laid claim to it. Not culturally. Or emotionally. Certainly she had not reached Alan at any level, not even sexually. At least all that anti-climatic writhing was behind her. She drained her piggies and returned to the kitchen to refill the cup.

The flat had a stale smell. She had been away for so long. She opened the window. There on the sill was the TV remote control. How on earth had it got there? Back in front of the TV she realised she had missed Duncan's new show which he had told her about in the car. Instead, she quickly discovered a lifestyle programme for women in exactly her frame of mind. A rather posh lady was showing you how to slow-bake slices of lemons and limes into dried ornaments or wind them onto wreaths or glue them to pots of home-made marmalade. Cindy shortly found herself switching on the oven and heading for the corner shop. That was all their runtish little fruit was fit for. Slicing, baking, gluing. She bought a jar of luxury marmalade. She had a golden ribbon in her drawer of gift wrap. She would copy the posh lady. It beat working. It beat boredom. It was something to do. Something to do well. And Cindy did it well. She remembered the step-by-step instructions and an hour and a half later she had a gorgeous jar of home-made-looking thick-cut Seville marmalade topped with an extravaganza of dried citrus and gift-wrapped with a flourishing golden bow. But she had no one to give it to. She had no one even to show it to. She had had to do it by herself. She was on her own. She was all alone. She admired her handiwork. It was wonderful to be home.

Karen Myhill tried to slice her over-ripe orange with her over-blunt knife. It squashed in the middle like a children's hollow ball and the peel split. Pith and pips emerged. They weren't meant to. There was juice all over the counter top. That hadn't happened on TV either, but Karen cared not. She hacked away. She was happy enough. The posh lady's limes had sliced into five or six pieces each. Karen was getting a maximum of four semi-usable slices from her huge oranges. Still she was happy. She had had the day at home. Sister Verity had played well again today. The instant tracking on the ratings phoned through to her office by Briony Linden were up again. Duncan had produced the show. For once she had it in the bag. For once she had a series that was short and simple and successful and self-sustaining and which didn't require her to stand over it and strain over it and spit over it. Then The Station had made her day with its follow-on to Sister Verity, *Lovely Afternoon*. Remarkably, for once, she had all the ingredients she needed to go domestic. That was, of course, the secret formula of the show. There was almost nothing to do but you felt clever. Max would be home from college soon and she would show him her handiwork. She would be a proper apple pie and cookies mom. She even had an apron and she even had it on. She checked the oven. What had the posh lady said? One hour at two hundred or two hours at one hundred? Well, she didn't really have two hours and her slices were awfully thick. It was all very simple really and it didn't absolutely matter if they weren't exactly right. The presenter had made that point herself. It was about the effort, the gesture, the individuality, the self-expression. Jesus. How could you possibly express yourself through oven-dried citrus segments? Karen laughed aloud. Honestly. Afternoon TV was daft. But it was horribly true. A woman could express herself through making and baking. God, she thought. I've turned into my own mother. I've turned into an old woman.

Karen stood dead still. She was stopped by a distinctly desperate knock at the front door. It resounded with somebody's presence. Whose? Max? Surely not. He would let himself in. But it couldn't be anybody else. Something must be wrong. She made for the hall and then instinctively put her priorities in order. She didn't want Max to pooh-pooh her hacked-at Outspan oranges. It would make more of an impression if she brought them out dried and aged and countrified from the oven in an hour or so. She turned and quickly slipped the tray onto the top shelf. Or should it be the bottom shelf? The trouble with *Lovely Afternoon* was that it was all done with one camera and bugger all cutaways, so although the woman told you, you didn't see every step. Didn't they know TV is about pictures? That eighty per cent of communication is visual. Karen compromised. Middle shelf. Knob to 150. She sped after the rap at the knocker. She pulled it open. It was not Max. It was not an old dear collecting for charity. It was not a tradesman. It was that Collins girl. Again. Karen attempted pleasantness.

'Max isn't here.'

'Isn't he?'

'No, he's not. It's the middle of the afternoon. He's out. You'll have to go away. I'm busy. I'm writing.'

The girl looked at her apron.

'I'm writing and I'm baking too. For Max. Don't look so surprised. I'm a housewife superstar, whatever you may think. They show you how to achieve it all on afternoon TV. You should try it. Your ideas look as if they could do with bucking up.'

The girl looked close to tears. Her eyes were imploring. What they were imploring, Karen knew not. Although Karen had never liked her, she found a little more sympathy.

'I'm sorry. Max isn't here. Excuse me for asking, but do you have a lock or something on your family phone. It's just that you never seem to use it. This is the third time in as many weeks you've dropped over for nothing. I could have told you he wasn't here. If we're not in, leave a message on the answering machine. That's what they were designed for.'

The girl said nothing.

'What time is it? Why are you never at school or college or wherever you are these days?'

'I didn't come to see Max.'

'Didn't you?'

'No.'

'Oh.'

'I came to see you.'

'Me? Why? What's up?'

The girl sniffed and composed herself. She seemed to change her mind.

'Nothing. I think I'd better go.'

'Oh, no you don't, young lady. I know you.'

'You . . . you do that new show *Sister Verity*, don't you?'

'Yes. Good, isn't it?'

'Max mentioned it to me. He said you had a whole team of people sorting out people's problems.'

'We do. But Sister Verity does most of it herself. She's what we in television call a natural.'

'I tried calling in on the responder.'

'At last! Someone who knows what that bloody thing is called.'

'Max told me. I didn't get through. I tried all afternoon, but it kept saying the system was full.'

'The ratings are up, that's why.'

'I wondered if you could help me?'

'Me? How could I help you?'

'You could tell me Sister Verity's home number or something and I could talk to her.'

'I don't think I could do that. She's like the agony aunts in those teen magazines. Sister Verity does not enter into individual correspondence. And she doesn't do haircare advice if that's what you're after, which is what you should be. I can't understand why other women put all that whale blubber on their face but they avoid getting a decent haircut. You could do with one. We've been snowed in with letters. We do read them. Then we choose callers in to the show who best represent what seem to be the trends. It's early days yet, of course, and we have such a choice of subject matter—'

'Please can I come in?'

Despite the softness of the voice, Karen was taken aback by the intensity of the request.

'Why?'

'I could tell *you*.'

'Well—' Karen tutted. She had managed to get herself into a happy frame of mind for the first time in ages. She couldn't be bothered with this little drama princess. But whatever she was thinking, her mouth said yes and her arm held wide open the door.

Minutes later Karen was contenting herself with her retrieved teapot and the chance to make some Earl Grey for an unexpected visitor. The girl had even taken off the black nylon bomber anoraky thing she seemed to have been glued inside for the last two years.

The girl sipped her tea. 'How old were you when you had Max?'

'How old was I?'

'Yeah.'

'In my thirties. I'm over fifty now. A dinosaur to you, I suppose. I'm an old woman to myself so I must be.'

'And you weren't married?'

'No.'

'And you brought him up all by yourself?'

'Yes. He's all my own doing. You can blame me for bringing such a wonderful boy into the world.'

'And could you cope?'

'Yes.'

'I mean, did you go to social services?'

'Social services? Is this for a project at school?'

'Whose? Mine?'

'I wasn't talking to your imaginary friend.'

'I mean, where did you get all your money from? Bringing up a child costs a fortune. My mum nags on and on about that. She never shuts up about it.'

'She's right . . . I was very lucky, actually. I had a very highly paid job and, I can't believe I'm saying this, TV people are very liberal and actually most people were supportive and helped out with my timetable and one fits everything in around one's career if one is very senior and can call the shots. I was never obliged to work a regular day or anything, so I could always cater for Max. When he was a baby I took him into the office. It was a very stimulating environment for him and all the girls would coo over him.' Karen looked into the golden distance of enhanced memory and smiled. 'I think they were jealous of me.'

'Because you had a baby?'

'Because I had a baby all by and all to myself. Your generation will benefit enormously from our trail blazing, you know. You don't need to have a husband or a man in your life to have a very good time. I mean, I would have had more friends maybe, and more dinners out and more sex, well any sex at all actually, if I hadn't had Max, but I did have him and Max was all I wanted. I believe, that you, young lady once made some very disparaging remarks about my relationship with my son. Well, you were wrong.'

'I don't know what you're on about.'

'It's of no consequence'

'I never said it whatever it was. Max twists your words a lot. He's ever so clever.'

'I know.' Karen beamed. She rose and looked into the oven. The citrus slices seemed to be frying. She was not sure whether to turn them over or not, but the girl called her back and she let them be.

'Mrs Myhill?'

'What?'

'What are those?'

'Oranges and lemons. I'm oven-drying them.'

''You understand about getting pregnant, don't you?'

Karen was conscious of the change of tone. She resumed her seat next to the girl.

'Y – e – e– s.'

'I mean and not being married and everyone being against you.'

'If you put it like that . . . I'll go along with that for a moment. What's your name? I don't even know your first name.'

'Ginny.'

'Ginny, I have this awful feeling you're going to confide in me and tell me something and expect me to know how to handle it. I'm just going to warn you first that rather a lot of people in this city we live in don't go along with the way I approach things. You can tell me anything you like and I won't be angry, but I can't promise not to tell your parents.'

A stream of tears began its flow down the girl's face.

'You mustn't. You mustn't tell them. You mustn't. They'll kill me.'

'They won't. They love you whatever you may have done.'

'You don't know them!'

'One loves one's child unconditionally.'

'They hate me.'

'They don't hate you.'

'They do hate me. They think I'm an embarrassment – I'm going to have a baby.' She broke down.

'Hush.' Karen took Ginny in her arms and she wept into her shoulder. It would be easier for her now. She could talk into Karen's apron strings and not have to look her in the eye. With a jolt of guilt, Karen realised that Sister Verity was not just about good cheap churn-it-out afternoon telly. She was a lifeline to real people in real need. She would have to confront Duncan with this fact tomorrow morning. Sister Verity would have to have a back-up team. No caller must ever be turned away. Perhaps they could do a link with the Samaritans or something. This girl had tried to get through and hadn't made it. She had no one to turn to. She could do something silly like try to kill herself or try to abort her baby. No woman should ever abort her baby, according to Karen. She had stared that option in the face herself, and liberal and left-leaning as she was, it was simply something she did not believe that any rational woman could contemplate. The girl sobbed in her arms. Karen took slow deep breaths and willed her to calm down. She stroked her hair. It did need cutting and conditioning. It was strange to have a girl depend on you, even if it was for just a moment. This was the problem of being the mother of girls. You worried about what they let boys do to them. But you didn't need to worry about boys. It wasn't as if Max could ever get pregnant. Were he ever to get a girl pregnant it would not be their problem, it would not be—

A charge of electricity, of terminal urgency, shot through Karen. Her whole body spasmed. She pushed the girl back from her shoulder. Ginny's face was red and creased, her eyes bloodshot and now filled with terror. She took Ginny by the shoulders and shook her vigorously, violently even. This was the girl whom Max hung around with, whom he sloped off down the garden path with, whom he hid from his mother with. What had she led him into? What had she led him on with? Why had she come to Karen?

'Who's the father? Who's the father?' Karen was screaming. 'Who's the father?' She shook the girl violently.

'I – I – don't – I – mustn't – please!'

'Who's the father? Tell me! Tell me! Tell me!'

'It's Max. It's Max. Oh God, I'm sorry. I'm so sorry. It's Max. I didn't mean for it to happen. Don't hit me. Please don't hit me. It's Max.'

'Oh my God! Oh my God!' wailed Karen. She instinctively pulled the girl into her arms and they sobbed together. She pressed the girl's heaving body into her own.

'Oh, Max. Oh my precious baby.'

On the other side of the kitchen, now ignored and best forgotten, inside the oven Karen's best efforts at happy homemaking turned to a sour and sticky blackness that Max's mother would never let him see.

41

And on the first day of September it rained. After a never-ending run of hot dry sunny days that had lasted and lasted and lasted, the rain came down in buckets. There was so much of it that the guttering shrugged its shoulders, gave up, and let the water flood out over the edge from the tops of buildings. There was so much of it that the Underground flooded at the edges and came to a standstill at the heart of town. There was so much of it that white clinging linen trousers became dogged around the base of the legs by dalmation spatterings. But the water companies were grateful for it. And the gardeners loved it. And the tourists had expected it and quite liked it as long as it didn't last.

Alan Josling, on the other hand, hated the rain. He detested it because, on the other hand, the left hand to be precise, he had to put up with a painful spasm. He had been in a car accident the previous year, and broken most of the useful bones in his body. Whenever the water table had risen since, the level of pain in his arm had risen in direct proportion. His doctor told him this was an impossibility, that it was something people read in Father Brown books or saw in Carry On films, where cardboard cutout characters went momentarily limp with lumbago or some such comedy illness brought on by damp. Alan Josling was not the imaginative type. He was not making it up. He believed it because he knew it was true. Rain spelt pain.

He pulled over for a second and used the twingeing arm to press the button to raise the roof on his new convertible car. A flight across the central reservation of the M11 in his last little sports number had not put him off hand-built, high-powered TVRs in the slightest. His new one, the 'Newy' as he referred to it, was as lovely as the last, as red as the last, as fast as the last, but this one was longer, though not higher. It was one of the lowest slung cars on the road, a Chimaera. There were women who were sex on legs. There were financial deals that were the business. There were goals that were droplet moments of pure joy. And there was the Chimaera. That was Alan Josling's hierarchy of happiness. He was not the imaginative type.

In the car's interior the noise of the rain on the roof was deafening. Turning up the volume on Phil Collins in quadraphony could not disguise it. He turned the music back down lower than it was before. The traffic lights changed. Alan pulled down on the left-hand side of the leather steering wheel. Ow. That hurt. He turned left and round and along into Wardour Street. Fuck off, he mouthed. Why was it, when it rained, pedestrians assumed they had the God-given right to walk out into the traffic and, worse, put their great big greasy unwashed hands on the bonnet of your baby? The Newy had to look lovely at all costs. It was one complete circle in his ring of confidence. The Newy glided into the Wardour Street car park, under the dog-leg barrier and round and up and along and into its place. In the dim interior Alan adjusted his vision and switched off the ignition and the car electrics. He paused to think.

Perhaps he should not park here. Perhaps his car would be seen, his number plate recognised, his inimitable style spotted. After all, no two TVRs were alike. On the other hand, nobody knew about the Newy yet, did they? It had taken seven months for the Newy to turn up, hand-built to his personal specification. You had to wait. It was worth it. The Newy was well worth waiting for. You got a fill-in MG from the garage while you waited, so that was OK. Did Nigel and Serena think he still had an MG or had he told them about the Newy? Had he told them about the MG? When had he last seen them or spoken to them? He couldn't remember. Anyway, they didn't park here. It wasn't good enough for old Fatboy. The junior board of MCN parked here in the Wardour Street NCP, but the executive board had private parking around the corner. Somewhere underground. Somewhere hidden. Was he hidden enough? He hoped so.

He unclipped his seat belt and leant over to the passenger seat and flicked the lock on his briefcase. For a second he contemplated the photo of Cindy he still carried there. Then he pulled out a steel comb and, angling his face into the rear-view mirror, he swiped the comb through a couple of times. Thinning, but not too much. Not as much as Fatboy. He hoped to God they weren't there. The guys from MCN New York had promised that they would not be. This was ridiculous. It was lunacy. Why he had to walk into the MCN International building he didn't know. They claimed it was simply because they couldn't take the risk of bringing original documents out of the building. This was the strictest, most confidential, most crucial run of figures there was. It was Alan himself who had insisted on seeing originals and not copies. Not even Nigel and Serena got to see these. But they didn't need to. They already ran Clancey and Bennett. They were not planning on making changes. But he was. They were not planning on restructuring. But he was. They were not planning to buy their own company behind their own backs. But he was. Alan Josling was planning to buy his way into the international big time and claw his way back up from below the line. Alan Josling, on the other, painful, twingeing, throbbing hand, was planning on selling a fifty per cent stake of his business to MCN International and merging Josling and Thurrock into Clancey and Bennett. He would personally create a new, strengthened MCN subsidiary under his own sole directorship. Nigel Gainsborough and Serena Sark – and Colin Thurrock for that matter – would be pushed out into the cold wet wide world where they belonged.

He slipped his comb away and knotted up his loose Hermès tie. He opened the car door and swung his legs out and, under the guise of his little black umbrella, headed for Dean Street and his date with destiny.

42

'Max!'
There was no reply.
'Max!'

Still he did not appear.

'Max! There's someone at the front door. Answer it please.'
Karen was fed up with that door. Nothing but trouble seemed to
cross its threshold these days. But Max did not appear and she
found herself in the hall alone and unprepared as ever. Late to
respond, she drew breath and opened her portal to God knows
what this time. Two men stood there. One in white overalls, the
other in T-shirt and jeans and carrying a set of folding steps. The
decorators.

'Oh piss! Fuck! Shit!'

The man in the T-shirt laughed. 'Forgotten we were coming,
darlin'?'

'I had, actually.'

One of the men propped the folding steps up against the hall
wall and the two began a short repeating procession back and
forth, bringing in painting cloths and boxes of filler and brushes
and all their things. Karen, meanwhile, crept upstairs.

She detected water running in the bathroom.

'Max!'

The sound of running water continued.

'Max! Are you in there?'

Silently and slowly the door drew back. A wet face appeared
in the crack. 'It is I.'

Karen looked at her son. He seemed so tall, so broad, so
powerful, so capable of protecting, so capable of threatening,
perhaps not yet a man but certainly no longer a boy. Overnight
he was grown-up, grown away from her. She no longer knew
what to expect. She no longer knew her son. She no longer knew
anything about him. Where he went. Whom he associated with.
What he got up to. What he held back from her, what he hid
from her, what he hoped she would not discover. Karen winced
at the prospect of the conversation they would have to have.
Max had swung in late the previous night, the night she had
meant to clear up for the decorators, so Karen had not set eyes
on him since Ginny Collins had delivered her little bombshell, if
not an actual live and screaming grandchild there and then on
the kitchen table.

'What is it?'

Karen faltered. She who was never lost for words was all

afumble, desperately trying to observe her son objectively, to see
him as others might see him and to judge what he was capable
of. But Max's newly washed face was clean of expression. His
hair was wet and pushed back from his smooth, white, high
forehead. His eyes were big and bright and clear as only a
youth's can be at this ungodly hour. The bloom was still on
his cheek. He was still so young. He was still her little boy. He
was still her precious baby. It couldn't be that there was now
another precious baby on the way. Karen could barely believe
it. Sunrise, sunset. Swiftly pass the years. Jesus. That was the
last straw. She was finally old enough to empathise with *Fiddler
on the Roof*. She didn't trust that Collins girl and she did not know
whether to believe her. She didn't trust herself with handling this
the right way either. She had not necessarily handled the issue of
Max's father the right way with him. It had been a wedge driven
between her and her son for most of his life. Having finally prised
it away just a half-year before, Karen had no wish to replace it
with another. She had to find the right time and the right place
to question Max. Not to confront him or to challenge him, but
to help him. Their relationship had become so testy of late she
knew that the once-passionless Max would explode and walk
out. Walk out of her home. Walk out of her life. Damn his father
for placing money in a fund and damn her for telling him about
it. Max could not get the money until he was twenty-five. That
was supposed to be the law, but Max had always been cleverer
than anyone who made up any rules. He was a young man of
independent means and she could not afford to push him.

'Come on, come on. I need to get dressed. I'll be late.'

'Oh, I . . .'

A horrible thought struck Karen. Some time back, that awful
stuck-up man had telephoned her and asked her about Max.
What was his name? Max's father's solicitor. Tim Lutyens. It
was not beyond the wit of Max to approach him and wheedle
his inheritance out of him. A million pounds. It would not
require the full sum to pay off that girl and buy her silence.
Or, God forbid, it would hardly require the full sum to pay
for an abortion. Or, hell's teeth, to pay to raise the child. Max
to raise a child? Surely not.

'Max. Max . . .'

'Come on, mum. Get to the point. You're turning into a gibbering idiot. Did you know women get more forgetful as they get older?'

'Could you help the decorators move our things upstairs? Please.'

'Decorators?'

'I'm sorry Max. It's all mummy's fault. Mummy completely forgot they were coming last night.'

'Oh did Mummy? Well tell Mummy she can go and tell the decorators it's part of their job to move the furniture.'

'Not the furniture, Max. Just our personal things. They won't care about them and they'll damage them. You know what workmen are like.'

'Why are we having decorators anyway? The place is fine as it is.'

'Max! Don't let me down.'

'You do it.'

'Oh, I'll help darling. But you know I can't carry anything. You're so big and strong.'

Max tutted in annoyance.

'You're so much better organised. You'll know where to put everything.'

Max tutted again.

'They're our precious things.'

'Precious. What do we have that's precious?'

'Our heirlooms. Granny's things. You'll want to pass those on . . . to your child.'

'No I won't.'

'You will darling. When he's born you'll know what I mean. There's granny's tea set and teapot and everything.'

'Granny's teapot? Who wants that old tat?'

'The child will. The child will. It might be a girl.'

Max glared at her. 'Any daughter of mine will be a career woman. Not some demented housewife into tea and scones.'

He disappeared back into the bathroom and immediately re-appeared, embedded in a huge towelling dressing-gown. He hid his body from his mother. Karen had no idea what Max's body looked like. The little baby she had held naked at her breast was almost never seen by her now, and when he was, he was fully clothed, let alone undressed. She half-followed Max to his room. It was embarrassing for her but a peek, a prying sneak at him might help her decide if he was capable of fathering a child. Of course he was. She knew that. But . . . She knelt down and put one lens of her spectacles to the keyhole of the panelled door. Damn. The key was stuck in from the other side. She could see only black.

'Excuse me, love? Where d'you want this?'

She turned to see the decorator behind her on the landing. He was holding her mother's mock Ming urn thing, so big it had stood in the hall for years as an umbrella stand that never got used. He was obviously wondering what she was doing. Getting a perverted kick from spying on her teenage son with no togs on, was no doubt what it looked like.

'I'll take it,' she said. She stood up and smiled pathetically to cover her embarrassment. She took the huge vase from him and he hovered and then realised she wasn't going anywhere with it so he left her to it and returned downstairs.

She leant back against the wall and hugged the vase like she had once hugged her precious baby. Every day there were pictures of children years younger than Max holding up their babies in the British tabloids. Jesus fucking Christ! What was she doing? Was she crazy? But thank God it had struck her now. That conniving Collins girl, that manipulating minx, that harlot of Hampstead, that *femme fatale* of Flask Walk, that nubile Little Nell of NW3, had not made something clear to Karen, had kept something from Karen, had perhaps left it deliberately unsaid to Karen and Karen realised that she had not had the wit or ken or presence of mind to ask her. God! God! Karen was suddenly blatantly aware that she did not know whether Max knew. The girl had blurted everything out to Karen because she had no one to share her desperation with. Max could be cold. Max could be calculating. Max could be cruel. Max could be comfortless. Karen loved her son but she knew his character. Perhaps Ginny simply could not turn to Max in her time of helplessness. Perhaps the poor child simply could not bring herself to tell Max about it at all. Karen pulled back from the brink. She had to rethink how to handle this. To tell Max he had fathered a child could devastate his life. To tell him he had if he hadn't, would devastate their relationship and in turn destroy

Karen's life. If Max did know, then he was keeping it from her. If he didn't know, then there were things Karen could do first to make the best of the situation. It could wait. She turned to go downstairs when Max appeared behind her and filled the door frame.

'Mum.' He said it softly and sympathetically.

She turned back.

'Yes?' Her heart was leaping already.

'Mum. I have something dreadful to tell you.'

Karen was gasping for breath.

'What? What?'

'I'm giving in.'

Karen was dying.

'Giving in?'

'Yeah. You're right. About the stuff.'

'The stuff?'

'Yeah. I'll go and move it. Otherwise I'll never hear the end of it if they break anything. And you know what workmen are like. That's as good as guaranteed.'

He pressed past his mother, not catching sight of her catching her breath. He turned fleetingly, took the huge vase from her cradling arms and departed with it.

'Sister Verity. My son . . . he's still at school and his girlfriend is pregnant.'

'Och, never! You know, every Sunday when I should be saying my prayers, I take a wee break and watch Formula One and that Damon Hill – I might even have a wee bet on it if I've been out – and, you know, I say to myself, whatever speed Damon gets up to, he'll never match the speed of a boy's sperm racing up a young girl's vagina.'

'It'll ruin both their lives.'

'It may do and it may not. Just think of the problems you *haven't* got there and you're winning already. You're not the young lady's mother, are you, so that's a blessing for you. I use the term young lady loosely, of course, for a loose young lady she would appear to be.'

'I disapprove of abortion.'

'Well, if I have anything to do with it she won't be having one of those, so we're ahead of the game on that one too. Are you too young, do you think, to be a grandmother?'

'No—'

'So that's something else not to bother your head with. There, three things you don't have to worry about and we've barely started. Your duty is to see that baby in, born fit and well. Sit that cocky boy of yours down and talk some sense into him. Sure, you'll love him and stand by him but you don't approve of him makin' a one-off donation to the local inseminary. To love her and leave her is not an option. If he's too young to marry her then he's too young to care and if he's too young to care for a child then there are many a barren couple the length o' the land who would give their best limb for a bairn. Nobody's life will be ruined m'dear. A gorgeous new life is a gift from God and a splendid gift it will make for the right couple. Your son and his wee girlfriend will have learnt their lesson and grown up in the process but they won't be burdened. God bless you. You're a lovely lady, so you are.'

43

'Hello, Charlotte?'

The phone turned to stone in Charlotte's hand. She recognised that voice.

'Hel-lo.'

'It's Serena, Charlotte.'

'Yes. I know.'

'Do you always answer the telephone like that? It won't impress your clients. At least it didn't impress me. But then, as we all know, I'm a hard act to follow.'

Hard wasn't the word Charlotte would have chosen herself.

Why had this horrendous woman called her? To criticise the way she picked up the telephone?

'I was surprised it was you, Serena. That's all.'

'Oh good. I'm ringing about two things. I'm very put out – actually rather hurt – that you didn't call either Nigel or myself to congratulate us on winning the other half of the Verity business.'

Half? Charlotte estimated it was worth barely fifteen per cent of the sanpro account.

'I didn't realise that's what you're meant to do. Congratulations, then. We're supposed to be competitors now, aren't we?'

'Absolutely not. You and I will always be friends, Charlotte.' Friends! 'At a personal level. And professionally. We're going to continue working side by side on Verity. Which is the first thing I was ringing about.' Serena continued. 'We need to have a co-ordination meeting. I have to say I was very put out, no not put out that's not the right phrase, I was angry, actually, about that dreadful nun woman person you've got plastered all over television.'

'That had nothing to do with me, Serena. She's entirely wrong for the brand.'

'I'm glad to hear it. Good. We're off to a good start.'

'I quite like her personally.'

'I'm sure we all would if we knew her. I know our old friend Duncan Cairns had a hand in this somewhere. I would have thought that he of all people, with his proclivities, would not have a personal interest in promoting the Roman Catholic Church.'

'That's not really what she does, actually , Serena. If you listen to her—'

Serena carried on regardless. 'It amazes me how someone can just swan off into television like that. He has no experience and if you ask me it shows. But you're absolutely right. She is wrong for the brand entirely and when I say entirely I'm including the predictor kits business at Clancey and Bennett. That's my patch and I have to look out for it. So I've been thinking. I think it is necessary for the HQ team and the C&B team to have a co-ordination meeting in the the next fortnight or so and sort out what our long-term dual strategy is going to be.

The clients are not to be told. If we're just going to compete with each other, we'll end up damaging each other's franchise which is plainly silly. I think we're all grown-up enough to know that since we've both just won Verity business we should make the most of it and make sure nobody's toes are getting stepped on. I know Hector very well. In fact I've seen quite a bit of him recently and I'm sure he'll agree I'm right. And so will you, of course, Charlotte. Hector seems to like you. I did say that I thought it was a tad early to make you an account director, but I'm sure you'll grow into it.'

Charlotte fumed silently. She did not want Serena Sark discussing her behind her back with anyone, least of all Hector. Was she really that chummy with him? Were those two cooking something up together or was Serena just name-dropping? She heard footsteps to her rear. It was Daniel. She turned and looked at him. He saw the strain on her face and gave her a sympathetic smile. She ignored Serena's talk and found herself realising that her warnings to Daniel on becoming his boss were first-day-in-the-job bluster. She had wanted to establish status, not ward him off. What the hell. She liked him. She smiled back and reached out with her left hand. He stroked her arm gently and sat down behind her.

'Nigel and I can make Wednesday, Thursday and Friday of the week after next,' continued Serena. 'I'll leave you to come back to Margaret. And confirm with a fax because Margaret'll no doubt get it wrong. We'll need two hours.'

'I'll see what I can do, Serena.' Charlotte spoke through gritted teeth. She didn't want Daniel and Maria to meet Nigel and Serena and discover what a hell hole she had sprung from.

'Now, Charlotte, I'm sorry to call you so late in the day. What time is it?'

'Nearly five.'

'There are other things afoot which I need to talk to you about a bit more privately and as it happens I'm throwing a dinner party tonight at my home and two very old friends have fallen by the wayside and I thought you could bring someone along with you and make up the numbers.'

Charlotte went into trauma. Serena Sark had just invited her to her home. This was unheard of.

'I . . . I . . .'

'It's eight for eight-thirty. And I don't need to tell you to dress smartly because you will. But obviously my husband's and my circle are mainly quite prominent and you'll want to make an impression.'

'I can't come'

'Charlotte! Don't let me down at the last minute!'

'You've only just asked me.'

Serena laughed. 'I couldn't ask you earlier because I didn't know the others were cancelling. Don't be silly. What were you going to be doing?'

Charlotte was caught on the hop. 'I was . . . going to play tennis.'

'Easily cancelled. Now bring along a nice young man. Otherwise there'll be thirteen of us around the table and some people are funny about things like that. I've just had my garden redesigned. If it's warm we'll have drinks outside. You must know a boy who went to the right sort of school. You don't have a boyfriend, do you? Hector said you didn't.'

Charlotte smarted. How the hell did he know? She really didn't want them gossiping about her behind her back.

'. . . Er . . .'

She had no idea what to say and found herself writing down Serena's address. Serena began to chortle with an auspicious merriment which was making her feel nauseous. After she had closed the call, Charlotte turned to Daniel.

'Shitty day?'

'Too fucking right,' she said. She began to whizz through her personal oraniser.'I suppose I could ask Rupert. Oh, he won't come. There's Julian but he's boring. Mark has got married. William will want me to sleep with him . . . Oh, Daniel what am I going to do?'

'What about?'

'I need to find a presentable young man.'

'Whoah. Look no further!'

Charlotte laughed. 'She'd die if I took you along.'

'Fuck off then.'

'I didn't mean it like that. Oh . . . sod it. Why not. She might as well meet you because we're going to be meeting her on

Verity anyway. And I need the protection. But you're not my boyfriend, understood?'

'So I'm not to mention what a great shag you are then?'

Charlotte scowled and then giggled.

'When is it?'

'What?'

'This thing we're going to where I'm not you're boyfriend and you're not a great shag.'

'It's tonight at eight-thirty.'

'Bunch of arse.'

'Why?'

'No can do.'

'What?!'

'Sorry, matey, but it's Bonzo's and my night for a bevvy and a curry.'

'Daniel. You can't let me down at the last minute!' She was adopting Serena's line.

'I can't cancel Bonzo.' He stretched his arms and shook his long-haired head in wild mock disbelief. Charlotte recognised the argument and the solution.

'Look. Don't cancel him. Meet him for a quick drink. I'll give you Serena's address and you join us at eight-thirty. I'll get there on my own on the Ducati.'

'Nah!'

'Three line whip!'

'Nah!'

'Daniel . . .'

'All right. Right you are. But I might be a bit late.'

'No you won't. You'll be on time.'

The clock in the street chimed. It was five p.m. Charlotte's telephone rang. She looked at Daniel.

'Five o'clock,' he said.

Chime.

The telephone continued to ring.

'So?'

Chime.

'Five o'clock car.'

Chime. Ring ring.

'Fuck off, Daniel. Don't wind me up!'

Chime. Ring ring.
'Don't answer it.'
'I have to.'
Chime. Ring ring.
Charlotte laughed nervously. It couldn't possibly be the five o'clock car. What had she done? Nothing? Well not quite. She had been talking to the enemy. She had agreed to co-ordinate with Serena, to gang up against the client. She had bad-mouthed Sister Verity. Serena and Hector had been back-stabbing her. Perhaps Marsha Blow-job listened in to phone calls. Everyone said she did.
   Ring ring.
   Charlotte lifted the receiver.

44

'Come on, come on. Start will you!'
   Cindy could not choose between rage or tears. She sat back in the driver's seat of her little green Mini and drummed her fingers on the steering wheel. She waited until she had had time to breathe deeply and to calm down. If only she had not left her lights on. All day. She turned the knob on the radio. Nothing happened. She flicked the switch for the windscreen wipers. Nothing happened. She tried flashing her headlights. Nothing happened. The story of my life, she thought – nothing happened. She sighed and her shoulders fell back heavily into place. She would have one last go at turning the wretched ignition and depressing herself further with the worst sound in the world, the sound of a dead engine's stuttering, sneering laugh. Your oh-oh-oh-oh-oh-own fault it, it said. Your oh-oh-oh-oh-oh-own fault. She pursed her lips. She looked in her shoulder bag. Again.

Surely she had her mobile phone on her. But it had not magically appeared since she had last looked. She looked in the glove compartment again, but there was still only the car manual with the coffee ring on it. She felt around the deep interior door pockets that feature in Mini advertising. There was no phone in there either. She knew she hadn't brought it. She never used it. She had got it free with her stereo system. She knew it was still at home sitting upright on its charger where it had sat untouched for months.

There was nothing for it but to get out and look for someone with jump leads. She'd pop back to W. G. Edmond's, the little hand-made soap company she had come to all the way out here, on this godforsaken industrial estate in East London. If it still was East London. The postcode must be at least E one hundred and something. At least it felt like it. Billy Edmond might have jump leads, though no doubt he'd want a reduction on her bill for the favour. It hadn't been a successful day at all. Spending nine hours on a crash course in marketing, coaching Neanderthal man in a hellish wasteland way out east, when you have Antipodean jet-lag – I must learn to turn down work, thought Cindy.

By the time she got back to the little brick building where W. G. Edmond's hand-made soaps were produced, Billy-boy had gone, fucked off. Shit. All of the other premises were unoccupied. They looked like they were used to store drugs. The whole set-up wasn't very legit. Cindy's visit was probably to cover for some illegal trading. Billy-boy had seemed to know nothing whatsoever about marketing and was more interested in looking up her skirt. At least he hadn't stooped to dropping his pen on the floor to assist his viewpoint. That and that alone had set him apart from the boys at school.

In her court shoes she clattered over the cobbles and past a stack of smelly, bulging black binliners. Shit. Deep shit this time. The man in the Portakabin at the gate had fucked off home too. Buggeration. Cindy would have to hoof it out onto the street.

The street was deserted. No cars, no pedestrians, no public, no people. The surrounding premises were vast warehouses with no windows and seemingly no doors. The entire planet seemed devoid of life. Cindy changed plans. It was still light but already she did not feel safe here. After all, if you could get raped in a ticket hall of the London Underground at rush hour, and, according to an article she had read, you could, then you were not safe in broad daylight anywhere. Particularly here. If only she had not come. If only she did not need the money. She decided to find a black cab or a bus stop or an Underground station or . . . she realised she had left her A-Z in the car. She wasn't sure its maps covered this far out of Central London anyway. She turned a corner. Then another. Then another. Winding her way around a tangle of empty streets lined with faceless brick and tin buildings, gradually, she became confused over which direction she was heading in.

She heard a sound. It was a car. It was coming her way. She could flag it down. Perhaps they had jump leads. They could tell her where the bus stop was. Or where the Underground was, if it came out this far. Didn't someone say it went all the way into Essex? So it should do. If it was a woman driver she would cadge a lift. She turned. To her delight she saw that the car was slowing down anyway. It was an old Zephyr, bright metallic blue with steel trim and a corner panel badly dented. Well, she wasn't expecting a Ferrari, was she? It would do.

Behind something furry dangling from the windscreen mirror, Cindy could see that it was not a woman driver. Instead, there were two occupants. Both of them were young men. Both of them were grinning. They looked like skinheads. Fuck, fuck, fuck. This was not what she had in mind at all. She was trying desperately not to panic but alarm bells were going off in every sensory part of her body. Her pulsating head. Her drying throat. Her racing heart. Her queasy stomach. Her twisting gut. Her shaking knees. For God's sake, Lucinda. Don't be so silly. Nonetheless, she checked the number plate quickly. She might have to remember it at their trial. She felt awfully frightened. She felt lacking in confidence. She felt unsure. Possibly you really could smell fear.

She turned and began to walk briskly away. Perhaps if she turned and ran all the way back to her car and locked herself in and . . . yeah, great thinking, Lucinda. Run into a deserted dead end and scream and scream like Joan Collins in her slack period. She seemed to have drifted into one of those seventies B-movie plots.

The Zephyr glided past and she could hear the two young men laughing inside. The passenger looked back. She tried not to catch his eye but hers were wide with fear and it was impossible not to. She saw his arm moving vigorously in the car interior. She was terrified he was loading a gun, then she realised he was winding down the window. He stuck his head out. The car cruised just ahead of her. For the first time ever Cindy imagined she was going to die.

'Lost, sweetheart?'

Cindy put her head down and stomped on.

'Hey, darlin', it's you I'm talkin' to. I asked if you was lost.'

Cindy tried to look confident. 'No. I'm not.'

'I think you are.'

'I think you're wrong.' She narrowed her eyes at him. He turned and said something no doubt unsubtle to his partner and they creased up with laughter.

'Where's the tube?' called Cindy. 'I'm meeting my boyfriend there.' She hoped it would sound more convincing to them than it did to herself.

'Which station you lookin' for?'

'. . . the local one.'

'I'm not sure I know where you mean. What time are you meeting your boyfriend?'

'Now. He's there now, waiting for me.'

'We'll give you a ride.'

'No thanks.'

'Come on.'

'No thank you.'

'Just get in the fucking car.' The change in tone was drastic. Cindy had palpitations.

'No way!' She abruptly turned round and began to run like hell, or at least as fast as her court shoes would carry her. She was sweating buckets. Her pulse was racing as erratically as she was. She was plain terrified even before she heard the car turn around and follow her back.

'Where's your boyfriend? I don't see him,' called the passenger. The driver was high on laughter.

'How big is your boyfriend's knob? Not as big as mine, I'll bet.'

Cindy's fright turned to horror. Jesus. She ran on. She was panting. She was short of breath. She had a stitch in her side. If she didn't get out of here quickly she was going to get raped. Gang raped. Nightmare. She hadn't run anywhere this fast since she had left school, which was twenty years ago and she hadn't worn court shoes in those days and she had still come second last. Her brain was in a flurry. She had to find a turning down which the car could not go and just hope to God they didn't jump out of the car and try to catch up with her.

'Hey,' called the guy. 'Where's the fire?' She heard them crease up again in hysterics. 'Ever sucked two guys off together? Bet you give great head.'

It entered her mind that they could be high on crack cocaine. They had lost control of themselves. There was no chance to reason with them, to plead with them. They were beyond persuasion. She tried to think what she might have in her shoulder bag which was hard and heavy and she could fight them with. But she couldn't think of anything except her mobile phone which, if she had brought it with her, would have meant she wouldn't have got into this fucking mess in the first place. Cindy tried as hard as she could to block out the tide of filth. The second guy was shouting something about pussy now and both men were screeching maniacally with laughter.

She careered towards an alleyway. Thank God, thank God. This end was blocked to cars by three black iron Victorian posts. She pulled off a neat trick. She ran past it so that the car passed beyond her. She then doubled back and ran like fuck down the alleyway. The car would have to turn full circle and that would take it half a minute longer.

But the two skinheads didn't plan on staying inside the Zephyr. They abandoned it and ran like lightning after her. In a second they were right behind her. She could hear their panting as they ran to catch up with her. One of them was literally breathing down her neck. She loosened her bag and reached from her shoulder and dipped into it as she ran. She pulled out a thick notebook and flung it hard behind her. It missed. They sensed her hysteria and sneered at her humiliation. Cindy had no idea what else she could do. She could not outrun them. Either side of the alleyway was lined with redundant buildings. There was nothing here. Through her acrid tears, to left and right and straight ahead, all Cindy could make out was brick walls. Her heart leapt as a hand touched her on her back. She bounded forward from it.

The tears were streaming down her face now as she tugged off her bag. Unbearable though it was to part with it she let fly with it over her shoulder at the feet of her attackers. They would settle for her money. Surely they would. Surely. But they kept on running and kept on laughing. They were catching up. Cindy felt the hand on her shoulder and this time its power and weight was overwhelming. She tripped and fell head first into the dirty road. Her attacker fell too. She used up every last breath left in her body to crawl out from underneath him and to sidestep his accomplice, who was bent over laughing at his partner.

'Man. You are one sad fucker.'

'Fuck off,' said the other.

Cindy saw neither of them. She ran on. Beads of a warm redness dripped in front of her eyes. She was bleeding. She had cut her forehead. Her wound stung with the grit of the road. The blood ran over her eyelid, down her cheek, into her mouth. With the wetness of it on her tongue she was aware just how dry her mouth had become.

The two men were closing in again. She kept going, drawing on some deep-seated reserve of energy. Adrenalin. Head down, she could not check out what lay ahead. Was this a dead end or not? She prayed it was not. She was so near. Around the corner lay the hope of help. If there was a corner.

But this time there were two, too-powerful hands upon her shoulders. She came hurtling down, falling hard. It hurt like hell. For the first time she heard the sound of herself shrieking. She could not bear to give them the satisfaction of hearing her voice or having any intimate knowledge of her person that she could deny them. But her wails were involuntary and uncontrollable. She dug her nails into the silver-ringed fingers on one shoulder and tried to drag herself forward. She could see only red, the red of the blood flowing freely from her forehead. She felt her legs being pinned down and Jesus only knew how many hands were on her thighs and at her knickers as all three wrestled on the ground.

'I smell pussy.' One of the men was saying it repeatedly and snorting with laughter. For whatever reason, they loosened their grip for a micro-second. It was enough for Cindy to take her chance and wriggle forward, just a bit. She had lost her bag. She had lost her shoes. She had lost her dignity. But she hadn't lost completely. Not yet.

She looked ahead. The blood fell across her eyes again. All she could see was red. But it was not the red of the blood from her head. It was not the red of her attacker's T-shirt. It was the red of a lovely little TVR Chimaera. The two men spotted it too.

'Fuckin' 'ell, man!'

'Shit!'

They released their grip and upped and scarpered back along the alley.

Cindy stumbled upwards and from side to side as the passenger car of the door swung open.

'Bad hair day?' asked Alan from the driver's seat.

'It's that just gang-raped look. It's all the rage around here.'

She broke into the uncontrolled, violent sobbing of total relief as she fell into the car and into her lover's arms.

45

'Shall we go through?'

Serena led the way, followed by her eleven dinner guests, her husband Alec bringing up the rear. Charlotte had wondered what Dr Sark would be like. She had imagined he would be a dead ringer for Nigel, if not in looks, at least in buffoonery. But he was not. He was charming, intelligent, good-looking and good company. What he was doing stuck with Serena, Charlotte could only begin to guess at. When she did think about it she realised that the Serena Sark of Soho was not the same Serena Sark of Wimbledon. She slipped off her sharp edges with her sharp suits when she got home of an evening and turned into the near-perfect hostess. Still, with the woman-who-does doing it, how difficult was it to pull off a successful dinner party? Charlotte moved ahead of the others and caught up with her erstwhile boss.

'I'm so sorry, Serena.'

'It's quite all right, Charlotte. People frequently assume Wimbledon is a lot nearer than it really is.'

'I'm sure Daniel will be here soon.'

'In the circles we move in Alec and I are quite used to our guests running a little late due to a political crisis or some such thing.' Serena smiled graciously, although it was quite clear that she was going to be put out if there were thirteen around the table. That, after all, was the only reason Daniel had been invited.

The dining room was one of gracious proportions at the rear of the between-the-wars house. In the centre, a circular table reflected the shape of a huge bay window over which was drawn an impressive sweep of pale cream curtains, shutting out the chill of the night. Serena had in her hand a set of handwritten place names and proceeded to lay them out.

'Eleanor, you're here next to Alec. Jim, you're on the other side with Deirdre. Susan and Dennis this side. Charlotte, you're here beside me. Dr and Mrs McReady are opposite each other over there. I'll sit here. Even though the table is round, Alec and I pretend we have a top and a bottom.'

The guests laughed politely at Serena's tired joke.

Serena finished ordering everyone about, which she did very well, and they sat down. Diagonally opposite Charlotte, a space remained for Daniel. Right now she could throttle him. Serena was prattling on about being delayed by political crises when all Daniel was being delayed by was boring old Bonzo and a pint of Guinness. She glanced at her giant Swatch. It was past nine.

Serena made a gesture and the woman attendant turned to the sideboard and produced a huge bowl of dense salad which she handed to Serena. The woman left the room and Serena held out the bowl to Charlotte.

'We're very informal here. Do help yourself everybody.'

Charlotte felt it was anything but informal and really did not want to go first. She didn't have to. The front door buzzed.

'That'll be Daniel. I'll go and collect him and bring him in.'

Although it was not the done thing, Serena understood that Charlotte would want to leave the table to prep Daniel in private. When she got to the polished oak front door, the woman who did was already letting Daniel in.

'Hi,' he said. 'Where's Selena?'

'Serena,' hissed Charlotte. She smiled at the woman, who acknowledged her and scuttled back into the kitchen.

'You reek of alcohol,' whispered Charlotte. 'Look at your hair.' She used both hands to straighten him out. 'Where have you been?'

'Sorry. I forgot.'

'You *forgot*?'

'Whoah. Bonzo and me went for a curry – right bunch of arse that was – and I—'

'Keep your voice down. You went for a curry?! You must be out of your mind! She's made enough food to feed the Red Army. Are you fit to go in?'

'Yeah, of course. Who's here?'

'No idea. They're all old and boring.'

'That Nige guy, is he here?'

'No, of course not. Don't even mention him.'

'Why not?'

'Not in front of her husband.'

'Why, are they shagging?'

Charlotte suddenly realised that, now she had seen Dr Sark firsthand, they – Nigel and Serena – were almost certainly not.

'No. It just doesn't seem right. Show an interest in her husband.'

'What's he do?'

'His name's Alec. He's in cancer research. He works for some Swiss company. He's developed some drug or something that's going to cure cancer and make the Sarks stinking rich.'

'Stinking, eh?'

'Not as stinking as you are of alcohol. If I'd known you were going to be pissed out of your tiny brain I wouldn't have asked you. I shouldn't have asked you anyway. I must be losing my touch. Go upstairs and clean your teeth.'

'I didn't bring me toothbrush.'

'Use theirs.'

Daniel looked incredulous. 'I'd rather eat out the cat's bowl. I'll pass. Stop fretting. You're not my bird.'

'No, but I'm your account director.'

'And a nine out of ten shag, as I was just saying to Bonzo. No names mentioned, of course.'

Charlotte shot him a look of total fury, but they had to go in and in they went. At the deep end.

Daniel shuffled from one buttock to the other. After the pained expression that arrived on Charlotte's face every time he chipped in, he had stopped talking, and then later he had stopped listening, and now he was observing how Charlotte would cock her head to one side and smile and then cock it to the other and laugh and all the time not quite cover up the fact that she was bored. Not as much as he was, though. With this lot you couldn't have a blarney about football, drugs or shagging.

If only he had not eaten that long boozy lunch with the clients. If only he had not nibbled that high-in-fat snack at the pub. If only he had not consumed that congealed chicken rogash at the takeaway. It was all repeating on him now, but it had not been when he had been pouring three types of white wine down his throat and stuffing his face with pink fish risotto and a mousse à deux chocolats which Serena repeatedly presented to him. He had only realised that the wry expression on the crumpled up chip wrapper that passed for her face was not one of encouragement when Charlotte had mouthed at him across the table to stop.

No one had identified that it was he who was farting. You can only keep it in so long, the fermenting aftermath of an undercooked takeaway Indian meal swilling inside a bellyful of beer. Sooner or later it erupts. You know it's going to even when you're packing it in. You don't care then. Normally you just go home to your pit of a flat-share, climb into the heap of unmade linen and rolled-up socks that resembles your bed and, when it turns over inside you, kicks you in the back of the stomach and decides to make a rush for freedom, you wake up and charge for the bog. In the best cases the expanding gases blow out of you at one end and you can pass the night inflating the bedsheets. In most cases the alcohol propels itself up your gullet and out your gob and if you get your timing right you can still make the dead centre of the lavatory bowl and not spatter the bathroom tiles. The worst cases are if you get the runs, because then you have to go and squat and squirt for hours in the dead of night and whenever you rise to leave your backside starts to spray again. Jesus. He hoped to God that wouldn't happen to him now.

'No thank you.'

Selena Scragg, or whatever her name was, was offering Bendick's Bitter Mints. She was giving him the evil eye. If he farted any more he'd blow the curtain behind him high off the ground and away from the bay window. Give them all a view of the garden she seemed so proud of. The frump opposite was rising. She was going for a slash. He hoped she wasn't going to be too long. He was next in there. He listened to Serena's instructions on where it was. Funny how somebody who was obviously a stickler for social niceties should bawl in foghorn tones the compass point directions of where to go and piss.

It was more than a leak he needed. He farted again. If he thought about his rectum, which he did not much care to, he sensed the old Graf Zeppelin had reinflated inside him and was desperate to sally forth back onto the world stage any minute now out, sailing out of his rear end with trumpets playing. Thank you, Mary, for the sphincter's apathy towards the seductive power of alcohol. He squeezed tight and the airship backed off. He watched Charlotte sip her coffee and brace herself as Serena floated gaily into the place of the lady who'd gone for a widdle. She was being all girly-flirtatious with Charlotte. What for? What were they talking about? He knew Serena was up to something. You could tell. She was that obvious. It was something to do with Sister Verity. Sister Verity. Laugh. You had to. What a little triumph she was. A disaster, of course, in the making. Who cared? The minute it all went wrong they'd all fuck off to the next top twenty agency and the next top twenty job. That's what you did in advertising. Look after number one. Leave the dickhead client to pick up the pieces of their own shattered strategy. He'd look after Charlotte though. She was a nice girl. She was a good account director. She was a stonking good shag. He would play her game in the short term, but in the longer one he knew he'd get her back into bed. Or at least over the bonnet of Bonzo's car. It was just a matter of time and timing.

'How old do *you* think he is?' Daniel eventually came round to the conclusion that Serena's question must have been asked of him. All eyes appeared to be on his. He was not sure how far out of it all he was and how long he had been drunk.

'Who are we talking about then?'

'Hector Quigley, of course.'

''Bout your age I should have thought.'

Serena's expression was rum. 'I think he must be a *great* deal older than me.'

'How old are you?'

'Really! Is HQ really as profitable as everyone says? Charlotte, do you know the income projections for next year?'

'I'm not on the board, Serena.'

'No, I suppose not. Do you have access, by any chance, to HQ's three-year plan, Charlotte? Does Hector have one?'

'I don't know. I think he makes quite a lot of it up as he goes along.'

'Surely that is only an illusion? Do you rate the quality of the board account management? And what about their media buying? Apparently there is a sort of loose international arrangement too. Do you know anything about that, Daniel?'

'Might do. How much are you paying for the info?'

'Paying?!'

'You're a competitor.'

'Goodness me. I'm hardly a competitor. I'm your hostess. I'm just showing an interest in your careers.'

'Likely as not.' Daniel failed to see Charlotte's very cross expression.

'I'm just chatting. It's just nice to know if an old friend such as Hector is doing as well as everyone says he is. Have you noticed if any assets have been sold off recently? Any little wisps of gossip on the wind?'

'Apparently one of the account directors is sleeping with her manager.' Daniel winked.

Charlotte's eyes narrowed, but Serena closed the conversation.

'That was not exactly the sort of thing I had in mind. Another mint anybody?'

'Don't mind if I do, Selena.' Daniel tore off the foil wrapper and dropped it into his plate. Thank Jesus Christ for fuck all. The old cow who'd trekked off for the longest piss in the northern hemisphere since Niagara Falls first fell off its cliff had deigned to come back from the dead, all fresh lippy and readjusted shoulder straps. Daniel cleared his throat. He said a loud excuse me to no one in particular and lurched off, out of the dining room. The corridor swooned around him. The floor seemed to roll like the deck of a seagoing schooner on a bad run on the Atlantic. Turn at the stairs and up to the first half-landing, Selena Scragg had said. He tripped on the first stair and fell face first into the hall carpet. He guffawed at himself. From the corner of his unfocussing eye he saw he had fallen beside a small vanity case placed neatly in front of a cupboard. Selena must be off on some international business freebie in the morning.

Thank fuck. Here it was and none too soon. The bog. Wooden panelled walls, white fluffy hand towel on miniature heated towel rail and, gleaming in white porcelain, lid raised in salute, smiling mouth agape and all ready and willing to be dumped in, our faithful old friend the toilet bowl. Inside four seconds Daniel had dropped his trousers and pants and was bum first in there, releasing the pent up forces of a day's all-expenses-paid calorific indulgence. The relief was magnificent. The raspberry fanfare was startling. The spectacle was extraordinary. For it was not the great Graf Zeppelin that launched from between his well-aimed buttocks but its arch-rival, the sleek, dynamic, pretentious Queen Mary. There she goes. It splashed into the receptive water, an ocean liner of a turd, slipping out effortlessly, gliding in one long uninterrupted movement from anus to U-bend, from back passage to sea passage, from a life completely constrained to one of fabulous freedom. Only it seemed not to have got the message.

Daniel pressed the flush lever. Nothing happened. He tried again. Well, that was par for the course. Nothing happened and it never did in other people's lavatories, particularly people you didn't know. There is a knack to flushing someone else's toilet and it is simply impossible to pick it up first time. He released the lever a third time. He rose, adjusted his dishabille and looked down. His deposit was still squatting there in the toilet bowl. For all the effort he had put into it, the all guns blazing squeeze, the downward thrusting energy, the full pressure on the flush, that which he had just shat out of his bottom remained there in front of him. Would it go round the U-bend? Would it hell. It was too long. It must be eighteen inches if it was a day. It was firm and solid and brown and full of itself and terribly tangible and thoroughly three-dimensional and very much there. It was quite simply the hugest turd he had ever set eyes upon. It was the Queen Mother of all missiles. The permanent secretary of shits. It was the biggest jobby in the world and it was not going anywhere.

Daniel drew breath. He could hear the dinner party guests laughing below. The cistern had refilled. He had flushed three times already. They must have heard him downstairs. This was his last chance. He firmly and fully depressed the lever. The pipes whirred, the water let rip and a full flush took place. The splishing splashing noise was music to his ears, Debussy probably. He looked through the torrent into the whirlpool. The giant jobby was drowning, spinning round and round, being sucked into the vortex. It descended in a viscous spiral and disappeared. Daniel sighed with relief. That was it. Now he could wash his hands, literally and metaphorically, of the crappiest crap of all time.

After he had run his hands under the tap and wiped them on the warm fluffy towel, he leant over to switch out the light and to make his descent to the dining room. But something caught him out of the corner of his eye. Jesus. What a bunch of arse. The biggest jobby in the world had clawed its way back round the bend and was sitting there alive and well and performing a synchronised swimming routine with the broad-shouldered glamour of an over-tanned Esther Williams.

Daniel gulped. What was he going to do? He could not just leave it there. The next occupant would know it was his. He could not flush again. They would all hear him. They would know he had given birth to a monster and be embarrassed for him. He wanted to escape. He wanted to jump out the window. But instead he had an idea. A stonkingly brilliant idea.

'Big bunch of arse, matey.' He wagged his finger at the jobby. He had better get a move on. He fell to his knees and reached out for the double-thickness duvet-soft toilet paper. He took a long white stretch and carefully wound it around his hand. He leant into the toilet bowl and placed his protected hand firmly on the head of the turd. He gave it a shove. It slipped right down and then slipped right back up again. He tried again. It did the same thing. It would not leave home. There was only one thing for it.

Daniel took the roll of toilet paper and spun out a huge quantity of it onto the floor. He had not seen this much unravelled bog paper since the Andrex puppy last bounded through the sitting room in a ten per cent extra promotion. Carefully regloving his hand, he slipped it beneath the turd and lifted it out of the water. He laid it out on the paper on the floor and wound and wound it around in the paper until it rocked there by itself, a little brown baby in swaddling clothes. Then he picked up the package, slipped to the window, opened it and wanged it out as hard and as far away as he possibly could. Rubbing his hands in satisfied dismissal, the remaining paper fell from his fingers to the garden below. It was caught on the wind. The window closed behind him, Daniel washed his hands one last time and, sobering up, took the trip back to the dinner table.

As he joined them in the dining room he saw that his fellow diners had abandoned the side of the table where they had been sitting. Instead, they had lined up on the other side and all eyes were on Serena, who stood at the edge of the long sweep of curtains around the bay window. Charlotte smiled at Daniel. He was horrified at her news.

'Serena's just spent a fortune on her garden apparently. She's going to show us,' she said.

Serena slipped both hands in behind the curtains and pulled on hidden strings. They drew back on both sides. It was the grand opening of a new stage production. Serena flashed her gypsy grin.

'Alec and I have had lighting put in. It makes such a spectacle at night. I'd forgotten tonight was the first time we could show it off.'

Her guests applauded at the sight. An illuminated patio of York stone and herringbone brick. Versailles tubs of bay trees and white geraniums twinkling with fairy lights. A moonshine-effect lawn with croquet hoops silhouetted on the horizon. A Victorian wrought-iron love bench picked out in white. All beneath a spreading oak underlit in green. Daniel shivered. He hoped to God that none of them looked up. For there, nestling in its cradle of comforting, two-ply duvet-soft toilet paper and hanging in a low-slung spiral from a mid-level branch, swinging shakily from side to side and catching the full beam of the spotlights, was that which should have been wanged across the garden wall and well on its way to oblivion. Not fallen two feet from the window and left dangling for all to see. It was the proud and public contents of his bottom; it was the biggest jobby in the world.

'Shall we go through for coffee?' asked Serena.

'Yeah!' yelped Daniel. He smartly led the way.

46

'Duncan?'

'What?'

'I've been thinking.' Michael looked up from his papers.

'About what?'

He shuffled the last pages of a contract. 'It's very interesting how independent production companies always seem to think they should hang on to the rights for programmes which they come up with the ideas for, but which would never see the light of day without our money.'

'You wouldn't have a channel without their shows. They

deserve the rights. Authors retain the rights to their books. Why shouldn't producers keep theirs to their programmes? Broadcasters are greedy.'

'No they're not. They invest in the product. Without that investment there would be no product. Therefore they should get a share.'

'It isn't a share they want. It's the whole damn one hundred per cent. That's what infuriates people like Karen and me. We do all the work and then because The Station or whoever gives you twenty thousand pounds for the pilot, they demand ownership of the product in perpetuity. There's a word for that. It's called exploitation.'

'It's not exploitation.'

'It is. It's the same way that record companies treat teenagers. Over here Elton. Over here Liam. Just sign this piece of paper and we'll look after your best interests. Those contracts are illegal now, they're no longer allowed to exploit the artists and buy out all their work before they've even written it.'

'That's not what broadcasters do.'

'It is. But it's ending soon. When there were only a handful of companies doing the commissioning they could get away with it. I mean, there was supposed to be competition but there wasn't.'

'There was.'

'There wasn't. If you were trying to sell a programme to Channel Four and they turned it down it would be very unlikely that it would be suitable for BBC1.'

'You could take it to BBC2.'

'In some cases you could. But in most you couldn't. But now . . .'

'What?'

'Oh nothing. This is boring.'

'No it's not.'

'It is. Why you have to bring your work home with you I don't know.'

'You do too.'

'I do not.'

'You do. You did when you worked in advertising.'

'That was different.'

'How was it different?'

'It was different because I worked in advertising and you didn't.'

'Eh?'

'When we used to discuss work at home it was different work. It was interesting. Now everything's interconnected.'

'Like this?' Michael held up a document.

'What's that?'

'The *Sister Verity* contract.'

'She's under contract to us.'

'No. I meant the contract for the series.'

'Are you only looking at that now? It's been on air for weeks.'

'I've not had a chance to see it yet. The preliminaries have been signed. The juniors do that. But it's not actually *bona fide* until I sign it and the chief executive signs it.'

'Well, you'd better get a move on. We could change terms now I know it's not been done.'

'The preliminaries have been so you can't. Anyway, that's not how English law works. You've taken the money and have entered into a deed of faith and therefore you are obliged to behave by the standard practices of the industry.'

'Which are all over the place as we all know.' Duncan sighed.

'Stop being so moody.'

'I'm not being moody.'

'Oh yes you are. You're moody because you want to run off with those two lesbians and play doctors and nurses followed by house.'

Duncan tutted.

'Am I right or am I right?' asked Michael.

'I'm not moody. And if I am that's not why. I feel left alone at work if you must know. Karen has upped and abandoned me. I've no idea what I'm meant to be doing these days.'

'Do as you please, then.'

'I do but . . . well, it's her show and her company and . . . you know what she's like . . .'

'The Most Difficult Woman In Television.'

'I don't think so actually. You're the most difficult old woman in television these days.'

'Huh. Well, as I was going to say earlier until I was distracted—'

'Who by?'

'You. Look, just shut up, OK?'

Duncan scowled.

'I've thought through all the implications of this, Duncan. I am, or was, a solicitor and I know what I'm talking about.'

Duncan scowled some more.

'I think it is all right for you to help these women to conceive a child.'

Duncan sat bolt upright on the settee. Wow. That was a change of heart. He waited for the catch. Here it came.

'But it has to be providing that you do not see them or the child again. Or at least very often.'

'That's ridiculous. You're behaving like Hitler, as usual.'

'You and those two women are behaving like Hitler if you don't mind me saying so. Artificially planning the next super generation. Intelligence. Blue eyes. Blond hair. Healthy background. You've ticked off your little Aryan list, haven't you?'

'You're preposterous. One of these days I'm going to get a tape recorder and play back our conversations to you so you can hear just how ridiculous you are. Anyway, my eyes aren't blue, they're grey.'

'Hallelujah. A nation sighs in relief.'

'What's that meant to mean?'

Michael said nothing and returned to reading his papers.

Duncan tutted again. 'So what am I to do?'

'Think about it.'

'I'm not thinking about it. It doesn't merit thinking about.'

Michael put down his pen on the coffee table. 'I mean, why did they not consider me, that's what I want to know. I'm intelligent. I'm good-looking. I earn more money than you. And I'd do the business. I'd shag her, which is more than you would.'

Duncan's face contorted into creases of laughter. 'I knew I should have switched on the tape recorder. Shag her! She's a lesbian, for God's sake. That's the last thing she wants. You're so fucking precious! You're just jealous!'

'Yes I am jealous. Actually.'

'Think about it, Michael. You hate children.'

'I do not.'

'You do. You can't stand them. The youngest little boy you'd want to bounce up and down on your knee would be about seventeen.'

'This is true. But the lesbians don't know that.'

'That wasn't their reason for not picking you.' Whoops. He had let it slip out.

'Their reason? They have a reason for not picking me? What was it then?'

'You don't look like Lesley.'

'I don't believe that for a moment.'

'It's true.'

'I don't believe you.' Michael came over and stood over Duncan, menacingly. Duncan, lying on his back on the settee, adopted a half-foetal position in mock defence.

'They didn't want a child with . . . you know . . .'

'With what?'

Duncan tensed up with laughter and scrunched himself into a ball beneath Michael. 'They didn't want a child with a hairy little body and a bald head – particularly if it's a girl.'

Michael yelled with pretend hurt and fell onto Duncan and began to tickle him. His hands rummaged up under his shirt and roughly played with his hair. They embraced and kissed passionately for a few minutes. Duncan pulled away and sorted his shirt out. He wiped his hair back from his forehead. Michael snuggled up beside him on the settee. They both looked up at the ceiling.

'I was only joking.'

'No you weren't. I got the message. Don't go off with them, Duncan.' He took Duncan's hand in his. 'Please.'

'I won't go off with anyone, I promise. Least of all two women who don't like men. I love you.'

'Do you?'

'Of course I do.'

'Miaow.'

The shadow of Pushkin fell across their faces. Standing on top of the back of the settee, she yawned and stretched herself out by some three times her normal length then dug her claws into the seat fabric and began firing them into the cushion like a staple gun, part of her weapon-sharpening routine. The boys laughed.

'See Duncan. We have our own little baby already.'

'I know,' said Duncan. The smile flitted and faltered and fell from his face.

47

Cindy tried to smile. It seemed the only thing to do, but it wasn't working. It wasn't working because – though she would be eternally grateful to Alan for turning up like the seventh cavalry, or whoever it is who rides over the horizon in old movies – she was less than thrilled to be back with him and to have him back with her in her flat. She felt guilty about how she felt. She *was* grateful but now she wanted to say no thank you to what appeared to be part and parcel of the rescue package.

'Another drink?' asked Alan.

'Why not?' asked Cindy. She held out her champagne glass. It was not champagne which he poured in, but Marks and Spencer sparkling wine, all that she had found in her fridge when he had called around this evening. On any previous evening he would have been shown the door, the threshold of which he wouldn't have crossed in the first place. But on this evening, two nights after he had saved her, she had felt obliged to open up wide and let him back into her life.

'I can't believe you just turned up by coincidence.'

'I did. Well not quite. I found your car abandoned and you didn't answer your mobile phone and there was no sign of life anywhere, so I figured you had headed off to find a taxi or something and I knew you'd never find one out there, so I drove round looking for you for five minutes on the offchance I might catch you.'

'That doesn't explain what you were doing there in the first place. It's the middle of nowhere.'

'I still have some of your movements in my diary from when we were . . . you know, together. I knew it was a big contract for you because you made a fuss of it months ago when you fixed it up. When I checked my schedule I realised I'd be driving back from Essex about the time you'd be leaving that place. I wanted you to see the Newy. I had thought we might drive back into town in convoy and go for dinner.'

'God. Some men never get the message.' She felt mean. 'Well, I'm obviously glad that you did.'

'How's your head?'

'Can't say I've had any complaints.' It was tasteless and it went down like a lead balloon. Alan did not laugh. Instead he looked threatened. 'Oh, Alan, get real. There hasn't been anyone else other than you. Not for the want of me trying, mind you.'

Now he looked hurt. She hadn't even waited for the other emotions to vacate his face.

'I'm sorry, Alan. I'm trying very hard to be eternally grateful for your saving me from being gang-raped but it cannot change the status of where we were before. That wouldn't be realistic. It wouldn't work.'

'You've just decided that it wouldn't work.'

'I haven't just decided. I'm being honest with you.'

'I think maybe you're in shock from what's happened and it's put you off men. For the moment.'

'What?'

'Some women who have been raped never come to terms with sex again.'

'I haven't been raped. Nothing happened. We were even able to go back and get my bag. I didn't even lose any money.'

'You were nearly raped. It's psychological. You're having a delayed reaction or something. Take it out on me. I understand.'

'You must remind me what your hourly rate is, Dr Sigmund.'

'I don't know the technical terms but I know you, Cindy, and you're not yourself.'

'No, Alan. It's you who's not yourself, whoever yourself is. Nobody seems to know. Nobody can fathom you. You're a pretty hard-headed businessman and I find it faintly astonishing that someone who can spot a sting a mile off can't see that we don't belong with each other.'

'I know what it is. You're still hurt about that remark I made a few months back.'

'What remark?' Cindy had no idea what he was referring to.

'You know.'

'No.'

'That our relationship is inherently unstable.'

'Yeah, well, you weren't wrong there. I should have agreed with you instead of bleating on about wanting a baby. I must have been off my head.'

'It's only natural.'

'What? To be off my head?'

'No. To want a baby. Your internal clock is ticking away. You're in your late thirties.'

'Oh go on. Rub it in. Why don't you dress up in a long white beard and dance a pavane and swing a scythe?'

'I should have taken you more seriously.'

'Alan, it's too late.'

'No it's not. A baby is often the way to bring two people together.'

'It's often the way to trap two people together, you mean.'

'Don't be cynical.'

'I have every reason to be cynical, Alan. You don't want another child. You already have one. You said it yourself. You said you didn't much care for children. You said we couldn't afford one. You said I was not the maternal type. You said – I don't know what you said, but when I was really going for it you were totally dead set against it. Why you're bringing the subject up now I have no idea.'

'Because, Cindy, I would like to get back with you, that's why. And if you would like to have a child I'll go along with it. I'll help you to have one. I would certainly enjoy the first stage of the process!'

Cindy tutted. 'If you're after a quick screw on the floor as usual, now is not the time. And I'm not the person. I'm sorry.

If I do have a child I don't want you to be its father. That sounds horrible, but I think you were right before. I was wrong. Our relationship is inherently unstable.'

'Cindy! I have feelings too.'

'I forgot. You keep them so well hidden.'

'I do. I've just saved your life.'

'Alan, I am grateful. I've said I am. But you would have stopped just the same for a complete stranger. And tried it on with her, just like you're doing with me.'

Alan's face bled a furious crimson colour at that remark.

'I apologise. It was wrong of me to say that. I'm depressed. I'm a bit shaky still. Things aren't coming out the way I mean them to. God knows why I'm drinking this stuff. I'm turning into Shelley Winters ten years too soon.'

'Did you ever love me?'

'Yes. Yes, of course I did. Did you ever love me?'

'I have loved you since the moment you stepped into my life, Cindy. I still love you. More than I can ever say.'

'Alan!'

'What?'

'Why couldn't you say that before? You've never expressed your feelings for me. Your idea of a big gesture is to whip out two tickets to *La Bohème* and tell me to go on in on my own if you get stuck late in a meeting on the day.' She sighed.

Alan blushed.

'What is it now?'

'Guess what I have in my pocket?'

'An erection.'

'Not that pocket. This one.' He opened his jacket and produced two computer printed tickets bearing the red crest of the Royal Opera House.

Cindy's ears pricked up like a cat's at the sound of a rising can opener. If only she wasn't so shameless, so Pavlovian.

'Those look interesting.'

'Enticing?'

'Depends what's on.'

'*Turandot*. Is that how you pronounce it?'

'Who cares? The ice princess.'

'Oh, is she? Sorry, no offence intended.'

'None taken. Who's singing? I've not had time to read up on anything since I got back from Oz.'

'No idea.'

'What night?'

'Wednesday.'

'Will we still be talking?'

'Up to you.'

'I may not be free.'

Alan looked glum.

'It's not an excuse. I may genuinely not be free. I'll have to let you know.' Cindy stuck her face in her glass and drank down the dregs. Her head hurt like hell and her life was a mess, so why not swim in ersatz shimmering sparkling wine?

When Alan turned at the door half an hour later, he pecked her on the cheek. He dangled the tickets in front of her but, unusually, did not hand them over. He intended to hang onto them.

'Tempted?'

Cindy sighed. 'Alan . . .'

'I'll be in the foyer at seven-thirty.'

Cindy had almost completely closed the door behind him when she suddenly prised it open. He was standing by the Newy at the roadside.

'Alan!'

'What?'

'Don't be late.'

48

'Hello?'

'Hello. Mrs Collins?'

'Speaking.'

'Can I speak to Ginny, please?'

'What?'

'Ginny.'

'I can barely hear you. Do you have a cold?'

'Er . . . yes.'

'Well, it's all the rage this summer. Virginia? I don't know if she's in. I'm afraid I am not my daughter's keeper.' Ginny's mother turned from the mouthpiece. She had a voice that made her sound as if she broke boulders before breakfast. 'Virginia! *Virginia*!' She turned back. 'Who shall I say is calling?'

'A friend.'

'A friend? Do we have a name or are we one of the no names crowd?'

'I'm a schoolfriend.'

'Oh, are you? I hope you're not one of the ones involved in all that carry–on on the French trip.'

'Er . . . no.'

'There's no use denying it. *Virginia*! Ganging up on Virginia was very unfair, I'll have you know. I have no doubts whatsoever that my tearaway daughter was indeed the ringleader, but there is such a thing as shared responsibility. I have told Miss Martin that. Virginia may have bought that cognac. She can pass for eighteen. God knows she can pass for a woman of forty with a variable past. But you all drank it and you shouldn't have let her take the rap for it on her own. The thing about that Miss Martin, Oxbridge or no, is that she is only strong on discipline *after* the event. She should try prevention rather than the cure in my ever so humble opinion. She might find she travels further up her precious league table than up her own precious bottom. *Virginia*! I don't think she's in. No doubt you won't want to leave an incriminating message with me?'

'Er . . . no message.'

'Thought so! Children used to run to mothers. Now we're the last to know. Well I hope your cold clears up whoever you are. I'll ask Ginny who has a cold at school. Not that she'll tell me. She tells me nothing. Good bye.'

'Bye.'

Karen lifted her hand away from her mouth. She replaced the receiver. Well, that little piece of espionage hadn't worked.

'Children used to run to mothers. Now we're the last to know.'
Karen reflected on those words. How true they were. It was
a week now and she had caught neither sight nor sound of
Ginny Collins in that time. She was desperate to talk to her.
She was desperate to find out whether Max knew he was to
be the father of her child or not. Karen had been left straddling
the horns of a dilemma. She didn't want to be the person to
tell Max. If it wasn't true, it would backfire on her. On the
other hand if she did not tell Max and Ginny didn't summon
up the guts to tell him herself, time would tick over and before
they all knew it Ginny would become the great she-elephant
and they would all be confronting disaster with emotions and
relationships and hormones and after-birth all over the place.
Poor Ginny. Her mother sounded an old-fashioned battle-axe.
No wonder the girl had fallen into a life of drink-dependency on
school trips and slipped into precocious sexual experimentation.
For every action there is an equal and opposite reaction and
bringing your children up too strictly causes them to fly off
the rails at the earliest opportunity. Look at her and Max. She
had brought up Max in the most liberal and progressive manner
that a Hampstead media mother possibly could and how had he
turned out? About as wayward as a local railway timetable. No.
That was what she had thought until recently. But how much
of his life did she know about? What lay there fermenting under
the surface? How many local railway timetables got the local girls
pregnant? Karen sighed. Ginny's mother imagined the worst her
daughter had done was to buy a bottle of cheap French brandy.
She didn't know the half of it. Was there a half of it that
Karen didn't know? She felt trapped, trapped by circumstances.
Trapped by Max. Trapped by the decorators. Here she was locked
away, backed into a niche on the top floor of the house with just
a kettle and a word processor for company and the cracks in the
bare floorboards to occupy her mind. Her home was no longer
her own. Her life was no longer her own. Her precious baby was
no longer her own.

Max came into the kitchen in search of food. He pulled open the
fridge door and pulled out a block of cheddar cheese from the lit
interior.

'Would you like a cheese sandwich, darling?'

'This is fine as it is. What are you doing down here?'

'I couldn't work upstairs. It's too dusty. The dust was getting into the word processor.'

'I thought you had that Duncan Cairns writing on *Sister Verity*.'

'I have. He is.'

'So what are you doing?'

'Oh, nothing . . .'

'What?'

'A new series. Once the autumn schedule is on air everyone will be looking for new stuff again.'

'I hope you're not writing speculatively. I've told you it's a waste of time.'

'This is different.'

'You won't sell it.'

'You don't know what it is. And use a knife and a plate please. You shouldn't bite into the cheese like that. It's not nice.'

'It's not nice.' Max mimicked his mother. There was a clatter in the other room. They both stopped what they were doing and looked at each other.

'Decorators,' said Max.

'What have they broken now?' asked Karen.

'Sounded like they were moving the ladder. So, what is your new idea?'

'It's a secret.'

Max tutted. 'I don't want to know anyway.'

'Well why did you ask? . . . You keep secrets from me so I'm keeping secrets from you.'

'You're so childish sometimes.'

'I'm not being childish.'

'What secrets do I keep from you?'

'Well . . . I don't know, do I because if I did they wouldn't be secrets, would they?'

'You are being childish. Try a "for example".'

'Well, for example, I don't know where you go in the evenings and I don't know who you hang out with.'

'That's for good reason.'

'What good reason?'

'Because I don't want you tracking me down and turning up in the car and asking me if I need an extra jumper because it's getting cold in front of my friends.'

'You don't have any friends.'

'I do. You're the one with no friends.'

'That's not true.'

'Name one.'

'Max! You're a reptile.'

'You couldn't even stay friends with my father.'

'Don't drag all that up, please. Who's your best friend then?'

'There isn't a particular one. Just some of the guys from college.'

'They never come here.'

'They don't want to look at you and get turned to stone.'

'Don't be rude.'

'Look. Sixteen- and seventeen-year-olds don't come round to play with mummy. We do our own thing.'

'What about that Collins girl?'

Max shifted in his seat. 'What about her?'

'Is she your friend?'

'Sort of. I know her. She's just a kid. Well, obviously I know her.'

'Obviously?'

'Yeah. You've met her.'

Karen jumped. 'How d'you know that?'

'At the door. She came to the door.'

'Oh . . . yes. Is she your girlfriend?'

Max looked appalled. 'Mind your own business. I'm not discussing my sex life with you.'

'Your *sex* life!?'

'Oh come on. I'm sixteen. Old enough to get married.'

'*Married?!*'

'Don't panic. I'm not getting married. I'm just pointing out that it's legal to have kids and everything at sixteen.'

'Max, Max. Don't ruin your life!'

'What?'

'Just don't, my baby. Don't.'

'I have no intention of ruining my life. You're working hard enough at that already. I'm not encouraging you.'

'Don't be so hurtful, Max.'

'Are you making dinner or what?'

'Max . . .'

'What?' Max munched on his cheese. He picked up a copy of *Mother and Baby* from amongst the magazines Karen was using for source material. 'What on earth is this?'

'Noth-ing,' sang Karen. At last. He had fallen into her trap. 'Just some source material for the show I'm working on.'

'Which is?'

'Noth-ing,' she sang.

'Probably is if you're writing it. Get Duncan Cairns to create it for you.'

'D'you think he's better than me?'

'No, but you're paying him. You might as well squeeze the lifeblood out of him. I will when I'm running the company.'

'But that's exactly it, Max. You won't be unless things stay the way they are.'

'What things? I will run the company whatever happens.'

'Only if you can cope with adult life, Max. Only if you're responsible.'

'Eh?'

'I knew it. She hasn't told you, has she?'

'Who hasn't told me what? Sister Verity?'

'No, not Sister Verity. Oh. Max, I wish I knew what to do.'

'I wish I knew what you were talking about.'

'Hey, Mrs!' It was the decorator calling. The older one popped his head around the door. 'We're off now. Have to wait until tomorrow for the paint to dry.'

Karen went to see them out. Max surreptitiously swivelled around the monitor of the computer. What on earth was she writing? He peered into the light of the screen. A baby show? A baby show! A baby show . . .

Karen came back into the room.

'Hey, mum?'

'Don't look at that!' She rushed to the table and turned the screen away from Max's speed-reading eyes. She clicked on save and closed the file. 'That's not for you.'

'What? No babies for Max?'

'No. No babies for Max. What would *my* baby like for dinner?'

'Rusks. And mashed banana. Nah. Nothing. I'm going out.'

He upped and left Karen to roam alone around her half-bare, half-pulled apart, half-finished, half-happy house.

49

'Duncan!' What was he doing? Karen was impatient. 'Duncan!'

'Coming.'

Duncan had stalled in his progress across the office floor. It was strange to be back in the office after so many days in the *Sister Verity* studio and he was not at home there. But he was also disorientated by his post. He had collected it at the letterbox of his basement flat in Maida Vale and he had walked into Paddington with it unread in his hand. He had only just spotted the postmark at his desk and realised what he had. It was the result of his AIDS test. He drew a deep breath and plunged in.

'Duncan!'

'I've said I'm coming.'

It was not the result of his AIDS test, of course. He had known it would not be the result of his AIDS test. It was merely a card reporting that the result was in and requesting him to attend for final counselling. The old thumbs up or the old thumbs down. That, of course, was what the old thumbs up and thumbs down stood for literally. The selection between the option to go on living and the option to die.

'Duncan!'

'Yeah, yeah, yeah,' he muttered.

He made for Karen's office. He was more emotional about this than he had expected. He did not believe for a minute that the test would be positive. But then who did? Are we not all immortal?

'For fuck's sake, Duncan. I'll have grown old and died by the time you get in here.'

'At least you'll get the chance to grow old.'

She ignored him.

'I've decided to work up a mother and baby show.'

Duncan was taken by surprise. Ambushed. 'A mother and baby show?'

'For the afternoon.'

'Who for?'

'The Station. For after Sister Verity completes her run. Or put it on ITV daytime or anywhere. Women love three things on TV. Sex, weddings and babies. Babies aren't catered for.'

'I agree. Women love three things on TV. Sex, sex and sex.'

'Uh-uh. Weddings and babies come next.'

'It's too simple. Someone would have done it already if it was a ratings grabber.'

'Well they haven't because they're all blind. They're all mentally constipated. They're all men. There are too many men in this business, that's the real problem. And, nothing personal, too many gay men. Not one of you is interested in children.'

'You don't read the *Sun* then?'

'But women are. And what else have young mothers got to do other than stay at home and watch television? Here's my proposal. It's a sort of cross between education and entertainment.'

'Infotainment. That makes a nice change.' His sarcasm was lost on Karen.

'There are competitions too. I wonder who we could get to present it? Most of the harpies on TV are too horrific for anyone to believe they could have a baby which didn't hatch all scaly out of an egg.'

'What about Caron Keating. Hasn't she got a young baby?'

'God. Her. We'd get stuck with granny Gloria forcing her way onto centre stage every week dressed in fluorescent orange.'

'Daytime viewers might like a three generation approach.'

'Not right. There are too many Irish people on TV already.'

'Sister Verity is Irish.'

'She's good.'

Karen handed Duncan the proposal.

'Did Max help you with this?'

Duncan was startled by Karen's expression.

'What do you know about Max?'

'What do I know about him? He looks at your proposals doesn't he? Did he like this one?'

'I tried not to show it to him.'

'Tried?'

'He saw it anyway.'

'Didn't you want him to see it?'

'I didn't. I mean I didn't not want him to see it. I wanted him to see it but not until I'd found the right formula of words for the opening.'

Duncan read out the beginning. '"There is nothing as wonderful in all of human life as the birth of a baby and nothing as wonderful as sharing that news with those around you whom you love." It's a bit on the gushy side. Who were you thinking of sending it to? Beatrix Potter?'

'It's a woman's programme.'

'You're not really a woman's woman. I'm more of a woman's woman than you'll ever be.'

'You said it. Go away and read it. How's Sister Verity for this afternoon?'

'On autopilot. Now we've sorted out the technical hitches with the backgrounds and she's overcome her aversion to the ITC guidelines on taste and decency, there's nothing left to be produced really, just the selection of incoming calls and we can't plan those.'

'What does she do when she's not here with us?'

'Charity work, I suppose. And her Verity Tampon lectures. She goes round schools.'

'Well she can't go far. I'm not paying to helicopter her in just because she has some crappy school visit in Newcastle.'

'Verity pay for all that.'

'I mean, why do girls need all this help with their periods? Where are their mothers? It's the mothers that let them down. They don't talk to their daughters any longer and then the daughters go off on school trips to France and drink cognac and come home pregnant.'

'Well the sponsorship money is rolling in according to my friend Charlotte, so we should be thankful that mothers have a blockage when it comes to their daughters' periods, if you'll excuse the expression.' He looked down at Karen's mother and baby show. 'Karen?'

'What?'

'What was it like bringing up a child on your own? You know. Without a father.'

Karen pierced him with her gaze. Her eyes seemed magnified through her bejewelled glasses.

'Why are you asking me that? Why does everyone ask me that *now*?'

He was asking out of self-interest. He wanted to see what was in store for his baby being brought up without a man around. He wasn't going to reveal that to Karen, though. 'Because you've written a mother and baby show and you normally write from the heart. I just wondered why you're doing it now. Is it because Max is leaving home?'

'Leaving home?' She looked so down.

Duncan felt sympathetic but he had his own worries. Perhaps something was up with Karen and Max at home and that's why she was all over the place these days. Still, it was good for him.

'Karen, I've barely met Max. I have no idea what's going on in his life.'

'Neither have I. That's the problem. You said he was leaving.'

'Well, he'll go off to university soon, won't he? In the next couple of years . . . sorry.'

Karen sniffed.

'What would you know, Duncan? You lot – you and Michael and Jamie Hirst – what responsibilities have you got? When are you ever not selfish? When do you sacrifice your life for the next one down the line?'

Duncan retreated. Karen had shouted and screamed and pulled her famous peroxided hair and waved her trademark bejwelled glasses in the air before. But she had never got personal and hurtful. He returned to his desk and the letter from the clinic. He had responsibilities. He was not selfish. He did have sacrifices to make for the next one down the line.

Pushkin purred. She adored being groomed as long as there were no knots. If there were knots and the nylon brush got stuck and Duncan pulled too hard then she would give one miaow the first time and lash out with her claws the second. She rolled over onto her back, half-bent her paws and held them up. She threw her head back over Duncan's thigh and exposed her white throat, her mouth set in a smile.

'You and Marilyn Monroe, eh baby? What am I going to do with all this spare fur? Knit a blanket. You could lie on it. You'd like that, wouldn't you, my angel?'

Pushkin purred loudly in agreement. But, as Duncan defluffed the brush and placed the ball of hair onto a pile on the coffee table, the ringing of the telephone brought madam's hair appointment to an abrupt end. Duncan let the cat drop to the floor and half-tripped over her as he ran to pick up the call before the answering machine cut in.

'Duncan Cairns.'

'Hello, it's me.' It was Paul McCarthy.

'Oh, hi. I haven't heard from you in ages.'

'I've been busy.'

'What on?'

'Not working.'

'What then?'

'Oh, Duncan. I need to tell somebody. Something terrible has happened. It's ruined my life.'

'You're allergic to leather.'

'Be serious.'

'There's a strike in the chain mail industry.'

'Anton and I have had a row.'

'Is that all?'

'What do you mean, is that all? I ring up for sympathy

and get fucking Saddam Hussein without the mother of all moustaches.'

'Moustaches are passé, that's why. Other than that we're identical twins.' Paul tutted. 'Drama, drama, drama,' mocked Duncan. 'You weren't sympathetic last year when I told you Michael and I had had a big bust-up. I'm giving you a taste of your own medicine.'

'It's medicine I need. He virtually hospitalised me.'

'Anton did? My God. How?'

'Well, you know the sort of thing we're into?'

'His Rolex didn't slip off inside you, did it? Are you ticking?'

'Worse.'

'Worse?'

'I said something – I don't know what – which set him off. Next thing I know he's beating me black and blue. He broke every bone in my body.'

'Perhaps he thought you liked it.'

'We had a code word for when he should stop. I'm lying there in my sling shouting "Meringues, meringues, meringues," and he just goes on pounding away with his fists. Twisting my limbs. Striking me across the face. I thought he was going to kill me.'

Duncan was laughing at the image of Paul screaming "Meringues, meringues, meringues", but Paul had reduced himself to tears.

'What were you shouting "Meringues" for?'

'It was our code word to stop the pain. Meringues are delicate and easily smashed. Honestly, the way he was thumping me I might as well have been shouting fucking "rock cakes".'

'When was all this?'

'The other week. It's taken me this long to get over it. I've been bandaged up and on tranquillisers and been laid up at home with nothing to do other than wank myself silly watching porn films.'

'Ah. Not *every* bone was broken?'

'I knew I was on a highway to nothing asking you for sympathy. You're so brutal.'

'Butch is the word I think you're looking for. Anton is the one who's brutal. He sounds like a nasty piece of work.'

'I don't know. He came round to see me. To apologise.'

'To your flat?'

'Yes.'

'I hope you sent him packing.'

'I did. Right after the blow job.'

'Oh, for God's sake. You're your own worst enemy.'

'He said it was the drugs.'

'Huh.'

'Oh come on, Duncan. Everyone does drugs except you. You're so disapproving. You're so vanilla.'

'I'd rather stick with vanilla than try a session with your Mr Whippy.'

'All you're ever interested in is a quick reposte.'

'All you're ever interested in is a quick fix. Look where it's got you.'

'Hey, I tell you what.'

'What?'

'If you do get beaten black and blue you get these great tranquillisers on the NHS. They're free.'

'They're not free to those of us who pay taxes. Look, I am worried about you. Would you like me to come over and see you? I'll make you dinner or something. Or come over here. Whichever is easier.'

'No thank you. You are sweet sometimes. You're a funny boy.'

'Not as funny as you, I don't think.'

After he had completed the call the telephone rang again immediately.

'Duncan Cairns.'

'Hello, Duncan? It's Lesley.'

His heart skipped.

'Hi. How are you? Long time no speak.'

'I'm fine. We've been experimenting with our Verity ovulation predictor test. I'm so excited about this.'

'Yes. Me too.'

'Duncan, I need to see you again. At least once before we do the . . . thing.'

'The insemination procedure.' They needed a term for it.

'Any chance of you coming over, tomorrow?'

'I'll get my diary . Hang on ... yes, tomorrow evening is fine.'

'Come for a drink. I don't cook. We'll just have a beer or something.'

No hot food. Beer. You just knew she was a lesbian.

'I need to put you in the picture about something. I just want to make sure. You know how it is.'

'Of course. Hey, Lesley?'

'What?'

'I've had the HIV test but I don't have the result yet.' Duncan hoped that would impress her.

'You don't need it for this. This is bigger than that.'

'Oh.' He was disappointed by her muted reaction. What was bigger than whether he was HIV positive or not? Whether he would live or die or not? He had no idea of what it could be when he replaced the receiver on the voice of the girlfriend of the mother of the child of his dreams.

51

'God, Alan. No wonder you nearly killed yourself before.' The Australian notes in Cindy's voice sang out.

'We don't want to get stuck at those lights.'

'There's no rush. You've booked.'

'Even if you book for ten forty-five they still stop serving at eleven.'

In the dark Cindy lah-lahed Mussetta's aria.

'Happy?'

'Absolutely. I'm glad we swapped out of *Turandot*. *Bohème* is so uplifting. Strange, because it's a weepie. But you come out feeling all cosy.'

'There's hope for us yet.'

'Don't hold your breath. We should have gone somewhere nearer. Mezzo's.'

'Live music. I thought it would jar. With the opera.'

'I'd like to try the Oxo Tower. The views across the river are supposed to be spectacular.'

'Colin's been there. Says there was nowhere to park. I didn't think you'd want to traipse around dark and dingy alleyways so soon after your . . . incident.'

'Good choice of word. My incident. From now on I shall call it my incident. But I have you to protect me, Alan.'

'I'll buy a white horse first thing in the morning.'

'That's rather romantic. For you, anyway. They say it's only true love if you're prepared to lay down your life for your partner.'

'Really?'

'So would you lay down your life for me?'

'I don't answer hypothetical questions.'

'God! All you have to say is yes. You don't have to prove it. You sure know how to please me.'

'I do. *La Bohème*. Godiva truffles and Moët. Dinner at Coast.'

'All bribes received gratefully and checked in. Thank you. Now, getting back to my point, if we were on the *Titanic* and they said out of every couple one of you has to stay behind, would you volunteer to go down with the ship?'

'What a stupid question.'

'Just answer it. All you have to say is yes.'

'What would you do?'

'I'd look dreamily into your eyes and say, "Alan, I know how much you love me and how, were I to drown, so heartbroken would you be that you'd probably lose concentration driving and kill yourself, so nip off down to the bar, tank yourself up on Scotch and I'll always remember how you sacrificed your life for me."'

'Very funny. Here it is. Albemarle Street. There's even parking.'

Alan reverse-parked the Newy outside Coast.

'Baby, you're adoin' a great job,' he said to the car.

'Shame Cindy doesn't have your gleaming bodywork.'

'I never said that.'

'You love the car more than you love me.'

'It cost more.'

'Only so far!'

Cindy stayed in her seat and waited until Alan came around onto the pavement and opened her door for her. She swung out in her snug-fitting cream lace backless dress. Secret sequins on its bodice caught the lamplight.

'Look,' she said. 'We've parked between two Jaguar Sovereigns. Who says Britain is in decline?'

Alan wasn't listening. He was checking the number plates of the paired Jaguars. It was as bad as he thought. They were matching cars with adjacent numbers. He knew who that meant.

'Here, Cindy, take a look.'

Alan had walked over to the huge plate-glass engraved windows of the ultra-modern restaurant. At night the ascetic streamlined interior shone out into the Victorian street. Alan looked in.

'For God's sake, Alan. Have some class. People will think we're tourists.'

'Aagh!'

'Who is it? A client?'

'It's Nigel and Serena.'

'Really? Where? Let's see. I've never seen them.'

Cindy screwed up her eyes against the glass.

'What's that movie where they look in the window and they're starving and all the fat cats are sitting inside stuffing themselves?'

'Isn't it a Dickens?'

'Is that her? She's ghastly. She hasn't stopped for breath yet. Who does her hair? It's much too black for a woman of her age.'

'Who are they with?'

'A woman. I can't see her face.'

'I wonder who?'

'They're right over at the back. They won't see us when we go in.'

'Our table is downstairs. Fingers crossed we can slip past unnoticed.'

'Famous last words.'

They stepped back and grinned, brought closer by their espionage. They had to have eyes only for each other now so as to catch no others.

Alan pushed open the plate-glass door and let Cindy go first. He hid behind her. She walked the few feet to the light beech reception lectern.

'Table for two in the name of Josling. Downstairs.'

The smartly dressed man checked his pencil-crossed booking list and led them towards the spiral staircase at the back of the vast room.

Cindy snatched a discreet sideways look as she and Alan tripped lightly down the stairs. Serena's shrillness was high above the hub-bub.

'These stairs vibrate,' said Alan. 'They don't feel safe.'

On the floor below, the maître d' showed them to a small, circular table. It seemed more informal here. Other men were in very expensive suits like Alan's, but none wore ties.

'Well?' asked Cindy.

'I suppose you'd like more champagne?'

'No. Yes. I would like more champagne. But did you see who they were with?'

'I didn't dare look.'

'You're useless.'

'Sorry.'

'Well I did.'

'What did she look like?'

'I recognised her. I knew who it was.' They were both excited.

'Who?'

'Audrey Goldberg!'

'Audrey Goldberg? It couldn't have been. Serena Sark can't stand Audrey Goldberg.'

'Didn't look that way to me. They were getting along famously.'

'They must be recruiting.'

'Maybe. You wouldn't bring a headhunter to Coast though. Not for lunch, let alone dinner at this hour.'

'They're up to something, those two.'

'Don't let it bother you.'

'It doesn't bother me,' said Alan. But it bothered him a great deal. After his little chatette with his contacts on the board of MCN International about his little merger idea and after reading the little contract they had had drafted since, he didn't want Serena and Nigel to do anything else other than sit back and take the drop he was setting up for them.

52

Jamie Hirst examined the computer printout.

'Derek? What's seventeen seventeen?'

'Just after quarter past five,' replied his Oriental companion.

'What time is it now?'

'Just gone five.'

'Is it? You lose track of the time when you're writing.'

Derek gave a high-pitched laugh. 'I wouldn't call what we've just been doing writing.' He put his arms around Jamie and kissed him on the neck.

'I was before you turfed up early . . . there should be one in the next break.'

'On The Station?'

'On The Station. This is the issue with all the *Megabrek* promos. We need to get Briony to do a contra-deal with other channels. Then we won't just be preaching to the converted. The problem with the ratings on *Megabrek* is that we've reached saturation point with Station viewers. We need to bring a new audience in. And to reach them we need to get the promos on elsewhere.'

'Cost a bomb.'

'It wouldn't cost anything with a contra-deal.'

'Excuse me for asking, but as a mere politics, philosophy and economics student, I have only heard of the Iran Contra deal.'

'It's dead simple. The Station gives free advertising for, say, a series on The Paramount Channel. In return, Paramount show an equal number of promos for *Megabrek*. That way you get cross-cultural fertilisation of the two audiences.'

'Surely it's not in Paramount's interests to wean people off their own channel?'

'It's more sophisticated than that. To do a good contra-deal, The Station would pick another channel that is not regarded as directly competitive. Paramount would do it because they only broadcast at night. They would advertise *Megabrek* and wouldn't lose any viewers because they're not on air the next morning.'

'You have it all worked out, Mr Hirst.'

'Even if I say it myself, I do. Right. Make a note to call Briony Linden tomorrow. I won't call her now.'

'Why not?'

'Never introduce new business ideas in the late afternooon. People are tired and they want to go home. Shove over, and turn on the TV so we can see the promos we do have.'

Derek rolled over on the four poster bed. He found the remote control buried in the ripple of satin sheets. He switched on and flicked up until he came to The Station. Sister Verity was on air.

'Good God!' exclaimed Jamie.

'It's Karen Myhill in a wimple,' mocked Derek.

'I'm surprised you know what a wimple is.'

'Cross-cultural fertilisation,' laughed Derek. 'I've seen the Sisters of Perpetual Indulgence. She doesn't half prattle on.'

'This is such a bad idea. A nun. A phone-in. Agony. Misery. Let me correct myself. This is not an idea at all. It is a travesty. Why we didn't get the commission for this slot I'll never know.'

'How long has it been on air?'

'Since the middle of August. Three or four weeks. I don't understand why Martin Fox is commissioning out of season. Nobody starts a new series in the middle of August. Foxy is losing his touch.'

'Isn't he her boyfriend?

'No. But they're in cahoots.'

'I like the set. How do they do that?'

'Don't fall for it. It's a not very good piece of virtual reality bought off the shelf. For about a non-decimal shilling by the looks of it.'

'You're jealous.'

'I'm not jealous. I'm angry. Karen Myhill and Duncan Whatsisname have trumped us on this one and it pisses me off.'

'Come on, Jamie. We've got *Megabrek*. This is just a filler. They won't bring it back.'

'The ratings are soaring.'

'It's cheap crap.'

'Exactly. The ratings are soaring and it's cheap crap. The right ingredients and the right recipe at the right time.'

'We're going to take a break now, m'dears. But I'll be back to interfere in more of your lives after the break.'

Sister Verity beamed. Jamie's careful observation saw her eyeline waver just a fraction.

'Jesus. That's so unprofessional. They didn't cut away quickly enough.' The screen turned to a pink shimmering effect and in italic script in powder blue the name Sister Verity scrawled across the screen. 'What the fuck is this?' The "Sister" then dissolved and the word "Tampons" appeared beneath Verity to make the brand name of the sponsor. The voiceover spoke the catchline: The Truth is It's Verity.

Derek snorted. 'It's so tacky. A nun representing a tampon brand. I don't know why they don't have a tampon presenting it. They could get the next series sponsored by Anusol and have the show hosted by an arsehole.'

'They're all under contract to the BBC.'

Derek's giggle was caught up short as he let out a yelp. Jamie had grabbed him sharply by the scruff of the neck.

'What did you say?'

'Ow! Nothing. Hey, Jamie. The *Megabrek* promo.' He pointed at the acid-coloured animation on the screen. The familiar jungly music had been recently revamped with a house beat.

'Stuff the *Megabrek* promo.'

'Let go, will you. My hair.'

'Sorry. You've got Chinese hair. It doesn't do anything. Listen Derek, I've had an idea.'

'Something I said?'

'Yup.'

'We're going to do a bum show with someone talking out of their arse.'

'I don't think so. You see, Derek, I have misunderstood Karen Myhill. I don't think until this afternoon I had the measure of her. I thought she had creative integrity. I thought I was competing with her on creative ability. I thought her success was based on creative strategy. But looking at that tripe I see something else. Sister Verity is based on business strategy. Myhill didn't take her show and get Verity Tampons to sponsor it. She took Verity Tampons' money and built a show around it. What she did was come up with the finance rather than let the creative juices flow to meet old Foxy's requirements. Very clever . . .'

'Here. She's coming back. Does she do gay problems? I don't suppose so, being a nun.'

Jamie had pulled away and had walked to the tall sash window. He pulled up the ecru roller blind and looked down into the street.

'Sister Verity is sponsored by Verity Tampons,' said the TV voiceover. 'The Truth is It's Verity.'

'The truth is it's diabolical, said Derek.

'The truth is it *is* diabolical. Karen Myhill has supped with the devil and put up a nun as a smokescreen. She has sold her soul. She has shopped her standards to sponsorship. She brought in Duncan Cairns to bring in commercial money. Why else would she hire him? But that's not allowed . . .'

'Oh look! You can see clouds through the windows of the cathedral.'

'Karen Myhill has infringed the rules on editorial and sponsorship . . .' He paced the bedroom back and forth.

'You're standing in front of the screen. I know what you said about the set but I think it's brilliant. Saturn hasn't done anything like that.'

Jamie went to the top of the tallboy and picked up the radio phone. He pressed the memory button. 'Hi, it's me. I want you to fix up an interview. It's with the ITC. You need to find out who the person is who handles the sponsorship guidelines. I want them to come on *Megabrek*. Get some clips in. I want clips of sponsored programmes on ITV and Channel Four. Get

The Station to give you a clip of Sister Verity going in to the break . . . No, it's not boring for our audience. I think they'll find it interesting. But not half as interesting as the regulators will when we point out to them what's really going on . . .'

53

Charlotte sat quietly in her flat and studied her giant Swatch. She was not looking at the time. The big hand and the small hand could do what they liked for all Charlotte cared. They could race ahead of time. They could whir backwards. They could spin round in opposite directions. They could stretch out wide in disbelief. They could lie one upon the other, clapping. They could rise up together in shock and put their hands to their face, devastated. For Charlotte's eyes were on the little square where the date appeared. They had been for the last five days since her period had first been due. And now here it was, five days later and still no sign.

She drifted out of her trance. The watch face was shaking in her palm. No. It was her palm that was shaking, vibrating, quivering. In her other hand she clutched a small cardboard pack. It was a sample from the Verity range of products. It was a home pregnancy test kit from the office. She had helped herself to it. Helped herself? Half-inched it, as Daniel would have put it. It was Daniel's putting of considerably more inches than one half that had got her into this mess. Certain mess? Likely mess. Possible mess. Maybe no mess at all. Perhaps. Sort of. Hopefully not. Whoah, as a certain gentleman might say. He was no gentleman. But it wasn't his fault. It was hers.

She knew about safe sex. She was responsible. She was careful. Only it was funny how, with the best intentions in the world as soon as the champagne flew to your head and your knickers flew down to your ankles, your brain flew out of the window. Since she had worked the previous summer for a short spell for an AIDS charity she had somehow got it into her head that safe sex was all about not contracting AIDS, not getting an STD. Somehow she had forgotten about the possibility of getting pregnant. She had been on the Pill until quite recently, but had decided to come off it when her sex life took a dive. The rapid rise up the slippery runged ladder of advertising was inversely proportional to the decline in sexual escapadery. Until she had met Daniel Mainwaring. Dan the Man. She hoped he was man enough to stand by her.

She examined the pack. It was blue and pink like the Verity Tampons packs. Blue for a boy. Pink for a girl. She read the back-of-pack blurb. Then she slipped a nail underneath the join and flipped open the top. She emptied the contents onto the coffee table. God. It all looked so complicated. She hadn't seen anything like this since her brother had unpacked his home scientist kit one Christmas and threatened to blow them all up. Her little explosion would cause a bigger blast in the family, that was for sure. Only if she was preggers of course. Which she probably wasn't. But she might be. Or might not be . . .

She stood up. She was still in the T-shirt she had slept in. She leant over and took a last gulp of coffee. She tripped to the tiny bathroom of her tiny flat. No room for a baby here.

She wished she wasn't so period aware. She had only been thinking of periods because of Verity Tampons and Serena Sark and co-ordination meetings. If periods were not so top-of-mind, would she have noticed? The truth was that her periods had been regular as clockwork while she had been on the Pill. Then she had come off it and all hell had let loose. They had come and gone in dribbles and waves and gushes like a Cornish sea and about as predictable as the numbers on the National Lottery. But for the last three months things had settled down and all had been well. Each period twenty-eight days apart. Each period five days long. Each flow an average teaspoonful as it said it should be on the Verity packs. Who the hell had ever worked that out? She had the mental image of an old nurse holding a teaspoon between the legs of some unfortunate woman in the 1930s saying, 'It's all in the cause of progress.'

In the tiny bathroom she sat down on the toilet seat and read the instructions carefully again.

God. She was going to have to wee first. She yawned. She needed more coffee. One, to keep her awake and two, to give her more wee. Then she would watch the sample. Go from Verity Pink to Verity Red to Verity Blue to Very Big Trouble if it went any further. Charlotte had always hated purple. She had always dreaded its being in fashion, which it was apparently this autumn, and now she dreaded it more. Because if her Verity test went Verity Purple then she would be selecting from the Mothercare range of pregnancy frocks this autumn. Only if she was preggers, of course. Which she probably wasn't. Only if she had the baby. Which she probably wouldn't. Only if the test turned purple. Which it probably wouldn't. Would it?

54

Duncan pressed the buzzer. Through the crackle on the entry-phone he heard Lesley's voice.

'Hello?'

'It's Duncan.'

'Come on up. Second floor.'

Lesley and Sarah lived in a big house in Clapham with views of the Common. It had been converted into flats, some time ago judging by the dated look of the interior stairs and the poor standard of the conversion. The street had been elegant and grand once. It overlooked parkland, enjoying views and benefiting from clean air.

Outside their front door, Duncan could see through the glass that Lesley and Sarah were fond of primary colours. You entered straight into the zingy yellow kitchen of their spacious corner flat, a curious arrangement, and not one Duncan would have opted for. He would never have gone for such a functional kitchen or such a practical, jolly shade of yellow. He heard boots on bare floorboards and Sarah pulled up behind Lesley at the door.

'Hey. It's daddy.'

The women's smiles were broad and hearty and they stretched further when they closed in on him. Duncan smiled too. He felt he was going behind Michael's back a bit, but they had asked to see him, so here he was.

'Is this the bank?' he asked. 'I've come to register my deposit.'

They laughed.

'It's a shame they never made *Carry On IVF*,' said Sarah. 'They'd have had some great lines.'

The bright yellow kitchen led into an equally bright blue living room. Duncan would never have chosen blue for a living room. For a bedroom perhaps, even a bathroom. But not a cold colour for the living room. The colours were unsophisticated. Duncan thought a child might like them.

'Coffee?' asked Lesley.

'Yes please.'

'How do you take it?'

'Black and strong.'

'Which,' said Sarah, 'is how you like your men!'

'That's original,' said Duncan. It sounded critical rather than fly-away as he had intended. There was something about Sarah. He couldn't quite get it together with Sarah the way he was able to with Lesley. For a second he wished that Lesley was to be the mother and not Sarah. He felt guilty. It didn't matter. They'd got this far, hadn't they? There was nothing wrong with Sarah. She was attractive. She was clever. She was keen. She was probably nervous as hell about the whole thing. Terrified they'd do it all wrong. That explained her distance.

'Do you have many black friends?' she asked.

'Any?'

'Many?'

'Er . . . no.'

'I know Michael's a South African . . .'

'Of English descent. He's a Mandela supporter. He's not racist.'

'I didn't mean to suggest he was. We have several black lesbian friends. There's a club we go to in Brixton.'

'We're not really south of the river people.' God. Why did he sound such a crashing snob? He heard the whir of the coffee grinder. It blurred over the stilted edges of their conversation. 'There isn't such a high concentration of black people in St John's Wood.' Now he sounded like a Nazi statistician. God. Change subject, Dunky. 'I love your flat.' He didn't, of course.

'Would you like a tour?'

'I'd love one.' Duncan moved into the big bay window and looked out. It was a grey day. 'You have such fabulous views.'

'If you ignore the traffic.'

'You get traffic everywhere in London.'

'You used to have to be careful about the effect of lead on children's brains. At least we don't have to worry about that nowadays.'

'Is this the common where that woman was raped and murdered?' Now why did he say that? He felt awkward.

'Which one?'

'The blonde one, with her child.'

'Wasn't that Wimbledon?'

'I think it was. I'm sure it's safe round here.'

'It's not safe for women anywhere, Duncan. As long as all the politicians are fat old male bastards, women live in danger of rape, both penetrative and verbal, both real and symbolic.'

Duncan couldn't abide feminist claptrap.

'And there's queerbashing that goes on round here at night. We went on a march about it a few weeks ago. Fat lot of use it does, but you have to do it. The Anti-Nazi League people are very good about supporting us.'

'Are they?' Duncan gave an involuntary Wildean sneer. He wanted to click with Sarah. Lesley came through with the coffees. The atmosphere changed.

'Coffee's up.'

'It smells great.'

'It's not instant. I made it in the machine.'

'We went to Pride this year. We had the most fabulous day. Did you and Michael go?'

'It's not really our sort of thing. I think we were away at the time.'

'Where did you go?'

'We flew to San Francisco and drove all the way to Seattle. The architecture is stunning. It's the first place in America where they know the meaning of the word restraint.'

'We've not been to the States. Is it hot?'

'It wasn't in Seattle. Actually they have more rain there than we do.'

'Blimey.'

'Their skies are that sort of Calvin Klein grey.'

'I think you're more familiar with the colour of men's underpants than we are!'

'I should move to Pseud's Corner, shouldn't I? Then we flew down to Palm Springs for the sun . . . So . . . here we all are, to coin a phrase.'

Sarah settled on the arm of the settee and turned to Lesley. 'Have you got the book?'

'It's in the bedroom,' replied Lesley. 'I'll go and get it.'

She shot along the hall. Duncan and Sarah smiled nervously at each other. Lesley returned and handed a hardback book to Sarah. She didn't need it but it was her shield.

'We got this book. We bought it at a feminist convention we went to in Manchester at the start of this year. It's American.'

'I've never been to Manchester,' said Duncan.

'It tells you the experiences of lesbian couples having children.'

'Oh really?'

'Yes. It gives lots of advice and do's and don'ts and real-life examples of problems you have later in life. How to bring up your baby to be gender and sexuality aware. That sort of thing.'

'Oh, really?'

'Yes. And it's really practical. It's not a lot of crap American politically correct thinking.'

'Oh really?' Now that *was* a surprise.

'Anyway, that's why we asked you over because of what's in the book.'

'What *is* in the book?'

'Well. We want the baby to be ours. We want her to live with us. We want her to be our daughter. Mine and Lesley's. You would be the natural father but we need to define the parameters of your role with the child.'

'I understand that.'

'I'm sure you do. But, what we want to do, so there is absolutely no misunderstanding and so that everybody knows their rights and everything, is we want to draw up a contract and we want you to sign it.'

'A contract?'

'Yes. I'm a solicitor, as you know. To be scrupulously fair we'll get a colleague of mine to draw it up and then we'll ask her to come over here and she can talk you through it over a beer and you can sign it. We need to be sure that you and I agree what we're actually getting into.'

Duncan had not expected this. He cooled. 'I see. What sort of role for me did you have in mind?'

'Well, we want you to come here . . .'

'Yes?'

'Produce the sample . . .'

'Yes.'

'You wouldn't see me while I was pregnant . . .'

Duncan didn't like the sound of this. 'I wouldn't see you?'

'No. And if you wanted to make any financial arrangements like a trust fund or something . . .'

Duncan nodded. It was so amazingly typical how all these left-wing types who went on marches and shouted about social injustice were always the first to get the private income up and running.

'Yes?'

'And in the contract . . .'

'Yes?'

'Well, we would like her to be our child.'

'Ours meaning yours and mine.'

'That's not what we had in mind. We want her to be mine and Lesley's. We could write to you about her and keep you in touch but we want to raise her ourselves.'

'When would I see her? Him?'

'We would rather you didn't. That's what we want to have in the contract.'

'It's called an exclusion clause,' said Lesley.

'We want you to give up your right of access.'

Duncan was floored. He was winded. 'I thought you thought I'd be a good father?'

'We do.'

'That's partly it.'

'We think you'd be too good a father. We're worried that you would sort of, don't take this the wrong way, but take over – get in the way of us and our relationship and . . . you see, Lesley has to bond with the child equally to me and if you're part of a triangular thing it might not work out and . . . you know . . . d'you know what we mean?'

'I think I do.'

'So if you signed the contract we would allow you to send the child gifts and ask about progress and when she's older and beyond the formative years and if she wanted it, we'd introduce you. If I die before Lesley, she would be the baby's legal guardian. If we both die together in a plane crash or something we'd want the child to be brought up by my sister and her husband. It says in the book to organise something. They've agreed. Because she wouldn't know you as a father because Lesley would be her other parent. Do you see? It's nothing personal, Duncan. It's in the book.' Sarah was hugging it defensively to her breast.

Duncan was stunned. He was wounded, deeply wounded. He could father a child but never stroke its cheek or ruffle its hair or sing it to sleep or kiss its forehead or chase its nightmares away. His son or his daughter's heart could beat in unison with his in the same city and they would never know each other. In a few minutes Sarah had reduced his feather-bedded fantasy of fatherhood to a one-minute utilitarian wank into a cocktail glass.

'We would have to put father unknown on the birth certificate,' said Lesley. She had got to know Duncan well enough to realise that he was crushed and that it had all gone horribly wrong.

'But that wouldn't be true,' said Duncan.

'I know,' said Sarah. 'But in this fucked-up society you can't play by what the government's rules are. I mean what do they fucking know? Not the meaning of the truth, that's for sure.'

'Will you think about it? asked Lesley at the door. 'We'd be disappointed if it wasn't you.'

Whether it would be him or whether it would not be, Duncan was the disappointed one. He strolled onto the common and found an empty bench in front of some grey-green shrubs and wept there quietly to himself.

'Sister Verity, I'm gay.'

'Are you a Roman Catholic, young man?'

'No—'

'It's just that you may not know this but you can have a great wee career there in the Catholic Church if you're a homosexual because there's none of them there interested in a good woman, all the way up to the Pope, not that I'm making pretensions about the Holy Father, I'm not. But they're runnin' out of recruits and before you know it you could be blessin' the populace of St Peter's Square. And if you like paradin' around in dresses made of cloth of gold then it could be for you. You'll notice the women stick to the black and white. It's the boys who sport the jewellery and go swingin' that incense.'

'Actually, I wondered what you thought about gay couples having children.'

'I take it we're not just talkin' about over for the afternoon sort of thing?'

'No. I mean having them by surrogates and bringing them up.'

'Darlin', now look, I'm a nun and an old timer and though I don't stick with the good book always for my advice, it would seem to me that if God intended for you to have children you'd be out there lustin' after women and not your own type. Are you in a relationship with a man?'

'Yes.'

'And are you happy together?'

'Yes. Very.'

'Heavens above. Don't go spoilin' it all with a screaming bairn. What on God's earth makes you think having a child will make you happier or make the child happier? It will not. Children should be raised by their mothers and whatever you may be, me darlin', a mother you never can be. But I'm glad for you to hear that you are happy. Not many of my callers are, which is statin' the obvious, but that is my job. To state the obvious and no wonder they don't go paying me for it. Now, who's next?'

55

Daniel Mainwaring stretched in his seat. His yawn was cavernous. Without Charlotte here to crack the whip or shimmy her sweet little ass around the office he was off the hook for the afternoon. He might have slipped out for a few sly beers with Bonzo, but Bonzo had pissed off to set up some sales conference presentation with one of his clients. Boring old farting Bonzo. Never around when you wanted him. So Daniel had taken to reading *Viz* and was guffawing at it. His hands were behind his head and his boots on his desk top when Maria Handley burst in.

'Whoah. You gave me a heart attack. What's up with the face like sour milk?'

'I suppose you're doing the least amount humanly possible. As usual?'

'I have my business and my clients under control. Unlike some.'

'I don't believe that for a second. You're not proactive. You need to think ahead if you want to get promoted.'

'Bad mood. In one, are we?'

'Don't be insolent. Where is Charlotte this afternoon?'

'Search me. Search my underpants.'

'I am searching you. The two of you are far too close for comfort.'

'She was frozen out and she felt the big chill.'

'Do you have any respect for my status?'

'All it deserves.'

'You and Charlotte go hunting in pairs. That's a waste of resources.'

'Come again?'

'You're always doubling up in meetings and on trips to the client. You have different roles. She doesn't need a crutch.'

'She's a woman isn't she?' Daniel snorted.

'You work for me, not her.'

'That's not how Hecka put it to me.'

'Must you be so antagonistic?'

'No, but I enjoy it.'

'Young man, you are out of line.'

'Look, Maria, you only notice me to talk down to me. Every time you have something to say it's a criticism or an accusation. How do you think I feel?'

'I make no criticisms. Only observations.'

'Yeah, well, you should look at things differently.'

'My way suits me, I think you'll find.'

'Charlotte and I only share one account. I have two others. I virtually run Japanair on my own.'

'That's nothing to do with me. I can only judge on what you do in my team. If you see that proper little madam send her into my office.'

She snapped the door shut in its frame behind her.

'And don't close the fucking door,' muttered Daniel. He picked up the phone and rang Charlotte's extension. He got her voice mail and hung up. He decided to leave her a message at home. He checked in his organiser and rang her number. Instead of the machine, though, Charlotte answered.

'Boss lady! What are you doing at home?'

'I'm not well. Daniel something's come up. We need to talk.'

'We do?'

'We do.'

'Whoah. When?'

'As soon as.'

'I'm not doing anything now. What time is it? Almost five. There. Finished early.'

'Finished early? I've never heard of anyone in advertising finishing early.'

'You'd never heard of me until recently.'

'I wish I'd never heard of you.'

'You don't mean that.'

'You'd better come over. You may wish you'd never heard of me.'

Maria Handley had called and left a message on Charlotte's office voice mail. Now she tried her at home. The telephone was engaged, which meant that she was either skiving at home yacking or somebody else was leaving a message already. She had a good mind to give Charlotte a balling out. They were supposed to be getting a sanitary protection relaunch campaign out on national television and in the women's press. And where was everyone? At home or with their boots on the desk. They had a sexist old bastard as a boss. They had no secretary to answer client calls. Worse, appearing nationally on a cult cable TV show was the horrifically incorrect brand symbol of a nun with unpredictable views. That was Charlotte's doing. It was her fault. She had not stood up to Hector as Maria would have done. She had simply dialled a friend in TV and got a counter-productive television series up and running.

She jotted down a list of things to do next week. Internal status meeting on Monday morning at nine. Dan to be taken to task over getting status reports out on time. Dan to be taken to task over flawed contact reports. Dan to be taken to task over late billing on press production, the worst in the agency. Charlotte to be taken to task over inaccurate income forecasts. Charlotte to be taken to task over clumsy creative briefs. Charlotte to be taken to task over incorrect approval procedures on presenting ads to client. Also, somebody, it looked like Charlotte's careless hand, had put a co-ordination meeting in her diary with Clancey and Bennett. What was that about? The client appeared to know nothing of it either when she had rung them. Doubtless the client didn't mind being excluded, but clients are always happy until it all goes wrong, when they blame you. And fire your agency. There was much which could go wrong with Verity Tampons and there was much which could go wrong with Maria Handley's international career progress. She needed troubleshooters and all she had were trouble makers. Tense and angry, she reached for the phone again but before she could pick it up it rang.

'Maria Handley.'

'Maria, it's Marsha.'

'Hi.'

'Do you think you could pop over to the main building?'

'Sure. Why?'

'Hecka wants to see you.'

'What about? Do I need to bring anything?'

'No. But bearing in mind the time, I'd bring my jacket and handbag or whatever, if I were you. Save you the trip back later.'

'I'll do that. Thanks.'

'See you in a mo.'

'See ya.'

Maria slipped on her citrus jacket. It was possibly too hot for today but she wanted to look smart for Hector, who appeared to judge on presentation alone. She picked up her bag and slipped out a pocket mirror. She checked her make-up. She could do with more blusher. She sat back down and felt around inside her bag for her make-up tote. She took out a brush only slightly smaller than the one used to paint the Forth Bridge and dunked it into a berry-brown powder. She then flicked along below the line of her cheekbones. She put her things away and as she left her office she fluffed up her hair. Big hair for big meetings with big people.

She didn't hear the clock on Marylebone Road strike the first of its charmless chimes, nor did she hear the fifth and last as she came out of the side door and was stopped in her tracks at the sight of Marsha Blow standing in the mews opposite, clipboard clutched to her breast, grim expression on her face and chauffeur-driven car to her right.

'Michael!'

He lifted his head from his sports bag and looked around. He did not instantly recognise who it was. This was someone he had previously seen only fully clothed. It was Jamie Hirst. His body was bigger and better than he would have thought.

'What are you doing here?' asked Jamie.

'Same as you. Swimming.' Michael took his towel and vigorously rubbed it across the back of his head, about the only bit where there was any hair left these days. 'Or are you just here for a wank in the showers like the rest?'

'Not my scene. I do a few laps of the pool here once a month or so.'

'It's difficult to find the time, isn't it?'

'Or the inclination.'

'Are you here on your own? What's your boyfriend's name . . . ?'

'Derek. He's not here. He's gone off with some student friends for a few days. Something to do with his course.'

'Something to do with beer and shagging if it's got students involved.'

'I don't think he's the type. He's Chinese. I trust him.'

Now Michael was rubbing his chest and starting to dry off his legs.

'I hadn't realised how hairy you were,' said Jamie.

'Some of us have none of it on our heads and all of it on our bodies. I don't shave my body like those great mincing queens you see round here.'

'I can't stand that either.'

'Even though you like a smooth-bottomed boy yourself. Rice queens do.'

'That's a terrible thing to say. I love Derek for his personality and his brain.'

'Pull the other one. Have you just been in the pool or are you just going in?'

'I'm just going in. If you don't mind waiting I'll meet you in twenty minutes or so. We could have a drink.'

'I'd like to but I have to meet Duncan.'

'How is he?'

'Fine. Busy on an afternoon series he's putting out for us.'

'*Sister Verity.*'

'Have you seen it?'

'Who hasn't? Where on earth did they find her?'

'Karen's idea. She heard about her and Duncan fixed it through this girl he used to work with. She runs the Verity brand at one of the big agencies.'

'Oh does she? That's interesting.'

Michael laughed. He put his towel down for a second on the bench and whipped off his shorts, then began the last stages of drying his body.

'You know, Jamie, when you're fully dressed I can see your brain going click, click, click and it's even more obvious when you're stripped to your thong.'

Jamie looked sheepish. 'This is not a thong.'

'Looks like one. Turn round.'

'Fuck off. I'm not having you checking out my backside.'

'I'll just stick with the packet pointing this way then, shall I? I can read you like a centrefold with the staples removed. You're up to something. What are you planning now?'

'Nothing.'

'That's not true. You're always planning something. You probably planned on bumping into me here, for all I know. I say. Look at that beautiful boy over there.' Jamie turned to see a young blond man disrobing to reveal a six-pack stomach. 'Do you think if I flash him my cock I'm in with a chance?'

'I wouldn't have thought so. You've been flashing it at me for the last five minutes and I'm not exactly salivating.'

'Cheeky bastard. Anyway, you're into Orientals. You prefer a bite-sized chipolata to a full kilo of liverwurst. And who's flashing? I don't notice you draping your towel over yourself.'

'I have my shorts on.'

'That is a thong. I've seen more fabric on an eyepatch. It disappears right up the crack of your arse.'

'You've been checking me out, you bastard.'

'Only before I realised who you were.'

'How did I do?'

'I'm the Head of the Legal Team at The Station and that, along with everything else, is confidential. I don't want your lot gossiping about it on *Megabrek*. How is *Megabrek* these days anyway?'

'Doing very nicely.'

'Anyone good on recently?'

'I'm trying a new approach. More educational. We're going in for a series of experts to inform and advise our audience on behind the scenes things in the media, advertising, TV shows, sponsorship, that sort of thing.'

'What are you trying to do? Close the channel down?'

'Oh, I think there'll be a lot of interest. In next Wednesday's show, there will be.'

'There will? That'll make a change. Who's on?'

Michael pulled on his underpants and pulled a T-shirt over his head.

'You should wear more white, Michael. It highlights your silver colouring.'

'Fuck off. My hair is black.'

'Not even your body hair is black these days. I know. I've just seen it.'

'God. I'll have to shave it off then. Sorry. I have to sit down to put my socks on. So?'

'So what?'

'So who's the big celeb on Wednesday's show?'

'Dorothy Copeland Charming.'

'Who?'

'Dorothy Copeland Charming.'

'Who's she?'

'I'm surprised you don't know.'

'I've heard of Bjork. And Enya. Is she one of that lot?'

'No.' Jamie looked at his watch. 'I'll have to get a move on or I'll run out of pool time. No. She isn't. I'd watch the programme if I were you. You'll find Dorothy very interesting.'

'I'm sure I will. I like Dorothies. In fact, I think you'll find that, like you, I'm already a very good friend of a certain Dorothy.'

'I'm glad you're able to laugh, Michael. I hope Duncan has as good a sense of humour as you.'

'Why shouldn't he have?'

'Oh, no reason,' said Jamie and turned to take the plunge, leaving Michael mystified and facing his bare cheeks.

57

'You look dog tired.'

'Woof woof. How did you get here so quickly?'

'I had my car with me. Some old cow gave me a filthy look for parking my old banger in your street. Everyone in St John's Wood seems to have a Porsche or a Merc.'

Charlotte pulled back the door and let Daniel in. He took off his dark green jacket and folded it with its dayglo pink lining showing out. He placed it on the settee and lay back beside it, his long legs spread. He patted his thigh. He looked even taller inside Charlotte's tiny flat.

'Come and sit here, Charlie.'

'I'm supposed to be your account director.' That remark did not stop her from crossing the room and falling into his arms. They kissed for a second and then she laid her head on his chest and he stroked her hair.

'It needs cutting,' she said.

'Seems OK to me.'

'Yes, well, everything is not OK, Dan.'

'You called me Dan.'

'I'm lying in your arms. I thought I'd try to be less formal. Don't bother, by the way, to issue a contact report from this meeting.'

'What's the big problem?'

'The big problem is . . . Look. You won't tell Bonzo?'

'Why should I tell Fartbreath?'

'You tell him everything. At least I get the impression you do. You were out with him last night, weren't you?'

'Only as far as the rugby club.'

'The rugby club? I didn't know you two played rugby.'

'We don't. Never have. But there's a good bar and it's boys only and they have stand-up and strippers on weeknights.'

Charlotte stopped caressing Daniel's chest. 'I hope you weren't watching strippers last night.'

'What is it about birds and strippers and porn? Anyone would think I'd been out collecting for the IRA. Course I was watching them get their kit off. Free totty and Bonzo and I are there. Last night was such a laugh.'

'I'm sure it was hilarous.'

'Dead right.'

'Tell me, then.'

'I can't.'

'Why not?'

'Boys' stuff.'

'I'm quite progressive, you know.'

'That's the problem. It's not your political correct outing.'

'I want to know what you and Bonzo get up to.'

'Well . . . we just had a few beers and then this fat bloke with crusty armpits gets up on stage and tells terrible jokes.'

'He sounds revolting. All centred on gynaecology, no doubt.'

'Pretty much.'

'How revolting. Example?'

'Can't remember.'

'I'm not falling for that.'

'OK. Er . . . there's this Englishman, Irishman and Scotsman in the desert.'

'Sophisticated crowd in last night, was it?'

'And they're desperate. They're lost. Parched. Going crazy. And this mirage appears before their eyes. A belly dancer.'

'God!'

'And she's dancing away, topless, fucking huge pendulums swinging, all jewels and see-through veils and they're all slavering for it. Only she's wearing these golden knickers.'

Charlotte tisked. 'But how long for?'

'Not long. She dances around and suddenly she whips them off and underneath she has another pair on, showing a thistle.'

'A thistle?'

'Yeah. And the Scotsman cries, "Och aye! By the thistle of Scotland, she is mine!" And he rushes forward to snatch a kiss, only she dances on and whips them off and underneath she has another pair of knickers bearing a shamrock. And the Irishman jumps up and cries, "To be sure, by the shamrock of Ireland, she is mine!". Only he too is frustrated because she strips off those and underneath she has yet another pair. This time with a rose—'

'And the Englishman says, "By the rose of England she is mine."?'

'How did you guess? And he runs forward ready to shag her when she whips them off again and this time she's stark blooming naked. And at this point an Arab suddenly passes by and cries out, "By the beard of Allah, she is mine!" and disappears off with her on the hump of his camel. Good eh?'

'That is so infantile.' But Charlotte giggled and wormed her way further into Daniel's big body. 'She should have waxed her bikini line more throughly.'

'Yeah, well that was later.'

'What do you mean?'

'The strippers.'

'Oh yes. I'd forgotten about the strippers. I hope you did the decent thing and left before they came on.'

'Did I fuck. I did the decent thing and hung around . . .'

'Spill the beans, Danny boy.'

'Bonzo always stays for the strippers on account of his being desperate to empty his nuts so we had a few jars and then I went next door to the takeaway place to get us each a bag of chips.'

'Chips!'

'I'm a big boy. I gotta eat. And Craterface needs to keep up his grease intake or he'd be in danger of looking half-human. So when I get back there's this old dog writhing away on stage with a shaved fanny.'

'Poor woman. I feel sorry for her. I mean I'm very liberal about sex but she's probably only doing it because she's desperate to pay her council flat rent. They all look so bored. She's probably a single mother.'

'This one was probably a single grandmother. I thought Hugh Scully was going to come out and announce she was a rare old piece with a bad crack.'

'Don't be so horrible.'

'She gets good money for it. Anyway, I sits down beside Bonzo who's stuck to his chair on account of his hard-on—'

'Bonzo with an erection! Over some old woman!'

'He's not much to look at but he has a knob on him like a baby's arm holding an orange.'

'Daniel! Bonzo has? How would you know?'

'Cos he comes through in the mornings when I'm having my brekkers wearing this smeggy old dressing-gown he's got, only he never ties it properly and it splits open sometimes. I never eat sausage and eggs of a morning in case he's got his on display. You see things if you live with people. Anyway, I sits down and hands him his chips, for which he's desperate, and he digs right in and rams a whole mouthful of mushy potato into his gob, only at this point the old dog glides right off the stage and into the audience and since he's grinning in the front she spreads her legs right in our faces and swings up and clamps her fanny right over his mouth. And everybody's roaring away, particularly me because only I know Bonzo's chewing the cud and getting fish in with his chips.'

'Daniel! That's completely uncalled for!'

'Well, you asked.'

'I hope to God you don't talk to him about me that way.'

'No way. Of course not.'

'Where does he think you are when you're here?'

'I'm always out. He doesn't ask.'

'Well . . .'

'Well what? No chance of a cuppa tea or a drink?'

'We need to talk first.'

'What's up? What have I done now?'

'Look.' She caught his eye and tried to communicate the seriousness of what she had to say. She felt beneath the settee and pulled out the vial from the Verity home pregnancy testing kit.

'What's that? Don't tell me you're dyeing your hair purple. It won't go with your citrus outfit.'

'It's the test tube bit out of a Verity kit. It tells you if you're pregnant or not. And this,' she picked up the shade chart from the box, 'is what you match it against.'

Daniel's body shrank away beneath her. His face fell. His voice and vowels were neutered. 'You're not telling me you're pregnant?'

'I think we may be expecting a baby, Daniel.'

'Jesus.'

'Jesus indeed. That wasn't going to be my first choice of name but I'm sure with us as his parents he'll be an exceptional child. I'll get the tea. You look like you need it. You can look after me when the morning sickness starts.'

'Now, m'dears, who is my next new friend?'

'Sister Verity, I'm pregnant.'

'Congratulations!'

'But I'm not in a long-term relationship and it's extremely inconvenient to my career at this stage and the father is totally the wrong type for me.'

'If you don't mind me saying so, obviously he is not the wrong type for you, dear, if you are happy to share his bed and his genitals with him. He sounds like quite the right type to me. And the only career in which it is ever inconvenient to be carrying a child is, dare I say it, my own. Now, you're not a bride of Christ yourself are you?'

'No.'

'So there you are. You sound quite posh. Do you have money, m'dear?'

'A bit. I earn quite a bit.'

'Well there you are. Problems are like prostitutes, throw money at them and you can strip them bare and give them a good seeing to. A young executive type such as yourself can afford a nanny no doubt, and raising a child is a boon to any woman's abilities of organisation and problem solving. You'll no doubt end up top banana in the company and have the wee fellow to thank for it. Will the man stand by you? When he's not lying on top of you, by the sound of things.'

'I don't know. I just don't know.'

'Well, in my long experience that usually means yes. Good luck to you. You've done well to squeeze in there in front of the commercial break we have to have. I'll be back after this.'

58

There was a tap at the door. Cindy made for it, then returned and slipped the gossamer negligee over her nightdress. She swirled her way across the gleaming painted floor to her visitor.

'Oh, it's you.'

'Don't look so disappointed,' said Alan.

'I thought it was room service with the champagne. The boys here are just to die for. Anouska must have hand-picked them personally.'

'If I'd realised the competition was going to be that tough I wouldn't have chosen the Hempel. Here, these are for you.' Alan had been hiding a corsage of camellias behind his back. 'I knew everything was white here so I got white.'

'They're absolutely divine, Alan. Thank you.' She pecked him on the cheek. 'The Hempel. The camellias. And the man on time for once. What have I done to deserve this?'

'I'm just trying a bit harder, that's all.' He came in, removed his jacket and folded it outwards to show the Armani label. He noticed a citrus-coloured thread hanging through one of the button holes. He picked it out and secreted it away into his trouser pocket, but not before Cindy had clocked it. She made no comment. It was probably nothing. She would only pick a fight and ruin the evening she had so been looking forward to. Alan searched the room for somewhere suitable to lay the jacket down. 'It's a bit bare,' he said. 'You don't get much for your money, do you?'

'Bare is in. Bare-faced luxury.'

'Bare-faced cheek at this price.'

'It was good enough for George Michael. You're paying for the harmony of the space and the open aesthetic. You should see the bathroom.'

'It's too Japanese-looking. We're English.'

'You may be. I'm Australian.'

'Really? I hadn't noticed.' Alan skidded on the floor as he set out towards a standing soapstone sculpture of an oriental official in the corner. 'Here, hold this,' he said and neatly lobbed his folded jacket into its folded arms. He sat down on a bench and removed his black shoes. 'I have to make a few phone calls, first, before dinner.'

'Oh *Alan*,' Cindy whined.

'Well it was either that or go back to the office and see Colin.'

'Were you out this afternoon?'

'Yes.'

'Where?'

'Nowhere.'

'Alan Josling, the man of mystery.'

'I was just out.'

'Just out? What do you mean just out?'

'Confidential business.'

'You can tell me.'

'No I can't.'

'Alan!'

'I can't. This is the big one. If I pull this off we'll be set up for all time, you and me.'

'You and me? I don't know if I want to be set up for all time you-and-me-style.'

'Cindy, it's costing me an arm and a leg to dine and stay here tonight. Don't spoil it.'

'You're the one who's spoiling it. You're the one who wants to make phone calls.'

'I run a small business.'

'So do I.'

'Yours is just a consultancy—'

'Don't denigrate what I do for a living—'

'I'm not—'

'You always think your business is more important than mine. Or me for that matter.'

'Cindy let's not argue.'

'You started it.'

'I did not.'

'You did. You waltz in here. You try to fob me off with flowers. You pick threads off your clothes.'

'What?!'

'You don't even notice I happen to be got up like Zsa Zsa Gabor on hallucinatory drugs. You want to make phone calls. You won't tell me where you've been all day. Well how do you think I feel after all the effort I've gone to to make this nice for us?'

'I booked the hotel.'

'Big deal.'

'I'm paying for it.'

'You're putting it all through on expenses, cheapskate.'

Alan sat red-faced and silent for a moment. He had one shoe on and one shoe off.

'Would you like me to leave?'

Cindy said nothing. Instead, she glided upwards in her flowing negligee into the upper half of the split-level suite to a platform laden with natural cushions and a fireplace of Californian driftwood. She ran her fingers along the ledge over the fireplace and into a designer line-up of parchment-covered tomes. She tugged one out and opened it. She sighed.

'These books have no pages in them.'

'They're just for effect.'

'There's no colour in this room.'

She looked down towards Alan and at the same time he looked up to her. They exchanged eye contact but no emotion passed between them. There was a prominent knock at the door.

'Who's that?' asked Alan.

'Moët and Chandon,' said Cindy. 'Our therapists.'

She came up for air. She stretched out her neck and let her head

and her hair hang backwards down the side of the bed. It was
suspended from the ceiling on bamboo poles. She caught sight
of her negligee lying draped across the back of the white chair
where it reflected the halogen twinkle of the recessed lighting.
Her slip nightdress lay in a pool of satin where Alan had pulled
it from her shoulders and she had let it drizzle to the floor. She
wanted to rise and retrieve it, tidy up, but Alan was slurping
away on her breasts. He was making a dreadful noise, like a
child draining a milk shake. She patted the top of his head. He
looked up.

'I'm a puppy,' he said, and let his tongue hang out, red and
hot. He wriggled it from side to side. 'What would you like me
to do with it?' he asked. He wiped the sweat from his brow.

'Talk to me.'

'Cindy,' he warned. 'Fuck first. Argue later. There are many
men my age who wouldn't go down on a woman, you know.'

'I can't do it in here.'

'What?'

'I can't do it in here. It's too designed.'

'Is it me?'

'No. It's too minimalist for me. There's too much space. I keep
feeling we're being watched.'

'Watched?'

'I know. It sounds silly. That slitty eyed statue thing keeps
looking at me. I preferred Blakes. I prefer all that black. All that
fussiness. The lines are too clean in here.'

'I can think of a few dirty ones if you like. How about "Suck
me off."'

'That's not what I meant.'

'It's what I meant.' He began to travel up the bed towards
her face.

'I don't think I could manage it.'

Alan sighed. 'You're still in rape trauma.'

'Don't be ridiculous. I wasn't raped and I'm not in trauma.
I'm in the Hempel and I'm full up from dinner. I don't feel like
making love. I'm sorry, Alan, but it's all too contrived.'

'You'd better get used to it if we're going to try for a baby.'

There was a pause, one of the pregnant variety.

'A baby?'

'You wanted one the other day. If you want to conceive we're not going to leave it to chance. We can do ovulation prediction and all that. I learnt all about it for the Verity pitch. The one I lost to those two dickheads at Clancey and Bennett.'

'Alan . . . don't let's talk about it now. And don't let's talk about advertising either. You're asking me to make too many leaps at once.'

'I haven't even asked you to swing from that bamboo pole. Yet. What leaps?'

'Alan let's get one thing clear. We're not here to conceive a baby. You've tried very hard and I appreciate it, but I can't get off on it. I'm just not like that.'

Alan sighed. He could feel from the flapping against his thigh that he had lost half his erection anyway. He'd let her doze for a while and maybe she could whack him off later or something. She could read *Hello!* with one hand and do him with the other, even, he wouldn't mind.

She pushed her hair under the nape of her neck and stuffed it into the pillow.

'Alan?'

'What?' He lay bedside her, his hands behind her head.

'Where were you this afternoon?'

'I can't tell you.'

'Were you with another woman?'

'No.'

'Tell me.'

'Of course not.'

'You were picking threads off your suit when you came in. I saw you.'

'For God's sake. It was one thread. It could have been off anything.'

'Or anyone. I want to know who.'

'You're being stupid. I was out on business.'

'I think you were with another woman.'

'Jesus, Cindy, how stupid do you think I am? Do you honestly think I would come back wooing you and spending money on you and sweet-talking you and then on the day of our big reunion at The Hempel nip off for a quick poke in the afternoon with some tart? Not to put too fine a point on it, I can barely crank up an erection once a day let alone poke like a bunny rabbit. And look down there. There's the proof.'

Cindy looked at his semi-erect cock which he had wave to her with help from his hand. She giggled.

'I'm being silly, aren't I?'

'I'm afraid so. I can't say where I was. But . . .'

'But? I like buts.'

'I like butts too.' He squeezed hers.

'I'm not getting fat, am I?' she asked, giggling again.

'Course not. The only fat arse I know is Nigel Gainsborough. He and his sidekick Serena Sark should look out. They may think they've pinched the Verity predictor business off me. Well they have. But I intend to blow a few trumpets and bring the walls of their little citadel tumbling down and that's one thing they'll never predict.'

59

'Hi, this is Duncan. I'm good-looking, early thirties, fair colouring. I'm extremely well-equipped in the genitals department. Into anything as long as it's rough and rude and raunchy. So go on. Send me a message.'

'Press one to listen, two to send, three to re-record. Do it now.'

Paul pressed two and sent his message onto the line. He looked nothing like Duncan, but that was hardly the point of the Maletalk cruise line. And nobody used their real name and nobody else ever seemed to select Duncan as their choice. He wondered what the most regular names were and what their selection signified about the gay sensibility. He didn't wonder about it for too long. Instead, he pressed his way back through the series of instructions and onto the recorded messages of the men cruising the line with him now. He fast forwarded through those he was not interested in.

'Hi. I'm a Greek guy—'

Yuck. Beep.

'Hi. Couple in Earl's Court seeking other couples. You must have a gym-trained body—'

Beep. Earl's Court? Girl's Court, surely. Paul preferred his men big and dirty and slightly to the side of sicko. Earl's Court was too 'nice'. They were all on the Internet these days anyway. The cruise lines there were pulling the business off the phones, but Paul could not afford the cost of a modem let alone a PC. He was stuck with the paupers, the middle-aged, the tourists and the old-fashioned.

'Good evening.'

Now here was a voice that knew how to make an announcement. It was plummy. It was mature. It intoned. It dictated. Literally. It sounded as if he expected his every utterance to be written down. Paul had once been a secretary and had taken a bit of dictation then. In fact he had been taking a bit of dick ever since.

'There *is* a doctor in the house. If you are intrigued by the concept of medical sex please leave a message.'

Hello.

'To respond to this message press one. To skip to the next message press two. To listen to this message again press three. Do it now.'

Paul decided to be dutiful and send a reply. He pressed one. Beep.

'Record your message after the tone.'

Beep.

'Hello. My name is Duncan. I would like to make an appointment with the doctor. What exactly is medical sex? Will you strip me down in your surgery? How well hung is your stethoscope? Do you wear rubber gloves for exploratory internal examinations? Do tell, doctor.'

Beep.

'To listen to your message press one. To send your message press two. To re-record your message press three.'

Paul pressed two and sent his message on its way.

Beep.

He would have to wait to see if the doctor posted a reply back. A few moments passed. Then there came another beep, although trumpets would have been more appropriate for Paul.

'You *have* a message,' said the American voice. 'Press one to retrieve your message.' Paul pressed and pulled the receiver closer to his ear.

'There would appear to be a misunderstanding. I am not a general practitioner. I am a surgeon. I perform operations. Would you care for a consultation?'

Beep. Operations? Kinky dinky.

'Will you give me a big injection?'

Beep.

'I am an extremely important professional. If you are not going to take this seriously I will have to terminate your call.'

Beep.

Oooh. He sounded ever so masterful. Paul sent a conciliatory message.

'What sort of operation would you perform on me?'

Beep.

'Well, as an example, do you by any chance possess a foreskin?'

Beep.

By any chance! Possess? He didn't mean pickled in a jar of alcohol did he? Paul did indeed possess a foreskin of considerable dimensions.

'Do I have a foreskin? Does the Royal Opera House have curtains?'

Beep.

'Good. Well, in the interests of research the sort of operation I might perform on you might be to attach the forementioned foreskin to four points. I would then stretch it wide open in a square formation and pour in, for example, molten wax.'

Beep.

Yikes, thought Paul. Molten wax. He had made plenty of use of candles for sexual purposes in the past – church ones were particularly suitable – but he had never thought of lighting them. For the first time ever somebody had suggested something sexual to Paul McCarthy of which he had never heard. He must get out more.

'Doesn't molten wax hurt?'

Beep.

'There is much pleasure to be produced in pain. Several of my previous patients have asked me to sew up their foreskins. This I do when they arrive at my practice. One leaves only a small gap. One does it without anaesthetic. One *can* use surgical staples but I am skilled with a needle and thread. I then instruct the patient to drink profuse amounts prior to participating in what a medical man such as myself might term restricted urination. I find this fascinating to watch. I record the result on my camcorder for my research library.'

Beep.

Paul gulped and instinctively stuffed his hand in his pants and pulled back his own foreskin just to make sure it hadn't somehow superglued itself together. He began to wonder what sort of weirdos the BMA was taking on these days. If the plummy voice belonged to a real doctor at all, that was. It was extremely unlikely that it did. There was something exceptional about the way this man talked. He was obviously older and someone quite authoritative, but also someone quite theatrical who revelled in dominant role play. Paul suddenly seized on the idea that perhaps Anton was playing a joke on him.

'Anton, it's Duncan, I mean it's Paul. Is that you? Are you winding me up or what?'

Beep.

Paul waited. He ran through the list of other callers and waited. He checked through the adverts on the bulletin board and waited. He skipped through the personal confessions on another section and waited. But no post arrived. There were no further mailshots, no more medical messages. Whoever it was had no more to say. Whoever it was had gone off line. Whoever it was had been frightened away by the impatient patient.

60

Karen removed her trademark spectacles and rubbed her eye. The thin lines on her face were thicker this morning.

'I hope you haven't got me in here at the crack of dawn for nothing.'

'Actually,' replied Duncan, 'I hope I have. Here. I picked up a cappuccino for you.'

He placed a polystyrene cup in front of Karen and, while she flipped off the plastic lid and licked the chocolate foam off its underside, Duncan slipped out of his jacket. He made for the door of Karen's office.

'Where are you going?' she asked.

'To hang up my jacket.'

'Just dump it here.'

'It's wool. It will crease. I have a hanger by my desk.'

'For God's sake!' Karen found it droll.

It was the first time in a long while that Duncan had seen her amused. It didn't stop him going though. He returned a moment later.

'Is it time yet?' asked Karen.

'Should be. Why haven't you switched on the television?'

'And put up Jamie Hirst's ratings? Why would I want to do that?'

'Because he has every intention of bringing ours down. If what he said to Michael is to be believed.'

'What were he and Michael doing cavorting at that pool anyway?'

'Just that, no doubt. Cavorting. That's what gay men do around pools.'

'They just bumped into each other? I bet Jamie planned it.'

'I thought that too. Where's the remote?'

'Here somewhere,' said Karen. She rummaged into some

documents and newpapers in the heap on her desk. 'I can't believe you've got me in the office at seven-thirty in the morning. Oh look, here's that file I was searching for. I was wondering where that had got to. Why couldn't I have stayed at home and watched it with Max?' She handed Duncan the remote.

'Because I'm your consultant on sponsorship and advertising as well as your producer and you have to do some things with me occasionally and not with Max.' He pressed the up button until he came to The Station. He turned on the mute so that the television was silent.

'Fucking hell! They've changed the set. What does it look like?'

'Breakfast TV, that's what it looks like.' Duncan sipped through the foam of his cappuccino. 'Who's the presenter?'

'I think she was someone big on MTV.'

'Now she's someone mega on *Megabrek*.'

'I think not. All the breakfast shows have lost their edge,' Karen tutted. 'Commercial break. I thought they had lots of interactive bits.'

'They do, but they save most of them for later on when the audience peaks. You have to schedule items within programme running orders as much as you have to schedule programmes throughout the day.'

'I know that. So what is this person's name?'

'Dorothy Copeland Charming. She's the executive in charge of sponsorship deals at the ITC. Ah. They're back.'

Karen sat down at her desk and pulled in her seat. She leant forward. She wagged a left hand for Duncan to turn up the volume. He obliged.

'Something new on the show today. Over the next few weeks I'll be meeting some of the people behind the scenes in TV to find out, with all the new channel launches and new technology, what new things are going on. Something you're bound to have noticed creeping in over the last few years is a form of advertising linked directly to programmes. Sponsorship. Old favourites like *Coronation Street* are now brought to you by Cadbury's and newer programmes like *Gladiators* are endorsed by Del Monte . . .'

'She's quite good, isn't she?' said Duncan.

'She can walk backwards and read an autocue. Shh.'

'... Well that's all called sponsorship. And someone who knows more about it than anyone else is my guest today, Dorothy Copeland Charming of the Independent Television Commission, the ITC.'

'Hello.'

'Aaagh. Look at that!' Karen pointed at the screen.

'What?'

'She's wearing my citrus suit.'

'It looks better on you.'

'If she got it from Julie Anne Brain Bypass I want my money back.'

'Shh.'

'Dorothy, you are the person responsible for making sure that sponsors obey all the rules and regulations.'

'That's right. As we say, we're here to ITC they get it right.'

'Yeah. Cool. And do they get it right?'

'Usually they do, yes. Almost always. Here in the UK we have one of the strictest advertising and sponsorship codes of practice in the world.'

'Boring,' said Karen.

'Shh,' said Duncan.

'So why is there all this sponsorship stuff happening all of a sudden?'

'For a number of reasons really. Basically commercial channels rely on only a few sources of revenue – advertising, subscription and programme sales to other broadcasters. There are new channels almost every week now, but there aren't any more advertisers or any more viewers. Those have reached saturation point. So encouraging sponsorship is a way of helping channels to gain more revenue and to help give viewers more choice.'

'I see. Now—'

'You see, our research shows that viewers want more programmes and more channels, but they don't want to have to pay for them through subscription or pay-per-view schemes.'

'I see. But why don't they just have like more ads in the breaks?'

'Because that would devalue the breaks as we have them now. Advertisers want to be one of a few advertising in the break, not one of about twenty. Viewers wouldn't be able to remember all those commercials and if the breaks were too long they would start surfing.'

'What's surfing?'

'Channel hopping.'

'Right. Cool. Surfing. Must remember that one. That's what we all do, don't we? We surf or get up and make a cuppa.'

'The system we have at the moment is one of the most successful in the world. In America, for example, where they have twelve minutes of advertising per hour, well, I find any programme chopped up like that unwatchable. One minute you're watching Eliza Bennett and Mr Darcy embracing, the next it's the Sheba cat getting a kiss and a cuddle. There is a balance and we're here to see they get it right.'

'To ITC they get it right. Plug your own catchline, our Dorothy!'

'Indeed.'

'So let's get to the bottom of this. What's the difference between sponsoring a programme and placing an ad in the break?'

'Well, an ad is an ad is an ad.'

'Greased lightning, Dorothy! Now we all know why you're the expert!'

'Hah hah. But with a sponsored programme there's a relationship between the sponsor and the show. So while ads come and go and move around programmes, the sponsor's message is always in the same place at the same time and built into the programme in the titles and what we call the break bumpers around the commercials.'

'Break bumpers! Fabby dabby!'

'And the real advantage of sponsorship is that the sponsor, who I must reassure your viewers has no influence over the programme content, has a link with a programme which they can, shall we say, exploit elsewhere off screen. You know, in newspaper ads or in free meals at McDonald's or gladiator visits at Safeway's or whatever it might be.'

'Fantastic. That links me into some clips I wanted to show you.'

Karen sighed. 'This is boring. It's way over the heads of the kids.'

'That's not why they're doing it.'

There followed video tape of some sponsorship idents: *Coronation Street* and Cadbury's; *Quizzine* and Crosse and Blackwell: *Sister Verity* and Verity Tampons.

'Where the fuck did they get that from?' Karen was about to bite through her polystyrene cup. 'If any one of the silly fuckers in this company as much as lifted a finger to help Saturn Productions I'll pull their brain out through their earhole and ram it down their throat and choke them on it!'

'Don't shout at me, I didn't give it to them. They'll have got it from The Station.'

'If Jamie Hirst or his henchmen had asked me I'd have told them exactly where to fuck off to.'

'Which is why they didn't.'

'Now, Dorothy, those last two. You said that the product wasn't allowed to influence the programme?'

'Absolutely. We're very rigid about that. There must be no connection at all between editorial and advertising. It's against the rules. Not so long ago, *This Morning* was fined half a million pounds for allowing commercial values to encroach on its editorial integrity.'

'So how can Crosse and Blackwell sponsor that *Quizzine* programme? They're a food company and it's a quiz show all about food. Isn't that a conflict of interest?'

'No. It's a series all about cooking from raw ingredients. No brand names are mentioned and no example of processed food is used. Crosse and Blackwell is a processed food manufacturer and any product areas in which they operate are excluded from the series.'

'So why sponsor it ?'

'Well . . . you really ought to put that question to them. I assume they wish to associate their sauces and canned products with the very high standard of cooking achieved on *Quizzine*.'

'Good answer, our Dorothy. Now what about *Sister Verity*?'

'I'm afraid I'm not aware of the *Sister Verity* show.'

'Well let me fill you in, Dotty—'

Karen's face ran like molten lead. 'Bitch.'

'—you see, Sister Verity is a nun who works for Verity Tampons. She's under contract to them to front a campaign aimed at schoolgirls. She's their brand symbol on pack. She also has this TV show which Verity Tampons have put all the money up for and which they sponsor and in which Sister Verity the brand symbol appears. How is that not a conflict of interest?'

'Fucking hell! Shit! I'll fucking kill that bastard Jamie Hirst.'

'Well I should point out that we make most of our judgements following broadcast rather than prior . . . I wasn't personally aware of this sponsorship. But we look into these things all the time and if there were any form of breach of guidelines then we would want to have an investigation.'

'Because you're here to ITC they get it right!'

'We are indeed.'

'Well Dotty, it's been huge fun having you on *Megabrek* . . .'

'It's been a total fucking barrel of laughs! Turn it *off*, Duncan!'

'. . . Ta very much for coming in. And now, let's look at a rundown of this week's top ten video releases . . .'

'Jesus Fucking Christ!' Karen went ballistic. She was meltdown mad. She was ready to break the desk in two across her thigh. 'Duncan, this is all your fault!'

'My fault?'

'Your friend dug up Sister Verity. She wanted to sponsor the show.'

'Excuse me, but Sister Verity was already under contract to Verity Tampons when you spotted her on L!VE TV and decided we *had* to have her.'

'Well, what about Michael Farnham and what's that woman's name you're friendly with at The Station?'

'Briony Linden. I don't know, Karen. But with all of us involved it's impossible that we've broken the guidelines. Jamie Hirst is just stirring it. The ITC would have done something about it before now, surely.'

'Of course they wouldn't have done. It's daytime TV. How do they know what's on every channel? Stations let alone programmes are coming and going at a rate of knots. That old bag could hardly keep up, could she?'

'She must have a monitoring department.'

'She does. It's called Saturn Productions. How could Jamie Hirst do this to me?'

'He's just winding us all up. He wants you to keep you on your toes and to fall out with Briony and Martin and me and Michael. Don't you see?'

'What did she say that other show got fined?'

'Half a million pounds.'

'Half a million pounds! Where are we going to get that sort of money? That'll wipe us out once and for all. And if it does, Duncan Cairns, I hold you responsible.'

With germ warfare on her mind, Karen Myhill swept out past her office door and slammed it resoundingly shut behind her.

61

Briony Linden peeked out from the third-floor balcony overlooking the atrium space of The Station's spectacular reception area. She wanted to catch sight of Dorothy Copeland Charming before she could see the whites of her eyes in the meeting. Briony made a face. The woman was wearing the same sour citrus suit which she had just seen on the video of *Megabrek*. Everyone was of the opinion that Jamie Hirst had set all this up deliberately, but Briony did not agree. She tended to think well of people. It was hardly in Jamie's vested interests to stir up trouble at The Station which he relied on for about twenty million pounds of his income.

'Let me see, Mummy.' Briony felt her younger daughter tug at the thigh of her trousers. 'Hold me up.'

'I can't darling. You're too big.'

'Please.'

'You might drop your crayons. Imagine how everybody would feel if they had pencils landing on their heads.'

Her daughter giggled. 'Please, Mummy.'

'All right.' It was not every day she brought the six-year-old into the office. In fact, it was only the second time ever. Briony's husband worked part-time from home, so their two daughters were normally safe with him. But today he had to go to a meeting and there was no school for Megan, their younger child – education cuts meant there was no relief teacher for this one day – so Briony had decided to bring her daughter to work. She thought that all those secretaries who had previously pictured you as a ghastly old bag softened to you. Perhaps it would have the same effect on Dorothy Copeland Charming. Megan put her paper and crayons on the floor and Briony lifted her and held her against the rail.

'It's far away to the ground . . .'

'I know, darling.' Briony wobbled.

'Don't drop me!'

'I won't, darling.'

'Mummy?'

'What?'

'If I were a fairy could I fly?'

'Not without an aeroplane, sweetheart. OK. Time to stand on our own two feet again. Pick up your things, Meg. Now, listen.' She crouched down and looked into Megan's eyes. She had the same white skin and white hair as her mother. 'Mummy is going into a very important meeting with her boss and a lady from outside. You just sit in the corner and draw Mummy a lovely picture and don't say anything, OK?'

'Can I have a drink?'

'You've had too much Coca-Cola already from those blasted girls. Promise me one thing, darling. When you grow up don't be a secretary. I couldn't bear it.'

'I want to be a fairy.'

'I know, darling, but they're low-tech. They've been outmoded by the digital revolution. Perhaps something with computers? Do you want to go to the toilet? Say now because I can't leave the meeting for at least an hour.'

Megan shook her head. Briony took her hand and walked slowly around the open balcony area to one of the huge projecting wings of the building where a glass-walled meeting room overlooked a piazza. On the outside glass curtain wall, two cylindrical glass viewing lifts bobbed up and down. Martin was already in the room, pacing.

'Briony. It's not like you to be late. Who's this?'

Megan hung back shy and stared at the terracotta carpet.

'She'll be very quiet, I promise. My husband isn't at home today so I brought her in for a few hours. Megan, sweetheart, come over here into the corner. Look. Look at the people in the lifts. Can you see them? Now sit down on the floor, put your paper there and draw Mummy a lovely picture.'

'I don't want to draw a picture.'

'Well do something. Quietly.'

'Hello. Dorothy Copeland Charming.' The sour citrus suit filled the door-frame. In her left hand she carried what looked to Briony like a small vanity case. Briony stood up and gave her most official of smiles. She stepped forward and extended her hand.

'Briony Linden, head of marketing. And this is—'

'Martin Fox.'

'Hello, Briony. Hello Martin. And who's this?'

'That's my daughter, Megan.'

'Don't you have a crèche?'

'No, we don't, do we Martin?'

'We have every other bloody thing. Can't afford it.'

'It's expensive isn't it? We don't have one at the ITC either. I can't say I personally approve of people bringing their children into the office.'

'I've not done it before,' said Briony, defensively. Dorothy Copeland Charming could fuck off if she was going to kick the meeting off like that, horrendous woman. 'Well, just one time before.'

'I suppose The Station is a very relaxed sort of working environment, which is probably a good way of leading straight into the topic which I asked to see you about today. I think you have taken far too relaxed a view to something of very serious concern. *Very* serious concern.'

Martin gestured for Dorothy to sit down at a long glass table, which she did. She placed her case discreetly to one side of her linked ankles. He offered her coffee from a plastic thermos jug. She declined. Briony helped herself when she realised Martin wasn't going to have one either.

'As I informed you on the telephone, I did not want to put anything in writing at this stage. I do not want to put either of you in a difficult situation so I thought this off-the-record chat would provide an opportunity to clear the air.'

'Does the air need clearing?' asked Martin.

'I'm afraid it does. I'll have to write to you in the strongest possible terms when I get back to the office. I'm just warning you of that now.' She waited for their thanks but none came. 'Our observations of *Sister Verity* are that you have contravened the ITC guidelines on sponsorship.'

'We weren't aware that we had.'

'Well you have. Blatantly. I'm afraid it's so blatant as to be beyond the normal fudge that the TV authorities could even think of settling for. There has simply been the most gross infringement of the rules regarding the separation of editorial from commercial interests.'

'We don't see it that way,' said Briony.

'I'm sure you don't. I'm sure the petty thief isn't aware of his wrongdoing or of the full text of the law but that doesn't make it right. The smaller cable companies seem to think they can get away with anything but I'm surprised that The Station would, to put it colloquially, try it on.'

'We haven't,' said Martin firmly.

'It's not a question of how *you* see it. It's a question of how *I* see it. Sister Verity is effectively a brand symbol advertising a product – and a product, no less, with rather a lot of restrictions around it due to its personal nature – and you have had her wholly in vision, bang in the middle of a twenty-four minute long programme every afternoon for the last six weeks. That constitutes what we call prominence. And since Verity also funds the series it also constitutes product placement.'

'Sister Verity,' said Briony, 'is a person in her own right. She's never advertised Verity Tampons. In fact they've never done any TV advertising on any channel ever, let alone this one.'

'I'm afraid you're being disingenuous, Briony. Dissembling, I think, is what they call it. Sister Verity is not a real person. That is a stage name which she adopted at the request of the Hector Quigley advertising agency in order to promote Verity Tampons. She is under contract to them.'

'We don't pay her,' explained Martin. 'Nor does the production company. She's a nun. She receives only expenses. It's a while since I've checked the contracts but I remember that.'

'That's irrelevant. The contracts I have had sight of were authorised with the nominal sum of one pound changing hands. I mean, she doesn't even wear a real nun's habit on television.'

'So?' asked Martin.

'Well, it's symptomatic of all the things that are wrong. The use of the typeface, the use of the same blue and pink colours as the packaging, the—'

'But,' protested Briony, 'Sister Verity has never appeared in a commercial. They don't use her to flog the product.'

'I'm afraid they do. She appears on the back of the pack and in the text on the information inside and she has a recorded phone line if you call Verity Tampons Consumer Services and last and not least, she goes around secondary schools preaching health and hygiene to young teenage girls and dishing out free samples. I was appalled when I found that out. I had no idea privatisation had gone that far.'

Briony argued on. 'That age group aren't usually at home at five p.m. to catch the show.'

'They might be. Well, certainly it's a possibility. There are truants . . .'

Martin rubbed his brow and sighed.

'Mummy?' It was Megan.

'What darling?'

'Can you take me for a wee?'

'No, Meg, I cannot. Sweetheart, the grown-ups are talking. Wait two seconds. We're nearly through.'

'We're nearly through our careers by the sounds of things,' joked Martin to Dorothy, who seemed horrified that the child should not only be seen *and* heard but interrupt too. She didn't see the funny side.

'Dismissals are not part of my remit. That's for your management to decide. Basically, what I would like you to do now is to tell me what is practical for you to achieve and I will then relate that back to you in a letter asking you to guarantee that it gets done.'

'I don't understand,' said Martin.

'Well, you will obviously have to either take the programme off air or Sister Verity will have to change her name and her image and her typeface and the blue and pink colours in the title and credits sequences. And you'll have to drop the sponsorship.'

'Jesus.'

'But the ITC is very reasonable. We will give you a period in which you have to take the show off air.'

Briony shot a look of despairing helplessness at Martin. White of face and hair by nature, what little colour she had been visibly ebbing away. Now Martin had turned puce in panic. He stuttered.

'B . . . b . . . b . . .'

'It won't have to be tomorrow,' said Dorothy. She sounded as if she thought she was being encouraging.

'I'm glad to hear it,' gasped Martin. 'We're still a new channel. We don't have a vast library of suitable material which we can just fling on air at a moment's notice.'

'How long will it take to find a replacement?'

'I don't know. Six or seven weeks.'

'That's too long. The series has got nine weeks to run. I must be seen to have got you to truncate the series.'

'Four weeks, then.'

'Say three. OK. Three weeks tomorrow, Sister Verity must either come off air or drop all obvious and subliminal references to Verity Tampons.'

'My God. Perhaps you could tell Karen Myhill.'

'She's the woman who created the programme?'

'She is.'

'I'm surprised she's not here today to face the music.'

'It's preferable, believe me. She never faces the music. She enjoys discord.'

'Well that settles it. I shall have our lawyers draw up a letter and hand-deliver it to you tomorrow. I'll also notify you of the fact that you will be publicly censured and that that will have to be announced on air. And I'll let you know the parameters of the potential fine.'

'Fine?'

'That will be payable later after legal procedures have been gone through.'

'How much?'

'It's not for me to say.'

'Well, like what? One thousand? Ten thousand? Fifty thousand?'

'Oh no.' Dorothy gave a contemptuous wave of her sour citrus arm. 'More likely half a million.'

'Jesus,' said Briony.

'They're a big brand. You're a big TV station. It's a very big infringement.'

'Who pays?' asked Martin, complexion paling.

'You do. Technically. But it usually comes down to the contracts you have with your partners. That's not my area.'

Not my area, thought Briony wryly to herself as they rose. Martin obviously felt as she did. Dorothy could see herself out. As she reached for the door handle Megan suddenly scampered across the floor from her corner and presented Dorothy with a piece of paper. Briony looked on, too floored to do anything.

'Goodness me, dear. What's this?' asked Dorothy.

'I've drawn a picture of you,' said Megan.

'Have you dear? And who's this?'

'That's me. I'm a fairy. And that's you. You're a witch.'

Martin Fox lowered his brow onto the glass table top and groaned.

'Dorothy Copeland *Not* Charming,' said Briony. She produced a slightly squashed pack of Camel Lights from her pocket.

'Don't,' said Martin.

'Right now I don't give a flying fu– flying fairy,' said Briony, just remembering Megan was still in the room with them. In majestic defiance of the company rules, she lit up a cigarette and nervously puffed away. She was actually shaking now. It was delayed reaction.

'Well, Briony, I hope I'm not going to get the blame for this.' Martin was searching in his trouser pocket for something.

'I won't set off the alarms. I've learnt how not to.'

'I didn't mean that. I meant the half million pound fine.' He produced a white handkerchief from his pocket and put it to the beads of sweat on his forehead.

'Old iron knickers was laying it on thick. It might not be that much.'

'Terrific. That takes a whole load off my mind.' He dabbed away.

'On the other hand it might be more.'

'Christ.'

'Well don't blame me.'

'I didn't put the deal together.'

'Neither did I. Blame Karen Myhill.' Briony defiantly puffed away. Her hand shook as much as before.

'She'll blame Duncan Cairns. He organised it.'

'He'll blame the agency. They must have misled him.'

'They'll blame us. I blame Jamie Hirst. What in hell's name does he think he's playing at?' Martin waved his handkerchief, a flag of surrender.

'Do you think he did it deliberately?'

'Is the Duke of Edinburgh Greek? Of course he did it deliberately. He's probably got the replacement series shot and edited and ready to air from tomorrow. I – hmm . . . hah!'

'What is it?'

'Get Michael Farnham on the telephone.'

'There's no phone in here. Michael's brilliant. He'll sort something out.'

'If I'm not mistaken he already has.'

'What?'

'I seem to remember at some stage in the past him arguing about a clause in our standard commissioning contract. Anything like this, product placement problems etcetera, and the liability lies with the production company. Much as I respect her, Karen Myhill will have to pay the bloody fine on this one. Poor cow.' He grinned in hope if not relief.

'I thought you and she were meant to be great mates?'

'That won't prevent me from making her pay. It was her error. It'll finish her and her company off. '

'Are you sure?'

'Sure. How much will she turn over in a year? Bugger all, I should think. Perhaps she can countersue the agency. Or Verity Tampons may just put up the money, if they're allowed to.'

''No. I mean are you sure what you just said is in the standard contract?'

'I think it is. It ought to be.The important thing is that we have to make sure the buck doesn't stop with us, Briony. Michael Farnham better sort this whole thing out. All of our heads are on the block.'

'We'll get censured. It'll be on the news. It'll be in the papers.'

'A censure can lead to the loss of the franchise. The Station could get closed down even if we could sort out the money thing. I'll have to advise the Chief Executive immediately.' He rose to leave.

'Mummy?'

The two adults looked at Megan.

'Can we go and play in the lifts?'

Briony laughed through a puff of smoke. 'Good idea, darling. Let's go and play in the lifts. Coming Martin?'

'Why the hell not? We might not get another chance.'

62

'You're sure your mother doesn't shop here?'

'She wouldn't be caught dead in Tesco's. She wouldn't know where Neasden was. She shops in Waitrose.'

'It's rather expensive.'

'She can afford it.'

Karen screwed up her eyes behind her bejewelled glasses and examined the girl limping languidly half a pace ahead of her. That was the third dismissive reference Ginny Collins had made to one or other or either of her parents. Karen didn't much like going behind their back and she didn't much like Ginny's attitude.

'It's just,' said Karen, 'that I don't think she should see us together. Which is why I suggested meeting here like this.'

'Took me all of an hour to get here on the bus. It's off the A to Z almost.'

'I can hardly move in my own home since the decorators arrived. I can get our shopping done for this week. Excuse me.' Karen let go of the trolley and reached up onto the shelf. She picked out two cans of own label chopped tomatoes and threw them into the empty metal trolley where they landed with a clatter.

'Do you normally shop here?'

'No. Which is why so far I haven't found one damn thing I'm looking for. I hadn't realised this place was so vast. I didn't know Tesco sold clothes.'

'You don't want to.'

'Why do they lay out every store differently?'

'Dunno. Market research.'

'Yes, well, I'm Sainsbury woman. God knows what that says about me. It's just that I have to run a home and a business and I do it all on my own and I haven't got the time to coo and purr at new products in the supermarket. If I could press a button and have the food delivered into my home, I would.'

'Is it that hard being a single mother?'

'It's tough, Ginny. I'm in my fifties and I make money and it's still tough. You won't be in that position.'

'I mean the image we get off the telly is always some drug-addicted slag with a fag hanging from her mouth stuck on the twentieth floor of some concrete estate dragging a screaming pramful of half-black children up the stairs because the lift's been vandalised. I mean, that's how they're seen.'

'That's TV for you. It doesn't suit to show the other side. That would be boring.' Karen said it sarcastically, making clear her opinion of her peers.

'I've been looking into it because I'm doing media studies. I'd like to be a film director or maybe a TV director like you.'

'Ambitious. I'm a producer.'

'What's the difference?'

'Well . . . it's hard to explain it really. The director does all the directing on the programme which the producer has . . . you know . . . produced.'

Flummoxed, Karen smiled at her inability to describe her own job. It seemed obvious to her. But then she had been doing it for the best part of thirty years. She wheeled on, scanning the shelves of the chiller cabinet.

'Fromage frais. I need fromage frais.'

For once, Ginny looked up and paid attention. She sidled along the illuminated display. The fluorescence lit up the down on her flushed cheeks and Karen was struck by how young this girl really was, how pretty, how virginal looking, if not, perhaps, literally intacta. Her stomach rumbled. She felt sick at the prospect of it all.

'Here.'

'Thank you. Only, sorry, but that's not the right one. I should have said. I need eight per cent fat. It'll say "low fat" on it.'

'Why do old women always care about fat? It's not as if anybody bothers if they're overweight or not.'

Karen gripped the bar of the trolley handle very tightly indeed. She could have buckled it so shot through with hurt was she at the insensitivity of the throwaway remark. Was that how they saw her, Ginny and Max? As an old woman? One past caring about? She suddenly possessed a poor appetite for shopping. Ginny returned with the right tub, unaware of the pangs she had caused her potential protector. She scuffed her feet on the tiled floor.

'You can't go on wearing platform shoes like that if you're pregnant.'

'You're not my mother.'

Karen ground her teeth. 'Of that I am well aware. It's not a fashion tip. It'll just kill your back, that's all.'

'See if I care.'

'Oh fuck you, Ginny! See if I care either!'

Pushed too far, Karen swerved the trolley round. It crashed into the back of a startled woman's calves. She squealed in pain.

'I'm so sorry,' muttered Karen, fraught and embarrassed.

She swept off down the aisle towards the long queues at the checkouts. Ginny soon caught up with her, terrified.

'I'm sorry, Mrs Myhill. I'm sorry.'

An obese woman in front of Karen turned and gave them a filthy look.

'Call me Karen, for God's sake.'

'Karen.'

'Look, Ginny. I'll pay for these things. You go over to the cafeteria and get us a coffee each or a tea or anything and I'll join you at the table. OK?'

'I don't want coffee here. I'd rather dye my hair orange than eat in Tesco's.'

'Do I look like the sort of woman who eats in Tesco's either? Just do it!'

The obese woman turned with an even filthier look, tutted at Karen's shouting, then muttered something under her breath. Alarmed, Ginny dashed off smartly. Karen clocked the plump woman's white bread and lemon curd shopping basket and dismissed her in her mind.

The cafeteria was smart and clean, if too much of a living tribute to wipe-clean surfaces and operating theatre lighting. Karen knew how old and tired she must look under these lights. Still, the coffee was good. And, thankfully, the place was empty at this odd hour. She decided to take Ginny head on.

'The reason I made you get on a bus and come all the way out to Neasden is because we need to talk. I haven't mentioned this to Max yet—'

'Oh, don't tell him!'

'That answers my first question. Max doesn't know.'

'No.'

'Why not?'

'Because . . .'

'Because *what*, Ginny? Look Ginny, I'm sorry but you're going to have to grow up very fast here and now and face the facts. You're pregnant and you're going to have a baby or not have a baby and if you do, you need proper medical care and attention and support. You can't stick your head in a bucket of sand and not let on and hope it goes away. It's not going away. It's going to come kicking and screaming and scratching and ripping its way out of your vagina before you know it and it'll hurt like hell and it'll ruin your life and my son's and I won't let you do that. Understood?'

Tears streamed down the girl's face.

'Why have you not told Max?'

'Because – I don't know what to do. My mother will kill me.'

'She'll be lucky to get the chance if you don't stop being so evasive.'

'I want an abortion.'

Karen was hooded with gloom. An abortion was a terribly good idea. An abortion was the one-stop solution they sought. The nightmare would end. Except that Karen simply did not sanction abortion. She could not abort her own child when she became pregnant after a moment of madness. She could not advise this girl to do it either. Max had been the biggest and the best thing in her whole life. He had made her life worth living. He was the point of her life. He was the purpose of her life. He *was* her life. How could she possibly advise this girl to kill her own baby? It was not just hers. It was Max's flesh and blood too. And through him it was Karen's as well. God.

'You must confront your parents.'

'I can't.'

'You must.'

'I can't.'

'You must.'

'Stop pressuring me.'

'I'm not pressuring you, Ginny.'

'They'll make me have an abortion.'

'I thought you wanted an abortion.'

'I don't know what I want. I'm not murdering my child. I can take care of a baby. Lots of girls do it. They still get their A Levels.'

'Be realistic.'

'They do. I can take care of a baby.'

'It's Max's baby too. You must talk to him about it. You can't make any decisions on your own. He must have an equal say.'

'He's not interested.'

'That's hardly surprising. You haven't told him.'

'He'll want it aborted.'

'He may not.'

'He will. He's a killer.'

'What?!'

'You don't know your own son, that's your problem. He's clinical. He's cold. He's calculating. He sees everything as a problem of principle that he's got a clever solution for. Well, he's not slaughtering my child.'

'Don't talk about Max like that. Max is a good boy. He's clever and he's kind. I'm proud of my son.'

'You shouldn't be. Look at what he's done to me. Ruined my life. You said so yourself. He took advantage of me.'

'I find that very hard to believe. You must have led him on.'

'The hell I did. He was all over me. He's an animal.'

'You're lying.'

'I am not.'

'You are. Max is not like that.'

'Max is. Max is a bastard – he has *you* to thank for that.'

'You little minx. Look at you.'

'Look at yourself.'

'You have all the charm of a common little trollope, d'you know that? What did you do to lure my son into bed? You're little better than a slut.'

'You're in no position to judge me, Mrs Myhill. You're the bastard's mother.'

'Where did you do it? I hope to God it wasn't in my home? How come your parents don't know?'

'It was on the heath.'

'The heath. That's disgusting.'

'I couldn't care less what you think.'

'That's your trouble, Ginny. You need to start caring.'

'I do care. I'm not having you so-called grown-ups make me have an abortion.'

'No one's forcing you to have an abortion. I'm not, anyway.'

'I will bring up this child on my own. I don't need you or my parents and I don't need Max. I just need his money and I'm entitled to it.'

Karen gulped. 'His money? What money?'

'Don't pretend. I'm not a moron. Max has a trust fund. Me

and my baby are entitled to at least half of it. He can pay me a lump sum and maintenance.'

Karen was so outraged she could barely draw the breath required to respond. 'How in fuck's name did you hear about Max's trust fund?'

'That's the first time I've seen you genuinely concerned, Mrs Myhill. At the prospect of losing some of your son's grubby stash of unearned money. Well you should have told him to keep his pants on and to put his prick away before he started poking about with it. I'm entitled to at least half of his million pounds and I have every intention of getting it.'

'You scheming little bitch.'

'You scheming big bitch.'

'I'm warning you, Ginny Collins. If you as much as even mention Max's trust fund or see him ever again or have anything to do with him, it won't be any baby that ruins your life. It'll be me. That's a promise.'

Karen stood up and started to run for the supermarket revolving door. She was going to burst into tears and she wasn't going to give the evil young woman who had duped both her and her son the pleasure of seeing her do so. But the girl's words shouted after her hit her smack on the side of her head and there was nothing she could do to stop them from reverberating inside it.

'I don't think you'll do anything of the sort, Mrs Myhill. Because I'm carrying your grandchild.'

63

'I'm hurt you don't think I'm the perfect mother for your child.'

'You're hurt?'

'Yeah. You could have asked me.' Cindy smiled and took Duncan's arm. She led him out of the ethereal eighteenth-century orangery of Kensington Palace where they had just taken tea amongst the neo-classical statues, and back into the royally manicured grounds.

'You're not a lesbian.'

'Don't tempt me. I might become one. Men are so difficult. Anyway, I didn't realise you needed to be one.'

'It seemed like a good idea to me.'

'It seems like a lousy idea to me.' She stopped and they admired the elegant façade of the stately brick palace. 'Which windows are Di's d'you think? And which are Princess Margaret's and Princess Michael's? You'd think you'd be able to tell by their choice in curtains.'

'I think they have to have the originals don't they?'

'Do they wear Doc Martens? The lesbians, I mean. Bet they did their own electrics.'

'They're not like that.'

'Oh. The lipstick sort. Play tennis, do they?'

'I have no idea.'

'It was a joke. You must have heard of what goes on on the tennis circuit.'

'I didn't realise that they covered that sort of thing in *Hello!* magazine.'

'*Hello!* magazine?'

'Your exclusive reading matter.'

'Piss off. So, these two diesel dykes—'

'I don't know any diesel dykes. They're just two nice girls.'

'There was this girl in my class at school. She was very dykey. She became a lumberjack for the New South Wales government or something. She was the last girl in our year to wear a bra.'

'And you were the first.'

'I was the second. 32A.'

'Is that very small?'

'Spot the man who knows his way around a woman's body.'

'I've been reading up on it. On ovulation and pregnancy.'

'Yuk.'

'You're not very maternal. I thought you just offered your services as a surrogate.'

'I am maternal. But I'm a single woman. I know I'm very modern in some ways but in others I'm old-fashioned. I don't think children should be brought up in households where there isn't a mother and father, married or at least . . . no. Married. I mean married.'

'So what are we doing touring Kensington Palace? This is the biggest broken home in Britain.'

'That's different. There were three of them in that marriage, remember? Personally, I'm with Di. Come on. I'll take you to her water garden. Have you never been? It's hidden by high hedges like a well-kept secret. You can't go into it. You just catch glimpses of it through windows they've cut in the yew. You can only see from a distance. It's very romantic.' She led on.

'So,' said Duncan, 'basically, when we get down to my situation you don't approve.'

'I didn't say that. Everyone who knows you knows you would make a good father. But that's not what's on the cards here is it?'

'Isn't it?'

'Stop deluding yourself, Duncan. God, you're normally so focused about everything, this time you've gone blind. These two women want your sperm and then they want you to fuck off. Can't you see that? They don't want you as a father. Not the sort you have in mind. They don't want you as a father figure either. There's all this research that feminists read, it's a lot of crap probably, but they believe it, and it says that role models are a thing of the nineteen sixties and that it's the child's general environment that matters and not whether it's got one parent or two and that as long as the child is with its mother everything will be fine. It doesn't need a father.'

'I don't believe that.'

'I don't either. I'm just telling you that a lot of "wimmin" do.'

'Where did you read this?'

'It was in *Hello!* magazine.'

'It wasn't!'

'No of course it wasn't. Which only goes to prove I read other things. I do run my own business, you know. And I am a single woman and I do sometimes think of having children, although

I don't think I ever will. But I do think about it and therefore I read. There. Surprised you, didn't it?'

'I rate your intelligence, actually.'

'Really. I always thought you thought I was some sort of stupid person you could try out your arguments on.'

'It's because I think precisely the opposite I try them out on you. But why pick me if they know that I'm keen to be involved with the child's upbringing?'

'You fitted the bill. They had a list of requirements, you said.'

'But lots of men would fit them.'

'Well they found you first. Also they wanted a gay man.'

'I didn't say that.'

'I know you didn't. But that's what they were looking for.'

'How do you draw that conclusion?'

'They are two lesbians. Somebody reports them to the council. There's two dykes bringing up a baby all weird. Have it put into care.'

'The authorities would never take a child from its natural parents unless it was being maltreated.'

'Exactly. But they could give the child to the father. But a father who has never seen his child wouldn't get the kid. And a father who was gay and living with another man absolutely wouldn't have a snowball in hell's chance of ever getting hold of the child legally.'

Duncan looked dejected.

'That's why they picked you, Dunky.'

Duncan looked miserable.

'Truth hurts, doesn't it?'

Duncan looked heartbroken. 'Do you think I've been foolish?'

'Not as big a fool as I've been.'

'Why? What have you done now?'

'I don't think I liked that "now" at the end of that sentence. You make me feel like a serial failure.'

'I'm sorry.'

'It's just that I seem to have sort of half got back together with Alan.'

'Why?'

'Why not?'

'When you were in Australia I had lunch with him.'

'Did you?'

'Not intentionally.'

'Conniving behind my back?'

'No.'

'And?'

'And he said he loved you.'

'Well if he told you it *must* be true!'

'Why else would he tell me?'

'So that you'd tell me.'

'You're surprisingly cynical.'

'You're surprisingly naive.'

Duncan looked downcast. 'I don't want to do the wrong thing.'

'Don't do anything at all.'

'Do you think I shouldn't?'

'Leave them to come back to you and see what they suggest next. Treat it like a business deal. I mean, you try never to look desperate in business because then you have no negotiating position. You may look too keen to them.'

'Perhaps. You're not really hurt about that perfect mother thing.'

'Of course not.'

'You may have kids. With Alan. There's plenty of time yet.'

'There isn't plenty. Only yesterday I was twenty-one. Today I'm in my late thirties. Tomorrow I'll be laid out on the slab.'

'Death is a much longer way off than that.'

'I didn't mean death. I meant laid out getting myself nipped and tucked.'

When they reached the high yew hedge of the palace water garden Duncan leant over the parapet ledge of the first square window cut into it. It was like a room inside, a perfectly clipped garden arranged around a still, formal pool, an exemplar of man's complete control over nature. Duncan hankered after such symmetry and order. He watched affectionately as a grey squirrel scrambled along the edge of the pond, darting from one lead fountain tub to another, unaware of the geometric sophistry of its home. Cindy looked beyond, far away. Duncan wasn't sure whether she was searching the future or the distant past. He wondered if her advice was coloured by her own situation. A bit galling to have no children of your own when even your gay friends are having them. He wondered if he should call Lesley. He wondered if he should call Michael. She wondered if she should call Alan. He wondered. She wondered. They wandered on.

64

'That looks interesting. Dunky and I should go.' Michael picked up a pamphlet on Martin Fox's desk. The logo of the Royal Shakespeare Company was emblazoned upon it. 'What are they doing this season, anything good? We haven't been for ages.'

'I haven't had time to look. Sit down, please.'

Michael pulled up one of the comfortable visitor's chairs around the low coffee table in Martin's office. He neatly placed his folder of contracts on it and flicked through the pamphlet.

'They keep sending me all that crap. I've told my secretary to bin it. The trouble is when you're the head of programmes for a TV channel everyone invites you to everything for free in the asinine hope you'll make it into a series. I mean Shakespeare? Does this look like the BBC?'

'The trouble is when you're the company lawyer nobody invites you to anything because everybody knows you have no influence.'

'Count me out. I *know* you have influence, which is why I asked you to this meeting. Where is Briony? I hope she hasn't got that ruddy child in tow with her again. I hate children.'

'It was just for the one day, Martin.' The two men looked up. Briony was in the doorway. She turned to Martin's secretary outside. 'Coffee please. What about you two?' The two men nodded. 'Make it three. Thank you.'

Briony was wearing a light brown shirt and wide pants ensemble with a long trailing lilac scarf.

'You're looking very Isadora Duncan today,' complimented Michael.

'Somebody else said that. It must be the scarf. I hadn't realised she got strangled by hers.'

'Did she?'

'Apparently it got caught in the wheel of her car and when she drove off it choked her to death. Of course, here I don't need to hit the car park. I can rely on my colleagues to do it with their bare hands.'

'That's rather uncharitable, Briony,' said Martin. 'We have a good atmosphere here.'

'Yeah, well, wait till the Americans hear about *Sister Verity*.'

'Sister Verity? They'd love her in the States,' said Michael.

Briony had seen the RSC pamphlet in Michael's hands. 'What's that?'

'Martin's theatre brochure.'

'I'm surprised he has the time.'

Martin made a face. The secretary entered and distributed the coffees and then departed. Martin gave them a grey, resigned look. Michael wondered why. He was about to learn.

'Look, you people. What I have to say this morning is to go no further. This is strictly private and confidential. Understood?'

'Yes,' said Briony.

Michael looked puzzled. 'I suppose so.'

'We have a problem with *Sister Verity*. I'm sorry Michael but it takes in your partner as producer and I'm asking for there to be no pillow talk on this one. I've no idea what is politically correct, but I have to ask you and you have to promise to keep it to yourself.'

'What's the problem?'

'I have in my hand a piece of paper. It's a letter from the ITC. From Dorothy Copeland Charming.'

'Dorothy Copeland *Not* Charming,' said Briony.

'She came in to see us yesterday.'

'She's the one that Jamie Hirst was on about?'

'Don't mention his name, please. She had this letter hand-delivered this afternoon. It repeats what she told us yesterday. I tried to get hold of you but you were out of the office. What Dorothy has to say basically is that the ITC have viewed the Myhill series and regard the use of Sister Verity as a breach of the guidelines on commercial involvement in editorial. She's the direct symbol of a brand and, worse, the brand which sponsors the show. The deal was effectively brokered by the production company, which is apparently also a conflict of interest, and although the sponsorship money is paid to us what we essentially do is simply give it straight back to Karen Myhill who arranged it all in the first place and who looks as if she's in cahoots with the brand. If not criminals, we're accomplices.'

'Shit,' said Michael.

'Don't they have to prove that Verity have influenced the content of the programme? To make the allegations stick?' asked Briony.

'No,' said Michael.

'They don't need to,' said Martin. 'But as it happens quite a lot of young teenage girls have indeed called in and Sister Verity has given them the party line on periods and ovulation and when you can get pregnant and how to do a home test. I didn't even know they made those ruddy products.'

'They've just launched, I think,' said Briony. 'It's through Clancey and Bennett. Our agency.'

'Jesus. That's all we need.'

'Duncan used to work there,' added Michael.

'Oh, for fuck's sake. We're all up to our necks with this one. What I need you to do, Michael, is to talk us through the Myhill commissioning contract and the Verity sponsorship contract. There's no way there isn't going to be a fine on this and a public censuring. The chief executive has done his nut already and I haven't even had the guts to say the fine might be half a million quid.'

'Half a million?' Michael was staggered. He looked decidedly uncomfortable for one normally so cool.

'Probably. You try standing up and telling our shareholders that at the AGM. Basically, Michael, someone's going to get stung pretty badly around here. Briony and I could both lose our jobs. What I want you to do, Michael, is weave some of your legal magic over the contracts and dig us out of the hole we're in. Are those them?'

'Yup . . . I was wondering why you asked me to bring them . . . The point about the Myhill contract is . . .'

'What?'

Michael gulped. There was a catch of uncharacteristic shyness in his voice. 'It isn't finalised.'

'*What*?!' Martin was visibly shocked.

'We haven't signed it and neither has Karen Myhill.'

'*I don't fucking believe it!*'

'Well, I'm sorry. It's true.'

'Sorry? What fucking use is sorry, Michael? *Je-sus*. Why not?'

'It shouldn't be a problem.'

'Shouldn't be? *Shouldn't be*?'

'We've hired her before and she's proceeded on our standard terms. We are covered by a letter saying standard terms are to be assumed.'

'Assumed!'

Briony looked at Michael. Martin looked at Michael. Michael looked at Martin.

'Would another assumption be that my job is on the line as well?'

'Too fucking right. What the fuck have you been playing at? The show is up and running and on air and we haven't got a signed contract. I don't believe it!'

'But—'

'And all we've got is some crappy little memo with vague promises on it, no doubt. Jesus . . .'

'Yes, but—'

'I mean, for fuck's sake, Michael, what have you been doing all this time?'

'Contracts never get finalised before shows go on air. It's the nature of the business.'

'Try telling that to the Yanks. The CEO will want my balls for his Newton's cradle.'

'The Verity sponsorship deal is signed and sealed.'

'Thank God for small mercies.'

'Well that's actually the difficult one to do. So I did that one first.'

'Well unfortunately, it was the wrong one.'

'No it wasn't, otherwise you wouldn't have got the budget to finance the series. Karen's contract is more standard, so I thought I'd do it second but she's not known as The Most Difficult Woman In Television for nothing. She and her accountant are tough negotiators.'

'You're breaking my heart.'

'They are.' Michael's pitch heightened in self-defence. 'And I happen to be very short-staffed and I have to delegate the standard stuff to the juniors. They're slow. I just can't read every line of every contract myself. Not for the whole channel.'

'I don't expect you to. But if I lose my job because of you, I'll fucking kill you.'

'What about mine?' asked Briony. But the two men were so heated they had almost welded into contact.

Michael became visibly aggressive. 'If you lose your job, Martin, it'll only be because you lost your nerve. Don't blame me. You commissioned the series at very short notice. You were the last person to go round saying "take your time". You wanted the programme on air straightaway. Who was I to hold it up?'

'Your role is to batten down the hatches, Michael. It seems you have singularly failed to do that here. This is just plain incompetence.'

'No it is not. It wouldn't matter one iota, Martin, if you hadn't commissioned a series which blatantly broke the guidelines in the first place. It's your responsibility to comply with the editorial guidelines. Programme content is nothing to do with me. You're not asking me how to get round the guidelines. You're asking me to get you off the hook of paying a fine. One which you brought on yourself.'

'The hell I did. Your mincing little boyfriend stitched me up. So as far as I'm concerned the blame lies at your door.'

Michael was furious. His eyes flashed with fury. His skin burnt with anger. Briony could sense the temperaure rising to combustion point.

'Don't you think you're getting a bit overheated you two?' She tried a soft smile. 'Let's not get personal, shall we? We need to stay rational. And quiet. There's a row of secretaries lined up outside fascinated at who's doing all the shouting.'

'Lazy bitches at the best of times,' muttered Martin.

'Martin! I've never seen you like this.' Briony was appalled. 'You're turning into a misogynistic homophobe.'

'I happen to be under a great deal of pressure.'

'Well, give Michael a chance to suggest a solution.'

Michael was shifting through his papers. 'Hang on a minute.' He sorted and read some more and then drew breath. Martin looked grim but remained silent.

'Well, I think this is the position. Let's assume that the ITC fines us as the broadcaster for breaking the rules and it's half a million pounds? OK. The position is that we can contractually pass the responsibility back to Myhill Productions. She has to pay the half-million.'

'Except that she hasn't signed the fucking contract.'

'She will argue that. But she's had sight of it and she's taken the money for the series which, as far as I am concerned, is the equivalent to signing on the dotted line. Her lawyer has sent me letters quibbling some points but not that one. So effectively that's an admission they've seen the contract and have not disputed that point. They've also been commsisioned by us before on a similar contract and agreed the same point then.'

'It's not watertight.'

'Not as we would like it to be. I concede that. But we can argue that those are our standard terms of business with her. So she knew what she was getting into. If she takes us to court I'd say we'd have a forty to sixty per cent chance of winning.'

'Fuck. Is that all?'

'Those are good odds. I'm being conservative. I have to be.'

'What about Verity Tampons?'

'They're in the clear. Their contract is to do with finance and slogans and that sort of thing. They can't be responsible for what is broadcast because the very nature of their deal means they're not meant to have any influence on the programme. If anyone were to sue them for the money it would have to be Karen.'

'She'll have to. It'll bankrupt her, a half a million pound fine.'

'Well, she'll have the income from the series.'

'Not all of it. The ITC want it taken off air in three weeks.'

'We still have to pay Karen.'

'Why?'

'It's a fixed-price contract.'

'What does that mean?'

'We still have to pay Myhill Productions the whole cost of the series, even if we cancel it.'

'But we haven't signed it.'

'Yes,' said Briony, 'but neither has she. You can't pin the fine on her and then wriggle out of paying her for the series. That wouldn't be fair.'

'Fair? Who cares about fair? Oh for fuck's sake this is a disaster. There's nine weeks still to run. The cost per hour is low but there's a lot of shows. It's three hundred grand for the six cancelled weeks.'

'It's better than a half-million pound fine.'

'But, said Briony, ' if the fine is less than three hundred thousand, we'd be better off paying it ourselves. It would be cheaper than paying for the series.'

'Then you'd be paying the fine and for the series. You still have to pay for the series, stupid,' Martin snapped at her.

'I'm not stupid,' said Briony, hurt.

'This is a no-win situation. Goddammit.' Martin thumped the table. 'Look, people, I need a solution. I need one fast. Or we're all facing the sack.'

Michael looked white. Briony gulped. She tried another approach. 'Why don't we drop Sister Verity. Replace her with another presenter?'

'Then,' said Michael, 'you have to give all the sponsorhip money back to Verity Tampons. So you'd lose three hundred thousand that way. And Karen will have to build a new set and new titles and new credits and you'd have to pay for all of that.'

'Fuck,' said Martin. 'Isn't this what the Americans call a lose-lose situation?'

'It sounds more like a lose-lose-lose situation,' observed Briony. 'Well, what are we going to do?'

'Reconvene on Monday morning, here,' said Martin. 'I will

talk some more to Dorothy Copeland Charming and get a steer on how this whole thing works and you two try to come up with as many solutions as you can. At worst we have to do a massive damage limitation exercise. And Michael?'

'What?'

'Not a word. I can't have Karen tipped off so that she has all her options covered ahead of us.'

'Isn't that cruel?' asked Briony. She still had a lot to learn about TV.

'Hey. It's a jungle out there, isn't it? And I'm a—'

'Bastard?' offered Briony.

'Eh?' Martin looked unpleasantly surprised.

'A shit?' proffered Michael.

'I was going to say lion, actually,' said Martin, wounded.

'A sly fox is the real expression you're looking for,' said Michael.

'I haven't been called that for years.'

'Not to your face,' said Briony.

Outside Martin's door Michael realised he was still carrying the RSC pamphlet. He held it up for Briony to see.

'*A Comedy of Errors*,' he said.

'A shame it can't be *All's Well That Ends Well*' she sighed. 'Somehow I doubt it.'

65

'I *can't* get rid of him. He won't go away.' The secretary shook out her hands in frustration. 'Why don't you try?'

From behind his huge desk of honest English oak, Tim Lutyens gave her a weary look under one raised fine eyebrow. He sighed.

'I'm sorry, Mr Lutyens, but he's not a normal person. He's very sinister-looking. He's frightening me.'

'He's threatened violence?'

'No. He's not that sort. He's the psychological sort. You know. Silent and creepy. He's been sitting there for over two hours.'

Tim Lutyens sighed once more.

'And he has still not said who he is?'

'No he bloody well hasn't.'

'Miss Snell!'

The secretary blushed at her boss's reprimand. 'Well he's driving me up the wall. And so are you for not seeing him. And it's my going-home time. I can't throw him out. Not physically. He's too big.'

Tim Lutyens sighed yet again. 'Very well. I think I know who this young gentleman is. There is only one person it could be. Send him in.'

Relieved, the secretary marched to the magnificent panelled door and, leaving it ajar behind her, slipped outside with trepidation. A moment later, slowly and smoothly, the door swung back and a tall, broad youth stood glowering underneath the heavily carved architrave.

'Maximilian. It is, isn't it?'

Tim Lutyens had never before set eyes on Max Myhill. He had met his father many times and he had met his mother once. He was surprised that Max resembled neither. But then Max Myhill was his own creation. And one which detested being called Maximilian.

'No one calls me that. I don't like it.'

'It's your name, isn't it?'

'It's what's inscribed on my birth certificate. Names are established by frequency of use. My name is what I call myself and what I allow people to call me.'

'Your father always called you Maximilian.'

'My father never knew me. He never cared to meet me.'

'It's how you are referred to in all the legal documents concerning the trust fund he established in your name. I take it that is what you have come to see me about, Maximilian.' Max bristled menacingly. Tim Lutyens knew almost no teenagers but he had never before seen one with the sheer electrical presence of this one. 'I'm sorry. Max. Or shall I call you Mr Myhill?'

Max did not answer. His eyes were staring and his face was motionless. He reminded the solicitor of a distinguished city banker he had once represented who had gone to prison for fraud. His behaviour there had led him to solitary confinement and after his release he had never moved a facial muscle until the day he died. Max Myhill was such a person, brilliant, calculating, behind a mask. There are those who wear their heart on their sleeve and who give everything away and those who wear a hat on their heart and who give nothing away. Was Max that latter type? For some reason Tim's mind ran on to a third category. Those who have no heart at all. This boy, this young man, made him nervous. And no one had ever made Tim Lutyens nervous. Not even Max's mother, The Most Difficult Woman In Television.

'Please be seated, Mr Myhill.'

'I'll stand. This will not take long.'

'What will? What brings you unannounced to the Piccadilly offices of Lutyens Kleiner? I understand you have been waiting for over two hours.'

'I understand I have been kept waiting for over two hours.'

Once more Tim Lutyens raised one fine eyebrow. 'You wouldn't give my secretary your name.'

'She's a frightened rabbit, that one.'

'Her job is to control access to me.'

'Would you have agreed to see me?'

'I am seeing you now. I knew it was you.'

'I'm sure you don't have many clients of my age and physical description.'

'That is true. I do not. But I am also aware that you have telephoned these offices recently on a number of occasions, leaving no name or message then either.'

'That may or may not be true.'

'So what's the mystery?'

'No mystery. I need to talk to you about my trust fund.'

'Are you sure you would not like to sit down?'

'I'm fine standing.'

'Well let me request that you do sit down, Mr Myhill. I have a strained neck and you are very tall.'

Max strode forward across the polished floor and drew out a leather-backed chair from the front of the oak desk. He slouched unwillingly into it. He flicked his eyes sideways, taking in the strong architectonic lines of the heavily moulded dado around the room. His eyes flicked back and bored into the solicitor's gaze.

'Does it make you feel powerful working in this room?'

Tim Lutyens was reminded of Max's mother. He could see more of her in him now.

'I beg your pardon?'

'The architecture. The big desk. The frightened rabbit. The power politics?'

'I beg your pardon?'

'You make me sit down so I feel smaller. So you don't look up to me.'

'That was not my intention at all. I only intended to make the meeting more comfortable.' Tim Lutyens could not believe he was on the defensive. It was not he, but Max, who controlled the power politics. He struggled to regain the initiative. 'Shall we cut to the chase? In what way can I be of help, Mr Myhill?'

'You are a trustee of my trust fund.'

'I am.'

'Are you allowed to tell me how much money is in it?'

'I'm afraid I am not at liberty to reveal specific figures.'

'You told my mother last year there was a million pounds in it.'

'I think you'll find she deduced that from our conversation. Your mother is a remarkable woman.'

'People make remarks about her, that's true. So I'm due a million quid or thereabouts.'

'You have no access to the money until you are twenty-five years old.'

'How strict is that rule?'

'It is the rule of law.'

'The rule of law can be flexible.'

'Not in this case. It is a secure trust fund. It is not your flexible friend to be drawn on and diminished.'

'But it's my money. I need to have access to it now.'

'I'm afraid that's impossible.'

'We'll see about that.'

'Allow *me* to tell *you* what the law is, Mr Myhill.'

'I don't care what the law is. You're a trustee. You must have access to the money. You must be able to change the rules.'

'I could not and would not do that. It simply could not be recommended. Your father's idea – quite correctly in my opinion – was that not until you attained the age of twenty-five would you know fully your own mind and be mature enough to take the correct actions with such a substantial endowment.'

'I don't need it all at the moment. Half of it will do.'

'Half?! I really wouldn't counsel your ever withdrawing half of the funds whatever age you might attain, Mr Myhill.'

Max returned the solicitor's wilting look with a filthy one of his own.

'Look, if you're not preprared to help me then I need to know who the other trustees are.'

'For what reason?'

'So I can get you all sacked and stop you standing in my way. You're supposed to represent my best interests, not stall on me.'

'Not quite, Mr Myhill. We are supposed to represent the best interests of the fund established by your father. That is the law. It may seem a subtle distinction in your eyes but it is a crucial one. I might add that not only are you not yet twenty-five years old but you are not yet eighteen. You have not yet come of age.'

'I'm over sixteen. I'm old enough to go to work and to marry and to have a child even under your precious laws you care so much about.'

'But you are contemplating none of those things so that is an irrelevance, isn't it? . . . Or is it?'

Max looked down at the oak floor. His desert boots looked scruffy against the polished surface.

'I'm sorry, Mr Myhill, I cannot be of assistance on this occasion.'

Max stood up. 'Because of the way you have treated me today, Mr Lutyens, as soon as I am old enough I am going to have you fired as a trustee.'

Tim Lutyens raised both eyebrows this time. 'I think that's rather a dramatic and unfair reaction. One reminiscent of your mother if I may be so bold. But it will not be necessary to call for my dismissal. As soon as you reach twenty five the three trustees will relinquish their roles. I'm sorry if that will deny you any pleasure.'

'Who are the other trustees?'

'I am not at liberty to say.'

'Can't say. Won't say. You love it, don't you? Having the power.'

'That is not how I feel, Mr Myhill. I have no power. But what you have is an absence of power and you dislike that. I can see that. Like mother like son. She has had a strong influence on you.'

'You can leave out the comments about my mother and me.' Max stood up, rising to his full height. 'I knew this would be waste of time. At least I tried. I need that money and I'll find a way of getting my hands on it. Law or no law. Thanks for nothing, Mr Lutyens.' Max turned his back on the solicitor and strode to the door.

'Oh, Maximilian! I'm sorry, Max.'

Max stopped and turned.

'I know it's none of my busines, but what on earth does somebody of your age need half a million pounds for?'

'You're right, Mr Lutyens. It's none of your business.'

Max turned the big brass handle on the panelled door and propelled himself out of the room. The door banged behind him. A moment later, Miss Snell returned.

'Goodness me, Miss Snell. I thought you were long gone.'

'I came back, Mr Lutyens. I felt obliged. I was worried for your safety. I've been sitting there with my finger on the nine button ready to call for an ambulance.'

'Goodness me. Everyone is behaving so dramatically today.' She did have the look of a frightened rabbit.

Deep in thought, Tim Lutyens puckered his lips. He reached for the roll organiser on his desk and twirled through the letters. J.K.L.M. At the back he found the home telephone number for Max's mother. He tapped it into his black telephone and while he waited for an answer he addressed either Miss Snell or possibly the great cornice from days of Empire that ran around the ceiling. They were each an equally solid, reliable and permanent part of Lutyens Kleiner. And, in his opinion, equally thick.

'Interesting young man.'

'Is he? What did he want?'

'I really couldn't say. Truly a most difficult son of a most difficult woman. Asked nothing of his father. Strange. Whatever, I think she should be told.'

66

Wentworth Golf Club. In the late September afternoon sun, life member Hector Quigley stood at the first tee dressed in pink. Raspberry pink. Raspberry cashmere sweater. Raspberries and cream checked shirt poking through at neck and cuff. Raspberry trousers. Raspberry-faced too, he examined the bullet-hard, white golf ball rolling in his great fleshy palm. It was a monogrammed ball. As it turned over, it flashed Hector's initials back at him, miniature HQs embossed six or seven times around the patterned surface of the ball. He held it out in front of the partner assigned to him for the afternoon.

'I have no middle initial. Hector Quigley. HQ. That is what I am. No more, no less. No trappings with me. What you see is what you get.'

His partner looked on mystified, incredulous and impatient. They were playing in a fund raising tournament for the advertising industry charity NABS, which raised money for former employees of the industry fallen on hard times. Not that either of these players would end up anything other than very comfortably off indeed.

'Look at that,' Hector continued. He closed his hand around

the ball. 'I can look at it and examine it. I can hold it in my palm. I can dominate it. I can circle it and cover it and squeeze it hard. But I cannot destroy it or ever change it. Not with my bare hands. Do you know what that is?'

'A golf ball,' said his partner. Nigel Gainsborough was baffled and bored as usual.

'It is a metaphor for the advertising industry. That's what it is. And now I am going to place it on the tee and drive it as far and as fast forward as I can.'

'Well get a bloody move on will you? Drive it to buggery.'

'I have no intention of driving it to buggery or bugger anywhere for that matter. I intend to be very precise – as I am in everything I do – and land it on the green in one go.'

'Hole in one, old chap?' chortled Nigel. 'I'll bet you one hundred pounds you won't achieve that.'

'This hole or the whole round?'

'Oh – the whole round. Why not?' Nigel guffawed and rested even more of his weight on his black-and-burgundy leather golf bag. It tipped forward on its big wheeled trolley and he stumbled.

'Better make it one thousand. And, just for good measure, I'll also pay out should you get one. If you don't get one it doesn't matter.'

'You're on! Hah! I hope you have the readies on you. I won't take a cheque.'

'I do indeed. I'll borrow it off Philip if it comes to it. He carries my cash.'

'So it's not under the weight of your clubs he's staggering then! Ever had a hole in one, old boy?'

'Not yet.'

'Thought so. I have. Once.'

'There is a first time for everything. The thousand pounds goes to NABS of course. I'm not giving you a thousand quid, you greedy old bastard.'

Nigel looked crestfallen. 'Oh, of course, old boy. Charity, charity, charity, that's my motto.' He was disappointed. He had already pictured fanning out the notes in front of Serena and bragging it around the office. How he'd grabbed a grand off old Hector Quigley, the tightest-fisted man in town.

'Where in hell's name is Philip?' asked Hector. He did a little tap dance in his black-and-white patent golf shoes. He had swapped snakeskin for studs though, and the effect was less smooth than he would have liked. 'Fred Astaire,' he said.

'As long as you golf like Fred Astaire, I don't mind.'

A cough behind them stopped their sniping. Nigel turned round. It was Alan Josling, looking dapper in tartan trews and a lurid combination Pringle sweater bought for the occasion. In a leather-gloved hand he dragged a gleaming large Slazenger golf bag on a trolley identical to Nigel's. With him was a man Nigel did not recognise. They all grinned and puffed themselves up and looked as self-confident and as self-made and as self-centred as is humanly possible when attired in the colours of a Mary Baker icing set.

'Are you teeing off or what?' asked Alan. His might be the smallest agency, but he wasn't going to let Hector Quigley boss him around on the golf course.

'I'm waiting for my chauffeur,' stated Hector grandly.

'Taking the Rolls to the first green are you?'

'Actually it's a Bentley. No. He acts as my caddy. He should be here any moment.'

'Would you mind if we played through? It's just that everyone else will be held up. We have to set off at ten-minute intervals.'

'In my opinion that is too tight. They have us banked up like adverts in a commercial break, one after the other.'

'All the more reason for Gilbert and I to play through. You don't mind?'

'I can't see Hector carrying his own bag down the fairway,' chortled Nigel. 'Though everyone else is.'

'Well I am not everyone else. And no one is carrying their own bag. They're using trolleys and using trolleys is naff. Naff, naff, naff.'

He stood back with Nigel and Alan Josling stepped into the centre of the tee and stabbed the ground with a fluorescent tee and ball. From his bag he unsheathed a number two wood. He stood astride over the ball, looked down the length of the fairway to the red flag on the horizon and swung wide. He gave the ball a cracking shot and the four men watched it arc into the sky. It fell forward and appeared to land on the edge of the green, dead centre. Alan turned smugly to Nigel.

'Beat that!'

'I'm playing old Hecka here. That's for your chum to beat, not me.'

'It's a tournament. We're all against each other.'

'Doesn't stop at the office door, does it?' observed Hector.

'Why did they make it singles and not doubles this year?' asked Nigel.

Alan's partner answered him. 'There aren't enough players anymore. That's why they're letting clients like me in as well now. Too many young people in the business. Can't play golf.'

'Too many bloody women in the business, if you ask me,' replied Nigel. 'Can't play any damn thing.'

Gilbert set up his shot and took aim and gave the ball a good whack, brute force if not a stylish swing.

'Well done.' said Alan.

'You're only saying that because I'm twenty yards behind you.'

'He's only saying that because you're his client,' guffawed Nigel. 'Sorry old boy,' he added, when he saw Alan's look.

'As in advertising, as on the course, as in life, as in everything,' jested Alan. 'Anyway. Nigel, what are you complaining about women for? You work with one. Where is our very own "Muffin" today?'

'Gone to one of our clients. Women's business. Actually, Hecka, that one we share with you. The up-yer-fanny Verity account.'

Alan bristled at the mention of the brand he had failed to win. At least Nigel did not know.

'Ah. Verity. How is the delightful Serena getting on with her pregnancy predictions?'

'Yeah?' said Alan. 'Up the duff yet?'

Nigel was cross. 'Your friend has made a large divot on the tee. I hope you're going to put it back.' That's what Serena would have said.

Gilbert attended to the piece of split turf and he and Alan pulled ahead of Nigel and Hector, just where Alan desired to be in real life and just what he was working on now.

As they pounded off down the fairway, Philip caught up with Hector and Nigel. He was bent double with the full weight of Hector's huge golf bag and extensive collection of clubs across his back. He had changed out of his uniform into a black wool ensemble. At Hector's insistence he kept his peaked cap on, the gold HQ logo glinting in the afternoon sun.

'Where the hell have you been? You're holding everyone up and making me look slack, which is worse.'

'I'm very sorry sir.'

'Quickly then. What say you?'

'Summa driver.'

'Summa driver then.'

Philip unsleeved the driver from the hand-stitched Tom Auchterlonie brushed-calf bag. With a small grey duster he polished the head and handed it to Hector. Hector took it in his right hand and, with his left, shielded his eyes from the sun. He looked long and hard down the fairway to the red flag.

'What sort of club is that then, old boy?'

Hector beamed. 'This is my Summa driver. Look at that.' He up-ended the club and caressed its head in his gloved hand. 'The inside is made from ceramic.'

'Won't it smash?'

'Ten times harder than steel that is. Deluxe bronze-boron graphite. Only diamond is harder. A forgiving one hundred per cent sweetspot across the entire hitting face of the golf club. Adds forty yards to every shot.'

'I say. Isn't that cheating, old boy?'

'The rules of golf have changed since your day, Nigel. You really must try to keep up with the pace of the game.'

Nigel was annoyed. He found Hector's constant one-upmanship wearing. 'Hurry up, Hector, you're dawdling. The next lot'll be along. You really must try to keep up with the pace of the game.'

'I am quite aware of that. They can bloody well wait as far as I'm concerned.'

He signalled to Philip, who stepped forward and took the monogrammed ball from him. He crouched down and, producing a solid gold tee from his pocket, he stuck it into the ground and placed the ball upon it.

Hector stood over the ball, legs spread, and loosely rolled the club in his hands. He held the head to the top of the tee and took a soft practice swing. Unfortunately it touched the ball as it returned and knocked it from its perch.

'Counting that shot!' squealed Nigel gleefully. 'No thousand pounds for the first hole!'

'Bugger off. No one was looking. It was a practice shot.'

Hector took a full swing this time and walloped the ball halfway down the fairway and a considerably shorter distance than that achieved by the two previous men.

Nigel roared and slapped his plump thigh. 'Does that include the forty extra yards you were bragging about, or do you add those on later?'

'I haven't warmed up yet.'

'Better find a three-bar heater then, hadn't you! You'll have to hit a lot harder than that if you intend to win today,' Nigel stepped into the breach, 'or you'll lose your thousand quid.'

He quickly swung and, with all those years of practice behind him, it was not a bad shot for a big-bellied man already out of breath.

'Goodness me,' said Hector. Philip was already marching ahead of them.

'Thousand quid,' teased Nigel, pleased. He strode after Philip.

'Didn't we say one hundred?' protested Hector. But Nigel was feigning the useful deafness he had honed over the years of working with Serena Sark. It was going to be a jolly afternoon.

'Hah!' Nigel chuckled.

Hector's ball had landed just beyond the bunker on the tenth hole. It rolled back perilously close to the edge. It did not fall in.

'I wasn't using the Summa driver,' was Hector's excuse this time.

'Does it make any difference?' giggled Nigel. 'Your shot next, Hecka.'

'It's your turn.'

'Still yours. You have to play first. You're furthest from the hole.'

'Farther. Not furthest. There are only two of us.'

They set off from the tee.

'No sign of Josling now,' said Nigel searching the horizon. 'Racing ahead, they are. You're a slowcoach, Hector.'

Hector puffed while Nigel dragged his trolley behind him. He was at home on the course. As he had grown more reluctant and more uncomfortable tied up in the agency, so he had grown happier and healthier let loose on the golf course.

'One thousand big smackers.' Nigel laughed.

Hector snarled. 'To coin a phrase, you're beginning to get on my tits, Gainsborough.'

'Ho ho! Can't stand the heat of the fairway, can you Hecka? Not used to being number two. One thousand big smackers. Should have had your financial boys to neg the deal for you. One thousand big smackers.'

'I'll give you a big smack in the chops if you're not careful, you great lump. It might be pertinent for you to know that I can afford one thousand pounds several hundred times over. *If* I have to pay out, which I have no intention of doing.'

'We'll see. Ho ho! He's quick off the mark your man.' Nigel was referring to Philip, who was pacing ahead of them fast with Hector's golf bag over one shoulder. 'Big boy, isn't he? Barely bends under that weight. Bred into them of course, the darkies. Good at carrying things.'

The two men set off behind the chauffeur, their florid faces and florid woollens contrasting with his plain black face and plain black outfit.

'Doesn't look round.'

'He knows we're here.'

'Doesn't say much.'

'He knows his place.'

'Not so good at that as a species. I lock my car doors from the inside these days. You can't be too careful. As much as mug you as look at you, the Afros. How much does someone like that earn?'

'Thinking of hiring someone to carry your bags, Nigel? I thought you had Serena to do that for you.'

Nigel smarted. Hector was ready to get his own back now and it obviously wasn't going to be within the Royal and Ancient rules of the game. He could goad Nigel Gainsborough another way.

'Fill you in on our lunch, did she?'

'Who, old boy?'

'Serena.'

'What lunch?'

'The delightful Serena. The clever, calculating, co-operative Serena.'

'What are you on about, old boy? Serena doesn't keep secrets from me.'

'Doesn't she?'

'No she doesn't.'

'Tell you about the takeover of Clancey and Bennett by MCN International did she?'

'I knew all about that. She just handled the negotiations. She's better at that sort of thing.'

'She kick-started it. She didn't tell you that, did she?'

'I don't believe you.'

'Oh, that's what she was telling me the other day. Fair boasting about it. But then she needed to convince me.'

'Convince you of what?'

'Nigel, if she hasn't broken the news yet it would be wrong of me to break her confidence.'

Nigel was cross.

'You can break wind for all I care, Hecka. What are you two cooking up together? Something to do with Verity, no doubt. Suit yourselves. See if I care.'

'Verity? That little thing. No. This is much bigger than that.'

They had arrived at the edge of the bunker. Philip stood there looking blank and impassive. While Hector examined his monogrammed ball in close-up, Nigel raised his hand above his eyes and strained into the distance.

'I'm so much further ahead than you I can't see where I am. You'll have to hit it bloody hard to catch up.'

Hector turned to Philip. 'What say you, Philip?'

'Chipping iron, sir.'

Nigel scoffed. He pottered over behind Hector and stood at the edge of the bunker. It was cut deep and round into the green fairway. The sand was terribly un-English, raked in lines, white as if from a desert island in the Caribbean.

'Lot of that where you come from, is there?' Nigel smiled at Philip.

'No sir. Not in Tottenham.'

'Hottentottenham,' burbled Nigel. He did not mean to cause offence and Philip took none. When he had taken up Hector Quigley's offer to be his manservant he had expected to meet only the great and the good and the utterly unreconstructed and Nigel Gainsborough was obviously neither one of the great nor the good. He handed Hector the chipping iron.

Nigel sniggered behind them. He sang a little ditty. 'It's a long way to chip-a-golf-ball, It's a long way to go . . .'

Hector thrust the chipping iron forward into Philip's chest.

'Give me the Summa driver.'

'The Summa driver, sir?'

'The Summa driver. Are you deaf?'

'Are you sure that's wise?' asked the caddy.

'Since when was it your job to question me?' snapped Hector. 'Just give me the fucking Summa driver.'

Behind them Nigel laughed hee-haw like a donkey. '. . . Farewell Piccadilly, goodbye thousand quid . . .'

The caddy unsheathed the head of the Summa driver from its little bag and handed it to his boss. Hector found his footing between the edge of the bunker and Nigel's feet. He took a half-swing to test his stance. He turned round sharply to Nigel.

'You're in my eyeline. At least your fat stomach is.'

Nigel wiped a tear of hilarity from his eye. 'Touchy, touchy.' He stepped sideways.

Hector paused and took three, long-drawn, deep breaths. The full might of his huge hands gripped the steel-shafted handle of the club. His bright blue piggy eyes focused on the faraway fluttering flag. He took aim. He willed the ball to fly through the air and land in the hole. It would not be a hole in one but it would be a virtuoso shot and it would shut Nigel Gainsborough and his fat face up once and for all. He threw his full weight into it. He swung far back. With a crunching crack and a resounding thud, he walloped the ball up and into the sky in a perfect hoopline. Hector craned his neck. Philip lifted his hand to his eyes. With the bag already across his shoulders he set off furiously. Summa driver in hand, Hector bounded after him, puffing in pink. They saw the ball bounce once up in the air and onto the green. It rolled forward. It was headed straight for the hole.

'It's going in. *It's going in*,' squeaked Hector. He jumped for joy as he tried to catch up with his caddy. He shouted over his shoulder to Fatboy. 'I told you so. There. See. I told you so. *Hah*! That's one big surprise for you, Gainsborough, and you can expect the other when you get back to Clancey and goddamn Bennett and ask the saintly Serena Sark what shenanigans she and I have cooked up. There's mud in your eye.'

By the time Philip had raised the red flag from the hole and looked in, Hector was perspiring and more jam- than raspberry-faced. He rolled across the green. A giant pink ball, he almost fell into the hole.

'It's in! *It's in*! Beat *that* Gainsborough, you old bastard! *Beat that*!'

Philip calmly returned the flag to its upright position in the hole while Hector held on high his monogrammed ball for all to see. But apart from Philip, there was no one there to see. There was no one there at all. Hector and Philip stood absolutely alone on the green. Hector turned round. He revolved. He spun 360 degrees. He peered between the trees. He skimmed across the shrubs. He looked long down the fairways. No sign of life. Nobody. Nothing. Nigel Gainsborough, tall and round and overweight and overdressed from top to toe in dynamic dayglo lilac checks had disappeared off the face of the earth.

'The stupid bugger,' complained Hector, annoyed that not one provoking thing he had said had been heard by his rival and perplexed that the best shot of the day might be disbelieved by the boozers at the nineteenth hole. 'Where the *fuck* is he?'

68

'How can he do this to me, Michael?' Karen snatched her glasses from her face and dug in her pocket for her hanky. She dabbed her eyes. It was the first time Michael had seen Karen close to tears.

'Sorry. Who are we talking about? Martin or Max?'

'Martin Fucking Foxface, who do you think?' Karen slipped her spectacles back on. 'The Max thing is confidential. I just wanted to know what you thought. I thought you might have heard of Tim Lutyens.'

'I only qualified as a solicitor, Karen. I've always worked in TV. I know media and company law. Not trust funds. And not conveyancing either. If another person at The Station asks for help with buying their new house . . .'

'Do they do that?'

'Absolutely. There's a property boom on.'

'What about you and Duncan?'

'We're happy living as we are.'

'Apart. Huh.'

'Oh, Duncan has plans to bring us together.'

'You're moving in?'

'No. Something else . . .'

Michael had not told Karen about Duncan's planned baby and

she had not told Michael about Max's unplanned one. She had only asked him whether Tim Lutyens was right to inform her of her son's actions and what position Max might be in. She wasn't going to raise the rafters in tellyland by advertising the fact that another mad Myhill bouncing baby bombshell was about to hit town, this time hand in umbilical with the original vixen teenage mother from hell. Karen had been planning a quieter few decades ahead. But that seemed to have gone with the wind and tomorrow was not another day, it was here and now and it spelt the end for Myhill Productions.

'I have decorators in at the moment. My house is no longer my home.'

'They take over, don't they?'

'I go tiptoeing around frightened I might pick up something I've owned for twenty years and incur their wrath. Why am I afraid of a man in a white overall? I'm not afraid of John Birt or Michael Grade or David Elstein.'

'They don't wear white overalls. Not outside the clinic, anyway.'

Karen sighed. 'What oh what oh what oh what am I going to do, Michael? Martin Fox can't land five hundred thousand big fuckers on me. He's a big broadcaster. I'm only a little producer.'

'You have editorial responsibility.'

'He has the responsibility of a man beaming signals into people's homes. Why doesn't he fight them? He's running scared. If I had met that vindictive bitch from the ITC I'd have neutralised her in that meeting.'

'I think that's why you weren't asked. Television has moved on since Genghis Khan rode this way, Karen.'

'What do I care what some big-hipped bitch thinks? I bet she's never watched *Sister Verity*. Every day we turn away thousands of people desperate to talk to her. She's a breath of fresh air in their lives. A ray of hope. A shaft of light—'

'A dancing sunbeam of happiness otherwise known as Tinkerbell.'

'I'm doing afternoon TV. What do you expect? Anthropological analysis with Doctor Margaret Mead?'

'Well, not Enid Blyton.'

'Let me look at this contract again. I haven't signed it, you know.'

'I'll have to argue that makes no difference.'

'You'll have to argue . . . ?'

'We're bound to end up in court over this.'

'Court? Court or no court Michael, I'm not paying. I cannot pay. I'm not drawing a line under my career to save Fox's fat arse. His wife is big in the City. She's on a squillion a year. She's a top-table Tory. They don't need to rob me blind to live in comfort.'

'He doesn't get the money. It's not personal.'

'It is. It's fucking personal. I have no life, Michael. I only have my son. Now I don't even know what he's playing at. Everyone's ganging up on me. What have I done? Delivered a low-cost programme to The Station. One that's a hit. One that helps real people solve real problems. And what thanks do I get? Dumped on from a great height. Shat on by the biggest shit in TV. Fined and flayed alive. Made an example of. Proscribed. Well you can all fuck off! I'll see you all in hell before I dig into my pockets for one penny! You drew up a contract that stitched me up.'

'I did nothing of the sort.'

'You saw this coming and covered your own arse.'

'Balls. Karen—'

'You didn't bother to chase me to sign it because you knew if I looked at it I'd never agree to it.'

'That's rubbish Karen and you know it.'

'Too right. That contract *is* rubbish and *you* know it. I'm fighting you. All the way, Michael Farnham. You and Foxy and that no-brain marketing woman you hang around with. And Duncan will side with me.'

'Duncan can't take sides in this—'

'Duncan will have to. If you want to fight dirty you picked the wrong person. I'm not The Most Difficult Woman In Television. Not yet. I haven't even started being difficult. You and Martin Fox can take your whole cable network and shove it sideways up your arse. No doubt that'll give you particularly immense satisfaction!'

And with that she stormed out.

*   *   *

'I thought you cleared this with the ITVA?'

Charlotte had never seen Duncan angry before. There was an alligator snap in there which frightened her.

'Why should I? Sister Verity isn't an advert. She's an endorsement on packs only. She's not in any commercials.'

'God, Charlotte. How can you be so naive? You've landed everyone in it. Do you know that?'

'I'm sorry, Duncan, but I have much greater pressures on me than this right now and I really can't help you.'

'Such as?

'Such as none of your business.' Charlotte hardly wanted to tell him she might be pregnant. She felt irresponsible enough as it was.

'Top TV executives are losing their jobs because of you.'

'That's got nothing to do with me!'

'It has everything to do with you.'

'It was *you* who rang *me* up, Duncan Cairns!'

'You briefed me to meet your strategy. You told me that that nun was not part of the brand activity.'

'She's not.'

'She is.'

'Not part of the advertising. You left here with every document and every script and every piece of copy in existence. I told you everything. You met my clients. I can't be responsible for Hector Quigley. Go and see him.'

'I don't think you realise, Charlotte. Your nun friend could finish my career and my partner's.'

'Oh? Which partner is this? The old hag or the boyfriend?'

'Both.'

'Well, that's their lookout. I am not responsible for clearing the content of television programmes. It's not my name on the credits rolling up on the little ego trip at the end of every programme.'

'You're missing the point.'

'I'm missing a meeting.' Charlotte was on the verge of tears. 'I'm sorry it's all a mess, Duncan but it's nothing to do with me. You contacted me and I helped you. Now you're trying to cover your tracks. I thought you were decent when I met you, but now I know better. I came to work for you at Clancey and Bennett and you walked out on me and landed me in it. Now you're turning round and trying to pin this one on me too. Well it isn't my fault. I never wanted a fucking nun in the campaign in the first place. Jesus! Sometimes I can't believe the things that happen to me.'

And with that she stormed out.

'Duncan, you'll have to take my side.'

'Why?'

'What do you mean, "Why?"'

'Michael, the only thing that is obvious is that if I gang up with you and Martin and Briony against Karen she'll fire me and kill me and not necessarily in that order. I owe it to her to stand by her.'

'You owe it to me to stand by me, you little bugger.'

'Don't swear.'

'Well don't be so obstinate. I'm your lover.'

'You're also threatening to sue the production company I work for over the programme that I make for them which contains a woman I introduced to them through an ex-colleague of mine who also happens to be a friend, or was until your lot fucked everything up. You're the broadcaster. You have to check the guidelines. You should pay the fine. You can afford it.'

'All our capital is tied up.'

'Well untie it. Move out of that building. Try operating from a Nissen hut, I don't know. Karen Myhill obviously can't pay a fine of half a million pounds. Be reasonable.'

'I am reasonable. I'm the only one that's being reasonable. I'm a lawyer.'

'Bully for you.'

'I can't believe you'd put Karen before me.'

'I have to do the right thing.'

'Agree with me, then.'

'You know that it's morally wrong to pin this on Karen.'

'Morals and the law are not the same thing.'

'Oh here it is. I forgot you were raised a fascist in South Africa.'

'Don't pull that one.'

'Well I didn't have black servants waiting on me hand and foot in Edinburgh when I was a child.'

'Duncan! Karen will live to fight another day. You won't. You need to keep in with The Station. You need to keep in with your contacts in advertising. You need to keep in with me.'

'I need to do what is right, Michael. And making you look good in the office so you can wipe Martin Fox's arse for him doesn't come into that category.'

And with that he stormed out.

Briony leapt as she turned the corner of the corridor onto the balcony over the atrium. She thumped smack into Martin. Perhaps she should do herself a favour and throw herself to the reception floor below. He made her feel like a red rag to a bull.

'I hope you haven't got that bloody child on your arm?'

'Martin – no! I told you. I brought her in just that once.'

'If you had had her under control in that meeting instead of winding up Dorothy Copeland Charming we might not all be in this mess.'

'Oh, for God's sake. The Station has got a half-million pound fine because my six-year-old daughter drew a caricature? Get real!'

He waved a piece of fax paper. 'Look at this.'

'I'm looking at it. It's a piece of fax paper. I can't be expected to read it if you wave it around like that.'

'I've been ordered to New York.'

'New York? Why?'

'I'll give you one good guess, Briony Linden. I've to see the holding company president with the CEO for dinner in two weeks' time. I'm being flown out to be hung, drawn and quartered.'

'Hanged. Pictures are hung, people get hanged.'

'Fuck the grammar. If I get hanged you and Michael Farnham will be crucified on my return, I promise you. It's his legal incompetence and your money grubbing marketing madness that has landed me in this mess. I'm warning you, little Ms Linden, you won't work in television or marketing or advertising or even fucking whoring if I go down on this one.'

And with that he he stormed off. For the first time in her career Briony plunged into the ladies to weep in a cubicle.

'Now, m'dears. How are we all doin' today? Tickety boo. Doesn't that have a smashing ring to it? But if you have a wee problem, don't fret. You can count on your old Sister Verity. And you can call up your old Sister Verity. Pick up that wee piece of technology you've got there in your hand and press your bright-as-a-button now. Sister Verity who grew up with the leprechauns will wave her wee magic wand and banish those tears just as the good Paddy himself banished the snakes from Ireland. Shame he didn't banish the rain as well while he was goin' about his business, but who's countin' miracles? So give me a call and blessin' you all.'

69

'Alfa One Zero to base. Come in base. Over.'
  'We hear you Alfa One Zero. Over.'
  'Spotted them. Two figures, one in pink. Over.'
  'Sounds right. Over.'
  'They're on the eighth fairway, I think it is. I'll try to take her down and land there wind allowing. If we need further assistance I'll radio from the ground.'
  'Roger, Alfa One Zero. The course will remain closed until you're airborne again. Over.'
  'Roger. Over and out.'
The helicopter pitched slightly forward as it began its rapid descent. Below, the trees and shrubs of Wentworth flattened out with the blast of the propellors. The air ambulance came

to rest in the middle of the fairway. Two paramedics leapt out and ran forward, stretcher and first aid kit between them.

On the brow of the hill they saw heading towards them a sorry sight. A large fat man, with golden curly hair and dressed like a giant baby in Spam pink, was struggling to pull a big white-wheeled golf cart behind him. He was head-down, red in the face and out of puff. The trolley's other end was held off the ground by a slim black man bent double with the weight of another set of golf clubs on his back. They veered from side to side irregularly and erratically, though this appeared to be more a result of the panic of the man at the front, who was shouting slogans of encouragement into the wind. Laid out horizontal on the golf trolley was a fat set of golf clubs in a bag. And laid out horizontal on the bag was the fat body of a middle-aged man clothed in lilac checks. Flat on his back, his arms dangled down limp on either side. His knuckles dragged on the grass. At the brow of the hill the pink man looked up and spotted them. He stopped to wave his arms in the air. He appeared to be shouting, 'Mayday! Mayday!' But he had stopped too abruptly and, without warning, the black man at the rear was caught unawares and the golf cart upended, jettisoning the lilac body over the side. The two men put the trolley to rights and dragged their lumpen cargo back onto it before pushing forward again. The paramedics met the two exhausted porters and their patient halfway up the hill.

'*Quickly! Quickly!*' screamed the man in pink.

'Remain calm!' called one of the paramedics, a square-shaped woman in a black nylon jumpsuit. While the man in pink flustered inefficiently around them, they quickly unfolded their stretcher and laid the man in lilac on it.

'Why do you people always have to make such a fuss?' Despite being a nervous wreck, the man in pink was full of his own self-importance. 'Arriving in a helicopter for God's sake. Could you not have used a more discreet form of transport?'

The woman replied officiously. 'We've been asked before not to drive our ambulances over fairways. And it's too far from the clubhouse to come on foot.'

'Is he dead?' enquired the man.

'We'll just ascertain what's going on here.'

While one of the medical team strapped the body to the stetcher, his colleague pulled up the eyelids of their quarry. She put her head to his chest.

'Heart attack is it?' She began to tug open his lilac shirt at the neck.

'I suppose so. We found him flat out in the bunker. Jesus. I shall remember this unto my dying day.'

'Friend of yours, is he?'

'An aquaintance. Business associate.'

'History of heart trouble?'

'No. I'm as fit as a fiddle.'

'Not you. Him.'

'No. I don't know. No idea.'

The paramedics had by now finished trussing their victim.

'What's that mark on his forehead?'

'Where?'

'There. He's been bashed in the front of the head. Look at that. Jesus. That is brutal.'

'Good God. So he has. How on earth . . . ?'

Back at the side of the air ambulance, the paramedics winched the body upwards. The rotor blades once more whirred into action. The noise was absolutely deafening. The wind created around the base of the chopper flattened the grass. The two uniformed lifesavers pulled the stretcher off the winch and into the hold. They stored their booty to one side. The square-shaped woman gave the thumbs up and the helicopter began to lift gently off the ground.

'What about us?' shouted the man in pink.

The man called back this time. 'The police are on their way down the eighteenth from the clubhouse. Head back and they'll meet you. Don't—'

Anything else he shouted was lost to Hector and Philip as the noise drowned him out and the helicopter became airborne. They watched it rise vertically, directly above them and in just a few seconds it beetled off across the skies.

'Amazing things, helicopters,' said Hector. He wiped the sweat from his brow and plonked himself down on the grass. Philip sat down beside him and they lay back in exhaustion side by side. Never before had they been this close. Hector suddenly shot upright. He stood up. Philip watched him as he trotted over to the trolley which lay on its side. He slipped a club from its glove. He came back and sat down beside the chauffeur. He stroked the head of his Summa driver.

'No sign of blood. This thing is ten times harder than steel, you know.'

'Yes, sir.'

'Only diamond is harder. It's a Summa driver. Deluxe bronze-boron graphite.' He caressed the head of the club in his gloved hand. 'A forgiving one hundred per cent sweetspot across the entire hitting face of the club.'

'I know, sir.'

'Do you think he was dead?'

'I don't know, sir.'

'He might die still if he hasn't already. Or be left a vegetable. How would they tell the difference? It must have been one hell of a whack. Stupid bugger. How was I to know the old fucker was standing in my swing line?'

'It was an accident, sir.'

'There's only your and my word for it.'

Philip had never seen Hector look so lost. 'They won't dispute your word, sir.'

'Ah, but they might.' For once Hector dismounted his self-made pedestal and spoke straight to his chauffeur. 'A jury would take one look at me and think, "Robert Maxwell with blond hair. A man steeped in his own vanity." Twelve good men and true waiting to put the boot in. Nobody likes an old adman. Nobody trusts a millionaire. Look at my fucking layabout family. What sort of character witnesses do you think they would make?'

'It's not going to come to that.'

'Ah, but it might.'

'It was an accident.'

'Motive, you see. I have a motive.'

'A motive?'

'I wish to God I hadn't had that lunch with Serena Sark. I wish to God I'd never met the bloody woman. She'll get clean off and I'll get life. Terrible food they have in prison, you know, Philip.'

Philip absorbed the information. He had no idea what Hector

was talking about but he knew there were always sly schemes and dangerous plans afoot in high places. He tentatively offered his boss the comfort of his hand on his shoulder but withdrew before he made contact. Hector Quigley did not like to be touched and it was not the chauffeur's place to initiate a breach of protocol. He heard voices on the wind. He spotted figures through the trees. He stood up. Hector did not notice. Philip turned to him.

'Hey?'

'What is it?'

'It's the police. They're here.'

Hector gulped. He looked fearful for only a fraction. He quickly composed himself. By the time they came for him he was prepared to face the music.

70

Charlotte arrived back at the Clinique desk on the ground floor of Harrod's. She had whisked herself off on a tour of the fabled food halls. She had gone in search of a series of slight purchases while her mother took the chance of a freebie touch-up from the beautician behind the Clinique counter. As she sauntered through the archway back to her mother, Charlotte gaily swung her little plastic bags. Despite falling out with Duncan, she felt carefree. She had much to feel carefree about. She had tried two Boots own-brand pregnancy home tests and both had indicated she was definitely not preggers. The Verity one had been unclear. Perhaps it wasn't as accurate as the client claimed. The truth is it's Verity? The truth is you couldn't tell the truth, one way or the other. Dan had been out of the office this morning. She decided to wait until this evening to tell him and he could stop panicking too. Instead, to celebrate she had met up with her mother for a rush round Harrod's in her lunch hour. Her bags rose and fell in the air. They contained smoked fish, star fruit and hand-made Scottish oatmeal biscuits. She had no idea what she was going to do with them, but sensible shopping was not the objective of the trip to Knightsbridge.

'Mummy, you look wonderful.'

'Do I dear?'

Charlotte nodded.

'Well, that's a relief.' Morella reached for her daughter's hand and squeezed it. A relief it might be but, while the foundation on her face might hide the tiny imperfections of her middle-aged skin, it could not disguise the more substantial imperfections of her middle-aged life and her middle-aged crisis. She clung to Charlotte's grip and saw herself twenty-five years younger. But Charlotte was different. She had a career. She was independent. She was one of a generation of girls who did as she pleased and got away with it. Morella admired her daughter. If she were not her mother she might be jealous of her, except that Charlotte was so open and unassuming and appealing that no one could be spiteful towards her.

The beautician held up a magnifying mirror to Morella's face. It twinkled under the store lights. 'All these products are hypo-allergenic and not tested on animals,' she said.

'Yes, I know.' Morella patted her hair at the sides. Her face looked so lined. 'You've told me that at least a hundred times. You should speak to my daughter. She's in advertising too.'

'Oh really? Perfumes and cosmetics?'

'No. Sanitary—' Charlotte didn't want to tell the beautician she advertised tampons. 'I work for a big advertising agency.'

'Fascinating,' said the girl impassively. She turned on the spot to Charlotte's mother. 'There's no obligation to make a purchase.'

Morella was not going to but Charlotte stepped in and on her American Express card bought her mother a mini-bag of tester products. The beautician added a free eyebrow pencil for good measure. They bustled through the well-tailored and the tourists and pushed their way through the glass doors onto the street outside. More tourists were looking in the windows.

'Did you bring your car, Mummy?'

'No. I told you I spotted Margot hailing a taxi in Chelsea so I jumped in with her. I left the BMW at the house. What about you?'

'The bike is at the garage. Let's take a cab. I'll drop you off and then go back to the agency. I'll put it on my expenses.'

Her mother had no time to protest that The Boltons was hardly on the way to Marylebone before Charlotte was at the kerbside. A black cab with its yellow light lit was edging along the pavement.

'Taxi!' Charlotte craftily side-stepped the green-coated Harrod's commissionaire and pulled open the passenger door and stepped inside laughing.

'Oi,' shouted the commissionaire into the cab. 'These are for Harrod's customers.'

Charlotte leant forward in her seat. 'I am a Harrod's customer.' She held up her plastic bags to prove it. 'Anyway, it's first come first served when it comes to taxis.'

'Excuse me, if I could just get past.' Embarrassed, Morella sidled past the commissionaire. Her daughter bumped up along the back seat and she sat down tired beside her.

'Where to, love?'

'The Boltons, please,' replied Charlotte. 'You see, Mummy, working in agencies has its advantages. You learn how to get that cab under all circumstances.'

'It's not very dignified.'

'Advertising is not about being dignified. It's about winning.'

'Really! You're in your twenties now.'

'I'm not that far off thirty. Don't remind me.'

'Think how I feel.'

It started to rain and the cab chugged along in fits and starts.

'They'll have to do something about London,' said Morella. 'It's becoming unbearable. You can't move anymore. It was so much nicer in the sixties.

'You say that about everything, Mummy. You say the boys were nicer, the girls were nicer.'

'Well, they were.'

'I saw Tamara Beckwith in the fish hall at Harrods.'

'Really? Is she someone you work with?'

'No. She's famous. Mummy you must keep up. She's in *Hello!* She's a socialite.'

'No one's a socialite anymore. Not nowadays.'

'Mummy, you're so out of touch.'

'What has Tamara Beckstein done then?'

'With, not Stein. She's not Jewish. Well, perhaps she is, I don't know. She's not done anything. She's just famous for being famous. She's the daughter of this seriously rich guy and she passes the day going to openings of things. She has a child. She had it when she was still at school or something.'

'Highly likely.'

'I wish I didn't have to work for a living. Then again I like it. I wish it wasn't raining.'

'I, I, I. You all live in the me society. What about the rest of us, what about me, that's what I want to know?'

Charlotte laughed at her mother's unintended carelessness and prattled on while Morella became silent and sour. When they got to The Boltons Charlotte pointed out the house to the cabbie. 'I'll come in. I'll grab a coffee.'

'Darling, your job. You'll be late back. Take the cab on.'

'It's only one-thirty. There's no one there to notice. Hector Quigley was out all afternoon yesterday playing golf and didn't even bother to show up for a meeting this morning. Dan won't be back until four. I'll come in. Keep you company for a bit.'

'I have a headache.'

'Well go to bed and I'll bring you up smoked salmon on oatmeal biscuits. Come on, Mummy, I insist.'

Charlotte opened the door and bounced out. Before she knew it, Morella found herself standing beside her daughter on the pavement. The light rain pit-patted down.

'Charlotte, you mustn't be so bossy. I'm your mother.' She looked edgy.

'It's you I get it from. My God.' Charlotte looked startled.

'What?'

'Your car. Duncan's old car. I'd forgotten it was parked here.'

'It's a bit dirty, I'm afraid.'

'He always had it gleaming. MCN had someone to clean all the directors' cars for them. I bet you barely use it, Mummy, I know you.'

'You don't know me, Charlotte. I use it all the time.'

'Where do you go?'

'. . . I don't go anywhere.'

'Come on then.'

Charlotte pushed open the gate and headed in behind the high white stucco walls of the front garden.

'Charlotte!'

She turned. Her mother remained on the pavement. She had not crossed the threshold of the property. She looked ill. Charlotte came back.

'Don't go up the garden path.'

'Why ever not? Mummy, what is it? You look terrible.'

Underneath her make-up, she did. She burst into tears. Charlotte had never seen her mother like this before. She didn't look so much unhappy as miserable, not so much tragic as pathetic. Her shoulders didn't heave. She just stood in the light rain with tears streaming down her face. Charlotte put her arms around her, her little plastic bags dangling against her mother's back. Morella stood rigid. She had never been good at the tactile thing.

'Mummy, Mummy, Mummy. Please don't cry. You're making me cry. Stop it. What is it? Tell me.'

'Don't go into the house, darling.'

'What?'

'Don't go into the house.'

'Why ever not?'

'I can't bear it.'

'What can't you bear?'

Morella cried a bit more. She sniffed.

'What is it, Mummy? What's going on?'

'I don't know. I don't know what's going on.'

'Is it Tony?'

Her mother gulped. 'Yes.'

'Have you had an argument?'

'No. I haven't . . . Oh Charlotte, it's terrible.'

'What is, Mummy? For God's sake tell me. I'm trying to be sympathetic but the suspense is killing me.'

'I'll tell you in the car.'

Morella turned around and headed back to the convertible

BMW. When Charlotte got there she noticed a duvet stuffed on the back seat.

Morella opened the rear door and clambered in. She pushed up the bedding and Charlotte got inside beside her. She clunked the door shut. The floor space was taken up with a small vanity case which had tipped up and spilled out her mother's make-up and brushes and plastic cups and things.

'I can't go into the house, Charlotte . . .'

Charlotte felt chilled.

'I've . . . I've . . .'

'Did you spend last night in the car?'

'I've been sleeping in the car these last few weeks . . .'

'*Mummy*!'

'This is my home now.'

'. . . Good God.'

'I haven't any money, you know. Not a penny. Not since the Lloyds disaster. I haven't got the compensation yet. I didn't know what to do.'

'You should have called me. Come to the flat.'

'You don't want me there, sweetheart. You have a very important job to do. You're under so much pressure.'

'For God's sake, Mummy. I don't want my mother living in the street.'

'Do you know, dear, it's amazing what you can get for free from the shops if you look the part. I've had my hair done and had several makeovers and I always take the soap from the Ladies. You needn't pay for perfume because they squirt you and let you walk around for a while to see if you like it. I don't know why people bother to shoplift. You can even get food tastings in Marks and Spencer.'

'You hate Marks and Spencer.'

'The clothes, darling, not the food. The food is good. When I go out for lunch with the girls I just pretend I've left my cards at home. They pay. I don't suppose they will for ever, but I've got away with it so far. When I get the compensation I'll be able to fend for myself again.'

To hear her mother talking like this was unbelievable. Charlotte was bewildered. 'Mummy, you're effectively living rough. You've been sleeping in the car.'

'It's a BMW.'

'What difference does that make?'

'It's luxurious. Imagine if I had opted for that Nissan Micra we saw.'

They dissolved into pained laughter at the absurdity.

'One night I put the roof down and slept under the stars. Well, just for half an hour or so. It gets so bitter in the middle of the night even in the summer. It's never silent. Not even around here. There's always some traffic or some machinery or something going on in the distance.'

'The city that never sleeps.'

'Those poor people out there all the time. They never sleep either.' She rubbed the condensation on the window with the flat of her hand and looked up at the house. 'I just go in when he's not there. To go to the toilet or to change my clothes.'

'Is he having an affair?'

'I don't know, darling.'

'But you think he is?'

'I don't know what to think.'

Charlotte didn't like the sound of this. Perhaps her mother had had a breakdown. She was acting so out of character Charlotte barely recognised Morella as her own mother. 'Where is he? Tony?'

'He doesn't know. I haven't told him.'

'Doesn't know what? He must know. Mummy, what's going on? Are you sleeping with him?'

'I . . . I . . . Oh darling it's so difficult to discuss it with you.'

Charlotte swivelled in her seat and took a terrifyingly tight grip on her mother's elbow.

'Mummy, look at me. Look me in the eye. I'm your daughter and I'm sure as hell not getting out of this car until you tell me the whole fucking story and the whole fucking truth. Understand?'

'There's no need to use bad language, Charlotte. I may have lost my money and I may have lost my husband but I haven't lost my manners and neither should you.'

'This was a mistake. We haven't got enough time. I have to go over to the studio.'

Michael thought Duncan was being just a bit twitchy.

'Relax. Finish your lunch.'

'I'm not a very relaxed person.'

'Try to be. Try not to let this ITC thing come between us.'

'I have a live show going out this afternoon.'

'Sister Verity can do it with both arms handcuffed behind her back.'

'She may have to with this ITC investigation going on. It's not her I'm worried about. The whole team is falling apart. Karen was behaving strangely enough before, but now she's gone completely loopy. I think we'll almost certainly have to pull it, you know, whatever the outcome of all this wrangling.'

'Well don't blame me.'

'I don't blame you.'

'You do.'

'I don't. It is an error which the ITC have belatedly woken up to and decided to do something about. We're being victimised because they haven't kept up with the times.'

'What do you mean?'

'I mean, Michael, that there is lots more TV, lots more stations, lots more technology. But there aren't lots more viewers and there ain't any more money. So we're chasing a thinner and thinner slice of an ever-diminishing cake.'

'Do you fancy dessert?'

'Karen and I are playing the new game that everyone will have to play. We've matched our creativity and editorial abilities, The Station's scheduling requirements and editorial needs and the marketing strategy of a brand with finance – and packaged the lot. Verity loves it. The Station loves it. We love it. The audience adores it. We've even created a new star. But, oh no, the bloody regulators have to come in and say, "It's our party and we don't want uninvited guests even if they're paying their own way."'

'You must obey the rules even if you don't agree with them.'

'That attitude makes my blood boil. Britain will be run ragged by the USA or Australia or Germany or God knows who if we carry on being so precious.'

'Taking sponsorship money can destroy editorial independence.'

'"Can" being the operative word. It doesn't have to. The way Karen and I have produced *Sister Verity* is a signpost to the future of TV.'

'In that case, God help all of us, is all I can say.'

'Don't be so sniffy. You're not the target. You're an Oxbridge graduate.'

'We watch television too.'

'Hardly. Anyway, enough of this. I must get back. How are Martin and Briony coping? Bitching about me no doubt?'

'They wouldn't do that in front of me. They probably blame me. Karen blames me. You blame me. Everyone blames me.'

'Everyone is blaming everyone else. Still, as I've discovered, that's the biggest game-show in TV. Hello and come on down to another long-running series of *Nothing To Do with Me.*'

'God, you're cynical.'

'I've grown a thick skin. It goes with everyone else's thick head.'

'You may need a thicker one. Martin has gone to New York. Briony thinks he's getting fired.'

'You're joking?'

'She didn't seem to be. Said he accosted her in the corridor and left her in tears. She thinks she's up for the chop.'

'Well, if they let those two go they'll save enough on salaries to pay the fine. It'll all blow over. You know what it's like. If we compromise a bit and reduce the branding or restructure the finance we can get by. Mark my words the worst is over.'

'Words marked.'

'I keep saying this: I must go. This time I mean it.'

Duncan rose. His mobile phone rang. He pulled it from his pocket. 'Duncan Cairns.'

'Are you the man behind *Sister Verity*?'

Duncan did not recognise the whispering female voice.

'I am the series producer. '

'Can I talk to you on the quiet?'

'Who is this calling please?'

'I hope I'm doin' the right thing.'

'I don't know. Are you?'

'It's like . . . she's worried about bringing you all down with her.'

'Who is? Bringing us all down where?'

'You know it's not her real name and everything?'

'It's her stage name, yes. Who is this?'

'She's a very good person but I mean, you know . . . she came to me and she's ever so worried. She's been like a sister to me but she isn't a sister at all. Oh. Here they come. I have to leave it there. Sorry.' The line went dead. Duncan stood stone still for a second. For the first time in a few days his mind concentrated on just one thing for just one moment.

'Who was that?'

'I have no idea. It was an anonymous caller.'

'Wrong number.'

'It was a woman, in distress I think, sort of common-sounding—'

'Don't be such a snob.'

'I'm not a snob. You know what I mean. She said she hoped Sister Verity didn't bring us all down with her. I wonder if she meant she was giving out the wrong advice? She implied she wasn't a proper nun. Perhaps she was someone from the Catholics. Sister Verity's very ropey on the old theology. Probably failed her entrance exams, or something. God.'

'What order is she from?'

'I'm trying to remember. She did tell me . . . No, Charlotte did. All Hallow's or something. In North London. I wrote it down. I'll have to check. I'll have to check up on her. We'll need to confirm her independence for the ITC enquiry and the fact that she isn't paid or anything.'

'Could be embarrassing.'

'She's a created character called Sister Verity. That's the whole point of the show.'

'The whole point of the show is that she's a nun. The tabloids will have a field day if she turns out to have duffed up on her qualifications.'

'I wonder who she was, the woman who rang.'

'Try your phone. Does it store the number?'

Duncan pressed a few buttons.

'She's left a traceable number. Write this down.' As he repeated the number Michael wrote it down. As Duncan was about to call it the telephone rang. It was the production office at the studio.

'Duncan! Where the fuck are you?' said the production manager. 'Sister Verity is due in make-up. She's got her script to go through and everything. You know we've got to tighten up with the ITC breathing down our necks.'

'Excuse me. *I* am the series producer.'

'So where are you?'

'I'm at lunch. I'm not due in for another hour or so.'

'But you're bringing Sister Verity.'

'She has a limo.'

'But you're bringing her today.'

'Who told you that?'

'She did. She rang and cancelled the limo.'

'Well she must be coming some other way. I don't know where she is.'

'She said she was with you.'

'Someone's got their wires crossed. She hasn't called me. I've no idea where she is.'

'Well, nor have I and nor has anyone else. She's normally first here.'

'Well don't panic. She'll turn up. I'll be in shortly.'

Duncan put the phone back in his pocket. He felt weak at the knees.

'Problems?'

'Nothing I can't handle.'

But he was already wondering if he could handle what the hell was going on. Who the hell was the mysterious caller and where the hell was Sister Verity?

As usual there was no parking to be found in Paddington and Karen was forced to drive around for longer than usual. She dashed from the car through the rain to the blue door of Myhill Productions and made her way down the corridor and through the double doors into the office. She found herself alone. Everyone else was over at the studio. She paused at Duncan's desk and, searching for any titbits or developments of interest, she messed up his neat little piles of ordered filing. Karen didn't notice and if she had she wouldn't have cared. She trudged on to her own office and unlocked the door. She threw her coat upon the floor and flopped into her chair. She revolved round to the table behind where her word processor sat and leant behind it to switch it on. But she failed to see the screen flicker and light up because she was stopped by an observation she made from the corner of her eye. Her coat normally landed in an empty space by the corner of the room, but this time it had fallen with a different sound upon something placed there. Something not placed there by Karen.

Curious, Karen rose and moved to where her coat lay. It was draped over something oblong. A smallish case. A woman's case. A vanity case. Not hers. One she had not seen before. Karen peeled away the coat and looked at it. She pressed down the lock and the trigger sprang on it. The lid popped open and Karen lifted it up. She watched her own mystified expression revealed in the lid mirror.

Inside, on the top, was an envelope which bore the inscription: To the Good Lady Karen. Karen did not recognise the handwriting but she was instantly certain it was from Sister Verity. She picked it up. The letter had been lying on a thin summer jacket, pale citrus, not unlike her own from her makeover session. It had folded down to nothing. She pulled it out and underneath it uncovered a skirt. Karen dropped the jacket and skirt to one side and returned to her desk. She sat down. She stalled and then ferociously fought with the top of the envelope until it ripped open. It contained a one-page, handwritten, or rather scrawled, letter. Karen herself would never write a letter on lined paper torn from a spiral notebook and, if she ever were to, it would have to be only a one-line note on a piece this small. Just about everything was revealed by the size and shape and weight of the paper people chose to write on, even when selected in an emergency. Sister Verity had appeared to transcend class because of the uniform she wore, but it could not disguise her choice of paper which told its own story to so acute an observer as Karen Myhill. She had no idea what the letter might contain, but she knew that Sister Verity would deliver her little package wrapped in kindness and tied with humour. Karen pushed the bridge of her bejewelled glasses up her beaky nose and squinted at the sloping scrawl. The lines wobbled on the page. There were some words she could not decipher. But here it was anyway. Sister Verity's apology.

My dear good lady Karen
You know there is nothing in the world that would cause me to bring harm upon you. You are a fine lady. You have showed me only the kindness of your heart. When I agreed to become Sister Verity for the advertising people I never for a moment thought that it would lead to anything more than a few minutes of fun. But once I started I could not stop. It is the devil in me, you see. I should never have let you put me on the television. I should never have agreed to solve the people's problems. I should never have stayed. Now I come to my senses. The past is catching up with me. I have to go. I am sorry if I have let you down, my dear. Believe me, it was never my intention so to do. I return to you the little suit, not much worn. Your company paid for it and I saw you have one like it your good self and it might just fit you. The enclosed is for you. Do with it as you please. It is the ill gotten gains of my devilish career. The good people sent me money because the programme said that I was unpaid. I return it to you. Spend it on yourself, my dear. Do not give it to the charities as they are all a bunch of swindling cheats. So sorry. A sister to you always. Blessing you all. Sister Verity.

'She's run away,' said Karen out loud. 'I wonder who she was?' Her heart was thumping. She tiptoed back to her own desk. It was strange but she felt calm, still inside. She re-read the letter. Well, at least now she didn't have to confront Sister Verity with the prospect of truncating the series over the rules. How touching of her to leave her the suit. It wouldn't fit. It was too short and too wide. She'd find someone who would want it. No she would not. She would hang it up at home and keep it as a souvenir of Sister Verity. Karen realised she had no idea what Sister Verity really looked like. They did not know her age or the colour of her hair. They had seen only the habit. No one looks at the face of a nun. She recalled the reference to the enclosed which Sister Verity had written about. She turned the letter over in her hands but there was nothing with it. It must still be in the envelope. She had probably popped a tenner in as an afterthought. Sweet. A tenner was nothing to Karen, but it was a widow's mite of a fortune to Sister Verity. Karen was touched again. She was keen to keep it and fulfil Sister Verity's last wish. She retrieved the debris of the badly torn envelope from the heap of things on her desk. Her fingers told her that, sure enough, there was just the one note inside. Better to pop that into her purse before anyone else turned up. Particularly Duncan, who would be determined to do the right thing and give it back to the viewers who had sent it in to the show. Or worse, donate it to charity which is exactly where Sister Verity did not want it to go. She was amused that a nun should chastise charities but she agreed with her on that one. They were all a bunch of skivers.

She looked down at the folded note in her hand. Karen was surprised. It was not a tenner after all. It was not money. She must have misunderstood. Casually, she opened it out. It was computer printed in a pathetically characterless typeface on the meanest, thinnest paper Karen wouldn't have bought for toilet tissue. Slowly she read the message she found there. Her pulse quickened. Her hands shook. Her temperature soared. Her skin flushed. Her heart raced. Her glasses steamed up. Before anything had sunk in she heard a flurry of footsteps in the office beyond. Hastily, she pulled open her top drawer and hurriedly stuffed the piece of paper into it. She tried to ram it shut but it jammed. There was too much junk in there and it just wouldn't go. God dammit shut will you. The drawer duly obliged. Fearing discovery, she leapt in one bound from her desk and attempted to calm herself down. Nervously, she tiptoed to the ajar door and peeked out. It was Duncan. Thank God it was Duncan. His brow was shiny with sweat like he had been running. She saw him make a face at the disorder on his desk. Well, that was the least of what was wrong.

'Duncan! Duncan! Duncan!'

Duncan leapt, looking startled. He sped across the floor. 'I had no idea there was anyone else in the office.'

The two competed to cross-communicate their news.

'It's Sister Verity,' gasped Karen.

'You've heard.'

'What?'

'She's left,' replied Duncan. 'Left us and left the show.'

'That's not all she's left.'

'She's left the country?'

'Has she?'

'No idea. I thought you were telling me.'

'No. I meant that's not all she's left behind.'

'What?'

'She's left half a million pounds in the company account.'

'*What*?!'

'She's deposited half a million pounds into our bank account. Correction, my bank account. She wrote me a note and attached the thingy that confirms the transfer.'

'*How much*?!'

'Half a million. I suppose I should ring up and get the bank to verify it just to be sure. Shit. The overdraft. They'll not let me keep that on now. What's half a million minus twenty-four thousand? Why can't I count?'

Duncan grinned. 'A piece of piss, that's what it is.'

'I know! Solvency here I come!'

'You can't keep it.'

'Watch me. Any complaints from you and I fire you on the spot. You got me into this mess and we're going to get out of it my way.'

'Karen—'

'My way, Duncan. *My way*. I can repeat it more times than Frank fucking Sinatra.'

'Spare me, please. This you don't know.'

'What? *What*?'

'There never was a Sister Verity. She wasn't a nun at all.'

'Fuck.' Karen shot a look back at her desk drawer. 'She was a bank robber?'

'No time to explain now. Listen. It's gone three-thirty and we have a live show on at five and we've got no presenter.'

'Fuck,' said Karen. 'Fuck. Fuck. *Fuck*!'

73

'I'll leave this to you.' Karen hunched her shoulders into their routine droop and marched off towards the production office, leaving a breathless Duncan confronting several of the crew on the studio floor.

'None of us have any idea of what's going on,' complained a junior researcher.

'Join the club.'

'There are all these rumours,' said another.

'Are we all going to get fired?' asked the first. 'I'm really anxious. I never got paid what they owed me in the last company I worked for. Apparently this place is going bust over a half-million pound fine.'

Duncan followed a sigh with a smile.

'Why don't you get the others to come over here and I'll tell you all what's going on and what we're going to do about it.'

When the production team had gathered Duncan explained

to them that Sister Verity had disappeared and the position with The Station and the ITC. He wound up.

'The potential of a fine remains but the initial liability for paying it rests with The Station. If, for contractual reasons, Myhill Productions has to contribute towards it or even pay all of it then we have the resources to cover it.'

'Who are you trying to kid?'

'It's true. We do.'

'Where from?'

'I can't say.'

'We don't believe you. You're not a director of the company. You're freelance like the rest of us.'

'If you're freelance then it's not your problem, is it? Freewheel onto the next job. It'll be a year before a fine comes into operation and the money has to be found. But we've found it already anyway.'

'Where?'

'. . . let's just say we've had a windfall.'

'A windfall?'

'I'm not saying anymore.'

'Oh I hate that,' said one girl. 'It's like children. I've got a secret and I'm not telling you what it is.'

'You're acting like children. The company finances are not your concern and you're not liable for anything.'

'What are we doing about today's show? We're on in nearly an hour. Is Sister Verity coming back ever?'

Duncan puckered his lips. 'No. She's not.'

There was a dull groan from his audience.

'Duncan?'

The girl who controlled the teleprompter came charging down from the gallery. She held a cordless telephone in her hand.

'What?'

'There's a journalist on the phone. Asking about Sister Verity. Karen's hiding in the production office. She's locked herself in.'

'Here.' Duncan took the phone and gave a warning look to the staff. 'No sniggering.' His telephone rang and he picked it up. 'Duncan Cairns speaking . . . producer . . . I've no idea where you heard that . . . Well, if you can't reveal your sources I can't reveal anything either. I couldn't comment on innuendo contained in anonymous letters . . . I see . . . Well, whoever anonymous it was at Saturn Productions is wrong. Saturn Productions is a competitor of ours and an unlikely source of the unvarnished truth when it comes to *Sister Verity* . . . The series has been well received and it gets excellent ratings so I can't see why that would be the case . . . Sister Verity fronts the show but she is not a spokesperson for the production. I am. So she has nothing to add—'

'She's fucked off off the face of the earth,' interjected the researcher.

Duncan cupped the mouthpiece. 'Shut *up* . . . she's not on air today . . . there is nothing peculiar about that. We receive a lot of calls on the same subjects repeatedly and so I've decided to run a few episodes of the *Best of Sister Verity*. Sister Verity has done the show for months now daily without a break and as a nun she has to have a period for contemplation and spiritual renewal. She's on retreat and cannot be contacted until she returns . . . I know. Well, that's Saturn Productions for you. On another planet, as usual . . . Yes. Thank you. Goodbye.'

He replaced the receiver.

'Wow, that was brilliant, Duncan.'

'That was a free lesson on how to handle the press.'

'Karen would have told them to fuck off.'

'Entirely the wrong thing to say. Somebody – Jamie Hirst no doubt, though how he would know beats me – has alerted them to the fact that Sister Verity has done a runner. The way I explained it is the story you give out if anyone asks you. Any queries from the press must be handled directly by me. No one else is to be a self-appointed spokesman for the company. Understood?'

They nodded.

'What was that about *The Best of Sister Verity*?'

'I thought it up on the way here. We've still got one hour. What we'll do today is play out the recording of the pilot show we did. It only went out in Milton Keynes so almost no one has seen it. We need to modify the titles at the top of the show to match those in the broadcast series. Use the Harry to scribble on "The Best of" as an addition to the titles page. For however many more shows we do, what we need is to go into the edit suite and pick the best answers Sister Verity has given over the last few weeks, cut them together and put them out for the rest of the series.'

'That's brilliant,' said the researcher. 'Who'll edit them?'

'One of you lot, it doesn't matter who. Not me. Not having your background I don't self-drive in an edit suite.'

'There. There is something you can't do.'

'Not can't do. Don't do. There is a difference.'

'Smarmy bastard.'

Duncan laughed. 'You've got forty minutes to be back here with the revised titles on the pilot. There. Solved.'

'What about viewers calling in? They might not realise that it's not live.'

'You have a nice speaking voice. Write me a new script for the responder answering recordings. It should say that today's show is a "Best of" special by public demand and that Sister Verity is unable – no, is not in the studio – to take calls today. Thanks for calling. Thanks for watching. Enjoy today's programme. Something like that.'

'Will I say she's coming back or what?'

'Don't say anything. Write the script and bring it to me asap—'

Click.

They all turned as one as the production office door was unlocked from the inside. She appeared, a mirage in the frame.

'What are you all staring at?' asked Karen. 'Duncan, come in here.'

Duncan gave the rest a knowing look and headed over.

She looked down in the dumps. She flopped behind a desk. Duncan tripped in.

'I thought we were going have to contact you via ouija board.'

Karen looked at him incredulously.

'What did you say?'

'Sorry. I was just trying to be jolly amidst the panic.'

'Ouija board?'

'It's one of those things—'

'I know what it is. It's brilliant, that's what it is.' Karen had had an idea.

'Remember it was me who thought of it. What is it I have thought of anyway?'

'Duncan I've been sitting racking my brains here. I have to fulfil a contract for the next six weeks. Why the hell was this commissioned mid-season to mid-season? It's so awkward. I have to have a live daily half-hour show on air with one person sitting in the studio and she can't be Sister Verity. She can't be any nun at all and she mustn't have anything to do with tampons or pregnancies or whatever, otherwise we'll lose the sponsorship deal and The Station will be even more pissed off than they are now. And we've got to have it probably by next Monday.'

'This is Wednesday.'

'Duncan, you know what day of the week it is. Congratulations.'

'When you're not being quite so critical, Karen, we still have a half-hour slot this afternoon to fill.'

'Fuck.'

'Don't worry. It's all sorted. The *Best of Sister Verity* goes out at five p.m. The pilot. Followed tomorrow by highlights from the series. We're pretending it's a viewers' request.'

'Fantastic. Well done Duncan. Will Martin Fox buy that?'

'He has no alternative. The ITC can't cause a hole to appear in the schedule. I'll make sure none of the questions are about periods or preganancy or ovulation or anything like that. They're not the best ones anyway.'

'OK. Now onto Monday. Ouija boards.'

'What is this about ouija boards?'

'Find someone who can use one. Viewers call in and we get in touch with their dear departed live on TV for them.'

'Jesus. The dead, live on TV.'

'It's brilliant TV. Kids will love it. Teenagers will love it. Everyone will love it. And the architectural background and swirling mist effects will look fab. Shove on creepy music . . . we've got the weekend to cast and rehearse. Where's my secretary? I need to get this in writing to Martin Fox and I need a press release to go out to change the newspaper schedules. Get tabloid coverage.'

'Will it sustain?'

'What?'

'A medium with a ouija board on every day. Stripped across the week.'

'We'll ring the changes. Ouija on Monday, Tarot on Tuesday and if it's Wednesday – it must be runes. There. I've done three shows. You do the other two.'

'Thanks. Happy horoscopes on Thursday I suppose. Where will we find the people to do it?'

'Look in all the papers and magazines. They've all got columnists. And there must be a national society for contacting the dead?'

'It's called parliament, isn't it?'

'Hah! Duncan. I'm so excited. The best ideas are the spontaneous ones. I think we're onto a winner.'

'Where have I heard that before? '

For the first time in ages they grinned at each other, thrilled to be in TV.

74

'Are you coming to watch *Sister Verity*?'

Charlotte swung round in her seat.

'Oh, hi Dan. You're back.'

'You didn't call me Daniel.'

'I'm too tired to manage anything beyond the first syllable. You wore me out last night.'

'That's the trouble with toyboys.' He walked up behind her and placed his hands on her shoulders. 'You're tense.'

'I'm under a lot of pressure. Guess what?'

'What?'

'I'm not pregnant.'

'Whoah! Re-*sult*!' He punched the air behind her head.

'That Verity testing kit was more than a bit dodgy.'

Daniel began to massage the nape of her neck with both thumbs. 'You can say that again. Brill. Well, we have one thing off our minds now, at least. Come and watch *Sister Verity*.'

'I don't think I could face it. I saw my mother at lunchtime.'

'And?'

'And she's behaving oddly and she won't tell me why.'

'Mummies and daddies are peculiar things.'

'Tell me about it. You know the clients are in today?'

Daniel's voice registered surprise. 'Who are? Where?'

'The clients. They're in with Hector. Over the road.'

'I thought Hector wasn't in today.'

'He wasn't this morning. But he came in specially for this, apparently.'

'You're having me on. What for?'

'To sort out what to do about The Station and the show and the ITC.'

'Shouldn't you be in that meeting?' Daniel was worried. He kneaded harder.

'My thoughts exactly. Hector said it would be easier if he handled them on his own. From the plushness of his throne.'

'He's good at that. He does a little intimate show business special on them and they leave happy.'

'They're probably asking for my head on a plate right now. And he's saying, "And how would madam like it served? Off or on the bone?"'

'Nah.'

'They must be. Otherwise I'd be in the meeting with them. I should call Audrey Goldberg. I wish I'd never left Saatchi's.'

'You came here from Clancey and Bennett.'

'As I said, I wish I'd never left Saatchi's. I wouldn't have had the fiasco of MCN. Or the ghastly Serena Sark ringing me up every other Tuesday.'

'I thought she was all right.'

'You only met her for dinner. I am going to call Audrey up. Get another job. If anyone will have me.'

'I'll have you.'

She lifted and dropped her shoulders seductively. His firm hands and sensual handling were winning. Her blonde hair tumbled back as she dropped back her head and gazed directly up at him. He dropped his face to hers and kissed her slowly on the mouth. She lingered on it for a moment and then pulled out from under him.

'Somebody might come in.'

'No chance of a fuck then?'

'Not the remotest.'

'Blow job?'

'I'm too brittle. I'd bite it off.'

'It releases tension.'

'Yours you mean. You have a lot to learn young man. Sex isn't like that for women. We don't go in for passion as a form of release.'

'What *do* you go in for then? Knitting?'

'Firing insolent young account men. That helps me relax. For about five minutes. Then I just have to have another. Like Chinky food.'

'You'd be right up shit creek minus a paddle without me. No Dan. No Maria. Hecka on the hoof and in here every five minutes.'

'Instead of Daniel Mainwaring in here every five minutes. Daniel, I must finish these income forecasts and fire off a few memos. Go and turn on *Sister Verity* and I'll join you in a second.'

'I know I'm God's gift to women but even I couldn't turn on Sister Verity.'

'Go on!' Charlotte laughed and waved her young lover away.

After he had shut the door behind her she felt calmer and more able to concentrate. She put out of her mind thoughts of ringing her mother and thoughts of ringing her client and thoughts of ringing Duncan. She sat and typed at her keyboard. Since she had been on a Windows course she was quite proficient now. They would probably do away with secretaries altogether soon, and not just at HQ but everywhere. She sent her two memos to the printer and raked inside her untidy in-tray for the pre-printed income forecast forms she had received in the internal mail. She checked the form. The financial director had completed the figures for the year to date and all Charlotte had to do was estimate how the rest of the year's income would fall within the four months left. She swung open her filing cabinet beneath her desk and dug out the last forecast she had filled out and copied down the same figures. If she got this wrong she'd get fired. So? She was probably about to get fired anyway. *Mea culpa* did not have the happy ring of one of Hector's homilies. Whatever happened, she had not a clue as to whether Verity Tampons would continue to spend as before. How was she supposed to know whether Verity would still be their client after the fiasco of the TV sponsorship? It had been her idea to go onto TV in this way but certainly not hers to create the biggest nun event since Julie Andrews last warbled on a Salzburg mountain top doing a twirl in a dirndl.

'Flibbertygibbet,' she said. She sang softly. 'What are we going to do about Sister Verity?' Her words didn't fit the original melody so she extended it. 'How do you hold a moonbeam in your hand?'

The room fell silent. She could hear no traffic out on Marylebone Road. No trains over in Marylebone station. No sounds in the office. Just calm. Peace. Tranquillity. Ease . . . Just the rustle of her own hand on the sheet in front of her. Just the roll of the ball in the tip of her pen on the surface of the paper. Just the faint, steady hymn of the atmosphere and the presence of her own mind. In the distance, over the way, outside in the street, muffled by the double glazing, lost on the air of London, rounded and resonant she heard the silence break as the clock on the Landmark Hotel began to chime.

One . . .

She smiled to herself. She did like Dan. She was fond of him.

Two . . .

What time was it? She checked her watch. Time for Sister Verity.

Three . . .

Shrshrshrshr – !

Charlotte leapt almost out of her jacket. She jumped nearly out of her skin. The shrill ring of the telephone shattered the silence and pierced her ears.

Four . . .

'Hello?'

'Charlotte, it's Marsha. The Verity clients have just left. Can you come over to Hector's office. Straightaway.'

Five . . .

Stunned, Charlotte found herself by the window and looking down into the mews. A gleaming black chauffeur-driven Daimler rolled forward in the street below. She already knew what it was. Hearse-black, a modern metaphor for the shiny scythe of Old Father Time, just as dazzling, just as dangerous, just as deadly. It was the five o'clock car and it had come for her.

75

'Five o'clock and all's well.'

'Is it, Duncan?' Karen pulled her hair back severely from her brow, exposing its crossword pattern of worry lines.

'It is. *The Best of Sister Verity* has just gone on air and tomorrow's show is in editing right now. As long as Sister Verity herself doesn't actually show up anywhere or sell her story in the next five days we should just make it.'

'You haven't told me what you found out.'

'I haven't exactly had the time.' He sat down next to Karen in the production office and drew breath to fill her in.

'Can I bear to hear this? I suppose if I don't the suspense will kill me. Go on. Hit me.' She smiled at Duncan. At least he was avoiding looking smug with his scoop.

'I got this anonymous call on my mobile at lunch.'

'Predictable enough.'

'I was able to source the call because the caller did not one-four-one the number.'

'And?'

'You'll never guess where it was from.'

'I agree. I will never guess. So cut the theatrical pause.'

'Holloway. Holloway Prison.'

'Shit.' Karen's face took on an edgy smirk. 'I hope we haven't all been set up.' It looked as if she was enjoying the dénouement.

'On the contrary. I had exactly two hours to take a cab up to Holloway and get back here. I got in on the pretext we were making a news feature on women in custody.'

'We might be soon. Featuring me in a central role.'

'Inside the prison I tracked down the caller, a woman prisoner. She's doing time for inflicting grievous bodily harm on her drunken husband. She recognised Sister Verity. She seems to have been the only one.'

'Don't tell me . . .'

'Sister Verity used to share a cell with her and a bunch of others.'

'She was a criminal. It seems so unlikely.'

'That's just what the prisoners I spoke to said too. They pointed out she had carried out some simple financial frauds, victimless crimes. She didn't really harm anyone. She was a woman who had had personal misfortune and didn't want to live off the state. She was good at theatre and so utterly charming that getting companies to offload some of their profits on her came naturally. I spoke to three of her old friends. Only one of them had seen her on TV and she had only just recognised her. But they all agreed she should never have been in prison. She wasn't like them.'

'Not a nun but a saint?'

'She wasn't a nun at all. She was a loner. In and out of prison over the years. She suffered from ill health. A poor liver.'

'Rather a strong liver I should have said.'

'Well, isn't Irish Latin for alcoholic? They had to hospitalise her. They took her out of Holloway and put her in a secure ward or whatever you call them. And shortly after, with the luck of the Irish and a bit of charm she just walked out the front door.'

'How on earth is that possible?'

'They apparently had regular prison visitors. The great and the good and religious people. That gave her the idea to dress up as a nun and just walk out through the front door.'

'Just like that? Where did she get the outfit? She kidnapped a nun and stripped her naked did she? Didn't anybody notice? What am I paying my taxes for? Jesus!'

'She didn't do that. I was only able to find this out because she went back and visited the woman who called me. She saw her on TV and rang her up on the show. Sister Verity apparently went out and got herself another disguise. She had an amazing makeover. She waltzed back into Holloway in a sharp little suit with her hair stunningly cut looking a million dollars. None of the prison staff recognised her.'

'That explains the citrus suit she left me. She must have been mad.'

'She was mad, as we all know. She went back to help her old friend, be a shoulder to lean on, give her a few words of encouragement. In prison she was always the one that the others talked to. She'd been around and seen more than all of them put together and was full of worldly wisdom. Well, that we know. She did it for free on our show. That's where she learnt to do it. In Holloway. Only there, none of her advice could be acted upon. She apparently thought of doing our show as a way of giving something back to the community.'

'But didn't the prison warders recognise her when she popped back in to sign autographs after running amok on national TV? Or are they completely bloody blind?'

'They didn't recognise her because they had never seen her all dressed up like that. Just as the hospital staff didn't recognise her when she left her secured room. Her friend told me that Sister Verity nipped into the hospital laundry and pinched a spare nurse's uniform. She chose one too big and it was sort of lilacy and flowing. She felt she could pass herself off better as a nun so she took the apron and wrapped it around her head to hide her hair and change the shape of her face. She took the tube into Central London and it was while she was making up her mind whether to scarper to the left or the right that she was hit by a car and went into HQ for a lie down. The rest, as they say, is history.'

'The rest, as they say, is good TV, Duncan. Perhaps we can dramatise it. Who would make a good Irish nun?'

Duncan laughed.'

'I'm being serious.'

'Who would play *you*, Karen? That's the real question.'

That thought killed Karen's creativity for the moment. 'Clever Sister Verity. She fooled everyone.'

'Everyone wanted to be fooled. No one takes nuns seri-ously. Hector Quigley wanted a coup, Verity wanted a gimmick, Charlotte wanted to get off to a good start, we wanted a cheap TV series. She just played up to it all.'

'Why did this woman call you up?'

'Because Sister Verity was becoming terrified that she would be discovered and that she would land us as well as herself in trouble.'

'She did. Sort of. Though in a way none of us imagined.'

'She didn't know how to stop the rollercoaster. Apparently she had a real attack of the jitters when she suddenly found herself on live TV every day and in danger of being recognised. Then after a few weeks she realised she was getting away with it and felt guilty she was misleading you. That's what she told her friend in Holloway. That she was going to make a run for it. Her friend thought that if we knew we would choose to help her out. Once her real identity was exposed it would be out of our control.'

'Clever friend. Well good luck to Sister Verity. All I can say is thank God it wasn't Myra Hindley's liver playing up, otherwise I'd be in deep shit. Instead we filled a summer schedule and got another series off the back of it. I've already had my runes read down the phone.'

'When?'

'In the last hour.'

'That was quick.'

'No quicker than you were playing Philip Marlowe this after-noon. Nothing but blue skies, apparently, for Karen Myhill. What is that guy? Blind as well as barmy? So?'

'So? So what?'

'So who was Sister Verity then? What was her name?'

Duncan smiled. 'I never asked.'

'You never asked? Jesus. What sort of journalist are you?'

'I'm not a journalist, nor a detective. I don't want to know. She'll always be Sister Verity to me. Don't spoil the illusion.'

Karen smiled too. For the first time in a long time she flashed a lighthouse beam.

'Suits me,' she said. 'If we pass her in the street we'll never know. Good on you, sister.'

Charlotte stopped on the landing and turned to Daniel.

'You go first.'

Even a few whispered words couldn't conceal the catch in her voice. He stepped down beside her – he was so tall he might still have been stairs above – slipped into her space and pulled her thumping, pounding, beating body into his. She nestled in the warmth evaporating from his shirt, wrapping her arms around his great frame inside his green jacket. Security. He kissed her on the forehead and then on the mouth. His hand found its way into her hair and he caressed the back of her neck. The entire TV buying department could have thundered past, boisterous, blaspheming and baying like bloodhounds and these two wouldn't have bothered. They stood heat-sealed together for five seconds and then parted. She tried to send him a smile but her lips lost it. Only pain played upon them. He didn't tell her she looked like a shot rabbit slung on a hook to hang and putrefy.

'Fuck 'em,' he said. 'If they fire you I'm fucking off. Fuck the clients. Fuck Hector fucking Quigley. Fuck advertising.'

'Shhh. I don't want the huge-haired harpies on reception to hear. Let me depart with dignity.'

'Dignity? Hecka and his henchwoman can depart with a fucking broken broomhandle stuffed up their arses. Half each. I am so livid—' He was ugly with fury. He shook his fist.

'Daniel.' Charlotte placed her finger to her lips. 'Please.'

She regained her control and held up her head. She repositioned her bodyguard one stair behind her and made the descent with style into the Satellite reception area. She swept to the double glass doors and paused imperceptibly. She pushed her hair up with one hand, she pulled her sleeve down with the other. With both she gripped her lapels and tugged down on them sharply. She had resolved it in her mind. She would face the music and dance. Joan of Arc bravely being put to the torch, Edith Cavell unflinchingly facing the firing squad, Margaret

Thatcher proudly protesting 'I'm enjoying this.' Too damn good for the lot of them, Charlotte Reith, high-flying account director, daring bareback Ducati rider, seriously stunning girl about town – she was going to look them in the eye and walk out her way. They hadn't fired her: she quit. She thrust out her arms, rebelliously threw the doors open outwards and stepped into the street.

Anti-climax wasn't a big enough word for it. The black Daimler had left. There was no car. There was no Marsha. There was no P45. There was no send-off, no drum roll, no execution squad, no mourners. Just a big fat nothing.

'Bastards! *Bastards*!' hissed Daniel. 'What the fuck do they think they're playing at?'

'I don't know.' Charlotte felt faint. She tried to play Sherlock Holmes to his Watson but they were both hopelessly miscast. She did not know whether to feel dismayed or elated and delayed feeling anything for a moment. 'Come on.'

They picked up speed and ran into Quigley House and bombed through the atrium past the cappuccino bar. As one, they jumped into the cylindrical glass lift and watched the floor fall away as they shot up to the top level. The doors slid open with a hiss. They panted down the corridor, wading sluggishly through the deep pile of the carpet leading to Hector's haven. At Marsha's door Charlotte ran her fingers through her fine blonde hair.

'How do I look?'

'By 'eck, chuck, you look gorgeous,' Daniel mugged. They didn't bother to knock.

'Hi, Charlotte!' Marsha was beaming. She looked Daniel up and down the way men once gave women the once over. 'I see you've brought your puppy with you.'

'Be careful. I bite.'

'Snappy little thing, isn't he?' Marsha's eyes caught the overhead lights and sparkled. 'Your clients just left. Did you see them? He made me order the Daimler to take them to the station. He only does that when there's a crisis. I'll bring tea in for you both. It'll be a minute because his nibs can't have anything easily done, of course. Expect he'll soon want me to nip to India to pick the leaves personally. Can't have someone in a dodgy kaftan touching Hecka's spoonful with foreign fingers, can we? It'll kill me, this job.' Her eyes flicked across to the door to Hector's office and then back to Charlotte. She lowered her voice and leant forward to divulge. 'It's about Sister Verity.'

'I can guess.'

'No you can't.' She whispered, almost mouthed: 'She's done a runner.'

Incredulous, Charlotte mouthed back a *what*?!

'Now you see her, now you don't, apparently. I listened in to the meeting on the doobrie-doobrie. Gone up in a puff of smoke. Probably had a nervous breakdown – I know I would, made to don a crucifix every afternoon to sell tampons. Tampons! I mean she's a nun and they're internal, it makes no sense. And who thought of it? He'll have to eat his words. Sometimes I think he's half-witted.'

'What are they putting out instead then? Quick, have you a TV in here?'

'Do I look like someone who has time to watch TV in the office? I don't know. A repeat, probably. That's all you ever get now, repeats.'

'Marsha!'

'God. Everything's falling apart and he's happy as a sandman in there, for some reason. Something to do with a round of golf he had with your old boss, Charlotte. It's pathetic, isn't it, when they get like that.'

'My old boss?'

'Marsha!'

'I don't know. Go in. The old bugger doesn't like to be kept waiting as we all know. Might age five more minutes and lose the benefit of flashing his facelift one more time.'

They pushed their way through the heavy oak doors and made their way into the court of the king. Hector was perched on the piano stool looking more puffed up than usual. He turned, florid-faced.

'Did I ask for Daniel?'

'You did,' said Daniel. He was believed.

'Shall I sing for you? I have been writing a jingle for the Slip chocolate commercial. I think it will do marvellously but how do you compete against forty years of a campaign showing a girl performing fellatio on a Flake?'

'How about double penetration?' suggested Daniel.

'No thank yoo!' bawled Hector in his music-hall voice. 'I've just had my Vic vapour rub. Boom, boom!'

Hector ran his fingers over the middle register of the piano and pressed a chord. 'Take it away maestro. "Slip it in your pocket,"' he sang. '"Slip it out at work. Slip it to a lover. Slip it to a friend. Slip it at the start. Slip it at the end." – We'll see a couple sharing one at the movies at that point, so it will make sense. Cinema outlets as well as CTNs are key to introductory sampling in this market place. "Slip it in your handbag. Slip it out at night. Slip between the sheets. Slip it past your lips." Cut to extra big close-up of some tart tonguing up chocolate crumbs off her lower lip. Hah! Eat your heart out Cadbury's! "Sl-i-i-i-p it i-i-i-ns-i-i-i-de." That bit doesn't rhyme but then it has contemporary charm. Coca-Cola's lyrics don't rhyme. Bloody awful drink in my opinion, but one can't always be right.'

Daniel laughed. He had never before seen Hector this playful at the end of a day. 'You missed out, "Slip yourself a length."'

'Very good, Daniel, you young masturbater, you.' Hector addressed the air. 'Write that down, Marsha. I know you've been listening in all afternoon, you frustrated old cow.' He chuckled. Since she would hardly admit to it, he shouted at the door. 'Marsha!'

'Yes!'

'Tea!'

'It's coming.'

'So is Christmas. Get a move on. And send a get-well card to that old fat arse Gainsborough.'

'Nigel Gainsborough?' asked Charlotte. 'Is he ill?'

'He had, shall we say, a bad head. But the very good news for me and the very bad news for everybody else is that he has come round today without so much as a marginal loss of memory.'

'Why is that good news for you, Hecka?' asked Daniel, puzzled.

'Who are you? Emil and the Detectives? It is good news enough for you to know that I am in a very jolly mood and have hence composed a brilliant new commercial melody. Hector Quigley, Lord of the Jingle, I am.' He attempted a low-key

Tarzanish yell, which did not quite come off. 'Now. Charlotte Reith.'.

She looked at him nervously. She glanced at Daniel, who winked reassuringly, and looked back into Hector's sky blue eyes.

'It has not been an easy start for you. You've had to relaunch a dying brand, put up with a difficult client, organise a new foray for us into TV sponsorship, put up with an awkward group account structure which we have resolved with the departure of our American cousin and now our dear Sister Verity has buggered off somewhere.'

'What's happened?'

'She has, as they say, fucked orf. Don't blame 'er, meself, having to deal with the great unwashed every day. Appalling shower, the British lower classes. I know, I was one myself once before I crawled out from the mire.'

'Is she all right?'

'She is.'

'How do you know?'

'Because I have been in touch with her and with the woman at the TV company. Sister Verity has handed in her notice, if in an unconventional manner. But that was what we liked about her, her idiosyncracy. Character. That is why people admire me. Anyway, I asked you to come over to tell you what I have agreed with the client.'

Hector smiled. Charlotte did not yet feel totally reassured.

'We will bring in a new board director to co-ordinate the business at group account level. That will satisfy the client as to their importance in the grand scheme of things. It will no doubt take about six months to sort out. In the meantime I will personally supervise the business, which you will run on a day-to-day basis with young Daniel fellow-me-lad reporting to you. Just the three of us. The client is very happy with your performance.'

'Really?'

'Don't sound so surprised. Clients have no idea of the cracks in agencies. We only let them see the gloss on the surface. You talk a good story, Charlotte. You present well. You sound confident. You have credibility. The campaign has been got out on time and sales have matched targets to date. That's all that matters. I have been in this business longer than anybody else and I know which buttons to push for success.'

'What about *Sister Verity*? That's a fiasco.'

'Indeed it is not. Sister Verity is only a small part of what we do. Back-of-pack stuff.'

'She's a TV series.'

'She was. Past tense please. Sister Verity is a character created by my good self to play a role in communications. She's our Captain Bird's Eye. She's our Dulux dog. Not a reality but a symbol. We will continue to use her photograph on print work. For personality appearances we will find an actress to play the role. For the schools visits we will persuade Verity to recruit a team of nurses to do that. The kids will still believe there is a Sister Verity and will write to her and she will write back.'

'It'll be in all the papers.'

'It will be and it will pass quickly. I have persuaded the client to seek a PR company specialising in damage limitation exercises. Somebody who handles plane crashes for airlines, that sort of thing. Get a good spin doctor and we'll all get good press. Present the whole thing as a hoot.'

'What about the TV? What about The Station?'

'Fines and so on are their lookout, not ours. The series was drawing to a close.'

'It had six weeks to run,' insisted Charlotte.

'What is six weeks in the lifetime of a brand? I doubt it would have got recommissioned next year. *Sister Verity* will run no more. It was a pilot series on cable television during the lax late months of the summer. Verity are quite happy with the profile it raised. I have persuaded them to spend the remaining sponsorship funds through us in the next six months. We must always seek ways of persuading our clients not to put money into sponsorship and below-the-line activities when we can get our grubby little hands on it here for our own purposes. It will not surpise you to learn that Uncle Hector is a past master at diverting the spondoolies his way.'

'Wow,' said Charlotte. 'You're incredible.'

'I find myself highly credible.'

'You've sorted it all out yet nothing seems to have changed.'

'Most ideas fail, my dear Charlotte, not because they are not the right solution but because they address the wrong problem. Write that down, I can use it in my speech to the Institute of Directors. Why the hell they elevated Maurice Saatchi to the peerage and not me I shall never know. But then what have I done for government? Only by my example made it look weak and directionless while little Mo kept it there for years beyond its natural term. Who gets the gong? Not I. But no one has ever appreciated how good Hector Quigley is.' He leant forward from his throne. 'Well, my dear Charlotte, well my dear Daniel. Before this Christmas comes I will surprise you all. Now. Run along.'

'What did all that mean?' asked Daniel when they were back in Marsha's anteroom.

'I have no idea,' said Charlotte. 'At least we're off the hook. Champagne at the Atlantic to celebrate?'

'You know where that leads.' Daniel smirked. Charlotte smiled back.

Marsha's antennae were twitching, trying to pick up on what had happened. The telephone rang.

'Who shall I say is calling? . . . I see. No. I'm putting you through . . .' She tapped her phone and replaced the receiver. 'It's Hecka's fancy woman. I'm sure I know her voice but I can't place it.'

'Don't you know who she is yet?'

'No.'

'I'm surprised.'

'I think we all will be when we find out who it is.'

'Probably turn out to be Sister Verity,' said Daniel.

The two women looked at him, bemused.

'Who *is* Sister Verity?' asked Charlotte.

It was dark. It was squally. Karen was bent double at the front door of the house. Ostrich-like, she appeared to be about to stuff her head into her handbag. It was not an attempt to hide, though. One disappearance in one day was enough. She knew her keys were in her bag and they seemed to have slipped inside a tear in the lining and she was intent on getting them out even if it meant ripping the lining out of the bag. She felt like tearing something to shreds. She was angry. But she was also excited with the gossip about Sister Verity and the thrill of the new series. She was thinking of calling it *Face the Future*. It was something to tell Max. It was something to discuss with Max. She had had so little to say to Max recently when in reality she should have had so much.

It was amazing what collected at the bottom of your bag. A bus timetable from the 1980s. She had never used public transport so what that was doing there she had no idea. The stiff brush from inside a dried-up old bottle of Tippex correction fluid. It was unlikely she had put that loose into her handbag, but it was not impossible. A pre-decimal coin. She hadn't had the bag for a quarter of a century so there was no explaining that either. Her keys. Thank God. Her keys. Now at last she could get inside out of the snapping cold of the storm. She looked up at the nearly full moon through the branches of the plane trees in the street, through the lavender clouds. The branches looked like the cracks in a broken window silhouetted black against the deep grey of the sky. They swung from side to side in an irregular pattern. If Karen was not mistaken she could hear laughter on the wind. She could. It was getting closer and louder, the laughter of adolescence. She wondered if Max was approaching. The laughter came again and then she heard a snatch of argument. And that name. That damnable, trouble-steeped, cursable name.

'Ginny!'

Karen scowled maliciously in the shadows. She looked criminal enough to break into her own home, key or no key. She could hear them clearly now. It must be Max. It must be Ginny. Max and Ginny. She sidled down the path to see if it was. As she crept forward, so did deviousness into her mind. There was nothing for it. She had to do it. If not, she would be spotted. She dropped to her knees and began the painful cutting crawl across the unmown lawn towards and into the shrubby hedge that sat behind the low wall marking the street from the front garden. The ground was wet. Karen felt the damp earth filtering through her tights. It clamped itself to her luminous skin in leech-like clumps. Her legs were streaked with dirt. Her shoes were penetrated by water. Her palms were gloved in wet brown leaves which smelt of decay. No matter. She pushed her way into the damp murkiness of the shrubbery and, bar the occasional glint of diamanté as her spectacles reflected the moonlight, she blended seamlessly into the loose shapes against the wall. She held one ear up to the street. Though their voices were low it was not diffcult to hear.

'Come on. I've not had it for ages.'

'Fuck off.' That was Ginny Collins all right.

'I'm not getting it anywhere else, Ginny. I promise.' Who was that? It was certainly not Max.

'I'm not a tart. I'm fed up with you thinking I'm an easy lay.'

'I don't think that.'

'You don't love me.'

'I like you. I really do.'

They stopped in front of Karen's wall. From her monitoring base within the hedge all Karen could see were black shapes in the street. They stood a foot away. She daren't move. She daren't breathe. She daren't listen. She did all three.

'You don't love me.'

'I do.'

'You just use me for sex.'

'Love is sex.'

Karen realised Ginny was being picked up and lifted onto the wall. Her lower back almost touched Karen's ear. She was wearing a long silk scarf that dangled down and whose tasselled edges tickled the end of Karen's nose. She wanted to sneeze but if she leant any further backwards she would take her eye out with a thorn. She wished to God she hadn't climbed in here now. She felt horribly self-aware and downright embarrassed. But there was something going on here. The couple were silent for a moment. Then she heard them both breathe. Then silence. Then breathe. She heard squelching noises and lips being lubricated and tongues tangoing. Uggh. They were snogging. He was tonguing all the way down to her liver, for God's sake, inches from Karen's face. She wanted to wretch.

'Open your lips.'

'No.'

'Go on . . . Do this with your tongue . . . Now do that back to me . . . mmm . . . yeah.'

'Get your hand out of there.'

'Why? You like a good feel don't you?'

Ginny giggled. 'Higher. No lower. There.'

'Feels good. Hot. Hey. Put your hand down there . . . see . . . feel that. That's what you're doing to me . . . let me fuck you.'

'No.'

'Go on. You like it.'

'Snog me more first.'

'There isn't time. I have to get the tube home. I can't travel home with a hard-on.'

'Where?'

'Can't we go to your house?'

'Christ? Are you joking.'

'Fuck. If only I had my car. What about in here?'

Karen bristled in the bushes.

'Where?'

'Behind this hedge.'

Karen froze with fury.

'You're not fucking me in that old bitch's garden.'

Karen foamed with outrage.

'Hang on. Rub my cock a bit . . . mmm . . . good.'

There was more silence. Karen's blood boiled.

'You're making it so hard.'

'Got a condom?'

'Nuh. What about you?'

'I don't take condoms to school, stupid. You'll just have to go home and have a wank.'

The guy tutted. 'Do it for me.'

'It's boring.'

'It'll only take a second.'

'Well, don't come on my jacket, then. If my mother sees it she'll have a fit. She goes on and on about dry cleaning.'

'Oh, right. I thought you meant she'd see it was spunk.'

'She wouldn't know what that was. God. I'd rather kill myself than be old like her or the cow that owns this dump here.'

Karen was provoked into shaking her head. As a result something fell into the left lense of her spectacles. It was wet and clammy and cold as a cadaver. It wriggled a bit and fell still. It was a small, fawn-coloured slug. It left a trail of slime down the inside of the glass. Karen tried to poke it out with one finger but she daren't move much and gave up quickly.

'Go on.'

'Where?'

'Behind this hedge. Toss me off and then I'll fuck off and leave you alone.'

'Aw – I can't. I just can't.'

'Why not?'

'She might see us.'

'There's no one in. There's no lights on.'

'She might come home.'

'If you get a move on I'll have shot my wad before then.'

'How romantic. I can't. Not in there.'

'There's nowhere else.'

'No.'

'Why not?'

'Because . . . it's where Max lives.'

'Who's Max?'

'A poxy neighbour, that's who.'

Karen's ire ignited inside her shrub.

'You're not shagging him are you?'

Ginny laughed.

'Am I fuck. He's just a kid.'

Karen blinked in the darkness.

'Come on then.'

The figure of the girl upped and left the wall. For a moment Karen was left alone. In the squall she heard nothing. But then they came through the gate and round into the pitch black garden. Ginny stood, back to Karen who remained concealed. She still daren't move. To her abject horror the boy rapidly unbuttoned his flies and put his hand inside and tugged.

'I can't get it out. Too big, that's my problem.'

'You wish,' said Ginny. She yawned,

He pulled up his blouson and unbuttoned the top of his trousers. He pulled them and his pants a quarter way down his thighs. Karen caught the paleness of the shaft of his penis in the moonlight and averted her gaze. He hadn't lied about the size. 'Ginny, suck me off will you?'

Ginny sighed. As she squatted down in front, grabbed hold of the bobbing protuberance, the sordidness of it all became too much for Karen. In one jerky, stuttering stammering move, she half-leapt, half-fell out of her hiding place and grabbed Ginny roughly by the scruff of her neck in a plier–like grip that was so determined it surprised even herself. Ginny screamed and fell back from her boyfriend's groin. Karen yanked her hair down hard.

'Ow!'

'What the fuck do you think you're playing at, madam?'

'Ow! Let me go!' Ginny tried to stand up, but Karen held her thrust down. Even in the darkness and even through the slug in her lens Karen could see that the boy's expression mixed fear with sheepishness. Pants pulled down and cock pointing out is not most guys' idea of how to best present themselves to their middle-aged women neighbours in glasses. He fumbled in the dark with his trousers and pants and pulled them up. Karen realised it was the youth with long red hair she had once seen Ginny with before. He stood there hapless and helpless.

'Ow. Let me go you old bitch. You're hurting me. You're all mucky.'

'Not as mucky as your sordid sluttish mind, you little trollope.'

'Let me go. You shouldn't have been spying on us you nosey old parker. '

'You shouldn't have been in my garden. Are you in the habit of performing fellatio on my front lawn?'

'Ow! No. What are you on about? We don't like any classical music. Ow!'

'You're supposed to be the mother of my grandchild. Are you pregnant or aren't you? If this little fucker is the real father I'll flay you alive.'

The young man was taken aback. 'Hey? What's she on about? Ginny if you've got yourself up the duff I'll fucking kill you.'

Ginny sobbed. 'I skipped my period. Then it came back. I'm not pregnant. I thought I was. Honest. I thought I was.'

'Why the fuck didn't you tell me, Ginny?'

She gulped and coughed between howls of anguish. 'You said I was fat. I was trying to make myself slimmer. I went on a crash diet. Starving, I was. I didn't eat for weeks. I was so ill. My periods stopped. I thought I was going to have a baby.'

'I used rubbers.'

'I know. But I really thought I was pregnant.' Karen yanked her hair again. 'Ow! I really did.'

'Where does my son fit into all this? Tell me. Tell me, Ginny Collins or I'll go straight to your mother.'

'Nowhere.'

'Nowhere?'

'It had nothing to do with him. I wouldn't sleep with your son if you paid me. I hate him. He gives me the creeps. He's just a kid anyway. He's a virgin for all I know.'

Karen threw Ginny forward in contempt and the girl fell face first into the wet grass. She squealed.

'You've broken my neck, you old cow.'

'You've broken my heart, almost. Count yourself lucky I haven't broken every bone in your body in return. You thoughtless little swindler. What on earth do you think you've been playing at? You could have ruined everybody's lives. You selfish, selfish—'

'I didn't mean to. You said you would help me.'

'You stupid, stupid little girl.'

Ginny sobbed. Her boyfriend had a wry expression on his face.

'What's that in your glasses, Mrs?'

'It's a slug,' snapped Karen.

'A what?'

'It's a slug. A slimy little nasty moist thing like your slimy little nasty moist penis. Leave, you. Leave right now.'

'Ginny—'

'Leave!' screamed Karen. A light came on in the house next door and illuminated the corner of Karen's garden. She and Ginny instinctively stepped into the shadows. The young man turned on his heels and they heard his footsteps run off into the darkness. Ginny cried quietly.

'I used that Sister Verity's pregnancy prediction kit. Loada rubbish. I couldn't make head nor tail of it. I didn't make it up. Not the pregnant bit.'

'Maybe you didn't. But to drag Max into it?'

'I thought you could get Sister Verity to help me.'

'You wanted his money. You asked for his money. You demanded his money. You blackmailed us.'

'He told me about it. It's your fault.'

'My fault?'

'I couldn't believe it. I was terrified after I came to see you and then I saw Max and I realised you hadn't told him. I hadn't told my mother and you hadn't told your son.'

Karen's wine-bottle shoulders rose and slumped. She tutted.

'I thought you would help me. I thought you had the money to help me. I thought you would give me some money and tell me to go away to get rid of me . . . I don't know what I thought . . .'

Karen sighed. 'What's the use,' she said. She was at least relieved the baby issue had gone away and Max's money was safe. 'Go home Ginny. Go home to your mother. And take your knickers with you. Don't leave them on my lawn.'

'I haven't taken them off,' said Ginny defensively.

'Why are you with that horrible boy? He's just using you.'

'He loves me.'

'He doesn't love you. Men don't love you. They love football. They love beer. They love business. They don't love old bags like me and they don't love shag bags like you.'

Ginny's face caught the light from the next house. Karen saw how young and bewildered and lost and hurt she looked.

'Go home, Ginny. Go home to your mother. God knows why she allows you out at all hours of the day and night. I keep a firm rein on Max.'

'So where is he?'

Karen realised she had no idea. 'Never you mind.'

Ginny made to go but stopped. She spoke without turning round.

'I'm sorry for the trouble I've caused you.'

Karen said nothing.

'I know you don't believe me but I am. I won't see him again either. Bastard.'

'You have your whole life ahead of you, Ginny. I know you think I'm an ugly old witch who doesn't know anything, but try as hard as you can to believe me. You don't want to grow up too fast. Life can be fun. Life can be lovely. But it can also be a bigger bitch than I'll ever be. Stick with your family. Stick in at school. Stick up for yourself.'

Ginny turned around.

'Can I call Sister Verity tomorrow?'

Karen gave her an apologetic smile.

'Sister Verity ran away.'

Ginny look puzzled.

'I know,' said Karen. 'Me too. I don't understand it. Call me instead. Come round for tea. I'll make it in the pot.'

'Really?'

'Really. At least I'll know where you are.'

Ginny merged slowly into the blackness and Karen made for the door. She squinted at the lock. She realised she could not see through the slime on her left lense. She returned to the shrub and removed her glasses. She dabbed them onto a leaf several times until the little beige slug fell out into the night. With her glasses off she couldn't see exactly where.

'Slither away, little one,' she said softly. She felt sorry for it, the little slug. It wasn't its fault it was cast as one of nature's grubs in the garden. It was all part of the grand scheme of things and as far as Karen could see it was too tiny to pose a threat to her and too inconsequential to do her harm. Ginny Collins . . .

As she stood sad and alone and contemplating the slug and Ginny and the boy and Sister Verity and the half a million pounds and the new series and the order of the world in which they lived side by side, she heard the thump of footsteps on the pavement. She darted back into the shrubbery. It might be that young thug returning in revenge. But it was not. It was Max. Unseen, she watched him as he bombed up the path and into the house. He managed to close the door almost quietly.

'Oh, my precious baby,' she whispered and made to follow her son inside.

78

'Look at you. After all these years, still stuck in there looking back at me in black and white.' Hector pushed one half side of his navy blue velvet dressing-gown deep under the other and tautened the broad, tasselled belt. 'Well, what say you? Nothing, of course.'

He leant forward over the keyboard and picked up the silver framed photograph of his first wife from the lid of the Bernstein grand piano. Her cold, studio smile was frozen in time. He propped the portrait flat against the music stand and began to pick out a few notes of an old song. 'Play it again, Hector, eh? De di de di de di, de di de di de dee . . . The fundamental things apply-y-y as time goes by-y-y.'

He stopped playing and this time lifted his glass of Cragganmore from the piano. Around now, two o'clock in the morning, the night chill would seep into his bones.

'Is that our story?' he asked the photograph. 'Do the fundamental things still apply?' He drank deeply. His crystal beaker was filled to the brim. 'You made me so angry, Carol.' He swigged again. 'You made me so angry. You came all the way from Cardiff with me. You stood by my side, you put all your back into it, you took all the shit and then when you could have sat back and raked it in and lived the life of the lady muck you always aimed to be, you walked. Hah! Let me complete that sentence. You walked *out on me*. That I will never comprehend. I will never understand women, you said. I have known three wives and had three daughters so what could I possibly know about women? About as much as Lear. Probably you were right but you were not a woman. You were my friend. You were my partner. You were my wife. Business was not my life. Empire building was not my life. You were. But the minute you and I were on the cusp of all things great, you broke. You broke down. You let me down.' He took another gulp of scotch. 'Or did you? I don't know. All that fucking money I had to pay out for you to leave me and take Jackie with you. Half my worldly goods and, let's face it, the fabulously successful Hector and Carol Quigley were very worldly by that stage. Perhaps, then, you didn't let me down. You bled me dry. I like a fighter. I like spunk. Perhaps I should have expected it. You took me for what I had. I had always thought you would have flicked your hair that way you did and, with just a trace of lipstick and an upturn of your collar, would have fucked off quietly, decently, left me with Jackie. Funny how you think you know your own wife and daughter and you don't. But you see, you and I were never the same. Alike, but never the same. Oh, the same shit-start in life. The same crappy little hovel of a terraced home. The same outside toilet. Whatever happened to the outside toilet? One minute it defines and divides a nation, the next every damn bugger in town has their own vitreous enamel lavatory pan in fucking avocado to piss in. Should I blame socialism or conservatism for that grotesquery? Oh. Progress? I see. God help us. You know, when I was a boy I would don my coat and instead of saying, "I am going to spend a penny," which is what my aspiring mother hoped I would say, I would announce to all my aunties and suchlike, "I am just going to the country seat." I thought that was terribly amusing and much the finest euphemism. Eu-phrom-mism? No I'm from Albert Parade, boom boom! I was and am and always will be still from a back-to-back in South Wales no matter what SW the good City of Westminster sticks on the street signs of Belgravia. Carol. There is a name. One never meets a Carol now. They are all called Emma or Serena.

Well where's the money now, Carol? Spent is it? Invested in what? Oh deary me, how unfortunate. And whatshisface you married took some of it and fat-arsed off with it, did he? Better looking, I think you said he was, than me. Better looking. And is it better looking at the future now, Carol than at the past? Or is it worse? What does Jackie think, or are you still not talking? And you hurt me not. You knew me. Money is not my motivator. Power is. Advancement is. Social strata, entrance to it. I am not a kicker-in of doors. I wish to knock and be seen in and have a man take my coat. That's what made me tick. But you *did* know me. So perhaps the money thing was not meant to hurt. I've never worked that out. Do you remember, Carol, our first client? There was me all done up and sitting in their reception and they had the effrontery to send that ugly woman down to ask me if I would mind not wearing a pink shirt the next time, only they understood this time because I was from an advertising agency but not the next time. I took it then, Carol, because I had nothing. I only had you. We made it together. From Wales to Westminster. What a time. What a team.' He drained his glass and stood up. He toasted her goodbye with the empty glass. He padded over in his moccasins to the rococo drinks cabinet. He refilled his glass and knocked half back immediately. As he curved unsteadily around the nook of the piano his second wife caught his eye.

'Hello, my frail flower,' Hector whispered to her. He picked up the frame and gently puffed imaginary dust from the top. 'Is it heavenly in heaven or is it all too much to bear up there too?' He pulled the monochrome picture into the velvet of his gown, into his breast. 'Why oh why oh why, Tania? You wanted pearls and I draped you in diamonds. You wanted lace and I brought you furs. You wanted watercolours and I was out there bidding for oils. But you only had to say. I am not a tyrant. You only had to whisper in your dear Hector's ear. Perhaps you did. You were such a quiet little thing. A mouse's scurry of a girl. What life is it, to be a delicate thing? That sort of butterfly-wing fragility looks nice but touch it and you kill it. I only touched you, my angel, because you touched me. When I play now, it is the softness of your voice I hear la-la-ing behind my shoulder. So sweet and white and crisp your voice. Sugar it was. With the enhancement technology they have today I would have written a shampoo jingle for you and you would have sung it and it would have entered the culture, that sound.' It was the finest tribute Hector, Lord of the Jingle could pay her. He sighed. For a moment he recalled the fright of finding Nigel Gainsborough dead, or as good as, in the bunker at Wentworth. Then he thought of the anticlimax, of Marsha telling him that Nigel would live and that he had no memory of being struck on the head. Hector relived that moment of delicious, unbelievable, comic relief. Then he remembered instead Tania and the phone calls. The drama the first time. How that word had sped around the agency faster than he had followed the ambulance. Overdose. Truth travels fastest. It had got everywhere before he had got to the hospital and he had been doing ninety. He knew they had all been saying it behind his back, though he had let it be known he preferred 'collapse'. He was not ashamed. Why should he be? A wife does not try to kill herself because her husband who has much to give gives her everything. He was not ashamed, but he knew she would be and he was her protector so 'collapse' it was. He had filled their room with red red roses for her return. Or was that the second time? Then there was the year later. Then the rerun. Then the repeat. Then the final day. The word that did the rounds then was not 'overdose', it was 'again'. Hector could barely recall the dairy-based foods meeting that was more important than pacing a hospital corridor while your wife has her stomach pumped. Was it anyone's fault? Tania had called that bit more slowly. She had taken more but she had threatened less. The secretary was not so panicked. She had had three rounds of personal practice plus a precise briefing from her predecessor. They had all moved just that fraction slower. Tania. The hospital. The husband. 'It was the only thing you ever really pulled off,' mouthed Hector to the photograph. He remembered racing to the nursery in South Kensington to collect Alice and to lie to her and to bring her home. She had been only four then. He adored his daughter then because she was daddy's little princess and looked and acted like him. Later, with Tania buried, he was disappointed she took so little from her mother. He ran a huge finger across the non-reflective glass which sealed Tania in time. 'You bloomed and saw the sun and along came Hector and because he thought you were the loveliest of all the flowers in the field he picked you and took you home and placed you in his vase of water and accidently drowned you. I thought I could keep you for always,' and he pulled the brown cardboard prop out from the back of the picture and let it drop back. 'I thought I showed you love. I loved myself more? No. No, I do not subscribe to that theory. Funny how there are no photographs of us, Tania. Us together. Did you dispose of the lot? Some nights I still look through the old boxes to see. I have so many photographs of myself, with my family, with people I like, people I do not like, people I do not know, people I have no idea who the hell they are are. Category B celebrities and lord mayors and tombola people and old Tories and new Labour and Lord Callaghan of Cardiff and some fucking liberal demagogue or whatever that shower is called. But none with you, Tania. Gone, that's what you are.'

He raised his glass to his lips. It was empty once more. He laid the photograph of Tania back onto the piano beside that of his third wife. He dragged her from the top and took her to the bottle of Cragganmore and conversed with her while he emptied the dregs of it into his wet glass.

'What say you, Annabel? Jesus. You were hard work. Just hard, actually. Look at you. Even in soft focus and shot through twenty pairs of heavy duty gusset and all the vaseline Terence Donovan could smear on the lens and you still have the jaw of a fucking truck driver. Good in the sack, though. You were the best. Screwing you was like rowing for England. Enough to damn well near kill me but, oh what glory. Well, if you were trying to fuck me to death you damn well near succeeded. You killed me. You still do, every day. You and that girl. She's still my daughter too, you know. Remember that. Not your property, not your property at all. How old is she? Old enough to fail her degree and crash a Spider but not old enough to call her dad. What you two scheme up together egged on by your therapists beats me. Look at what I got from my father. A big fat nothing. Not as much as a lump of coal or a pot to piss in. Look at what I have given Portia. A start in life. The best school that money can buy. A home of her own that she can manage to make her way back to on the rare occasions she can't find anyone else's bed for the night. A fleet of unsuitable cars and unsuitable boyfriends she

seems quite capable of writing off faster than I can write out
the cheques to replace them. You are letting her, encouraging her, to squander her life. Revenge is not sweet, Annabel,
it is petty. And the revenge is not on me, it's on you and
Portia, can't you see that? And, Annabel, where is her fucking photograph? Did you half-inch it the last time you were
here?'

Hector searched the piano top for his third daughter but could
not see it. He fell into the yellow silk *chaise longue*. By the
lamplight there the shot of Annabel glowed in his hand. 'There
is something cheapening about colour photography. Strange.
The first two had taste and they had class but it was you who
had the upbringing. Brought up with horses, mind you. God
you were loud. Louder than me even. Those parties. Fun they
might have been had one not had the persistent feeling that half
the guests had had one's wife. The men *and* the women. A lot of
men would get off on that, you know. Not me. Straight as a die,
is old Hector Quigley. A bit too much aware of his skin tone and
his hair shade and his costume style, perhaps, but not a sexual
deviant. Never confuse the two things. But look at you, Annabel.
You had to be restrained from shagging every telegraph pole in
the Cotswolds. The working classes have always disapproved of
the sexual mores of the upper set and quite right too in my
opinion. I disagree with the working classes on everything but
that. How you hang onto Portia I shall never know. Because
she's sitting biding her time and waiting for her old man to
shuffle off and leave her all his money.' He wagged a finger at
the photograph. 'You've had as much as you're ever going to get,
either of you. There'll be a nice little shock in store for you when
they read out Hector Quigley's last will and testament. Try getting
the money off the Tania Quigley Trust for women of a nervous
disposition or whatever they end up calling it. Hah! Unless, of
couse, I am outlived by your successor. Yes I thought that would
surprise you. Hector Quigley is in love again. Again, if he ever
was before. Was he? I think he was, but who am I to judge. I am
at least in pursuit of a wife.' He thought out loud. 'I wonder if I
should call her.' From across the hall he heard the library clock
strike three. 'Perhaps not. Three o'clock. Three daughters. Three
wives. Three witches. Three stories. Three endings to three acts.

And barely three months until the curtain comes down on the whole damn show.'

79

Duncan had spent the day at one of the essential annual rituals of independent television production: the Channel Four/PACT Day held in the attractive surroundings of Regent's College at the heart of Regent's Park, the smartest in London. Hundreds of producers attend each year to hear those vital droplets of strategic wisdom fall from the lips of the commissioning editors structuring the schedules of the year to come. Misinterpret or, worse, miss the day itself and the following year is a barren one for the independent producer. Since the most repeated phrase from the platform was turning out to be, 'I don't want to be prescriptive,' Duncan, a trained reaper of information from his advertising days, left towards the end of the afternoon. He took the back exit from the college's Tuke Hall into the park.

It was a gorgeous autumnal October Wednesday. Duncan nonchalantly kicked his way through a drift of dried golden leaves on the path. It was a week and a half since *Face the Future* had gone on air. With Karen taking the helm on this one, Duncan was off the hook and free to get on with developing the next thing. Hence the day out. Once upon a time he would have felt guilty at sloping off early, but today he felt he had earned it. Ducks and geese and swans waddled amongst the tourists. He crossed the pretty little bridge over the pond and, apart from a bizarre moment staring nose to beak at a huge male swan, he was soon pounding down the Sherlock Holmes end of Baker Street and on his way.

He turned a few blocks down and wandered into the parallel Chiltern Street, with its little boutiques, including Julie Anne Bolton's *Re:Dress*! It was quiet here and there was nothing doing until, at the end of the road, the deafening siren of a London red fire engine blew out his eardrums as it rocketed from its grand early twentieth-century garage. He headed on until he reached the capital's busiest thoroughfare, Oxford Street. He doubled back towards Selfridges department store.

He had no intention of buying anything. Browsing. Touching. Picking up and criticising or standing back and admiring. Since he had entered the precarious world of TV he had kept his credit cards glued into his wallet. He just wanted to be inspired. Shops are great places to get ideas for TV. Themes, trends, storylines, presentation ideas, set design, the works. Retailing and television are similar in so many ways. A store *is* a TV station. It has goods for sale rather than programmes. It can choose to specialise in one area or it can provide variety. The question is how to lure the desired customer to visit your outlet in the first place. As difficult as getting that viewer to hit your button on the remote control. Duncan looked around. Selfridges knew how to get buttons pressed, that was for sure.

He ambled into the menswear department. When he had worked in advertising Duncan had bought his smartest clothes here. Classics in navy blue and black, casuals in the neutrals of stone, beige and khaki. These days he was still immaculately dressed, but less crisply so, with a softer silhouette. He followed a woman, who sashayed as she walked, into the men's underwear area, a semi-pornographic selection of eyebrow-raising styles of brand name undergear from around the world. What was it about underpants designers? There was a time when no one had heard of any. Now they had gone global. They had turned celebrities. They had become fêted. They had marched out of their private boxes and onto the world stage, trousers pulled down and hitherto undiscovered talents revealed. They had collectively entered an international commercial race of olympiad proportions in which they competed to elevate the male form to new heights. Or more correctly to elevate the scrotum and its tender contents to new heights with complexly engineered pouch tailoring while simultaneously racing up the back passage in an increasingly high percentage of form-asphyxiating lycra. It was debatable if they could reach any higher on both sides at the same time. Someone would go too far but you had to admire their chutzpah if not their jaw-dropping prices. The sashaying woman stopped at a stand and pulled out an Hom animal print thong and held it up in front of her. She was wearing sunglasses, which Duncan thought was just a trifle idiosyncratic in London in the autumn and indoors. She was wearing a small citrus suit. And she was carrying a vanity case.

Duncan ignored her. He was no longer the all-attention-to-detail wing commander of his management days. He was less of a perfectionist. Partly because it was not possible to be one, with Karen Myhill. Partly because it was not possible to be one in television anywhere. Partly because he was older and wiser and life no longer required to be played at that intensity anymore. There were better things to do with his spare time than prepare and plan and anticipate. Relaxing was an equally sound way of building strength to fight the battles ahead. Winding down was as essential as winding up.

He carried on into trunks. Now the woman in the little citrus suit was stretching out a pair of Calvin Klein grey striped shorts and putting her ringed hands inside the pouch. It seemed to Duncan peculiar that most men would allow their wives to buy their clothes for them, even those garments most intimate to them, particularly when they were not there. Duncan simply could not imagine buying clothes without trying them on and touching them and feeling them and looking in the mirror and comparing and contrasting them. To have your wife come back and dump them in a heap on the end of the bed saying 'There's your outfit for the next year,' seemed to Duncan like a very good reason for not being married and not being straight.

He followed the woman on into all-in-ones. There was something familiar about her. He had assumed she must be foreign. Why had he done that? Because she wore dark glasses? Because she was in a Central London department store? Because she was examining in detail the same underwear as him, which was obviously for sale only to gay boys or foreigners? After all, what straight, sensible, square, solid British bloke would wear a male body, a combination of T-shirt and testicle dividing knickers in one undergarment? This time, the woman pulled out on its hanger an Adonis stretch lycra number graced with a distinctive black-and-white piebald pattern. She held it up, dangling it against her own body. It was obscenely meanly cut, a hardcore dance aerobics go-go boy number by the looks of things. In her high stiletto shoes she clicked across to the mirror and posed in it. Duncan could just make out the reflection of her face but, with her heavy hairdo and Jackie Kennedy glasses he could decipher little about her. She did seem familiar. She *was* familiar. But it was surely an error on his part because he did not know her. Perhaps she was famous or had been once. There was something reminiscent about her. Her stance. Her gait. The tilt of her chin. The flick of her wrist. Duncan was first drawn to her but then retreated. He knew her not. He turned away and headed for socks.

'Duncan!'

He turned round sharply.

'I snatched sight of you over my shoulder. In the mirror.'

He knew that voice. He did know this woman but he could not think who it was. He back paced a couple of steps. A walking telephone directory with total recall, Duncan was embarrassed by his ignorance.

'Hello—'

'What are you doing in men's knickers, darling? Cruising around with a stonking big hard-on, no doubt.'

What an outrageous accusation. Worse, her voice carried. As far as the food hall, most likely.

'I beg your pardon?'

'Have you buggered off from the PACT day?'

'. . . Yes. . . . How did you know that?'

'You're carrying your brochure.'

'Oh yes.' Who the hell was she?

'I was there too. They say the same boring old thing year in year out. Don't write your propsal on more than two pages. It's like being back at kindergarten. Fancy a cappuccino on the mezzanine?'

Duncan was stumped. He still had no idea who she was. She was bloody strange whoever she was. She didn't seem to, well, fit together as a personality. He couldn't think why.

'I ought to be going.'

The woman held up the piebald all-in-one to her shoulders with one hand and with her vanity case in the other tugged down on the puffed-up crotch stretching it sensuously to the centre of her skirt.

'What do you think?'

'It looks like something from a porn film.'

'Divine. I could just munch my way through the between-the-legs bit.'

Duncan was wide-eyed. 'Who's it for?' He hoped it might give him a clue.

'Moi, of course.'

'It's for a man.'

The woman suddenly guffawed in a deep roar. She revealed a set of perfect, if prominent, upper teeth.

'You haven't twigged!'

'Er . . . no, I haven't.'

'Don't I seem familiar to you?'

'You do. But I can't think why.'

She roared again, delighted. 'It's me!' She whisked off her big shades. 'Paula.'

'Paula?' Staggered was simply not a strong enough term to describe Duncan's reaction. It was Paul McCarthy. In drag. In wig and glasses. In tights and nail varnish. In front of him. In Selfridges. In trouble, was how Duncan felt.

'Paula McCarthy. I'm getting in touch with my feminine side today.'

'*Jesus Christ*. You look ridiculous.' Duncan was aghast.

'Oh, God, he's off. All of Caledonia's righteousness condensed into one upright, uptight little Scotsman. I think I look very attractive, actually.'

'Your feet. Look at them.'

'It's impossible to get decent court shoes in eleven and a halfs. I had to go to one of those tranny places. I'm taking them back. They pinch worse than clothes pegs on your tits, I can tell you.'

A glamorous blonde shopper tried to slip past them.

'Excuse me,' she said as she pushed through. Duncan was convinced she was sniggering behind her hand.

'I'm getting in touch with my feminine side,' said Paul, again. Duncan began to back away. 'I got the message, thank you.'

'The caff's over this way.'

'I don't want coffee.'

'Oh, go on. It'll only take five minutes. I want to try out as many girlie things as possible. Girlies have coffee and confession with their mums when they go shopping. You be mum.'

'You piss off.'

'Duncan, you're to help me. I'm doing this because my therapist said I should.'

A camp little attendant with shiny slicked back hair and sporting a waistcoat flounced up beside them.

'Can I help madam with that. Is it for sir?'

Duncan realised it looked as if Paul or Paula was offering the minuscule aerobics outfit to him and he was rejecting it. Horribly for him, the salesman was going to close that sale.

'It's for my boyfriend,' said Paula. 'But he won't try it on. Perhaps you could persuade him.'

The attendant looked only too delighted to have a go. He battered his eyelashes at Duncan.

'The fitting rooms are over here, sir. You might like to try a tighter size.'

'It's barely big enough for a boy of twelve.'

'*Twelve*?' mugged Paula. 'You should be so lucky. Or did you mean years?'

He shrieked along with the attendant. Their hands flapped in formation.

'It stretches and moulds to your figure to show your body off in inch-by-inch detail,' said the salesman, sizing Duncan up and down.

'Inch by inch,' mocked Paula. 'Haven't you got one that does it by half-inches?'

Again they shrieked. Duncan's face was a mortified mixture of embarrassment and fury. He liked his body to be neither mocked nor referred to as his figure. Enough was enough.

'Come on, Paula, let's discuss it over a cappuccino, before I recommit you to the clinic,' and he dragged Paul up to the coffee bar on the mezzanine.

'The thing is,' said Paul licking the froth off the back of his spoon, ' – ooh look, my lipstick has come off on the cutlery – my therapist felt that with my whole thing about not penetrating I should see how I felt about the more feminine side of my nature. It wasn't her idea that I should dress up, of course, it was mine. I couldn't resist it. No one recognised me at PACT.'

'For God's sake! You didn't have that garb on in there, did you?'

'I have a change of clothes – and of gender – in my case, but actually I did go like this. I don't think they take women producers seriously, you know. I was dismissed more than once.'

'You don't look anything like a woman. You look like Arthur Mullard in lime.'

'Don't be cruel. It's how you feel inside that counts, not on the outside. That's the thing with penetration. One is a feeling on the outside, the other is on the inside. I'm more of an inside person.'

'I have no idea what you're burbling on about.'

'That's because you're so anal-brained, Duncan. You may wear your shirts out more these days but you're still a buttoned-up little queen inside.'

'I am not.'

'Haven't you ever done drag?'

'Of course not.'

'Well there you are. Speaks for itself, really.'

'Garbage. I don't have a gender identity crisis. I'm a man.'

'Hark. He's so butch.'

'I am butch.

'Balls. You love up-the-bum sex as much as the rest of us. Don't deny it.'

'Don't be crass.'

'Come out from behind your net curtains, Duncan.'

'I don't have net curtains.'

'You know what I mean. When were you last fisted in a sling on a Friday night?'

'Never. Paul, what you seem not to understand is there are straight people, gay people, bisexuals and you. The first three are normal, natural and conventional, and then there's you. An aberration.'

Paula looked as if she might cry. Her mascara moistened.

'That's so fucking typical. All you men are bastards.'

'For fuck's sake. You're a man too. Supposed to be.'

A tear ran into Paula's orangey brown tinted moisturiser. The waitress came to clear their cups away. She looked at Paula close up.

'You all right, love?' she asked. 'Is he giving you a hard time? Would you like me to fetch the store detective?'

'No thank you,' sniffed Paula. 'He's the brutal sort, my husband is.'

Duncan scowled. He looked heavenwards and ground his teeth.

When Duncan got home that evening he was tired. Behind the door of his basement flat lay a reminder of something he had forgotten about. He opened the envelope nervously. It was a request to return to the clinic for counselling and get the result of his HIV test. In all the fuss over Sister Verity, Duncan had pushed this to the back of his mind. That he had to be chased up irritated him. It irritated him a lot, but not as much as the prospect of the result worried him. He had to have this out with Michael and waiting for him to come back turned Duncan's happiness sour and ruffled his calm.

80

'I'm so glad I was able to drag you out of Selfridges.'

'Why, darling?'

'Because, Mummy, you are avoiding discussing with me what's going on.'

'What's that got to do with Selfridges?'

'I don't expect you to tell me your darkest secrets at the Godiva chocolate counter. Here, Mummy, you might just.'

Charlotte had skilfully detoured her mother off Oxford Street for an early evening drink in the quiet library of the Lanesborough Hotel on Hyde Park Corner. She intended to prise open her clam.

'It's not something one wants to discuss.' Morella was whispering.

'It's two weeks to the day that you told me you were living in the car, Mummy. That's two weeks too long that have passed. I need to know. I demand to know. Have you told any of your friends?'

Morella looked shocked. 'Of course not, darling.'

'You're worried they'll drop you from their bridge parties. Honestly, Mummy, I've been majorly concerned about you these last few weeks. You've virtually been living rough – cadging lunches off friends – freebie hunting in department stores. Next thing you'll be selling the *Big Issue*.'

'Don't exaggerate.'

'Have you seen Doctor Pendrake?'

'What on earth for? I'm not ill.'

'Are you sure?'

'Charlotte, I'm not ill. I'm sick with worry, that's all. I'm out of my mind with despair. But I'm not mentally imbalanced, if that's what you mean.'

'Moving out of your home and into your car and not telling anyone is not exactly normal behaviour, mother.'

'Don't call me mother.'

'Well you're making me cross. I'm trying to help you and you're rejecting me.'

'I'm not rejecting you.' Morella picked up a cashew nut. She didn't eat it. Instead she studied the panelling of the bar. 'It's all reproduction, isn't it?'

'You're changing the subject.' Charlotte swigged her vodka and tonic and waited for her mother.

'I'm just commenting. And don't drink so fast, it's not attractive in a young girl.' She reached out and ran her fingers along the dado rail of the pillar she had secreted herself behind. 'It's meant to look old but it lacks the patina of age. They might get away with it in California but not in London. We know fake when we see it.'

'We do, don't we? Perhaps you're having a nervous break-down. What *is* a nervous breakdown? Do you feel all weepy and can't go on-ish?'

Morella huffed. 'I'm *not* having a nervous breakdown.'

'You wouldn't know if you were.'

'*I* would. Look, it was a very rational thing to do in my opinion, moving into the car, while I get myself sorted out.'

'You can't sort yourself out in a car . . . Did he hit you?'

'No. . .'

'But . . . ?'

'I didn't say but.'

'No but you were going to.'

'You're so clever, aren't you? I hope you don't irritate your clients like this because they'll complain to that Hector man.'

'Hector Quigley thinks very highly of me.'

'I thought that thing with the nun had gone all wrong.'

'That wasn't my idea.'

'I told you not to get mixed up with tampons. Couldn't you do make-up or jewellery or something?'

'Don't be so old-fashioned and don't be so sexist and don't change the subject again. You're such an issue avoider, Mummy. You mustn't stifle this inside you or you'll grow inwardly bitter.'

'Amateur psychiatry will get you nowhere with me.'

'It's wrong, really wrong – not to mention out of date – to bottle up all your feelings and do the stiff upper lip bit and just lie back and think of the empire. I mean, women of your generation didn't do that anyway. Didn't they burn their bras and go on marches against Nam?'

'I hardly think so. We went to Pitman's and parties and wore pearls. I thought you were trying to be compassionate. Not critical.'

'You can be a real cold fish at times.'

Morella was visibly spiked by her daughter's remark.

'I'm sorry, Mummy. I didn't mean that.'

'You did.'

'I wasn't thinking.'

'I can see that. If you were thinking you'd have thought of

something nice to say but you didn't so the truth came out. It always does in the heat of the moment . . .' I *am* a cold fish, Charlotte, that's the truth. I don't like hugs and heartiness. I'm more the queen type than the Princess Diana type and I know which of those two I prefer. I don't intend to wash my dirty linen in public and I don't think they should either.'

'I'm not "public"—'

'I can't *stand* the let it all hang out society. Nobody respects anyone anymore. Dish, dish, dish that's all they all do. Well I'm fed up of it. And as for blabbing about my problems to other people, I won't.'

Charlotte spoke quietly. 'It's because you're ashamed of something. It's a black secret, the one you've got.'

'It's not *my* secret . . . This is your AIDS training coming out, I suppose.'

'No it's not.'

'It is. You girls all do that Diana compassion thing. I don't think it's sincere all that touchy feely kissie kissie stuff. So don't do it on me.'

'I'm not *doing* anything. Mummy, I'm your daughter. I'm supposed to care about you. What is it that's so terrible that you can't tell even me?'

'It's . . . no, I can't.'

'You can. It's something sexual, isn't it? That's why you won't tell me. I'm twenty-seven in two weeks, mother. I'm not a virgin, you know.'

'Well don't shout about it at the top of your voice in the middle of the Lanesborough Hotel. It's nothing to be proud of.'

'I'd kill myself if I was twenty-seven and still a virgin.'

Morella sighed. Charlotte laughed disbelievingly.

'Mummy, I can't believe you lived through the Swinging Sixties.'

'The sixties were very silly, not to say bloody boring. God knows they were. I married your father.'

'Don't let's talk about Daddy. You know we won't agree. Let's talk Tony.'

'I don't want to talk about him.'

'Did he hit you?'

'No . . . not me.'

• Douglas Chirnside

Charlotte was puzzled. 'Not you? He hit somebody else? Who?'

Morella looked miserable.

'Is he violent?'

'That's not the word for it.'

'Is he having an affair?'

'Yes. No. That's not the word either.'

'Is it something to do with a patient?'

'Not a patient. At least I don't think so.'

'His assistant? His receptionist?'

'It's nothing to do with them. They hardly see him. He's always away in the States or at that place in Switzerland, thank God. Then I can be alone in the house. But I can't be in the house by myself or with him either.'

'Why not?'

'Because of what's there.'

'In the house? What's in the house?'

'That . . . place.'

'What place? . . . What place? Tell me, Mummy, tell me.'

'I can't.'

'You've got to.'

'I can't.'

'You've got to. Look I'm taking you home right now and you're going to show me what it is you're talking about.'

'Absolutely not.'

'I'm coming with you. We'll get a taxi.'

'No.'

'I'll pay.'

'I can't!' Suddenly Morella was weeping. She broke down. Her humiliation was hidden only by the panelled pillar. 'I should never have married him! I'm trapped by my own breeding and cursed by my own vanity!' She composed herself. 'You go. You go on your own.' She fumbled in her hand bag. 'Here's the key.'

'You have to come with me.'

'Don't worry. Tony won't be there.'

'And what do I do? Look around the house? I don't know what I'm meant to be looking for.'

'Look . . .' Whatever it was, Morella was scared of it.

'Where? Where have I to look?'
'Under the stairs. Look in the cupboard under the stairs.'
She broke down again. Charlotte felt frightened.

81

Once the dome of St Paul's Cathedral was the largest in the world. It impressed because of its size. It *was* London. Then, in the last fifty years, Wren's great monument had been lost to the eye. It was built around densely and dwarfed by ugly office blocks. It became something you had to discover. It impressed because it was tucked away and you stumbled upon it, half-hidden around a corner. But now, at the turn of a new century the grand old lady in her bell skirt hailed once more, this time across the Thames to the other side of the water. As the fortunes of the river had waxed and waned and waxed again, on the south bank old buildings had been restored and revitalised. One was the Oxo building, whose thin brick tower now topped a dazzling restaurant and whose riverside windows afforded new glimpses of the City. The dome of St Paul's could be seen afresh. Now it impressed because of its elegance, because of its period, because it had survived. Now it shone because its diamond white stonework was brilliantly illuminated at night. This was the view of which Serena Sark dreamt on her way to share dinner with her partner Nigel Gainsborough.

'Sorry, love. Been a long day. Remind me where we're headed.' The cabbie threw his excuse cheerily over his shoulder into the back of the cab.

Serena smarted. 'I'm not your love so don't call me that,' she said shrilly.

''Scuse me, darlin'.'

'I'm not your darling either. Call me madam.'

'Call you bleedin' Ethel Merman if you're not careful,' muttered the cabbie under the motory chug of the taxi.

'Really, I can't think why you'd forget. It's just one simple thing to remember. The Oxo Tower Restaurant. It's much in demand.'

'Be there in five minutes.'

'Good.'

'I can't drive you all the way in though, love, there being building works in the area. I'll get you as near as I can, though.'

'Do that, please.'

Serena smiled in the dark. Tonight she was filled with fantasies of the future. She felt flushed with success. She had news for Nigel and they would toast each other over champagne. A *tête-à-tête* tonight. Tomorrow, or at least quite soon, they would be the toast of London. She had pulled it off with only a bit of help from Hector and none from Nigel. Still, he had been out of touch these last two weeks, off recuperating. Wheeler-dealering was not his forte. It had been wiser to go it alone. She had saved her sensational story for candlelight, the glistening Thames and the starlit views of St Paul's.

She peered into her lap. She had not been able to decide what to wear. Smart or glamorous, long or short, black or bright? Harvey Nichols these days seemed to have only brown. Brown was the new black, apparently. But brown was simply ghastly. Who was going to attend Christmas cocktails in their little *brown* dress? No one she knew. When the cabbie had turned up she had been wondering whether to don the little citrus suit or the little black dress. Both were special. In the end Alec had suggested a marvellous compromise. Wear the dress with the jacket of the suit over it. She felt fabulous. She had every reason to feel fabulous. When this news got out she would literally be fabulous, fabled in her profession.

'This is as near as I can get you.'

'You can't get closer? That's terrible. It's on account.'

They were one road back from the riverside walk leading to her destination. The red neon-lit Oxo windows loomed above. She jumped out. She walked briskly through a small park to the pedestrianised embankment. It was chilly there by the water and she hurried on. She touched her diamond ear clips. There they were, hard in place. She touched her dyed, jet-black hair. There it was, also hard in place. She arrived and entered the building. It was disapppointingly anonymous at ground level and taken up by offices. The place was deserted. With difficulty she found the plainly functional steel lift at the back and pressed the button for the eighth floor. She disembarked at the top. It was all modern. Too much bare glass and low leather bucket chairs in her opinion. She did acknowledge, however, that the deep blue ceiling of louvred sails sweeping overhead in a convex curve towards the panorama of the Thames was a great piece of drama. A handsome young man led her to her table and a river view.

Through the big glass panes the dome of St Pauls was reflected in the dark black water of the Thames. But that was not what brought Serena to a dead stop. Nor was it Nigel, sitting plumply and prodding a gherkin with a cocktail stick. Nor was it the bruise on his forehead, still yellow-purple around the edges. No. It was what was beside him. It was the last thing Serena wanted to see tonight or any other night. It was Tricia. It was Nigel's wife. It was Mrs Nigel Gainsborough. Serena's evening was destroyed before it had even begun. Nigel wiggled his fat fingers at her. Tricia smiled thinly.

She came over and took her seat opposite them. Nigel avoided her gaze and she avoided Tricia's. Tricia spoke.

'It's quite clever the way they sit you sideways so both sides can see the river. Solves disputes. I'd have resented giving up my view for you.'

Serena smiled. It was a cold smile. It was a frigid smile. It was the light coming on when the fridge is opened. Automatic, utilitarian, functional.

'I thought it was business partners. Not domestic ones. I'd have brought my husband if I'd known.'

'Nigel thought that I should come,' said Tricia.

'I thought we were going to talk business,' said Serena.

'I see so little of my husband, Serena. You work him so hard. Nigel has something to tell you and I thought it would be appropriate if I was here too. He's only been out of hospital for a week.' She raised her eyebrows. 'The waiter.'

Serena sensed the handsome young man at her elbow.

'Would madam care for an aperitif?'

Serena surveyed the table. 'You're on champagne.'

'He is. I'm having Kir Royale.'

Serena thought Kir Royale was common. 'I'll have champagne too, please.' She decided there and then to file her fabulous story for the future. Nigel would have to wait to hear her news. She couldn't have Tricia Gainsborough gossiping it all over Chelsea. Nothing was signed yet anyway.

The waiter brought Serena's champagne and they admired the views. They discussed the menu. They waited to order.

'I think we should tell her now,' said Tricia.

Her. Serena hated being called her. She glowered at Nigel.

'Nigel. What is it? You're keeping something from me.' She was keeping something from him but she was furious he was in cahoots with his wife and they weren't telling her.

'It's . . . er . . . not really, old girl.'

'Is it something to do with your yacht?'

'No,' said Tricia,

'You're moving house?'

'No.'

'You're selling your cottage?'

'No. Nigel, tell her.'

'Her.' Again. She hated the 'her' and she hated the her who was saying it.

'Well you know things have been a bit rough this last year with the staff problems and not much new business—'

'I'm on to all of that. I have news for you.'

'Oh really? What?'

'Can't say tonight, Nigel. Confidential.'

'Nigel tells me everything.'

'He may do, but I don't. Go on, tell me your news.'

'Well, I've been saying to myself recently, really, what's it all about?'

'What's what all about?'

'Life, old girl. The job. The career. The strain of it all. Since Hector Quigley nearly bashed me brains out I've been trying to get it all into focus.'

'Do you know, Serena, that Hector didn't visit Nigel in hospital once?'

'He's very busy,' replied Serena defensively.

'It was his fault.'

'He did send flowers,' said Nigel.

'You mean one of his lackeys sent flowers.'

'And a card. It's the thought that counts.'

'He could have killed you.' Tricia took a viscious sip of her Kir Royale.

'I know. That, Serena, is what set me thinking. One of the big boys paid a visit to my bedside. We did it on the quiet.'

'What big boys? Did what on the quiet?'

'One of the holding board.'

Serena shivered. News sprung on her was news she did not like. She wished she and Nigel had co-ordinated.

'Who?'

'Well . . . well . . . I don't . . . I mean . . .'

'Nigel is taking early retirement. At the end of the year.'

'He's on two years' notice. Like me.'

'MCN have made him an offer.'

Serena sat stunned, stupefied and silent. He could at least have got the words out himself. Then again perhaps not. She looked blankly at Tricia.

'I think you know my father died last April. Well, I'm an only daughter. My mother died many years ago. My father was quite wealthy and that's all sorted out now and we know exactly where we are and really there isn't any need for Nigel to go on working. He's got his final instalment coming out of MCN for the purchase of Clancey and Bennett on the thirty-first of December. Well you know that because you'll get yours too then. So that's it. The compulsory part of the MCN C&B merger deal will have been completed and Nigel will be free of those obligations. There's just the question of the notice and that's all been smoothed over too. And, the thing is, Serena, I know you've put what heart you have into it, but that wee agency within an agency thing is just not the same as the old Clancey and Bennett. Nigel's had enough, basically. I thought we might invest in a small hotel on the continent somewhere. Portugal.'

Nigel shook his head. 'Never trust a nation with green in their flag.'

'Well somewhere, darling. Get someone to run it for us. The thing is Serena, when I had Nigel all to myself at the hospital I realised that you get to see him more than I do and I don't want to have the best years of my marriage when I'm pushing seventy. He feels like *our* partner.' She gave a little gnashing laugh. 'Well he's not. He's *my* partner.'

Serena wasn't listening. She was looking at Nigel. Betrayal was what she smelled. Treason. Just at the moment when she needed him most he was abandoning her. Dumped like an old rag. After all these years. Put up to it by his wife. After all they'd been through together. After the ups, the downs, the fightback and now . . . the triumph? It no longer felt like it was going to be a triumph.

Serena sneered at Tricia. She watched her lips move but heard none of her words. She had put her on mute. Nigel was shrouded in the skirts of his wife. He was turning down the biggest opportunity of his career and didn't know it.

'What is madam having?' asked the waiter.

Serena looked up from her menu and glared. 'I'm having cold soup,' she replied.

'Awfully sorry, old girl,' said Nigel. He went to pat her arm but withdrew at one look from his wife.

82

'Wednesday night is footie night.'

'I'm a girl. I don't know these things.'

'I was just sitting down with Bonzo to watch Chelsea play Arsenal.'

'I'm so pleased you're here,' Charlotte gave Daniel a peck on the cheek. He carried on regardless.

'He'd got a six-pack in. You have no idea how rare an occurrence that is. That's what I'm missing.'

'I'm sorry, Daniel. I'm probably just being stupid. I was a bit frightened on my own. I didn't realise it would be this dark. I wish I'd waited until tomorrow now.'

'Now she tells me. What are you frightened of?'

'I don't know.'

'You birds are dead peculiar, you know that?'

'I'll explain once we're inside.'

'Inside where?'

'Here. It's my mother's house. Well, actually, it's her husband's house.'

'Whoah. Not short of a bob or two, are they?'

'Appearances can be deceptive.'

'Rich people always make excuses for their money. If I were rich like that I'd say, "Look at the fucking dosh, mate. Jealous or what?"'

'Stop it. It's not my money. It's not my mother's either. She lost all hers.'

'Is that why she married him?'

Charlottte stopped at the door and thought for a second. 'D'you know, I hadn't thought about it, but that probably had something to do with it. Relationships based on money never work.'

'Ours does. When do I get my monthly allowance?'

'Be serious.'

'Why?'

'I don't know why. Just stop ribbing me for one second, will you?' She put the mortice key in the lower lock and turned it twice as her mother had told her. Then she took the Yale key and inserted it into the upper lock. 'Here goes.'

She pushed open the door. She stood inside the dark hall and flicked back her hair. Suddenly she started. She seemed startled. A look of panic shot across her face. She almost screamed. '*Quickly*!'

Daniel jumped in fright. '*What? What?*'

But Charlotte had nipped behind the door. She pumped four numbers into a little box there. 'It's the burglar alarm,' she said apologetically, popping her head back round. 'I forgot I had to switch it off.'

'Jesus. You nearly made me dump standing up.' Charlotte switched on the hall lights.

'Nice pad.'

'If you like that sort of thing.'

'I do. Any beer?'

'I shouldn't have thought so.'

They searched the ground floor. The big double reception room. The hall. The conservatory. The toilet. The dining room.

'What are we looking for?' asked Daniel.

'I don't know exactly. It's not in here.'

'Look at this.'

'What?'

'This cupboard. It's built in. Must have cost a fortune.'

'Open it.'

'What's in it?'

'Look.'

Daniel opened one of the paired doors. 'My God. It's a miniature lift.'

'It's a dumb waiter. It goes down to the kitchen. Tony had a zillion little touches put in when he first bought the house. When they have dinner guests, the caterer sends all the food up that way. The other side is a fridge.'

'Beer.' Daniel opened it up. 'Yup. Christ. Kaliber. Good sense of humour your dad has.'

'He's not my father. He's my stepfather.'

'Oh yeah. What does he do?'

'He's a cosmetic surgeon.'

'Really?'

'Yes.'

'So we all know what you're getting for Christmas.'

'What?'

'Bigger tits.'

'Don't be vulgar.'

'My own little Pammy.'

'I wouldn't want to look like her in a million years. They look like balls stuck under her chin.'

'I wouldn't mind getting my balls stuck under her chin.' He pulled the ring on the can. 'Might as well. Do you have a bedroom here?'

'Daniel!' Charlotte was cross. 'This is not my home. Why do you always have sex on the brain?'

'Because I have rocks which I need to get off.'

'Well keep your rocks on for the moment. Daniel . . . ?'

He sipped his non-alcoholic beer and made a face. 'At least it's cold.'

'Daniel . . . ?'

'What?' He sounded irritated.

'I want you to look in the cupboard under the stairs.'

'What for?'

'My mother said something about it.'

'She asked you to ask me to look in the cupboard under the stairs?'

'No. She didn't. Look. I don't want to go into details but if you meet my mother in the future don't tell her I asked you to come here today, OK?'

'You've lost me. This is about as clear as your Verity TV strategy.'

'Don't be cruel. You're here as a friend not as an account manager.'

'Account damager.'

'Come on. We'll go together.'

Daniel gulped down some more beer and wiped his mouth with the back of his hand. He followed Charlotte to the hall. She stood by a painted panelled door under the high rising staircase. She itched with nervousness.

'What's up?'

'I don't know. My mother said if I looked in here I'd understand what her problem was.'

'Don't tell me. She's got a broken light on her Hoover.'

'Be serious. Look, if I open the door you stick your head in quickly and see what's there.'

'See what's there? OK, boss lady. If you say so. Get a move on.'

Gingerly, Charlotte pulled opened the door to the cupboard under the stairs. She felt uneasy. The interior cavern was huge and black. In the foreground was indeed a vacuum cleaner. Daniel craned. He could not see further. He stooped and crept inside. Charlotte stood in the hall, her stomach churning. She heard his shoes scrape on the dust. Then silence. Then nothing. Then her emotions erupted at a terrifying sound.

'*Aaaaagh*!' His sick-making scream echoed in the interior.

Her nerve snapped. She screamed back. '*Aaaaagh*!'

Daniel's head popped out sideways. His face was bright red. He was grinning. 'Fooled yah!' His grin turned into laughter.

'You bastard. You know I'm on edge!'

'Tee hee. Is there a light? I can't believe this thing is so big and there's no light. They've got every other mod con.'

'It's a big house but it's old. It probably needs rewiring.' She felt more relaxed now. Daniel was funny.

'Got a match?'

'I don't smoke. Neither does Mummy or Tony.'

'Me neither. Oh well, eat your heart out Indiana Jones.'

Daniel stooped over again and inched his way back into the cupboard. Charlotte stood alone in the hall. She waited until she could no longer hear him fumbling about in the dark. She became aware of the ticking of the grandfather clock. She continued to wait. She felt cold. She felt uneasy again. Daniel had been gone for ages.

'Daniel.' She said it softly.

'Daniel.' She whispered it into the empty space. Silence.

'Daniel.' She said it louder this time but still there was no reply. She was frightened again. She didn't want to go in after him. She knew he was playing a trick. But she was hating standing alone and exposed and unsure in the hall. She breathed in, ducked and dived into the darkness. She could see nothing. It was pitch black. Her thigh pressed against the vacuum cleaner. She dragged one hand across a dusty shelf which turned out to be the step of a ladder. Her other hand felt paint tins lined up to her right.

'Daniel.'

She expected him to jump on her in the dark. She wished he would hurry and do it and get it over and done with. She was trembling in anticipation. She was ready to scream and then have her jitters turn to laughter. But he didn't leap out. Instead she heard a click in front of her. A rectangle of artificial light lit up. Daniel's head was silhouetted against it.

'What . . . ?'

'You'd better come in here. I think your Mummy has a kinky streak.'

Intrigued more than she could ever have imagined, Charlotte

stumbled forward in the gloom and came to what she took for a small door where Daniel stood. He was lower down than her. She fell forward into his arms with enough force to slip between them and land on a floor about four feet below the level she had been on.

'Ow!' She was in pain.

'Whoops. I forgot to say be careful. There's two or three steps.'

'Thanks for warning me after the event. I think I've broken my ankle.'

'Well you've come to the right place.'

Charlotte sat up and looked around. They were in a small room of black shadows and steel bars and straps and hooks suspended from the ceiling. It was lit by a single infra-red light bulb.

'It's a secret room.'

'It wasn't just a dumb waiter your dad had built in.'

'He's not my father.'

'I keep forgetting.'

'What are those steel things on the wall?'

'D'you not know what this place is?'

'It smells. Is it a darkroom?'

'It's a playroom.'

'A playroom?'

'It's an S and M chamber.'

Charlotte gasped. Her hand shot to her mouth. 'You're joking.'

'It's a dungeon.'

'It's sick. How do *you* know?'

'I get Channel Four, don't I?'

'What's that?'

'A sling. Look there are hooks above it in the ceiling.'

'What do you do?'

'Climb in and I'll show you.'

'*Don't*! God. Yuk. The bastard. The dirty beast. No wonder Mummy couldn't bear to spend another night in the house. Daniel, I want out. Take me out.' She tried to stand up. 'Ow. My ankle hurts like hell.' She rubbed it then made for the door.

'Hey, Charlotte . . .'

'Yes?' She was concerned at the tone in his voice. She looked back but in the gloom she couldn't see his expression.

'You know what really goes on down here?'

'I can use my imagination. I'm trying not to, actually. How could he be into this sort of thing? It must have been a shock for poor Mummy. Do you think he still uses it?'

'Yup.'

'How can you tell?'

'There's a pile of magazines over here. They're quite recent.'

'He doesn't do anything with Mummy. I mean, I don't think they have sex. I don't think she's had sex for aeons. I can't imagine her and Tony doing it.'

'I can't either.'

'You don't know them. You've never met either of them.'

'I don't need to. Look.' He held up a magazine.

'I can't see it. It's just a black square in front of the light.'

'It's called *Spurt*. It's a male contact magazine.'

'What do you mean?'

'I mean unless your Mummy grows a big penis pretty quickly she's probably not got what your stepfather's looking for.'

Charlotte was absolutely stunned. 'Oh no. Oh no. Oh no. Poor Mummy.'

'I think your stepfather is a bit of an old sicko.'

'I think he's a bit of an old bastard. He's a shit. Come on, Daniel, please, let's go.'

'Sure. I'm having these handcuffs.'

'Daniel! You can't steal them. They're Tony's.'

He ignored her and raked around on a shelf. 'Eargh. Vomit.'

'What have you found?'

'An inflatable.'

'An inflatable what?'

'Exactly. An inflatable what. It's for opening up your back passage. For fisting.'

Charlotte's stomach turned. 'Jesus. That's sick.'

'Oh, I don't know . . .'

'Daniel! Come on. Please. I'll buy you a cappuccino.'

'Of course. I like my coffee like I like my victims. Whipped.'

Charlotte barely smiled. The whole episode was sordid and shocking. For the first time in ages she had no comeback line. And for the first time in ages her thoughts were not for herself. They were for her mother.

'Poor Mummy,' she said again.

83

'Martin! I thought you were never coming back from New York.'

Michael Farnham walked across the architectonic atrium of The Station. On a concrete wall a bank of steel-encased widescreen TVs was bolted onto exposed scaffolding. On-screen a family of four was running round a studio under stroboscopic lights to much hilarity from an audience who appeared to be trying to stop them doing something. The sound was turned off so it was impossible to detect what it was all about. Typical TV executives, neither man was interested in what his channel was broadcasting. On-air programmes are last year's work and these two felt that they had much to be concerned with for their future. Michael caught up with Martin as the head of programmes swiped the security turnstiles allowing access to the viewing lifts which shot up and down on either side of the building.

'You look glum. Got the old heave-ho then?'

Martin tutted. 'If you must know I've flown straight in on Concorde and I've no fucking idea what day it is.'

'Thursday. Give you a hard time did they?'

'Yes.'

'Oh.'

They waited at the base of the tube which carried the lifts.

'Yup. Wined and dined and clubbed and partied and bloody well socialised until the wee hours of the morning three days in a row. Then my wife joined me,' Martin pressed the button for the second floor. 'She rarely gets out of the City these days except on a trip to Wall Street. This is the first long weekend we've had together.'

'Long weekend! You've been away for whole week.'

'Michael, I am married to a monster. Bloomingdales, Tiffany's, Barney's, God knows bloody where. I have learnt the meaning of shop till you drop.'

'I've no idea what you're talking about, Martin.'

'You're not married. You wouldn't know about death by shopping.'

'I'm gay, Martin. I live death by shopping. We all thought you were going to get fired.'

Martin bulged his eyes in mock complaint. 'Don't sound so disappointed, you old bugger.'

'I'm not.'

'You are. You were all set to have a good gloat. The CEO sends you his love.'

'I didn't think they'd heard of me in New York.'

'They haven't. I lied.'

The lift arrived. The curved perspex doors parted and a young woman emerged in a tight lycra skirt and clinging angora top cut away at the waist to reveal her midriff and a pierced navel. As she trotted off towards reception Martin held his finger on the lift button, devouring her rear view.

'Now wouldn't you mind a piece of that?' he asked.

'No,' said Michael, matter of factly. 'Why don't the boys round here dress like that? In cutaway T-shirts.'

'You're sick,' said Martin. The lift shot upwards.

'You're being very politically incorrect today, Martin.'

'I'm knackered. And I'm not the head of programmes at fucking Channel Four so I don't have to be. Hhhhg.' As the lift crashed to a stop and their insides continued alarmingly upwards for that crucial extra stomach–churning second, Michael thought Martin was about to heave. He didn't. They got out and walked down the corridor to Martin's office.

'Get us two coffees,' he said to his secretary without as much as a hello. She looked frightened and caught Michael's eye. Behind Martin's back he gave her the thumbs up and she grinned and departed to get the caffeine injections.

Inside the office Martin dropped onto the settee and kicked his shoes off. 'Jesus Christ, why is it that your feet swell up so much on planes?'

'I don't know. It's normally my penis that swells up when *I'm* airborne.'

'Wheesht. I was with my wife and I don't want any of your sordid mile-high club stories. I shouldn't have thought that was Duncan's thing.'

'It's not. But then he doesn't feature in any of them! I thought you might have told your secretary you've survived the axe. She's been worried sick.'

'And spoil my fun. It's not her place to speculate about my position.'

'Like the rest of us, she was concerned.'

'I'm not responsible for your pay rise, Mr Farnham, so you can hold back with the faux compliments.'

'God, you're prickly this morning.'

'Oh morning, is it. I wondered what time of day it was.'

The door burst open and Briony burst in. Her mop of barley sugar hair flew behind her and then crashed into place on the top of her head. Pale of face, she peered through eyes lined in fluorescent blue mascara.

'Martin. You're back. What happened?'

'She's supposed to be making coffees. I suppose she ran straight round to you to tell you I was here.'

'She's my spy. How do you think I get anything done around here?'

'I didn't know that you did.'

'Martin! So what happened?'

'Sit down. Join the club.'

Briony perched on the arm of the settee. The secretary came in with three mugs of steaming coffee boiled to an inferno in the microwave. She left and Martin told them his news.

'Well the chaps in America are delighted with our performance. While we've been concentrating on minutiae like being fined for breaking the rules they've been looking at the big picture. That's the Yanks for you. That's why they're so successful. Britain is only a test market for them. They don't give a flying fuck about sponsorship regulations over here because we're about the only country that is tied up in the red tape of

• Douglas Chirnside

public service broadcasting. No. The main thing is they wanted to congratulate me on the mix of programmes and the use of interactive TV. We've cracked the formula over here and now they can launch it in the rest of Europe next year and in the States the year after.'

'But they flew you over at short notice.'

'It was their idea of a joke. My wife was in on it. They felt that because I'm a boring Brit I'd have no sense of humour and not want to go to their little party. I've turned down the last few invitations. They did a little award ceremony and . . . you know . . . It was just me and the chief executive.'

'That's unfair. I suppose they didn't invite me because I'm a woman. Marketing is half the success story of our launch year.'

'Send them a postcard then, Briony. I didn't know what they were up to.'

'So what about the fine?' asked Michael.

'A little local difficulty. But as you know, Karen Myhill has the funds – from what I shall term the the receipts of the programme – to meet anything they throw at us. She'll probably have change left over. If we get censured we'll broadcast an apology and it'll be in the papers. But the tabloids will tuck it away and those who read the qualiities don't watch cable TV so we'll survive. Anyone seen Sister Verity yet?'

'No,' said Michael. 'And we're not looking for her either.'

'How is *Face the Future* doing?'

'It's doing just great,' said Briony, 'all things considered. Bearing in mind you abandoned us on its fourth day on air.'

'I'm the head of programmes not the bloody hands-on producer. And I had good reason to go, as well you know. Anyway, we have all those soothsayers in our employ and not one of them was predicting disaster when I left.'

Michael laughed. 'I'm just working out the legal implications of viewers acting on advice given to them by old hags poking into chicken entrails.'

'I know Karen is The Most Difficult Woman In Television but there's no cause to get personal about her,' said Martin. They laughed again. 'Anyhow, what makes you think they're chicken entrails? I would have thought she'd be sifting through the guts of one Jamie Hirst.'

'What are we going to do about Jamie?' asked Briony. 'When is he going to get his comeuppance?'

Martin laughed. 'Don't worry about Jamie,' he said. 'I'll take care of him. It's just an idea I had on the plane but I rather fancied the editorial line on *Megabrek* was slipping. Slipping like a noose around his own neck. I think I might have to put the show out to early tender in the New Year. See if Jamie can handle a bit of unwelcome competition.'

'Nasty, nasty, ' said Michael.

'Too right.' Martin grinned. 'I didn't get to the top of the greasy pole without kicking a few others off on the way up and I'm still in good shape as young Jamie Hirst is going to discover. How about lunch?'

'It's not even nine-thirty,' said Briony.

'Isn't it? I haven't been to bed for three days. Well fuck it. There must be somewhere that does an all-day breakfast round here.'

'In King's Cross Station. Its very greasy. Like your pole.'

'Briony, leave my pole out of it. The Station to the station! And that's an executive order.'

84

'*Attention everyone. I repeat. Attention everyone.*'

Charlotte looked up at the sound of the disembodied female voice.

'What in God's name is that awful noise?'

'The tannoy,' replied Dan. 'I thought they'd stopped using it.'

'*All staff to Meeting Room One in five minutes. I repeat. All staff to Meeting Room One for an announcement by the chairman.*'

'God.' She faked concern. Charlotte was secretly thrilled there was to be some excitement to interrupt the writing of yet another presentation justifying the Verity advertising strategy. 'God, Daniel what can it be?' She was bristling with anticipation.

'No idea. Something big.' Daniel had goose-pimples.

'Has he done this before?'

'Before they introduced hot-desking and mobile phones they used the tannoy to track people down. I didn't realise they hadn't deactivated it.'

'I meant make an announcement.'

'When the last deputy chairman and financial director walked out and buggered up Hecka's plans for going global he did it then to put a three-line whip on the gossips. But no. I think it's something momentous.'

'We're all getting fired simultaneously.'

'Three hundred and forty-nine people? Nah. Come on.'

'I don't want to be first there.'

'Don't worry. Those of us in the Satellite will be last over.'

They took the stairs and in reception caught up with a silent stream of employees. They filed from Seymour Place into Old Marylebone Road. They poured through the revolving door, over the 'Good morning. Thursday.' mat, into the yellow reception area, across the atrium floor, past the cappuccino bar and towards the corridor which held HQ's principal meeting rooms. The door of Meeting Room One was open. On either side stood the two big-haired receptionists, each accompanied by a waitress holding a silver tray decked with glasses of champagne. The receptionists wished each person a cheery good morning and handed them a flute of bubbly.

'Air hostesses,' said Charlotte under her breath.

'Don't be cynical,' said Dan. 'Champagne means something to celebrate.'

Inside it was clear why Hector had called the meeting in the main building and not in the theatre. Charlotte had not realised before just how many employees there were, but once you saw them all together you realised how big the company was. The corridor of meeting rooms had moveable partition walls and these had been pulled back to create a hangar-sized space. There was a dais at the far end on which stood a low table draped in yellow silk and sporting a huge yellow vase of yellow roses. Daniel wormed his way into the crowd and with calls of 'Hi matey' was off in search of his chums. Charlotte studied her colleagues. She didn't know who everybody was. She felt like an outsider. Perhaps it was because she was young to be an account director and didn't fit the friendship bands of managers or directors. Perhaps it was because she had only the one account and hadn't worked across enough business yet to mix. Perhaps it was because she was based in the Satellite and the main building boys looked down on her. Perhaps it was because she'd been concentrating on Sister Verity and on her domestic problems with her mother's marriage. Perhaps it was because she just didn't fit in and didn't much care for these people.

'Good-morning-good-morning-good-morning-good-morning-good-*morning*!'

It was Hector. Cheery chortles tripped off his tongue like tap-dancing six-legged insects. His audience buzzed. Their leader was amongst his people, working the populace of his magic kingdom like Teddy Roosevelt running for office. The citizens rippled and parted as the Red Sea did for Moses and the prophet crossed through. Powerful, potent, piggy-eyed, he was in full flashy regalia this heady day. His immaculate three-piece pale yellow suit. His matching shirt and tie combination of powder pink and baby blue broad stripes. His white cuffs sticking out like down pipes and his gigantic cufflinks, the Roman sundial, the Spanish doubloon. His huge hands. Adorned with rings, they patted backs and stretched out and ahead, possibly to be kissed if not simply shaken by the excitable throng pressing around. His confectionery hair in gold and brass swept upwards. Today more than ever, Hector Quigley was a crisp, clean, cracking cliché. He was a caricature of himself. He was his own tribute, his own trumpet, his own take-it-away-please-maestro! He was Hecka, Lord of the Jingle. He was the happy hewer of Hector's Homilies. He was He-man Master of Hector's House. He had always been there and he always would be. Mr Fixit. Mr Self-Made Success Story. Mr Leave It To Me. Mr A. No.1. At the front. At the top. Over the top. He was Hector Quigley the longest-living legend in London advertising.

His snakeskin Chelsea boots reached the edge of the dais. He stepped up onto it. Marsha Blow appeared beneath him. He bent forward and had a word in her ear. She bustled self-importantly back into the crowd and beat a retreat to the back of the room. She squeezed her way in front of Charlotte. She gave her a broad grin and a wink.

'What's going on?' whispered Charlotte.

'Have I got news for *you*,' replied Marsha and bowed out. She seemed to be in a rush to collect something.

'Whatcha found out, boss lady?' It was Daniel.

'Nothing. What about you?'

'Zilch.'

A wave of shooshes began at the front and soon travelled to the rear of the room. The crowd was so silent you could have heard a name dropped. Hector began to speak in his James Robertson Justice tones. Holding his audience in the palm of his huge hand, each believed he spoke to them and to no other.

'Assembled before me what do I see?'

'A right bunch of lazy fuckers.' The audience laughed. Charlotte assumed it was Dan who had made the remark.

'And you're the laziest of the lot!' Laughter.

'I see you. I see my employees. I see my friends. I see three hundred and fifty of the hardest working people in advertising. I see HQ people. HQ people are cleverer and more committed and just plain better at their jobs than their counterparts in any other agency in this and any other town.'

'Here, here!' Laughter.

'Throw that lady a mutton chop for her efforts.' Hector was quick with his music hall repartee. More laughter. 'I do not jest. I believe that. For it is true. I don't just see a good group of workers standing beneath me. I see a dedicated band of intensely loyal followers. I have played like the Pied Piper and you have followed me wherever I have led.'

'That makes us a bunch of rats!' Laughter.

'No, but you, sir, are vermin!' Laughter. 'No. I think I have made a good Pied Piper. I think I have played a pretty tune. Each of you is in step with me and with my music of the mountain. Each of you, in your own way and in your own discipline, be it financial or media or creative or management or maybe in helping to run the office, each of you has made a contribution to our mutual success story. Each of you has climbed that mountain with me every day. Each of you has helped to turn a page in my book. Those of you who have been with the company longest – two of you since we started in the sixties – you know we have soldiered on together through times good and bad. More good than bad, I am pleased to say.'

He paused for a moment and looked away. He seemed sad now, wistful. He was choked. His audience stood silent to a man. They stilled. They studied his words. Slowly, the sensation crept over them that Hector Quigley was saying goodbye.

'When I look at you I see friends and family. You are my team, my boys, my girls. You are my children. You cannot do it on your own in this business. Advertising is teamwork. That is why I have been so successful. Because I have had the very best in my team.'

They thought for a minute he might cry. No one had seen Hector down like this before, but no one was surprised either. Underneath the make-up and the music and the showtime banter they knew there lived a loving man.

'I come to the business of today. The business of today affects you all and it will be the business of every day for all of you in the future. When I created the company three decades ago I laid the plans that would make this the most modern and dynamic agency in the advertising game. In those days we had only one television channel that took commercials and it was in black and white. You got ads long with copy. Copywriters were people who could write back then. But the business was changing. The colour supplement was invented. Photography was in. Colour television came along. Commercial radio stopped being something teenagers hid in the dark under their pillows . . . We were part of all those things and it was great fun to be there in the the forefront of Swinging London and its media. HQ grew. From myself and three friends and a dog over a butcher's in Covent Garden into the big business we have today. But the world moves on. Faster and faster it spins and so must we. Britain is no more an island. We stand on the pinnacle of this planet astride a global media culture. Our clients are international. They have brands that traverse the world.

'Now you know that a few years back, for their own reasons mystifying to me and to all of you, we lost our deputy chairman and our financial director whose task was to take us into Europe. That expansion, that deal fell through. Since then I have sought a solution to the loose liaisons we have with some of the independent continental agencies with whom we co-ordinate our international accounts. The day of the stand-alone agency is long gone. HQ is unique in being a privately owned top twenty agency. But our pole position is threatened. I cannot maintain our status for ever.'

'Rubbish.'

'That is very kind of you to say that, but it is not true. What I know and what you do not is that our core business is under threat. Our biggest clients have pointed a finger to show us the way. I have always kept my options open but finally they have run out. I don't just look at the foreseeable future. I am a man of vision and I peer far into the distance. Well, to cut a long story short, I have been in negotiations with an organisation, one of the best, one of worldwide ranking and I have found the firm friend, the perfect partner with whom, hand in hand, we will expand our base and increase our opportunities.'

'Who is it?'

'It is MCN International.'

Hector's people emitted a collective gasp. Charlotte was staggered. How hadn't she heard about this from MCN? They had a better lid on leaks these days.

'The first thing I want to do is to reassure you all that your jobs are safe. That is of priority importance to me and in the negotiations which will be finalised and come into effect on January the first next year there is a clause that guarantees each employee of mine their job for two years. I have not opted for a merger with MCN International. I could not bear to create an appalling hybrid like every other ghastly agency in this stuck together town. That is why I have held out so long. Instead, I have opted to sell HQ lock stock and barrel and to bring it into the MCN International group as a freestanding unit within their international network.'

'Not like Clancey and Bennett?' called somebody. Charlotte winced.

'Well it is appropriate that you should mention Clancey and Bennett. Clancey and Bennett is going to be absorbed into HQ.'

There was no audible reaction from anyone this time. But Charlotte felt contrary. She was amazed and depressed. Not half as depressed as she was about to be. Worse was to come.

'I think the time has come. Marsha! I would like to introduce to you the Managing Director of Clancey and Bennet who joins our board as Managing Director of HQ from January the first. Serena Sark.'

Charlotte revolved within the crowd. She was livid they were applauding. She was sickened. She saw the citrus-clad Serena make her entrance from the back of the room. Her heart sank. She felt dire now. She felt angry. She felt betrayed. It was blatantly clear now why Serena had invited her to dinner and pummelled her and Daniel all about the company. Serena flounced forward and joined Hector on the podium.

'Hello everybody. I'm Serena Sark.' Her voice was shrill and arch. 'I will be your managing director from next January and I can't tell you how excited everyone at MCN is about it.'

I can, thought Charlotte. They'll be positively gleeful to see the back of the old bag. If they were so thrilled about it why had no one called her? How on earth could Hector have delivered his baby into the strangling hands of serial slayer Serena Sark?

'I don't think I'm known to many of you here but I can see one protégé of mine.' Her gaze alighted on Charlotte.

Charlotte returned her smile grudgingly. She hated the looks she was getting. She would not have been surprised if thirty pieces of silver had landed at her feet. Her mind drifted from the meeting. She located Daniel in the scrum and pushed her way through to him. She found his hand hanging by her side and, concealed in the crush, clung onto it for comfort. Hector went on to promise them the biggest bash of all time at Christmas and a great send-off party. Today was Hector's day but tomorrow they would all feel as Charlotte did. They all knew the reality. They all knew the score. They all knew from their history books what happened when an agency is merged or is sold out or is taken over. They all knew what happened when an empire fell and its peoples were invaded and its property looted. They all knew of the Anschluss of Austria or the Fall of France or the decline and fall of the Romans. It was the end of an era. Hector Quigley had had a little secret. It wasn't his facelift. It was his little game of cards with MCN International enabling one Serena Sark to come up trumps.

85

'Hi.' Cindy pecked Alan on the cheek and sat down opposite him. 'This must be a first.'

'We've had lunch at Belgo before.' He folded away his copy of *Campaign* and placed it to one side.

'I meant you getting here before me. You're usually late.'

'I told you before. I'm making a special effort to stay in your good books these days.'

'Don't bother. I'm not keeping books, good or bad.'

'You say that but you don't mean it.'

'I don't mean it literally.' She was interrupted by a waiter dressed in monastic habit, the house style of this particular restaurant. Alan ordered a Belgian beer, Cindy a glass of dry white wine. 'What I mean is, Alan, if we are going to stay on seeing each other – and that is a very big if – you have to be yourself. I don't want you on special behaviour all the time because you won't be able to sustain it for ever and we'll both be wasting our time.'

'But you asked me to make an effort.'

'I asked you to love me and you either do or you don't. What's in *Campaign*?' She changed the subject and nodded to his paper. 'Anything?'

'Not the big story of the day. It was announced after they'd gone to press. Deliberately.'

'Yeah? What?'

'Hector Quigley has sold HQ to MCN International. He's retiring. Going for good. Nobody can believe it.'

'Really?' Cindy could. She smiled. 'You know there was a time when I was much younger and I worked in advertising and the earth would have moved when you had said that. Now I think "Advertising? Who gives a shit?" It's not as if Sainsbury's has taken over Marks and Spencer's and you might not be able to get those yummy little cappuccino bars at the checkouts any more.' She gave him her naughty smile from behind her menu. 'What are you having? I suppose I should have the mussels.'

'I've only told you half the news.'

'If the other half is half as exciting as the first half wake me up when you've run through it.'

'MCN are pulling Clancey and Bennett out of Dean Street and letting Serena Sark take over HQ.'

'Never! She's just running that pathetic little place. C&B isn't even a carbuncle on the backside of an old friend. How could she be in charge of a big organisation like HQ?'

'Don't be rude about people who run businesses of a medium size. After all, I do and you're not exactly running much yourself.'

'I'm a consultant. The size of my business is the size of my brain and that's big enough for me.'

'Look, Cindy, I have something to tell you.'

'God. Don't say it like that.'

'Well it's important and it's difficult to tell you because it's about a project that hasn't come off. I don't want you to think I'm a failure.'

Cindy laughed. 'Men. When will they realise that women are interested in them for who they are and not for what they do. Even material girls like me. Alan, if I'd been looking for a successful man I'd have aimed high. When I left Australia I'd have gone in search of Rupert Murdoch. On second thoughts, perhaps not.'

'Cindy, I've been in negotiations with MCN International to see about selling Thurrock and Josling to them. I've been hoping to do a deal in which my company would move into Dean Street and I would get to run a new division for them made up of T&J merged into C&B. I would have seen Nigel and Serena off. This time last week I was on the point of pulling it off.'

'Really? *Really*? You kept that under your hat.'

'When you're not living with somebody it's easy to miss what they're up to.'

'I'll buy that.'

'Then they slowed down. MCN did, on the contracts. I couldn't work out why. I guessed they must have a counter deal with somebody else. I couldn't think who. It never occurred to me it was within their own company. Now I know, of course. Serena Sark has somehow wangled her way in with Hector Quigley and is the first person to tempt him out of his tree in thirty years. Now she's come out on top and my endeavours – as usual – have led nowhere.'

'Was that the big glamorous future you had planned for us? You as head of balloons and whistles at MCN International?'

'Basically. I've lost out, once again, to that bloody woman.'

'Alan,' she took his hand across the table to comfort him, 'you haven't lost out at all.'

'I have.'

'Not the way I see it.'

'How come?'

'Well, admittedly you haven't gained anything but you haven't lost anything either. Not anything that you had before.'

'I suppose so. It doesn't feel that way.'

'I thought Colin Thurrock was going to retire or give up or go and stick his head in a bucket of sand or whatever.'

'Supposedly he is.

'Well then you'll have T&J to yourself and you can do whatever you like. If you had gone in with MCN you'd have the men in grey suits breathing down your neck. You'd have hated that. You're your own man, Alan.'

'I suppose so. I can't believe Serena Sark has pulled this off. It's a hundred times worse than her getting the Verity kits business.'

'Well thank God you weren't mixed up in that, Alan, with that nun jumping ship. Who wants to ask a nun for advice anyway, unless it's about wanting to grow a moustache? What is it about nuns that people like them so much? Look at this place. Waiters dressed as monks. Why?'

'It's Belgian.'

'That explains nothing. The dry cleaning bills must be a

scandal. Alan, I think you're doing pretty well. You've avoided having MCN ruin your average working day and you've avoided a scandal over a stupid brand symbol.'

'And avoided earning a few hundred thousand pounds for my trouble.'

'Money isn't everything. Most of it maybe, but not everything. Anyway, you've still got the Newy and you wine and dine in the best hostelries in town. You're not down and out yet. And you've got me.'

'Have I?'

'Not really, but right at this junction in time I'm trying to be your friend. You look like you need a shoulder to cry on.'

'Have you thought any more about us having a baby?'

'No.'

'Would you like to try?'

'What right now on a table for two in Belgo? You could drive me wild with a Belgian breadstick.'

'Be serious.'

'I could say the same thing to you. Alan, we discussed this in the Hempel.'

'We didn't get very far.'

'I *have* thought about it, I suppose, a bit. I'm not mother material. Not right now. And not with you. I saw you pluck those threads from your jacket that day.'

'I am not seeing another woman.'

'How do I know?'

'I was in a business meeting.'

'Who with? What man wears citrus as part of his work ensemble? And then rubs his jacket all over yours so the fibres come off on it?'

'Look, I'll tell you. I had lunch that day with a woman called Maria Handley. Hector Quigley fired her and she was offering to do some consultancy to help me pull the Verity tampon business out of there or the kits business out of C&B.'

'What, she just rang up and made the offer?'

'I've been trying to get a contact in HQ for ages. I thought Duncan would help me through his friend there but you know how prim and proper he is.'

'Alan, why don't you try and win a piece of business on your own merits just once instead of always trying to buy people? How far did you get with this woman?'

'Nowhere. She didn't have much to say.'

'Exactly. Where do you ever get by those means? It's the same with me. You're putting pressure on me to have a baby so that I end up being irrevocably linked to you for the rest of my life. Why can't you just settle for us trying to be together for the right reasons? That we like each other and that we're happy in each other's company. I do want a baby. I might want a baby. Well, if I choose later to have a baby it will only be with somebody who will be a proper old-fashioned father. I've thought about that. I know women who've done it on their own and I don't think I could cope – and . . .'

'What?'

'Fibres on the jacket.'

'I don't know how they got there.'

'How about you were lying on top of her and thrusting up and down. That might work a few threads loose.'

'How about it was a hot summer's day and she took her jacket off and when she rose to leave I held it up for her to slip into and it brushed against my own jacket.'

Cindy giggled. 'I'll buy that on one condition.'

'What?'

'You buy me lunch.'

'I was going to.'

'And dinner tomorrow night and tickets to *Elektra*.'

Alan huffed. 'You told me a minute ago to start doing things my way and to stop buying people.'

'I didn't mean me, I meant other people. Anyway, you don't want to listen to me. I'm a consultant but only because no one else would employ me. Here's the waiter. I'm having the mussels. And an affair with a man with a large breadstick.'

'I can't fucking believe it.' Charlotte reached her usual desk and propped her mobile phone in the corner. 'Her. Here. On my patch.'

'He didn't say what he was doing,' said Daniel. 'Is he going or staying or what?'

'Hector?'

'Yeah, Hecka.'

'Going. He must be. That's his big surprise. He's sold out. He's sold the company. And us. Down the river.'

'Whoah. Who'd have believed it?'

'Everybody said he was part and parcel of this place, that he would never leave, that this place was as safe as houses. Apparently the financial director is leaving.'

'Who told you that?'

'I listened in to some guy coming up the stairs behind me. I don't know who he is.'

'Probably somebody in accounts.'

'The money people are all getting out of here because the place is actually bankrupt.'

'Nah.'

'Appearances can be deceptive. Barings Bank didn't know they were about to crash until the day before.'

'We're not a bank.'

'We're worse. At least a bank has money. I heard this chap saying that Hector has been asset stripping the company for years to keep up his lifestyle. How many ex-wives has he got?'

'Three, I think.'

'Apparently they all have a stake in the company and he has huge payments to make to them and his son. He could never bear to let them think he was less rich and successful than he was. That's why he's done it.'

'It's all gossip.'

• Douglas Chirnside

'I know. They say eavesdroppers never hear good of themselves but you never hear good of anybody else either, do you?'

'Being part of MCN is good news.'

'Being sold is not. The first thing they'll do is rationalise the staff.'

'We're account management. We'll be all right.'

'I don't know. Hopefully we will be. It depends whether the company is on the verge of liquidation or not. Usually they turf out all the behind the scenes people straight away. Then they start trimming those of us up front.'

'Our jobs are protected for two years. Hecka promised.'

'Hecka doesn't live here anymore. They'll find a way round it.'

'I'm calling the clients now. Get them to ask for me to be kept on their business.'

'Good thinking, Boy Wonder.'

'Whoah. I think you'll find I'm Batman, actually.'

'Your legs are too thin.'

Charlotte's office mobile rang.

'Hello Charlotte, it's Stella Boddington. Remember me?'

'Of course I do, Stella.' She looked at Daniel. He blew her a kiss.

'Serena informed me last night of the proposed takeover of your company by MCN. Since she's going to be in charge of the merger I've asked her if it would be possible for you to work on my business again.'

'What did she say?'

'Well you know what she's like. I think she was saying yes but it could have been no. She's very brittle. Apart from anything I'd just like to have someone I like working on my business.'

'Stella, I would love to work on your account. I was just telling my account manager here that I hoped I got put on your business.'

After she had switched off the phone Daniel asked her who it was.

'Stella Boddington. She's very nice. She's the client on the Carpets Company. It was one of my accounts at C&B. Wants me to be her account director when the merger comes through.'

• 460

'So you're safe then.'

'You can be the manager on it. I need someone to handle the business while I look for another job.'

'Another job? Why?'

'Because my name is associated with hot-desking at MCN and I don't mean the office organisation.'

'Oh, yeah? That's something we haven't done. Yet.'

'What?'

'Shag in the office.'

'Well I'm not starting today.'

'I'm up for it.'

'You're up for anything that spells trouble. Serena will have bromide put in the coffee. She can't stand any of that sort of shenanigans in the office.'

'I wasn't planning on giving her a quick fuck in the art files, actually.'

Charlotte sighed. 'Oh Daniel, what are we going to do? I can't be seen to be sleeping with my account manager.'

'Can't you? Well, I'll have to give a refund on the tickets then.'

'You understand don't you?'

'No. I look after you. I take care of you. We're special together.'

'No Daniel. We're not special. Our relationship is based on a set of false – what's the word I'm looking for – well, things anyway.'

'I don't get it.'

'I know you don't get it. I mean that when I first met you I thought you were in movies.'

'I thought you were just some bird on the street.'

'I'm your account director. You lied to me.'

'You lied to me. You told me you were twenty-two.'

'I told you what you wanted to hear. Look, I'm supposed to be a grown up. I'm an account director. So far the only thing I've done this year is put a nun on television who turned out to be a criminal on the run, not to mention a hopelessly incorrect symbol for the brand, plus have the series axed for breaking commercial broadcasting rules and getting The Station a huge fine. That's one fuck of a contribution to the client's business in just a few months.'

'Hecka's responsible for all those errors, not you.'

'Hecka's leaving.'

'The clients are pleased.'

'The clients are barmy. But they won't go out of their way to keep me. Look at it from the point of view of new management. I'm young for the job, I left my last job at MCN embarrassingly early, I'm screwing my account manager—'

'I wish.'

Charlotte sighed again. 'What shall I do?'

'Come on darn the pub, matey.'

'Apart from all that there's my mother to sort out.'

'You've sorted her out. How long is she going to be sleeping in your flat? We can't shag there with her lying in the middle of the floor. Then again—'

'Stop it! She won't be there for long. She's found a little house in Chiswick that's rather nice. Tony's buying it for her.'

'So he's going to help her.'

'Until the divorce comes through and they sort the money out. He doesn't want his sexual proclivities to come out. And she will get her Lloyd's money. Eventually. Daniel?'

'What?'

'My mother never told me any of her problems before. We weren't that close. I mean she's not the sort to talk.'

'You're a good daughter.'

'It's changed how I see her. It makes me feel old, her turning to me for help. It shows you how lonely you can become. God. I hope I don't end up middle-aged and on my own.'

'She should marry Hecka, your mum.'

'What?!'

'Why not? Do them both a power of good.'

'She'd hate him,' said Charlotte. Then again, she wondered if she would. She knew her mother and Hector were connected through Anthony's magical skills.

'Do you still have a key to your mum's old place?'

'Yes. Why?'

'I thought we could go and try out the dungeon.'

'Daniel! You're a sad case.'

'Yeah, and you love it. Come on then.' He yawned and stretched himself up to his full six foot five inches in height.

'Everyone else has gone down the pub for the afternoon. I've said I'll meet Bonzo. No one will do any work at HQ today.'

'No one ever does any work round here.'

'Great, advertising, isn't it?!'

'Sheer bloody brilliant,' said Charlotte.

87

Of the summer and the winter sun, the latter is the more striking and all the more welcome for it. January is a depressing month. You get up in the dark. You arrive at work in the dark. You go home in the dark. For those who love life to be filled with light the beginning of the year is filled with gloom. Karen Myhill was no sun worshipper but even she was heartened to see her newly decorated living room fill with the blond colour of the morning sun of the first month of the year. She had had the room painted honey. She had had her sofas refurbished in blue. She had had the old carpet lifted and the old floor boards limed. She had laid out undyed wool rugs. She had placed poles over the windows and draped translucent muslin over them. She had positioned large pale terracotta pots in each corner. An antique bleached Spanish door was laid out flat on an iron stand to make an unusual coffee table. There she knelt, in chocolate brown oversized jersey and matching leggings, hugging her mug of coffee and staring into the blue flame of the gas fire in its original grate. The decorating may have given her home a makeover but it had not lifted her spirits. She was still angry with that Collins girl and she still had to face Max. At last he walked into the room sliding on the floor in his socks.

'Good morning,' she said. Her son seemed taller than ever from her low position on the floor. He had become a man. He was the new man in her life. He was the only man in her life.

'Good morning, sunshine,' he said. He made for the window. The sun was low in the sky and he squinted into it.

'What are your plans for today?' asked Karen.

'I haven't got anything planned.'

'Would you like some coffee?'

'I'd love some tea.'

She made to get up.

'Don't worry. I can get it myself.'

Karen listened to him in the kitchen and five minutes later he returned. He picked up the newspaper off the table.

'What's on TV today?'

'Nothing. Typical, isn't it? Two hundred channels and we can't find anything we like.'

'That's because we're in the business.'

'I expect other families are the same. Mrs Collins said something similar the other day.'

Max looked up. 'Mrs Collins? What were you doing talking to her?'

'She came to the door with some tickets for something.'

'What?'

'I don't know. I wasn't paying attention.'

'Mum! You're useless. You're on another planet.'

'I was examining her face.'

'Why? What's wrong with it? Apart from the obvious.'

'I was wondering about her and her daughter and their relationship.'

'Here it comes. And you and me and our relationship. Sons have different relationships from daughters with their mothers.'

'Do you think she knows what Ginny gets up to?'

'Doubt it.'

'And do you think I know what you get up to?'

'No. But I don't get up to anything.'

'How do I know?'

'Mum this is North London. Life is not that exciting.'

'This is one of the world's great capitals. Everything goes on here. Life. Death. A quarter of the world's music is recorded in this city. Drugs are consumed like sweeties. Sex is rampant.'

'Sorry, are we living in LA or North London?'

'North London is like Los Angeles.'

'No it's not. Kids here don't drive to school in convertibles and compare nose jobs. We've all got spots and homework and we spend our lives hanging around at bus stops. We don't have any money and we don't stay out late.'

'You have lots of money.'

'In a trust fund I can't get at.'

'And you stay out all hours.'

'I do not. I'm always home by midnight.'

'Where do you go?'

'Nowhere. To friends.'

'You don't have any friends.'

'College mates. You don't know them because they don't live around here. I go to their homes and do their homework for them in return for getting access to their computers. We should be on the Internet.'

'If we were on the Internet would you stay at home more?'

'Drag me away from it! There's so much stuff out there it's unreal.'

'What are you doing today?'

'Nothing. I told you.'

'OK. Let's go to wherever we have to and I'll buy us a modem.'

'Yo! Brilliant.'

'There are conditions attached.'

Max tutted.

'The first is that we have lunch together.'

Max relaxed. 'That's OK.'

'The second is that you agree now on a contract written in blood that I have equal access to the Internet in this household—'

'Oh, Mum!' Max whined.

'That's only fair.'

'Well, it's got to be equal *time*, not equal access because you'll be slow. You're not to sit on it all night and you're not to break it.'

'How could I break the information superhighway?'

'Because you're old and you won't understand it. It's for young people.'

'I am young at heart. I may have the body of a weak and feeble woman but I have the heart of a TV producer. I can charge it back to the business so we can use it as much as we like.'

'That's different. You didn't say that. If I can go on with no regard to cost then so can you. Deal agreed. What's the third thing?'

'What makes you think there is a third thing?'

'Because your strategy, as always, is patently obvious.'

'We have to have a serious talk.'

Max looked at her. His mother pushed her glasses up her nose.

'What about?'

'Things.'

'Things?'

'Yes. Things. Virginia Collins.'

'Who's she?'

'The Collins girl.'

'You mean, Ginny. I didn't realise that was her name. Bit of an ironic mislabelling, that one.'

'Why?'

'She's the school tart. She's only fifteen.'

'Do you mean by that that she's sleeping around?'

'She can't get much sleep. She's a shagbag. An easy lay.'

'I thought you were her friend.'

'I'm her neighbour. She's always asking me to help her with her homework and making very dubious offers in return. I tried to help her because I am a kind and generous soul.'

'Did you – how will I put this – take her up on her generous offers?'

Max looked embarrassed. 'Mum!'

'I'm curious.'

'I'm not that curious. I wouldn't touch her with a bargepole. She's probably riddled with VD.'

'So when she said you were the father of her child she was lying.'

'*What*? *What*?! You're making it up.'

'I'm not. But she was?'

'She's off her head. She's damaged what brain she had with drugs and drink. She's flipped. She's—'

'Never mind. I think you're right. She needs help. I don't think she'll get it from her family, though.'

'I can't believe she did that. She's not pregnant is she?'

'No. OK, I have one more question and then we can get ready and go out. Mr Lutyens called me.'

Max stirred uneasily. 'What about?'

'You've been to see him.'

'I called him twice. I saw him for a few minutes a while ago.'

'Why?'

'Why not? He handles my money.'

'Why did you not ask me to go with you?'

'Because I didn't want you to go with me.'

'Why not?'

'Because I'm old enough to go on my own. Because you know what you're like.'

'What did you need a half a million pounds for?'

'He's supposed to keep it confidential.'

'Answer the question.'

'Nothing.'

'Max.' She was warning him.

'That's true. *I* don't need half a million pounds. You needed half a million pounds to bail you out of the Sister Verity fiasco.'

Karen flushed with all the warmth she felt for her son. 'You mean you would give me the money in your trust to save me? Oh sweetheart.'

'Don't get slushy. It's less than half the money in the trust.'

'Oh, Max, you're so clever and so sweet.'

'I wouldn't have *given* you the money. I would have loaned it to you. It's in my own interest. I'll be taking over soon.'

'Not soon.'

'Not soon enough.'

'TV production companies are not handed down like family businesses.'

'I know. But anyone can be a TV producer. Look at Duncan Cairns. Look at Prince Edward.'

'I'd rather not. Life is tough enough without having to compete with the royal family. Why can't they stick to what they're good at, getting divorced and killing animals at the weekends?'

'Is that it?'

'I think so. Only . . .'

'Only what? There's always something.'

'You called Mr Lutyens *before* I started the *Sister Verity* show.'

'Only to keep him on his toes. I never went in to see him until I actually wanted access to it. It's my money he's looking after and there's a lot of it. I just like to breathe down his neck, make him do his sums.'

'Max, you were terrifying the poor man so much he called me. You mustn't be so user unfriendly.'

'I can't help it. It's genetic. Is that it now?'

'It is. That is it. Go upstairs and dry your hair and then we'll drive into town and connect ourselves to the world.'

'My hair is dry.'

'Max. Do as you're told.'

He stood up and towered over his mother. For just once she looked demure in her smart brown clothes, her neatly cut blonde hair and her big, wide, trademark bejewelled spectacles. Max looked down on her.

'Listen, Mum. I'll do as I'm told the day you do as you are told.'

He padded across the limed boards in his socks and out of the room leaving Karen smiling into her mug as she finished her coffee.

'Who can that be at this time of night?'

Michael was out of earshot and did not hear Duncan's rhetorical question. More worried that with such questions he was turning into a carbon copy of his mother than who might be on the phone, he carried Pushkin with him to take the call in the bedroom.

'Duncan, it's all over!'

It was Paul McCarthy in floods of tears.

'Would you like to speak to Michael?'

'Don't try to get rid of me. It's all *over*!'

'The whole world or just something in your life?'

'I don't know why I ever ring you two. You're so fucking unsympathetic.'

'Sorry. I'm a bit woozy. We're just clearing up from a dinner party.'

'A dinner party? Why wasn't I invited?' protested Paul through sniffles.

'They were straight people. We didn't need the floor show.'

'You're such a bitch. How could you strike me when I'm down?'

'How you normally like it. With a studded cat o' nine tails.' Duncan laughed. 'Oh, I'm only pulling your leg, Paul. What's the big problem?'

Paul wailed. 'Anton's chucked me.'

'Well, you're into all that S&M stuff.'

'I don't mean physically. He's called a halt to our relationship.'

'I'm sorry, Paul. Don't feel rejected. And don't take an overdose.'

'I can't afford to buy enough drugs to manage an overdose. And I don't feel rejected. It wasn't anything to do with me. It was his wife.'

'His *wife*?'

'No one was more surprised than me. She found the dungeon in the house and she's divorcing him and taking him for everything he's got.'

'Surely not everything? What would she want with a sling and a set of industrial tit clamps?'

'What am I going to do, Dunky?' Paul sniffed but he had already started to cheer up with the telling of his tale.

'Oh, I don't know. Hey, I know somebody you could go out with. They're just like you only different. And available. Quite sexy too.'

'Who? Who?' Paul's spirits were up. He was excited.

'Paula McCarthy.' Duncan was reduced to sniggering into Pushkin's back.

'Duncan Cairns, you're full of it.'

'Paul, you know I love you dearly. Go to sleep and I'll call you tomorrow. I promise.'

'I can't just yet.'

'Why?'

'This video's still got thirty minutes to run. It's a shave special.'

Duncan shook his head and was laughing when he replaced the receiver.

'My God.' Michael got up from the kitchen floor and, using his fist as a prop in the small of his back, arched rearwards over it.

'What is it?'

'I think I've got housemaid's knee.'

'Why aren't you clutching your knee, then?'

'Well, you know what I mean.'

'I do know what you mean. White South Africans weren't born to do housework.'

'I'm British and I have been for years. Anyway, I shouldn't be doing this. This is your flat.'

'It was your dinner party and your guests who made the mess.'

'Who was on the phone?'

'Paul. He and Anton have split up.'

'I hadn't realised they were together.'

'They tied the knot in private. Probably many knots, actually, those two.'

Michael went into the kitchen and put the cleaning things

away. When he returned Duncan was sitting on the settee trying to read the second section of *The Times*, only Pushkin was standing in his lap and spoiling his sightlines.

'Baby, I'm trying to read.'

'Miaow,' said Pushkin. She settled down into his lap, half-closed each eye and began to purr. He put down the paper and groomed her with his fingers.

'Are we ever going to live together?' asked Michael.

'Why are you asking that?'

'Because I would slightly less resent cleaning up if it was my own home.'

'Go and clean your own flat then.'

'Yours is nicer. I don't want to entertain in my flat. You're such a good cook.'

'Cooking is easy. I wish I had a dishwasher.'

'Why don't you get one?'

'The kitchen is too small. I wouldn't say no if you bought me one.'

'I will. Providing it's in a home we have together.'

'Don't rush me.'

'Waiting over ten years is not rushing. I know what it is.'

'What?'

'You're still planning to go off and shag that lesbian and bring up your Nazi love child.'

Duncan rolled his eyes to the ceiling. He tugged at a knot near Pushkin's tail. She made a complaining noise and tried to push him away with her rear right paw.

'You're annoying the cat.'

'Not as much as you're annoying me. I am not running off with a lesbian and I certainly have no intention of shagging one. I'm supposed to be in a relationship with you.'

'Supposed to be. Do you know that there's a statistic that says that gay men have much more sex than straight men.'

'That wouldn't be difficult.'

'But that straight men have more sex with their regular partner.'

'That wouldn't be difficult either.'

'Have you been unfaithful to me?'

'What brought all this on?'

'Aha! Avoiding answering.'

'I am not avoiding answering. I was, repeat was, thinking of fathering a child with Sarah and Lesley. We were not planning on using my sperm on draught. We had a champagne glass and a syringe in mind and a closed door between the two of us.'

'A champagne glass?'

'I upgraded it. She suggested sherry. '

'Jesus. Lesbians have no style.'

'Those two have. I just thought champagne was more celebratory. A child conceived in a sherry glass might be genetically predisposed to being a vicar's wife, irrespective of gender.'

'But you're not doing it now.'

'No.' Duncan stopped stroking Pushkin and instead leant forward and buried his face in the comforting fluffiness of her fur. She upped her rumbling purr.

Michael paused and then proceeded, pleased.

'Why not?'

'Because they were so goddamn clinical about the whole thing. They wanted a child with no father, basically. They didn't want any commitment. They didn't want me to have any rights or be named on the birth certificate or anything. They weren't looking for love.'

'That was obvious all along.'

'It wasn't obvious to me. And sometimes you can persuade people. I thought they might change their minds as they got to know me. But they didn't want to get to know me. They just wanted to make sure I had all my teeth and wasn't HIV positive. They were not interested in my personality. They were not interested in *me*. They were just interested in what was in my genes.'

'Sounds like any gay bar in London. People are just interested in what's in your jeans.'

'Hah, hah. That's original.'

'So why wouldn't you talk about it before?'

'Because you were against it.'

'I wasn't.'

'Of course you were.'

'Not in principal.'

'Eh?'

'Not in principal but in practice.'

'What does that mean?'

'If you would like a child and it would make you happy then I would like you to have one. But I don't want you to go off with someone else.'

'I'm not going off with anyone else.'

'Have you ever been unfaithful to me?'

'That's the second time you've asked me that question in five minutes. It's a question you should never ask and one I should never answer.'

'That means yes.'

'Well yes is the true answer.'

Michael looked hurt.

'You were there at the time.'

'Oh. Threesomes don't count.'

'They do in the tabloids.'

'We're not famous yet.'

'But we might be. Then see what comes out in the papers.'

'A gay baby with two lesbian mothers fathered by you would be much worse.'

'What makes you think it would be gay?'

'Wishful thinking.'

They laughed.

'I'm glad you didn't have that HIV test.'

'I did.'

Michael looked aghast a second time.

'I wish you wouldn't go behind my back like that.'

'As one poof said to the other.'

I'm being serious.'

'I know. I can tell. You're the world heavyweight champion when it comes to being serious.'

'It's dishonest to do something and not tell me about it.'

'Well don't worry. I'm negative.'

'I knew you would be.'

'So did I.'

'So you worried for nothing.'

'But you always worry that you might be positive even though you know you won't be. It's like when a plane takes off. You know there's almost no chance of it crashing but you always

think that it will. It's uncertainty. Living with uncertainty is hell. I'm glad I don't have to do it all the time.'

'I've lived with uncertainty.'

'Michael, you're the surest person I know.'

'That's my demeanour. I was frightened your life would change with a baby and you'd abandon me.'

'I'll never abandon you. Wake up in the middle of night and strangle you with my bare hands perhaps but I will never abandon you.'

'Promise.'

'I promise.'

'Then we can be our own family even without a child.'

Pushkin opened one sleepy eye and peeked at Duncan.

He laughed. 'You're included, little one,' he said, and hugged his baby.

89

Time changes everything. Almost. The landscape changes. The city changes. People come and people go and people pass you by. The hard working get promoted, the ambitous get self-promoted, the little folk never get any bigger. The great and the good grow old and are replaced by those seemingly less great and less good. London moves on. The map may stay the same, the streets never more congested – until you look at those old sepia photographs and it looks worse then than it does now – but as surely as does the great river at its pumping heart, London flows forward fast. Arterial roads may run on routes the Romans marched on, winding lanes in the City may evoke medieval trades long lost,

West End squares may bear the names of the distant Dukes and Duchesses who planned them, but each and every fresh day this dirty great capital reappraises and rebuilds and reinvents itself anew. This is a city that has lived and breathed and sighed and died almost, but survived to tell its tales across two millennia. Bodies change, appearances change, minds change, though heart and character remain the same.

Hector Quigley had stayed exactly the same, with a bit of help. His three-piece pale yellow suit, a virtuoso performance of unique distinction from Gieves and Hawkes, was, as always, as flawless as his face: equally tailored, equally well cut, equally bone-hugging. His matching shirt and tie combination of broad peach and lime stripes was a bespoke Thomas Pink creation, the usual thing. The cuffs of the shirt stuck out from under his jacket too, the same as they had always done. They were clamped in place by the cufflinks set, the Roman sundial and the Spanish doubloon. Nothing new there. Hector's hands looked huge, adorned as they were with popish rings, a ruby, a diamond, a sapphire – the ever-present ensemble. And to top the whole show off, his crown-like hair was cut and curled and dyed the identical shade of brassy yellow, just as it had always been. The same as always. The same as always. But time changes everything and while the mood of the man might not have altered one iota, the old world and the old order had blown away with the rattle of change.

  Hector Quigley had been away for a while and now he was back. He could not bear to keep away. The former ringmaster found it only marginally less difficult to draw up a ringside seat than to disappear to one in the back row. Retirement was a foreign country to one whose lifetime ticked to the cracking of the whip. After days stuffed full with lunches and launches and dinners and decisions, after years of balancing budgets and sorting out staff, after decades of having his opinion sought and giving them all a piece of his mind, now Hector was less troubled. In fact, he was never troubled at all. Nobody bothered. No one required his viewpoint, no one needed to know what he thought anymore. No one wanted to know. For the first time in his long life Hector Quigley, once tomorrow's story, was yesterday's news. Hector Quigley was the last in the line of showmen advertising agents and once he had made his exit the only comment on his performance was why on earth he had been left tap-dancing alone a generation after his peers had left the stage. Advertising is not about before. It is not about now. It is about the next big thing. There is only the future and ancient history. They would not put up a statue to Hector Quigley. Instead, they had assigned him to the stone age.

Portly and ebulliant, formal in an era of casualdom, elegant in a brutal age, he rolled out from the comfortable interior of his buttercup Bentley. These days there was a trace of grey on the underside of his snakeskin Chelsea boots that never used to walk on pavements. He stood there, outside Marylebone station, underneath its great Victorian decorative glass canopy. The old building looked clean and fancy and highly ornamental, much too pretty to be a terminal for public transport. Hector, of course, had never taken public transport. He had never been on a bus. He had never been on the Underground. He had never been on a train. He was getting out here because it was raining and because he could stand under the glass awning and be helped into his coat and be handed his umbrella and not get wet.

He intended to take a flight of fancy. He was going to stroll past the magic kingdom from which he had abdicated before he became dethroned. For old times' sake and because he was passing and because there was no rush to get to the next place and because he was an emotional, sentimental, wistful old thing Hector had decided to snatch a peek at Hector's House, to check out the HQ building, to glimpse his name in lights. Well on a piece of plastic signage at least. His memorial in the land of commerce. He wanted to do it secretly and quietly and anonymously – three ways of doing things that were pretty new to him – because he was . . . what? Bored? Lonely? Afraid?

The irreplaceable Philip held out Hector's broad black cash-mere coat with astrakhan collar. As Hector finished buttoning it up, a difficult procedure with his large fingers, Philip handed him his big black brolly. Hector looked what he was: rich and smart. Only the incongruous pale yellow trousers and snake-skin Chelsea boots showing beneath his coat drew attention to himself. But while Hector's dress declared outwardly that he wished to slip into the shadows, inwardly he yearned to be spotted and spotlit, waved to and flagged down, congratulated and remembered. Today was the day.

He turned the corner and strode down Lisson Grove to Marylebone Road. Here a flyover seemed to throw the traffic out of the sky onto the ground in front of him. Inexperienced, Hector stood too close the kerb. A bus splashed brown water up from the road and it spattered his shoes and trousers. So shiny and so patent were his shoes that they were impervious to water and it ran off instantly but his trousers were left speckled. Hector looked down sadly and stood back. He wanted to look perfect and now he did not. The red man changed to green and he began the race across the busy road before the lights turned against him. Safely on the opposite side all he had to do was walk a hundred yards and turn the corner into Seymour Place. From his target junction an open truck full of rubble and muck appeared and sat at the lights waiting to cart away its load of concrete and dirt.

Mucky old thing, thought Hector. He wondered what it was doing in his smart street. His old smart street. Another truck pulled up behind the first one and honked its horn. Its obese driver leant out of the window and waved to the driver in front who acknowledged him with a mock V sign. They laughed between them, one of the many minor meaningless communications between passing Londoners which happen every day.

Hector was enjoying walking on the pavement and being amongst real people. He was the sort of person that pedestrians thought might be famous and they looked at him as they passed in that peculiarly English way which avoids staring. Hector liked that. He felt light. He felt happy. He felt something might happen.

It was only when he turned the corner that he realised what the trucks were doing there. He stopped abruptly at the top end of the road and staggered back into the wall. He emitted a stifled yelp. It was as if he had been punched in the stomach and he had lost his wind.

The first thing he saw lay propped up against an articulated lorry at the far end of the road outside the Satellite building. Three four-foot-high blue plastic letters, an M, a C and an N, stacked up one on top of the other. They were rebranding the building. There, up on the front of the Satellite, on the third floor where the blacked-out windows of the new business theatre were, two men suspended from the top of the building in a cradle were using a blow torch to amputate the giant yellow Q that had sat up there for so many years. The H, Hector realised, was what lay in fragments in the street below. There they were. His initials. Separated. Isolated. Amputated. Cast down. Broken up. Smashed. Dead in the street. The fragmented pieces of all that remained of his fragmented dreams.

Worse, much worse, was happening nearer to him. If the removal of the initials from the Satellite building in Seymour Place was an amputation without anaesthetic what was happening to the frontage of Quigley's House on Old Marylebone Road was more than murder. It was a cold-blooded massacre.

After Hector had sold the agency and the businesses had been merged competitive client conflicts had reduced the number of accounts which could be kept. The administration, finance, support services and below the line departments had been rationalised back into MCN International in Dean Street and the staff axed. New business presentations were a lower key affair these days. Serena Sark did not dance or sing for her supper let alone her clients. There was no need for that huge theatre in the Satellite building. So it had been turned into offices, and, a substantial building in its own right, Serena had relocated Clancey and Bennett entirely into the Satellite.

Hector's House had been wholly owned by the company. It was a valuable asset in concrete and steel that could be usefully liquidated. It had been. It had been knocked off to a developer. The huge empty central space in the atrium was a waste. Only the most important architect-designed offices in the most prestigious areas can afford a huge atrium. The developers had decided to keep the back half of the building intact and turn the front portion into rabbit hutches for clerks of one kind or another.

Hector half-slumped down the wall and watched through work-weary eyes as his old home was sacked and looted and pulled down before him. They were crawling everywhere like ants in hard helmets, the builders. They were not builders though. They were destructionists. Vandals. Thieves. Scum.

Hector remembered it like yesterday, the day he had bought that building. He was three-quarters of the way through his career then but it had seemed he had the whole of his life still to live. Who else had owned their building outright? No one. Only he. Only Hecka, Lord of the Jingle. He remembered the arguments with the designers over the fitting out of the meeting rooms. He remembered the first cabling of the old phone system and the room that had had to be set aside to hold the switchboard. At the end its replacement sat in a box on the reception desk. Everything was shrinking all the time. The computers. The production technology. The campaigns. The world. The people. The legends. Hector looked at the palms of his huge hands. He was, literally, a great man. And he was a dinosaur, a larger than life, giant-sized scaly monster who had somehow not noticed the ice age and was left lumbering around on the periphery. He was too big for this world. His eyes moistened. He remembered the champagne at the front door on the first day and cutting the yellow ribbon and the excited babble of the girls from the typing pool.

There was a commotion in the street. A huge mobile crane-like vehicle, rusty and yellow in equal quantities edged up from the other end of the street. Hector could not avert his gaze. He was appalled. It circled around a truck which was receiving rubble tumbling down a shoot of inter-connecting black plastic buckets. It manouevered itself directly in front of the façade of the building. There was nothing behind it. Hector did not know the type of machine it was but he knew the nature of the beast. For suspended from its overhead arm was a massive, weighty, dangling concrete ball.

Sporting his umbrella as a shield, Hector watched uneasily as the sweaty driver inside the glass cab pulled back hard on the lever. He watched the mechanical arm lurch back. He watched the big boulder-like ball swing back. Then the whole system was released and the arm shot forward and, like some medieval siege weapon, the ball knocked a section of wall flat back into the rubble where the cappuccino bar had once stood at the bottom of the atrium. It collapsed with a terrible din. Then there was peace. Silence. The dust rose on the air like talcum powder. It floated far on the light wind and was breathed in by Hector. It passed up his nose. It entered his lungs. He coughed. He was choking on the stench of his own decomposing corpse. He was watching the vultures eat the carrion of his own cadaver. He was screaming out inside but no sound was escaping from his body. Hector could stand it no more. He turned to go then stopped for the last time. He could not bear to stay away but he would never return and he knew it now. One last look over his shoulder. Through the settling dust, beyond a steel window support, he spotted a sunshine yellow wall. On it was a panel. He knew what it said. It was one of his homilies.

The greatest brands last one hundred years.
So do the greatest selling ideas. At HQ those ideas are our ideas.
Campaigns that mean something not just today but for all the future.

Underneath was Hector's smiling face beneath his topper and below that his enlarged signature. They hadn't even bothered to take it down. He despised them. Go ahead. Destroy my words. Stamp on my face. Rip out my heart. Trail my guts across the street. Wipe me from the surface of the earth.

Hector spotted another piece of sunshine yellow. It was the hard hat of a builder. His gloved hand was scraping up some small chunks of concrete. With the other he reached for the panel on the wall. Hector swung away before the man tore it off and binned it with the rubble. The tears began their trip down Hector's face. So taut and perfect was his flawless face, so smooth his skin, so ceramic his cheeks, so chiselled his chin, those tears flowed straight, down and off the end of his jaw and onto his coat, quicksilver waterdrops skimming down a mirror.

He was a semblance of his old self when he reached the car. Philip neatly sprang out and opened the rear door. He stood behind Hector and waited to receive his coat and umbrella but was motioned to return to the driver's seat. Hector himself opened the passenger door. Inside was a middle-aged woman flicking the pages of *Hello!* On the cover Fergie hugged her children in Japanair branded T-shirts. The woman had rested the magazine on a small vanity case in her lap. She was wearing a little citrus suit. She looked up and smiled. It was Audrey Goldberg.

'Bump into anybody?' she asked. 'See anyone I know?'

'No,' said Hector quietly. He shuffled in beside her. Philip turned the key in the ignition.

'Oh, Philip. I will be getting out again in just a minute.'

'Where on earth are you going?' asked Audrey.

'I feel like a walk.'

'It's raining. Oh Hector. I knew we shouldn't have stopped. You mustn't mope about selling HQ.'

'I'm not.'

'You are. You're not exactly inscrutable. You're the most emotional man I've ever known. You went along with my plan and you can't bear it because it wasn't yours.'

'Balls.'

'I think I've done very well for us.'

'Us.'

'Yes. Us. Hector you were almost bankrupt. It's only a juggling act until you drop all the balls.'

'Bah!'

'You were running a company that was overstretched and overdrawn and overdue for the abattoir. I spotted that Serena was desperate to consolidate Clancey and Bennett's position within MCN International. I used my unique position as a go-between in the industry to bring all the relevant parties together and to negotiate the deal. You sold her a turkey. She bought a pig in a poke. But no one bothers because you both got what you wanted. You got out and she got in.'

Audrey was protesting the facts rather than summarising them. She took his hand in hers. He did not recoil.

'I thought you couldn't bear to be touched.'

'Today I can. I can bear to be touched by you.'

She stole her opportunity and clasped his hand the tighter for it.

'At least MCN got a huge physical asset in that building. You got the thirteen million pounds in cash.'

'I did not.'

'You did before Carol got her three, the Tania Quigley Foundation thingy got their two and your last wife got her one. Which leaves you with seven million still and your past is paid off. And I got my three quarters of a mil for brokering the deal.' She polished the lapel of her jacket with her free hand. 'Can he hear me through that thing?'

'He lip reads. He thinks I don't know but I do.'

'Can he? Here am I discussing my income. Oh, don't be ridiculous, of course he can't!' Unconsciously, she covered her mouth with her hand. 'Well, everybody is happy. Everything is fine in the garden. No one goes on for ever. You had to retire sometime. You went out at the top.' She let go of his hand and held out the magazine in front of her. 'Look at Fergie. I mean, she doesn't look anything like that in real life.' She folded the magazine on the vanity case and then slipped it inside. 'I don't know why I'm still lugging this stupid thing around with me. It made a good hidey hole for all the documents. The paperwork!' She placed the case at her feet and smoothed out her citrus skirt.

'I was the longest-living legend in London advertising.'

'That's your own catchphrase. You know what they say about believing your own publicity.'

'I *was*.'

'I know you were, darling. Everyone knows you were. But all that glitters is not gold, as you said to me. And HQ had a definite tinge of rust around the edges. Oh look. Here's an article on that woman who played Sister Verity. Barely out on parole and she's launching a perfume. You can get five pounds off with the coupon. Typical. I'll read it later.' She folded the magazine in her lap. Beside her was a little parcel. They both looked at it.

'Can I open it now?' asked Hector.

'Wait until we get home.'

'But I like surprises. I like presents.'

'I like surprises too,' replied Audrey and laughed more than she should have. 'It's my engagement gift to you. Open it with a bottle of champagne.'

Hector's huge hand tweaked the string around the brown paper parcel.

'You don't see string nowadays. Sellotape you see a lot of.'

'Times change, darling. Nothing is as good as it used to be.'

'I know. I'm an old man.'

'You don't look it.'

'There's a reason for that.'

'You're successful, forward thinking, young at heart. It shows in your face.' She studied it. It had finally lost the pinkness produced by the surgeon's laser.

Hector was touched. 'Thank you, my sweet,' he said. 'And now I am going for my walk.'

Audrey believed him this time. 'Where to? It's still raining.'

'Just a walk. On my own. Philip!' He knocked on the glass. 'Philip. Please take the future Mrs Hector Quigley home and I will join you shortly.'

He got out of the car and waved them off. Audrey laughed merrily out of the rear window, raising her citrus-sleeved arm in a victory salute. Hector came out from under the glass canopy of the station and stood in the rain. His hair became wet and flattened, his tear stains washed away. A despatch rider on a motor bike drew up at the side of the road.

'S'cuse me, matey. Any idea where Seymour Place is?'

Hector's face clouded for a second. 'Yes. It's—' He made to point with his huge hand and then dropped his arm. His expression brightened. He looked puffed-up pleased as punch. 'No. I've never heard of it,' he announced. His voice resonated with its hidden Welsh timbre. 'I am a stranger here myself.'

He turned and walked his snakeskin Chelsea boots into the station and towards the stairs leading down to the tube. There were things to be done that Hector Quigley had never done before. Fill his own time. Marry a woman he loved. Take a trip on the London Underground. Life still held out happiness for an old showman of seventy-two.

Basket Case

DOUGLAS CHIRNSIDE

It was a matchless combination of presence of mind and sheer nerve that had allowed Karen Myhill to launch herself from a semi-detached in Bedford to her place at the top of British commercial television. Now her subliminal survival instinct soared into overdrive. All was not lost. She flung her arms behind her head and frantically felt around the floor. In one decisive sweep, she grasped the waste-paper basket in both hands and propelled it upside down over the head of her oblivious lover.

In 1979 Karen Myhill's swift reactions conceal the mystery man's identity. But nine months on she gives birth: to her precious baby Max and to a myth. Who is Max's father. Who is Basket Case?

Sixteen years later, sharp young advertising executive Duncan Cairns is working on the launch of The Station, a new interactive cable TV channel. Then he gets a phone call. The Most Difficult Woman in Television needs him to keep her independent production company afloat. Duncan is tempted. It's just a shame no one's ever told him the story of Basket Case . . .

'What a good idea for a novel . . . If the media is not about excess, what is it about? This funny, bitchy read provides plenty'
Daily Mail

'Adland's favourite read'
Independent

'Entertaining first novel . . . Chirnside brings an insider's knowledge and waspish humour to his depiction of the interneccine rivalries of the media world'
The Times

∫

SCEPTRE

Goodbye, Johnny Thunders
TANIA KINDERSLEY

I met Jack at the start of my first summer in London. It was April, it was hot, I remember it. I was young and free and the whole world was just an oyster to me. It seems a long time ago now. I suppose it was a long time ago, in a way.

I wish I could have said that Johnny Thunders brought us together, that I met him by chance in one of those second-hand record stalls that cluster together under the Westway, sorting through the boxes with that look of frowning concentration that marks the vinyl buff from the casual browser, hunting for a bootleg album by the New York Dolls, or a late cut from the Heartbreakers. But I can't. I hadn't heard of Thunders in those days. I wasn't even a record buff.

Tania Kindersley's eloquent, evocative new novel is for everyone who has ever tried to stay cool through a hot summer in the city, for anyone who has ever been young, and for all those girls who know what it's like to fall in love with a bad boy . . .

The writing is fluent, snappy and contemporary, but the mood is elegiac and deeply romantic . . . the novel brilliantly catches the insubstantiality of young, doomed love'
Mail on Sunday

SCEPTRE

My Legendary Girlfriend
MIKE GAYLE

One thing really cracked me up though. 'It's like that song', she said, completely straightfaced. 'If You Love Somebody Set Them Free.' I couldn't believe it. It wasn't enough that she was wrecking my whole life. She was quoting Sting to me too.

Meet Will Kelly. English teacher. Film fan. King of sandwich construction. Chief curator in the National Museum of Ex-Girlfriends.

Still in love with The One, Will is desperate to discover if there can be An-Other One. In his decrepit flat where he can't even manage to cook spaghetti hoops without setting off the communal smoke alarm, his lifeline is the telephone. Will realises that with a single call friends can either lift him from the depths of depression or completely shatter his hopes.

There's Alice (who remembers his birthday), Simon (who doesn't), Martina (the one-night stand), Kate (the previous tenant of his rented hovel). And of course his Ex, Aggi – the inimitable Aggi. His Legendary Girlfriend.

Or is she?

Two men, three women and a donkey called Sandy . . . basically it's your classic love hexagon.

$\int$

SCEPTRE

The Tenth Justice
BRAD MELTZER

Ben Addison has got it made.

He's just finished law school. He's a new clerk at the Supreme Court. It's the first step on a golden career path.

But Ben is about to make a huge mistake. He's about to be tricked into leaking something he shouldn't. And he's about to land himself and his three best friends in really serious trouble.

'Compulsive'
Mail on Sunday

Meltzer's plot is well thought out, with a particularly vivid climax.
The Sunday Times

SCEPTRE

Sunstroke

MARC BLAKE

Sex, drugs, guns and money – everything you ever
wanted from a package holiday.

Sizzling summer in the Costa del Sol. Mike Trent's
holiday starts badly when his midnight swim in the
hotel pool is interrupted by a body plummeting from
a third floor balcony. Sarah Rutherford, using her job
as a travel rep as a cover, is investigating the mysterious
death of her party-loving sister.

When the two join forces they find themselves up
against the criminal community: a pint-sized skinhead,
the brothers Esteban, a slavering wolf, a hunchback
pornographer and an ex-pat villain with more than one
secret to hide. And their sun-baked paradise is teetering
on the verge of collapse.

SUNSTROKE. Catch it now.

$\int$

SCEPTRE